PRAISE FOR *CUTTING EDGE ADVERTISING II*

"There are three books about advertising I'd recommend. And I won't tell you what the other two are."

BOB BARRIE, Fallon McElligott, Minneapolis

"More creative inspiration than a ten-foot stack of One Show and D&AD annuals."

BRUCE BILDSTEN, Fallon McElligott, Minneapolis

"Jim has taken the moguls of advertising and got them captive for us, so we can take a journey into the deepest recesses of their incredible minds. The book is undoubtedly a bible for all copywriters at all levels. For a start, it will take them back to advertising."

THE BRIEF, India

"It succeeds with gusto ... Aitchison avoids the dull, lifeless form of 'How to' tomes. Intelligently structured ... it is a rare book in its homage to great print ads and how they are made."

BUSINESS REVIEW WEEKLY, Australia

"An absolutely excellent piece of work. Nowadays, young writers and art directors get precious little training once they've joined an agency, and books such as this do all of us in the industry a favour."

ADRIAN HOLMES, Chief Creative Officer, Lowe & Partners Worldwide

"It's the best I've ever read ... Unlike most books on advertising that are the thoughts of one person, these are the collective thoughts of so many great people. This is, in truth, the knowledge ... No writer, art director, account man, planner or client should be without it."

LIONEL HUNT, Lowe Hunt & Partners, Australia

"The multi-talented Aitchison, an Australian, is himself a former distinguished practitioner ... The author enjoys the advantage of not thinking that all the most creative ideas come out of London and New York."

PHILIP KLEINMAN, Market Leader, UK

"All you ever wanted to know, but never knew who to ask – a great read for anyone wanting more from their print advertising."

ANDREW THOMAS, International Herald Tribune

PRAISE FOR *CUTTING EDGE RADIO*

"Aitchison has managed to create the rare advertising text that simultaneously entertains, educates and most importantly, inspires. Aitchison is clever in intertwining his theory with practical examples – the real secret in maintaining any advertising professional's rapt attention."

ADOI magazine, Malaysia

"Jim Aitchison has done it again. With his trademark style of letting the greats do all the talking, he takes us on yet another journey, this time surpassing himself with an impressive list of 106 heavyweights in *Cutting Edge Radio*. Aitchison liberally sprinkles his book with comment after comment from great radio people. You can almost imagine yourself conversing with such talents as Lionel Hunt, Tony Hertz and Neil French as you read it. In every section, you can find about half a dozen scripts, many of them award-winning ones, as illustrations to Aitchison's tips. Every step of the process is given due thought – including how to sell your radio ideas ... If you're a writer who wants to come up with a great radio campaign, you'd better read it."

ADVOICE magazine, Singapore

"I wish this book had been written years ago. It's long overdue. It's a must for anyone who has an interest in radio advertising and is probably the most valuable investment any young writer could make."

BOB DENNIS, Vice President Creative Services,
MediaCorp Radio Singapore

"Jim's new book is much needed and deserves a place on the bookshelf of every ambitious creative team in the region."

DAVID GUERRERO, Chairman & Chief Executive Officer,
BBDO/Guerrero Ortega Manila

"... A powerful piece of work! It makes me feel great about belonging to a group of people that shares my passion ... Radio is often a lonely road to travel within the ad business, and although I have always known there are people who feel the way I do, to see them say the same things I say in print makes me feel good about what I do and the way I do it. (My) admiration and gratitude for what you've done, not only for the incredible amount of work and talent you've put in, but also – maybe even mostly – because you so obviously *get it*. You've taken in our passion and made it yours. It should be required reading in all creative departments."

TONY HERTZ, HERTZ:RADIO London

"This book really pissed me off. It pissed me off that it was so incredibly detailed and comprehensive, so practical, so inspiring and so useful. It pissed me off that it took so long for someone to actually write this book. It pissed me off that I didn't write it. But most of all, it pissed me off that I didn't have it when I was first starting out."

AUSTIN HOWE, Radioland Inc. Portland

"What a great book and learning tool. It should be required reading for anyone in advertising. It takes the reader through the process, explains and gives examples and excerpts by those who know. Brilliant."

THOMAS HRIPKO, The Radio Spot Dallas

"Radio is tricky. What's the answer? If you want to to know the good answers, talk to the best people. Lucky for you – Jim Aitchison already has."

ANDREW INGRAM, Radio Advertising Bureau UK

"By far the most interesting and instructive book on radio advertising I have ever read ... it removes some of the mystery and fear of the medium."

JOHN KYRIAKOU, Creative Director Toronto,
former Chairman & Executive Creative Director,
J. Walter Thompson Singapore

"*Cutting Edge Radio* is a burster. Congratulations on another definitive piece on our mad, mad industry. It's one helluva contribution."

STREET REMLEY, Street Noise Adelaide

PRAISE FOR *CUTTING EDGE COMMERCIALS*

"*Cutting Edge Commercials* is brilliant and on my desk."
MICHAEL CONRAD, Chief Creative Officer,
Leo Burnett Worldwide

"The beauty, and indeed the talent, of Jim Aitchison is his ability to not only let his subjects be heard clearly and sharply, but also to place their opinions in an overall context that guides the reader through the maze of television creativity, and tells a terrific story at the same time."
ROWAN DEAN, Rowan Dean Films and former Chairman,
Australian Writers and Art Directors Association

"*Cutting Edge Commercials* is a positive book of TV advertising experiences written with patience, diversity of perspectives and practical insights. Jim weaves his 'resource' for all advertising lovers and practitioners around interviews with creative masters around the world. Jim's book is of real experiences, insights, joys. Each TV advertising insight blows another bubble of hope for advertising everywhere."
ROBERT GIBRALTER in Ad Age Global

"An unusually impressive piece of work, and I shall recommend it widely."
PROFESSOR JOHN PHILIP JONES,
Syracuse University NY, USA

"Probably one of the best books ever written, not just about television advertising, but the business in general. I gobbled up each and every word. As it draws you inside the brilliant minds of its sources, it comes across more like a great chat over a couple of beers on the topics of what we do every day. You feel like you're in there with them all discussing opinions. Jim Aitchison has left no stone unturned when it comes to searching out the truth."
CHRIS KYME, AdAsia magazine

"So precise, so real and insightful, the best survival guide ever written for ad men. The only shame is that everyone else can get it, too."
CARY RUEDA, Creative Director,
Dentsu Young & Rubicam Malaysia

"Brilliant!"

SUTHISAK SUCHARITTANONTA,
Executive Creative Director, BBDO Bangkok

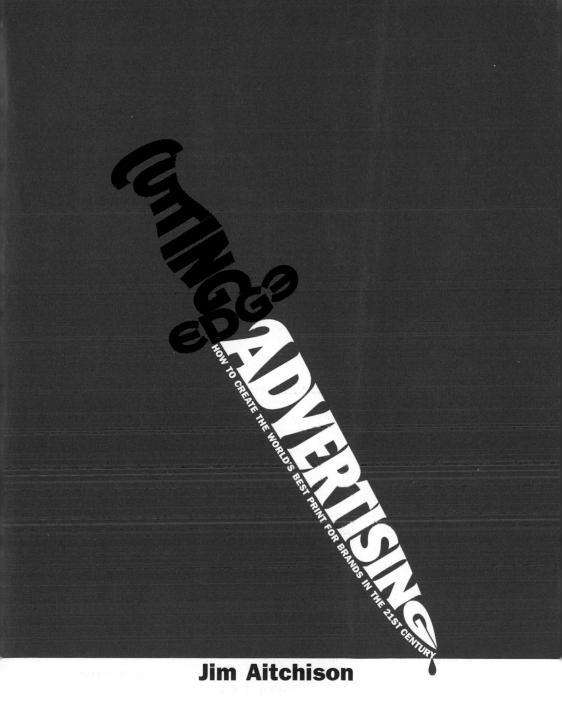

CUTTING edge ADVERTISING

HOW TO CREATE THE WORLD'S BEST PRINT FOR BRANDS IN THE 21ST CENTURY

Jim Aitchison

PEARSON

Prentice Hall

Singapore New York London Toronto Sydney Mexico City

Published in 2004 by
Prentice Hall
Pearson Education South Asia Pte Ltd
23/25 First Lok Yang Road, Jurong
Singapore 629733

Pearson Education offices in Asia: *Bangkok, Beijing, Hong Kong, Kuala Lumpur, Manila, New Delhi, Seoul, Singapore, Taipei, Tokyo*

Printed in Singapore

5 4 3 2
08 07 06 05 04

ISBN 981-244-557-9

National Library Board (Singapore) Cataloguing in Publication Data

Aitchison, Jim.
    Cutting edge advertising : how to create the world's best print for brands in the 21st century / Jim Aitchison. – 2nd ed. – Singapore : Prentice Hall, 2003.
        p. cm.

    ISBN : 981-244-557-9

1. Advertising.   2. Advertising copy.   3. Advertising layout and
typography.   I. Title.

HF5823
659.132 — dc21   SLS2003031552

CONTENTS

THE CAST
(In order of appearance)

Indra Sinha	Jonathan Bond
Roy Grace	Jim Mountjoy
Lionel Hunt	William Shakespeare
Graham Warsop	Bob Barrie
Hugh Mackay	Ron Mather
David Abbott	Saint Augustine
Tim Delaney	Bruce Bildsten
Neil Godfrey	Bertrand Russell
Mary Stow	Carl Jung
Mark Tutssel	Steve Browning
Neil French	Warren Brown
Gerard Stamp	Paul Fishlock
John Hegarty	Bill Bernbach
Nick Cohen	Ezra Pound
Steffan Postaer	Rod Wright
John Salmon	Will Self
Bill Oberlander	Jean-Marie Dru
Jeff Goodby	Fiona Clancy
Howard Gossage	Lee Clow
Kirk Souder	Antony Redman
Gary Goldsmith	David Mattingly
Siimon Reynolds	Dorothy Parker
David Droga	Robin Wight
Ed McCabe	Malcolm Pryce
Ian Batey	Frank Lowe
Leon Festinger	Steve Elrick
Dr Herbert Krugman	Dean Hanson
Andrew Ehrenberg	Danny Higgins
Oscar Wilde	John Messum
Simon Sherwood	Bill Gallacher
Bob Isherwood	Mike Lescarbeau
Garry Abbott	John Bevins
Steve Henry	Tony Brignull
Guido Heffels	George Lois
Richard Kirshenbaum	Andrew Clarke

Simon Mainwaring	Oakley Hall
Dean Mortenson	Jorge Luis Borges
Norman Alcuri	Ernest Hemingway
Ben Hunt	John Hersey
John Clang	William Wordsworth
Francis Tan	Eric Lomax
Steve Dunn	Richard Foster
Mark Fong	Raymond Chandler
Patrick Low	Rudyard Kipling
Scott Sheinberg	Dylan Thomas
Heintje Moo	Jack Kerouac
Gordon Tan	Malcolm Duffy
Yue Chee Guan	Peter Souter
Linda Leong	Charles Dickens
Paul Ruta	Daphne du Maurier
Len Cheeseman	Mike Boles
Nick Bell	Samuel Goldwyn
Robert McKee	Linda Locke
Helmut Krone	Robert Gibralter
Paul Arden	Andrew Bell
Jay Pond-Jones	Lim Sau Hoong
Chet Baker	Erik Heisholt
Tom Lichtenheld	Basil Mina
Daniel Lim	David Guerrero
Edmund Choe	Ali Smith
Jagdish Ramakrishnan	Michael Ball
David Fowler	Judy Wald
Tham Khai Meng	Sir Alec Guinness
Michael Lui	Ron Brown
Robin Heighway-Bury	Anthony Vagnoni
Janet Woolley	Gee Thomson
Theseus Chan	Michael Lynch
Kim Thorp	Ken McKenzie
Carl Ally	Lee Strasberg

FOREWORD

"You will, Oscar; you will."

I wish *I'd* said that.

I'm a sucker for quotation anthologies, aren't you? I've got dozens of them, and most are exactly the same.

But still I browse for an original thought, usually while on the bog, and the sense of achievement in finding *exactly* the phrase you're looking for is a pleasure that transcends the most spectacular of dumps.

Sorry, I was away there, for a moment. Happy days, happy days. Where were we? Right. Book review.

You know, when you consider how many excellent writers have spent at least a *little* time in ad agencies, it's rather odd that there are so few good books on the subject.

The first I read, when I was still grovelling for unpaid rents, in Birmingham's red-light district, was Vance Packard's *Hidden Persuaders*. It sounded like being a sort of spy, and I fancied the idea mightily, at the time. (It would sure beat being thumped by pimps on a daily basis, anyway.)

Then, too late, after I joined up, and my job consisted of scrabbling about in a damp cellar, looking for printing blocks, came *Those Wonderful People Who Gave You Pearl Harbour* by Jerry Della Femina.

OK, then! We weren't James Bonds. We were jolly, rollicking, devil-may-care iconoclasts, with a witty rejoinder for the dullest client. Even if we had names like a brand of sanitary napkins. *Much* better.

(I wonder if Jerry ever had to kill a rat with a printing block, to stop it making a nest in the media files. Just a thought.)

It was only *much* later, after I'd graduated to waisted suits with Jason Queen cuffs, that I read David Ogilvy's brilliantly disguised, direct-selling piece for his agency, *Confessions of an Advertising Man*. Even the *title* was a con. You *had* to love the old bugger, for his sheer audacity.

But that's about the lot. There have been others, too many others, but they've all been close relatives of these three. Or deadly dull, and utterly misleading, 'How To' tomes that must have been the cause of umpteen failed careers.

But Aitchison has cracked it, I reckon.

Look how thick this book is; Jim actually wrote about a quarter of it, at most. Money for jam!

His annoyingly simple idea was to allow *other* people to write the damn thing for him.

(Note, children, how the writer is finally bringing the piece round to the point where it has some vague relevance to the otherwise baffling 'headline'. You'll find this tip on ... whatever page it's on. Can't be bothered to look it up. I'm doing this for free, you know.)

Hang on. I've lost the thread again.

OK. Got it. The snag about David Ogilvy's books are that they're the firmly-held opinions of a single mind. However brilliant, that's limiting, by its own definition.

Aitchison has persuaded anyone who's anyone in this racket to turn over the tricks of their trade to him. In fact, if you look at the list of 'contributors' and find any glaring absentees, Jim probably asked them stuff, and they didn't bother to respond. Their loss, I tend to think.

This is destined to be essential reading for anyone in the business or thinking of getting into it. The book would be inestimably useful to any client who wondered how his money was spent, and wanted to get more bang for his buck. (Mind you, in the latter case, he'd have to concede that he didn't already know all there was to know, so perhaps not, after all.)

Finally, the *fun* thing about reading this is that Jim has quoted each contributor verbatim. As he put it to me, "letting the individual vocabularies and rhythms of the actual voices delineate the speakers". (Sorry, what's that in English, James?)

But it works. Only Indra Sinha burbles and booms *quite* like Indra, and you can hear him in these pages. Only Hegarty has *quite* such an icy mastery of clipped syntax, and the studied pause and throwaway; listen while you read.

And apparently only *I* sound like a rambling, babbling, incoherent twat.

Thanks a bundle, Jim.

I hope yer book rots on the remainder shelves.

Neil French
"Worldwide Creative Godfather"
to all the companies in the WPP Group

WITH SPECIAL THANKS

To Andrew Clarke, Saatchi & Saatchi, London, for designing the covers; to Jenny Wee, who typed everything between them; to Michael Larsen, literary agent and author, for invaluable advice; to Shutter Bug Photography Services and ProColor, Singapore, for all their professional help; and to everyone who generously contributed their time and talent in my quest for information.

Cover artwork: Paul Clarke

ACKNOWLEDGEMENTS

Extract from *The Confessions of Saint Augustine* by E. M. Blaiklock, Copyright © 1983 by E. M. Blaiklock, reproduced by permission of Hodder and Stoughton Limited and William Neill-Hall Ltd.

Extracts from *Why Don't People Listen?*, republished as *The Good Listener*, by Hugh Mackay, Copyright © Mackay Research Pty Limited 1994, published by Pan Macmillan Publishers Australia, permission granted by the copyright owner care of Curtis Brown (Aust) Pty Ltd.

Extracts from *The Art & Craft of Novel Writing* by Oakley Hall, Copyright © 1989 by Oakley Hall, used by permission of Story Press, an imprint of F&W Publications, Inc.

Extracts from interview with Will Self in *Publishers Weekly*, 8 September 1997, reprinted with permission of Publishers Weekly.

Extract from *Rebecca* by Daphne du Maurier reproduced with permission of Curtis Brown Ltd., London, on behalf of the Estate of Daphne du Maurier. Copyright © Daphne du Maurier.

Extract from *A Tale of Two Cities* by Charles Dickens, published by Penguin Books USA Inc., by courtesy of Penguin Putnam Inc.

Extracts from *Under Milk Wood* by Dylan Thomas, Copyright © 1952 by Dylan Thomas, published by J. M. Dent & Sons Ltd., reprinted by permission of the Trustees for the Copyrights of Dylan Thomas and New Directions Publishing Corporation.

Extracts from *The Railway Man* by Eric Lomax, Copyright © Eric Lomax 1995, reprinted by permission of the publishers, Random House UK Limited and W. W. Norton & Company, Inc.

Extract from *Strasberg at The Actors Studio* by Lee Strasberg, edited by Robert H. Hethmon, Copyright © 1965 by Lee Strasberg and Robert H. Hethmon, reprinted by permission of Theatre Communications Group, Inc.

THIS EDITION IS DEDICATED TO THE
MEMORY OF NORMAN ALCURI
(1953–2002)

1

UNCONVENTIONAL WISDOM

"The written word is the deepest dagger you can drive into a man's soul."

British writer Indra Sinha should know. His print campaigns for Amnesty International punctured public apathy and raised a fighting fund against oppression.

Ironically, print advertising itself has become a victim, burdened with more outdated rules and creative conventions than any other medium. The evidence of intellectual oppression is alarming. Hall of Fame art director Roy Grace calls it "a high level of mediocrity". Others are less kind.

But while print is the oldest advertising medium, it is also the most resilient. In the post-war years, it witnessed the transition from one type of advertising to another. It has again become the front line in the battle between the prevailing wisdom of one century, and the unconventional wisdom of the next.

Print exercises an irresistible charisma. It is the permanence of the page, the romance of paper and ink, the presses thundering at midnight. No television channel would dare call itself a *Tribune* or a *Chronicle* or a *Guardian*, nor claim to speak for the *Times* in which we live. Only the economy of print can *Telegraph* a message. Only the power of print can *Post* an image in the mind's eye. Only the pages of *Time*, *Newsweek*, *Fortune* and *The Economist* can report world events while shaping them at the same time. There could never be a *Viewer's Digest*, only a *Reader's Digest*. If television reduces us, print enlarges us.

"It's interesting that nothing has killed off the printed word," muses Lionel Hunt of Australia's Lowe Hunt & Partners. "Not radio, not cinema, not television, not even the Internet, which is still largely a print medium anyway. Whenever there's a new medium invented, there are always these dire predictions about the demise of the earlier ones, but it just doesn't happen. OK, so silent movies aren't that big at the moment, but Marcel Marceau still makes a living."

"It's not a crime to love print more than any other medium. I do," affirms Graham Warsop, chairman and executive creative director of South Africa's The Jupiter Drawing Room, ranked among the five most creative agencies in the world by *Advertising Age Creativity*. "Paper is the home of the written word. It has an impeccable pedigree. Equally, images on paper are like images on canvas. They have a formidable legacy of persuasion."

Print creativity is not the result of mystical inspiration. It is an art and, like every art, is the result of conscious effort and preparation. Developing a conscious understanding of the medium and its possibilities is the first step; individual ability and fickle inspiration will remain unconscious factors in this equation. At least for the time being.

DIMENSION

A cynic once called television a medium because it is neither rare nor well done. Yet, in comparison, print is often regarded as a passive, one-dimensional medium.

"It's a cretinous thing to say," asserts Sinha. "How much depth is there in one page of the *King James Bible*? How much depth is there in the opening line of *Lolita*?" Sinha believes the printed word has a greater capacity to free the imagination than television does. "Television imposes a visual on the viewer. It doesn't allow him the choice of imagining the world to be the way he wants it to be. Print can actually liberate the mind and create far more intense illusions, far deeper experiences, than any television or film ever will."

Australia's foremost social researcher, Hugh Mackay, agrees. "The words are asking *me* to make up the pictures, so they're *my* pictures.

There's a creative act within the reader. On television, the work's all done. I only receive; I don't construct and create the way I do with print."

Britain's David Abbott of Abbott Mead Vickers regards print's effect as an all-encompassing stimulus. "It's because of what words do. They engage the *whole* mind, and you don't think or feel in one dimension. Generally in advertising, I think it's the words you remember."

At Leagas Delaney, London, Tim Delaney argues that print's strength lies in its involvement with the reader. "Print is different from television and radio in that it's slower, more rational, in a number of areas. If you're trying to create a personality, or sustain a personality, print takes longer because of its rationality, because you need to engage the reader in more than just an assertive, image-based discussion. You've got to give them something which makes them stop, look, and respond. The whole process seems to be slightly *tougher* on the recipient. Because it's tougher, it's also *deeper*. If you do care to stop, if you do want to read, if you do get into an ad, even if you just look at an image and there are no words on it, just a logo, it's somehow deeper and more rewarding than something that lasts a few seconds on television or radio."

Perhaps the silence of print reinforces its depth. The reader's mind can concentrate on what is written, and on what is written between the lines. Print permits more subtlety, more verbal and visual nuances; what Britain's most highly awarded art director Neil Godfrey describes as "an elbow touching you".

"A print ad is a journey," says Mary Stow, head of planning at London's Howell Henry Chaldecott Lury & Partners. "You can read through it, flow with the logic. In print, things are written down in black and white. It means that people are much harder on print. You've got the evidence in front of you. With television advertising, people quite willingly accept what's being done to them. They collude with it. But if you're sitting reading a newspaper, the context all around the ad is pretty hard. Real life stories, facts. Therefore, the advertising has to acknowledge people are in that state of mind. They're not reading in the same way they watch TV."

"Print ads have incredible power of advocacy and persuasion," believes Mark Tutssel, vice chairman and deputy chief creative officer of Leo Burnett USA. Tutssel's awards include a Cannes Grand

Prix, a Clio Grand Prix, and four D&AD Silver Pencils. "The written word is alive and thriving. Magazine sales boom, as does text messaging, while the Internet is really one piece of copy. A great print ad makes the reader look at something in a whole new light or touches the reader in some fundamental way that alters their understanding."

PASSIVE OR ACTIVE? PUBLIC OR PRIVATE?

Print is the only medium we can hold and touch. Communication is one-to-one. The only barriers are those erected by advertisers, art directors and writers.

The physical reading experience, admits Neil French, "Worldwide Creative Godfather" to all the companies in the WPP Group, has coloured the way he creates for the medium. "Reading is governed by the length of your arms. Old blokes like me have either got their nose pressed up against the print, or they're holding their heads back and their arms out straight like they're driving a racing car." As a result, French believes these intimate, individualistic traits make print a very private medium. "The relationship between your eye and the page is a personal one. That's why people get stroppy when you read over their shoulders. It destroys the privacy of the moment."

Gerard Stamp, former creative director and chairman, Leo Burnett London, says print can be more intimate. "It *isn't* addressing an audience. It's speaking to an individual."

Describing print as a private, exclusive channel, Mackay cites research on the levels of involvement with advertising. "With the Internet, and with print, the message is very close to you. You're only about twelve inches away from the page or the screen. Both are very active communication experiences. You're reading what is on the screen, manipulating the mouse or the keyboard, or you're turning the pages, a very active relationship with the medium. Whereas with television, most of the time you're just sitting there, you're not even sitting forward, and the audio-visual waterfall just flows over you. Sometimes you're alert, sometimes you're quite soporific."

The intimacy of the relationship between the reader and the page does not exist between the viewer and the television screen. According to Mackay, another reason why readers love reading is their control of the process. "It's all on their terms. They're utterly in control. If I don't like you, I'll just turn the page and you're gone."

CONTROL

If the reader has control, so too do creatives. Each time a page is turned, a curtain rises to reveal a fresh scene. Print is a stage, a personal stage, where creativity can be stamped with individuality and soul. Creatives are alone and naked on that stage. Pretentious creativity is exposed. Superficiality becomes transparent. The inept cannot escape their fate.

There is *nowhere* to hide in a print ad, stresses Hunt, who is deeply suspicious of creative teams that only want to do television. "When I am interviewing writers or art directors, particularly art directors, I always ask to see their print work first. When you see a good TV spot, it's difficult to be sure who's responsible. It can be the writer, the art director, or both, or the director, or the talent. It doesn't matter for the end result, but it does matter if you're thinking of hiring someone on the strength of it."

"Although I like TV, I'm always drawn back to print," confesses Godfrey. "I think it's the control one has. Inevitably, a TV commercial is never quite like what you'd imagined. In print, I'm in control. It's my baby. All the decisions are mine."

In print, creative shortcomings cannot be ascribed to the director, the casting department, or even the catering company. "If there are flaws in your concept," cautions Sinha, "they're your flaws, your faults. If you take the client out of the equation, there's no one to blame but yourself. Everything is under your control and therefore can be changed and adjusted if you wish it to be so."

Being armed with absolute control over infinite possibilities is a tantalising prospect. Words can be words, words can be visuals. But the toy shop is not all it appears. If print creativity offers such freedom and depth, how does that explain the plethora of mediocrity and incest?

The next stage of conscious preparation should be to draw some parameters; to identify what constitutes great, cutting edge print.

CHAPTER 1

GREAT PRINT: WHAT IS IT?

Bartle Bogle Hegarty's John Hegarty is convinced that print has to do more, to work harder, to get noticed. "You could argue that it has to be more provocative. So if being more provocative means being more creative, then you have to be more creative in print."

Delaney looks for stopping power in either the headline or visual. "Not something gratuitously wacky, but something strong and relevant. And it isn't always that the strength of a line or image solves a problem. Life is more complex than that. Sometimes it's about the sixth ad in a series that stops you and clicks in."

For Abbott, the greatest print ideas are those which contain a human insight; an insight into human behaviour, for example, with which a reader can relate. "A spark of recognition is there at the root of most good communication," Abbott explains. "It's true of a painting or a novel. It's true of great advertising, too."

Nick Cohen of New York's Mad Dogs & Englishmen defines a great print ad as one that connects with people. "It's not about one that's simple, or one that's got a clever twist in it. It's one that people look at, that starts a relationship." In fact, Cohen sees connecting people with brands as the essence of all great advertising. "People have more choice than they ever did, but in the end, they vote with their dollar. They pick brands that they relate to, and that relate to them."

Insightful, impactful, provocative, connective: deceptively simple words, and any number of workmanlike ads could be rationalised to comply with them. But such debates are becoming increasingly academic. Print creativity is redefining itself.

A new generation of advertisers, the emergence of radical new marketing paradigms, the advent of planning, and a new wave of cutting edge agencies and creatives are challenging and changing the old, established order of things.

"Unlike television, print is *a written contract with the consumer*. It has an inherent integrity; it is not a good liar," maintains Steffan Postaer, chief creative officer at Leo Burnett's LBWorks. Postaer won the Kelly award for his Altoids print campaign. "Good print is not a storage space for logos and products and phone numbers and URL addresses; those ads look like an eight-year-old's closet. Print is not a political tool meant to appease some brand manager and his boss.

Print is a sales tool that needs to invite and seduce a person into buying or doing something. That tool needs to be sharp and simple, not fettered by a myriad of things." Nor is print static television, says Postaer. "Some agencies literally pull frames from their TV commercials and call it a print ad. I call it a travesty. I always tell my guys to do the print first. Print is its own thing because it endures. It does not go away like television, like a thief in the night."

Godfrey, whose career spanned over forty years at the cutting edge of British advertising, provides a craft perspective: "When I started, we were turning a corner from one type of advertising, mainly slogans and illustrations, to another. We needed to move away from the 1950s' dry brush illustrated feel where everything was a slogan that was shouted, to something much more modern. When I worked at Doyle Dane Bernbach (DDB), we did the very first full page ad. Until then, the biggest ads people had bought were half pages; mostly the ads were things like twelve-inch double columns, tiny ads. I remember doing the first double page spread in a newspaper, in colour, for Lufthansa. As the dimension of the ads grew bigger, we had to design a more angular, impactful way of doing them, no longer based on prissiness but said in a really strong way. We came into a period where we had something to say, not just showing the product."

Many of Godfrey's campaigns have become icons for the industry, slavishly imitated to this day. Yet Godfrey himself admits that if he was doing them now, they would probably look different. "I'd have to think in a completely different way, according to the style and mentality of life today. It's really quite different. There's a much broader, younger market. Things are sold directly to teenagers and younger children which, in the old days, were aimed at mothers and fathers."

John Salmon, creative director at London's Collett Dickenson Pearce, presided over that agency's golden years of creativity. His department was the legendary domain of Britain's reigning creative elite. "The advertising business is subject to fashion, there's no question about it, and a lot of the products that advertising sells have to do with fashion," he observes. "However, there are certain sorts of agencies who inch products into this arena of fashion, *regardless*. Cars, for example, are now sold on their visual appearance alone. The performance characteristics of the car, the price of the car, what

Avis is only No.2 in rent a cars. So why go with us?

We try harder.

(When you're not the biggest, you have to.)

We just can't afford dirty ashtrays. Or half-empty gas tanks. Or worn wipers. Or unwashed cars. Or low tires. Or anything less than seat–adjusters that adjust. Heaters that heat. Defrosters that defrost.

Obviously, the thing we try hardest for is just to be nice. To start you out right with a new car, like a lively, super-torque Ford, and a pleasant smile. To know, say, where you get a good pastrami sandwich in Duluth.

Why?

Because we can't afford to take you for granted.

Go with us next time.

The line at our counter is shorter.

Avis can't afford dirty ashtrays.

Or to start you out without a full gas tank, a new car like a lively, super-torque Ford, a smile.

Why?

When you're not the biggest in rent a cars, you have to try harder.

We do.

We're only No.2.

When you're only No.2, you try harder. Or else.

Little fish have to keep moving all of the time. The big ones never stop picking on them.

Avis knows all about the problems of little fish.

We're only No.2 in rent a cars. We'd be swallowed up if we didn't try harder.

Avis can't afford to relax.

There's no rest for us.

We're always emptying ashtrays. Making sure gas tanks are full before we rent our cars. Seeing that the batteries are full of life. Checking our windshield wipers.

And the cars we rent out can't be anything less than lively new super-torque Fords.

And since we're not the big fish, you won't feel like a sardine when you come to our counter.

We're not jammed with customers.

No. 2ism. The Avis Manifesto.

We are in the rent a car business, playing second fiddle to a giant.

Above all, we've had to learn how to stay alive.

In the struggle, we've also learned the basic difference between the No.1's and No.2's of the world.

The No.1 attitude is: "Don't do the wrong thing. Don't make mistakes and you'll be O.K."

The No.2 attitude is: "Do the right thing. Look for new ways. Try harder."

No.2ism is the Avis doctrine. And it works.

The Avis customer rents a clean, new Opel Rekord, with wipers wiping, ashtrays empty, gas tank full, from an Avis girl with smile firmly in place.

And Avis itself has come out of the red into the black.

Avis didn't invent No.2ism. Anyone is free to use it.

No. 2's of the world, arise!

Doyle Dane Bernbach's print advertising changed advertising forever. The agency's We try harder campaign for Avis is still an industry icon.

9

the car will do for you, these things have been subordinated to the salesman." The implication is that advertising creativity in many categories will be led by external forces like the fashion industry. In certain categories, though, Salmon foresees no change. "If you're selling plates with rabbits on them, and selling them off the page, there'll be a lot of copy and the ads will look pretty much the same now as they looked ten years ago, and ten years on I'm sure they'll still look very much the same."

"I think print advertising changes *superficially,*" reflects Abbott. "We go through fashions: borders, typography, coloured type, or whatever. Techniques change, but I don't think that the enduring principles of good communication will change that much. I haven't noticed them change that much in all the years I've been doing it. I don't see why they should change because it's all about human behaviour and reaction."

If Abbott is right, and human behaviour *is* immutable, will the fundamentals of great print creativity remain the same?

Delaney sheds further light: "It's not that there's one way of doing something that's right, and another one that's wrong. *It's what's appropriate at the time.* There are some learnings, and some things that people say. You still like Volkswagen ads because they're intelligent, and they show how simple a thought can be, and yet how compelling it can be. It isn't a rule, but it's certainly something you want to try and emulate. The writing on Avis was fresh and interesting, intelligent and accessible, and all kinds of other things that most ads still aren't today. They stand as campaigns that mean something to people because they've done what everyone else has done, but they've done it in a simple way."

Appropriate at the time. If Volkswagen and Avis were appropriate in Bill Bernbach's time, what is appropriate now?

NEW RULES?

There are no rules. Sooner or later, everything must become institutionalised and formulaic. At that point, creativity must move on. Fundamentals do not change; the way we address them does. Therein lies the problem.

Advertising has existed for centuries. As Sinha reminds us:

"Advertising is the second oldest profession and it arose directly out of the needs of the oldest."

Hegarty traces print advertising's lineage in order to identify the accumulation of conventions: "One can argue that the first poster was a food ad. It was a cave painting of a bison. Since that time, print has gathered around it a series of rules and attitudes that can be quite limiting to its development. As much as some people deplore the Apple Mac, it broke down the conventional layout that we'd all been paying homage to, the great Volkswagen layout done by Helmut Krone, the big picture, the small headline, the three columns of copy and the logo in the bottom right-hand corner. The versatility of the Mac broke that down. Things could be done in a different way."

Hegarty includes books and pamphlets in print's lineage. "Print is burdened by writing in a very profound way. There's a methodology about it which doesn't necessarily relate to the way the modern consumer approaches and touches advertising."

Hegarty argues that the art of advertising is about *reduction*: the ability to write less and say more.

"As an industry, we occupy the margins, the bits in between the editorial content, the bits in between the programmes. Therefore, our creativity is a kind of *guerilla* creativity. It comes in, makes a hit, and goes out again. It strikes me as odd that so often we make our work longer, rather than making it shorter. The French philosopher Pascal once wrote: *My apologies for this letter being so long; had I more time, it would have been shorter.* The fact is, it's harder to write less than it is to write more. Yet in our industry there's an idea that, somehow, length has a value. What we should be doing is reducing, because when you do that, you create an idea that is actually more powerful."

Hegarty's logic is that the only space he is trying to buy is inside the consumer's head. "The access point to it might be a print ad. If you take an idea down to its essentials, it has a chance of going in *faster*. The faster I can get my idea to go in there, the more likely it is to open out in there, like a seed. That's the place I want an idea to open out, *not* on the page. When I see ads where it's all written out, it's all long and complex. Sometimes, that's very much the case of what you need to do. But when you see awards for copywriting in the annuals, they always give it to a piece of long copy. They never actually give it to a very short piece of copy. If you believe Pascal, who is probably a more profound thinker than most people in advertising, it's the opposite of what it should be."

Sinha also questions current industry conventions. "We're talking to ourselves. We tend to be writing for award juries. After twenty years' experience of British advertising, anyone who says it isn't so is a liar. What you see is innovation often happening in fringe media, like compact disc sleeves, then it becomes trendy, then advertising picks it up. The distressed typefaces that punky publications put together with chewing gum and string ten years ago, which were picked up by art directors in trendy agencies five years ago, are now being picked up by art directors in mainstream agencies. It gets so boring. If we stopped being so self-regarding, so inward-looking, and looked at what the *consumer* is about, we will find new ways. If we set ourselves impossible tasks, if we tried to communicate things we might have thought were impossible to communicate, if we tried to achieve a level of impact we might have always considered to be impossible to achieve, if we made those our goals, we'd find that traditional methods are inadequate to cope with them. Therefore, by definition, we'd have to find some new ways to do it, like water running around an obstacle."

What, in fact, we are witnessing now is not so much a superficial, stylistic period of change in creative terms, but a revolution against self-imposed conventions and self-inflicted handicaps. Advertising methodology itself is being challenged, not merely its creative manifestation.

At New York's Kirshenbaum Bond & Partners, Bill Oberlander sums it up: "The Harvard Business School-Procter & Gamble matrix of how to do advertising that sells brands is *broken*. A lot of people are realising that books like Ogilvy's, and Leo Burnett's rules, even Doyle Dane Bernbach's rules, are *obsolete*. They're antiquated. There are sets of new paradigms about how to speak to consumers. You have to look at the entrepreneurs, the brands like Coke. These guys are the SWAT teams, the stealth bombers, of how to speak to consumers."

There is an ugliness about advertising, too, a crassness, which not only consumers reject.

"I'd call our philosophy *environmentalist*," says Jeff Goodby, chairman of Goodby, Silverstein & Partners, San Francisco. "I believe that advertising, like architecture or urban planning, is an unavoidable part of our environment. Thus, we want to create advertising that's intelligent, humorous, beautiful and moving. In general, a welcome and *respected* part of what we all have to walk through each day." Implicit in that belief is a rejection of the simplistic and banal. "It begins with a determination to find the *highest* common denominators, rather than the lowest, as most advertising unerringly does. We try to approach people with respect, out of a belief that if we expect a certain intelligence, attention and sense of humour on their part, we'll get it. There's a part of the circle we always leave for them to complete, which involves them in the advertising and makes it a more memorable experience." Goodby's philosophy opposes another pillar of formulaic advertising: mind-numbing repetition. "Our approach results in a kind of advertising that works, we think, without lots of repetition or exposure. As the infamous San Francisco copywriter Howard Gossage said, how many times do we have to read a book or see a movie? Once, maybe twice, even in the best cases. *Why* do we suppose that advertising must be seen over and over again to have an effect?"

Goodby's point is valid. We cannot divorce ourselves from what we inflict upon society. We should aspire to create and approve advertising of which we are not ashamed.

If we agree, then it is not an option; it becomes a responsibility.

For advertisers, agencies and creatives, the game is indeed changing. Long-held tenets and industry dogma distort our perspective, cobwebbing our view of what might be and what should be. All very well, but what is going to replace them? Anarchy?

In the search for cutting edge wisdom, it seems the new rulebook has yet to be written. There is more scope for intuitive thinking, for experimentation, for innovation. The fact that advertisers themselves are very often leading the charge has accelerated the revolution.

As Kirk Souder of Santa Monica agency Ground Zero observes: "If you ask people to create advertising, that's exactly what they'll create. If you ask people to do something more, then they'll do something more."

The question is, what are we consciously asking ourselves to do and be?

WHY BE CREATIVE?

Hegarty views creativity as the essence of humanity. "Humanity's leapt forward because it was creative; it could think, and it could put different thoughts together and come to different conclusions. It's part of what makes us what we are. It's always odd when people say to me, oh, you're creative, as though you're a different species." In Hegarty's book, everybody is creative. "You're creative when you put your clothes on in the morning, when you comb your hair, when you decide what car you're going to buy, what drink you're going to drink. It's all part of our creative persona."

Souder contends the reason for being creative has absolutely nothing to do with creating great advertising. "Being creative is about why we're here. The primary directive of existence must be growth. The moment that stops, we die. Either physically, intellectually, or spiritually." Souder draws an analogy with water. "Running water promotes life, stagnant water suffocates it. We can continue to grow by being like running water, through the experience and assimilation of new things. *By going where we haven't gone before.* That could be the execution of an ad, finding a new way home from work, or selling everything you have to live with an isolated tribe on a remote tributary of the Amazon for three years. Because the more things we *see*, the more things we *taste*, the more things we *try*, the more accurate our personal model of the universe is, and the closer we get to ultimate truth."

If Hegarty and Souder are right, and creativity is at our core, why is it that so many creative people seem prepared to accept a lesser standard?

Creativity is subjective. Some believe that writers and art directors are motivated by ego and awards. Others argue that achieving creative breakthroughs is a responsibility to their clients; the awards will follow, as French once said, like end-of-term prizes.

Cohen does not think people are happy to achieve mediocrity. "It's a very hard industry. You deal with a lot of rejection and therefore your optimism gets sucked out of you. You start second-guessing your clients, second-guessing what's possible. It grinds you down. I think they give up a little bit; they lose their optimism about why they got into the business in the first place."

Gary Goldsmith at Lowe & Partners Worldwide, New York, pinpoints unrealistic expectations and pain. "Young people coming in assume that there are great clients and bad clients, and if you happen to get a great one you'll do great work. They're really all the same; you just have to make something of it. It's very hard to do good work. There's a certain amount of pain involved. You've got to force yourself into a discomfort zone of working on something, day after day, and not having it. We all want to relieve that pain, so we come up with something and we convince ourselves it's pretty good and we move on to the next. You also tend to rationalise; you tend to look up and down a hallway and say, 'Well, my work's better than the guy's in the room next to me', or 'My work's better than some other agency's work', or 'That client will never buy anything good'. So you take the pressure off yourself and put it on anything around you, instead of forcing yourself to confront the fact that if it's not good, it's *your* fault."

"There is a kind of predisposition towards the acceptable rather than the remarkable," considers Salmon. "The emphasis of a lot of clients is not harnessed to the content of their advertising so much as to the economy of it. The emphasis is on buying media economically, on ads that are not going to be controversial, and on ads that will research well. Very few clients now have the ability to say, I know a good ad when I see one. Consequently, this has an effect on creative people who say, well, they'll never buy that, and on account people who say the same, without giving the client a chance to say whether he'll buy it or not." One result of this, Salmon believes, is the stress placed on visual techniques. "If an ad has a very uninteresting content, they hope it can be overcome by visual impact."

A month before starting legendary Australian agency OMON, Siimon Reynolds said that the two most popular words in his country's advertising industry were *"That's nice"*. "You show someone an okay job and you get 'That's Nice'. Ten times a week I hear it, that's nice, did a nice idea yesterday, that's nice! Nice, nice, nice, that's nice. And in a funny way, 'That's Nice' says everything about what *isn't* nice about our industry. There isn't enough 'Is it Great?' being said. 'That's Nice' has become the criteria at which we can stop work, satisfied."

David Droga, former executive creative director, Saatchi & Saatchi London, and now global creative director of Publicis Worldwide, warns that mediocrity is contagious. "It's easy to get opinions, it's hard to get great opinions. You've got to surround yourself with people you respect. If you surround yourself with morons who say everything you do is brilliant, you'll end up being just like the morons."

Roy Grace is a veteran of the Bill Bernbach-Volkswagen era at DDB. His stance is uncompromising. "A lot of creative people are capable only of mediocrity. They take perfect aim at it and hit it right between the eyes. Mediocrity is easy. Mediocrity means being easy on yourself, taking the easy way out, not suffering, not being obsessively and compulsively focused on excellence." Grace equates cutting edge work with basic talent, drive and intelligence. "I always wanted to be the best. In my mind I said I've got to be the best, I *need* to be the best."

The choice is clear. Creative people can leave behind landmarks in their industry, or spend a lifetime in bland obscurity. There are no ifs and buts; no shades of grey.

Beyond individual aspirations is a bigger picture. Creativity is the external face of the advertising agency. Creativity is the external manifestation of the agency's culture. Every piece of creative work builds the agency's brand as well as the client's brand. Therefore, it is an inescapable fact that every lesser ad lessens the agency's brand in the market as well as the client's brand. The results of agency brand building can be measured in five ways: by the number of clients who stay or leave; by the number of pitches to which the agency is invited; by the calibre of people the agency can attract; by what the agency's competitors say about it; and by the awards the agency wins.

It is no coincidence that those new agencies which registered meteoric growth in the past three decades have all been creatively driven: America's Chiat/Day, Fallon and Wieden & Kennedy; Britain's

Saatchi & Saatchi, Abbott Mead Vickers and Bartle Bogle Hegarty; France's BDDP; Australia's Campaign Palace; South Africa's Hunt Lascaris and The Jupiter Drawing Room. They, and dozens more, have cut through the ranks of the establishment with unconventional campaigns for blue chip advertisers.

Their voices will be heard in the next chapter.

WHY BUY CREATIVE?

Ed McCabe said: "To produce great advertising, you need three things in an agency. The management that wants it. The creative people who can produce it. And most important of all, the clients who will buy it."

What *are* clients buying?

Rather than view creativity as dangerous, many advertisers now deem it mandatory. Apple, Nike, Benetton and Absolut have become household names as the result of breakthrough advertising ideas.

"It's great clients who make agencies great, *not* the reverse," points out Ian Batey, founding chairman of Batey Ads, Singapore. "*They've* got to take the risk, *they've* got to buy the stuff and run with it. If you look around over the last twenty years, and look behind the great advertising, you'll find a great company. And behind the great company will be a great man. If you can find those guys early on, you've struck gold," says Batey. "A lot of clients treat advertising as a necessary evil. You could go through life as an advertising agency, having all those grey, boring accounts, but you've got to earn a living, so you do a decent job, the stuff works. Sometimes, in fifty or sixty accounts, there might be only ten that are really dancing, but those ten keep you electrified. Those guys knocked on your door, as much as you knocked on theirs. You connected with each other, you can relate. They've got to have trust in you, and vice versa. The entrepreneur who wants to lift his game also stimulates you. It *can't* be a one-way thing."

"At a lot of agencies," Goodby muses, "the clients are invariably treated as Neanderthal adversaries. Not only is life too short for that, but I've found that clients often have very good ideas that you can listen to, appropriate, and ultimately get credit for."

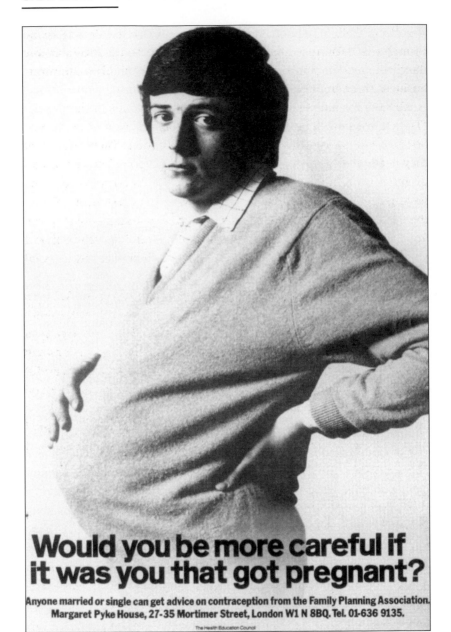

"Possibly the best press ad of all time," says Steve Henry.
The Pregnant Man *written by Jeremy Sinclair at Cramer Saatchi,*
London, in the late 1960s for the UK Health Education Council.

Abbott believes agencies *cannot expect* their clients to be courageous. "You must interest them in being effective, and educate them with evidence by the way you work with them. They are not in business to be brave."

Abbott sees a duality of interests in the agency-client relationship. "The clients you get in the early days are clients who come to you because you're small and you've got a reputation. They know that they need great work to compete, to make their pound or their dollar go further. I think the hard phase is when clients come to you who have got enough money to *blast* their way to recognition. Nevertheless, you want to use that budget, because you're the agency you are, to further your own creative reputation. You still believe that if you can make forty million look like eighty million, it's just as good as making two million look like four million."

Persuading a client to run cutting edge advertising, in Abbott's view, centres on trust. "It's about winning their confidence; it's about maybe proving yourself on some small things; it's about trying to think in terms of campaigns and not just ads, so that they understand this isn't just a one-shot piece of brilliance. It's also being careful about what clients you take; it's being honest about what you're good at, and what you're not good at. I always try and view new business in that light. 'Could we do a good job on it?' is one of the questions I think you should ask yourself, and you should be honest enough, if you say it's not really your bag, not to go for it."

THE CUTTING EDGE.
SOMETIMES, IT CAN HURT.

Life at the cutting edge is a heady mix of sacrilege and sacrifice.

The sacrilege first. Creativity is a destructive process, tearing down what has gone before and rebuilding afresh. We have to shift gears, from logic to intuition, and adjust perspectives in line with new realities. The fundamentals of human behaviour have not changed; simply the environment in which we find them, and the creative means by which we access them. To quote Delaney, it is what is appropriate at the time.

And so to the sacrifice. To create cutting edge work, to make a difference, you must first make a difference within yourself. You will need a strong, intense base for your advertising ideology. That follows in the next chapters. But do not expect an easy ride.

Sinha's advice says it all: "If you really, really, *really* are determined to get into advertising as a writer or an art director, then you'll find that you are entering a world where there are all sorts of conventions and rules already set. You can either play by those conventions and rules and try to win yourself fame and fortune that way, in which case you may not be stretching yourself. But if you're someone with protean creative urges inside you, someone who really wants to break the mould, and you want to do something that no one's ever seen before, then you've got to be prepared that the industry will not help you, because it's full of extremely conservative people who know the way it's been done since the year dot. Creative directors who have seen awards won on things for many years by doing it *their* way; clients who see that results are produced by doing it *their* way. And if you come in and say, I want to do it some *new* way that comes out of your spirit or some intuition of yours, there'll be a hell of a lot of resistance.

"But, by the same token, the people who do follow their own instincts, and fight for them, and *prevail*, they're the people who break new ground and end up setting the new standards and showing the new way forward. Like Graham Fink, they'll be the figureheads for the future."

It's in here. And it's no smaller than a tumor that's found in a real breast. The difference is, while searching for it in this ad could almost be considered fun and games, discovering the real thing could be a matter of life and death. Breast cancer is one of the most common forms of cancer to strike women. And, if detected at an early enough stage, it's also one of the most curable. That's why the American Cancer Society recommends that women over forty have a mammogram at least every other year, and women under forty have a baseline mammogram between the ages of 35 to 39. You see, a mammogram can discover a tumor or a cyst up to three years before you'd ever feel a lump. In fact, it can detect a tumor or a cyst no bigger than a pinhead. Which, incidentally, is about the size of what you are searching for on this page. At Charter Regional in Cleveland, you can have a mammogram performed for just $101. Your mammogram will be conducted in private, and your results will be held in complete confidence and sent directly to your doctor. After your mammogram, a trained radiology technician will meet with you individually and show you how to perform a breast self-examination at home. And, we'll provide you with a free sensor pad, a new exam tool that can amplify the feeling of anything underneath your breast. Something even as small as a grain of salt. If you would like to schedule a mammogram, just call Charter's Call for Health at 593-1210 or 1-800-537-8184. Oh, and by the way, if you haven't found the lump by now, chances are, you're not going to. It was in the 17th line. The period at the end of the sentence was slightly larger than the others. So think about it, if you couldn't find it with your eyes, imagine how hard it would be to find it with your hands.

CAN YOU FIND THE LUMP IN THIS BREAST?

CHARTER REGIONAL MEDICAL CENTER

CALL FOR HEALTH

5 9 3 - 1 2 1 0

Print creativity defies all rules. Words can be words, words can be visuals. There are no limits, as Henderson Advertising, Greenville, South Carolina, proves.

2

How to Find Your Voice

G reat advertising has never been produced by ambivalent minds.

Some very fundamental beliefs about advertising are now being questioned. At the root of it all are: how advertising works; whether or not traditional advertising research is still valid; and whether we should have more trust in our own intuitive skills as communicators.

As a cutting edge communicator, you will need a very strong, well-informed personal philosophy about advertising. You will need to take sides and take a stand. Understanding the fundamental elements of your craft does not mean simply intellectual comprehension. It means consciously accepting certain ideas, internalising them, and committing yourself to them. Otherwise your faith will not survive.

Once you have found your values, you will begin to find your true voice as a communicator.

Changing Consumer Attitudes Won't Change Consumer Behaviour

All too often, well-meaning souls write briefs asking for advertising which has to change consumer attitudes. It is an utterly fallacious objective.

Beware of believing that the way to change consumer behaviour is to first change consumer attitudes. Attitudes tend to be the *result* of behaviour, not the cause of it.

Psychologist Leon Festinger showed that attitudinal change tends to follow behavioural change, rather than precede it. His *Theory of Cognitive Dissonance*, published in 1957, recognised that people desire stable opinions. When that state is upset, they experience a kind of tension, or dissonance, which needs to be relieved. His experiments explained how people justify their actions by changing their beliefs. In this context, advertising plays a vital role by reinforcing a new pattern of attitudes *after* a change in consumer behaviour. The more advertising creates dissonance, the more people are likely to *reject* it.

Dr. Herbert Krugman's research into advertising showed that identifiable attitude change occurs *after the purchase* and not before it. Attitudes, therefore, are significant only when tied to experience.

A perfect example is anti-smoking advertising. After years of exposure to dissonant health warnings, many smokers will grudgingly admit that their habit is harmful. While their attitude to smoking has in some way changed, their behaviour has not. In fact, their negative behaviour could well have been reinforced. What would more likely change their behaviour is a tragic experience: the death of a close relative or friend from cancer. If they quit smoking as a result, then anti-smoking messages would support their new attitude.

AWARENESS: A WARNING

Another fallacy worth exploring is *awareness*. Advertising briefs are written *ad nauseum* calling for campaigns to create awareness, as though awareness itself will guarantee purchase.

Andrew Ehrenberg has researched the relationship between advertising and consumer behaviour in the supermarket. His point is that awareness is not a highly emotional state. Nor does it imply an active predisposition to buy the brand. Rather, it means just what it says, and it may just stop at that: pure awareness. Ehrenberg believes that the trigger to purchase is more likely to come from the external world, such as a cut-price offer or an in-store demonstration, than from the internal world of attitudes and dispositions. Like Festinger and Krugman, he concludes that advertising's main role is *reinforcing* feelings of satisfaction with brands already bought.

AND LET'S NOT FORGET RECALL

While we are about it, we should probably despatch that other old bogeyman: advertising recall.

The classroom model of advertising still lingers on. Sales managers still believe in selling points and like to list them in their ads. Researchers still believe ads can be assessed by measuring the amount of advertising content retained in the minds of consumers.

The theory sounds plausible enough: if the audience can remember what the advertising said, the advertising was effective. The reality, though, is completely different. The real test is how they *interpreted* the advertising, and what they did as a result.

For every study that shows a positive correlation between advertising recall and purchase behaviour, there is a study that shows a negative correlation. It is a lot wiser if you believe that consumer behaviour *cannot* be predicted by the recall of advertising, only by the recall of brand names.

HOW ADVERTISING *DOESN'T* WORK

Hugh Mackay explodes what he calls the Injection Myth. Advertising, he reminds us, does not work like a hypodermic needle.

In order to be effective communicators, the theory goes, we must first craft our messages carefully so as to maximise their impact on the audience. Then we choose a medium for injecting them into the minds of our target audience. We load our messages into the medium, inject them via the eye or ear, or both, and wait for them to work.

Mackay says: "We cling to the idea that messages are powerful and audiences are passive. We want people to absorb what we're saying without being distracted by their own opinions or by their feelings towards us. The things we want to communicate seem so interesting and important to us that it's hard for us to believe that they're not equally interesting and important to other people."

An equally dangerous delusion, Mackay explains, is the assumption that meanings are actually *in* our messages; that once our messages lodge in the minds of consumers, the meanings will, too.

"It's not what our message does to the reader, but what the reader does with our message, that determines our success. When we speak of a powerful message, we're really referring to the power of the message to evoke a response. *Communication occurs when the audience does something with the message.* The audience has the power to interpret the message. In communication terms, that's the ultimate power."

"People are not passive sponges just waiting there to receive your messages," warns Mary Stow. "There are a lot of misconceptions about shouting very loudly, and saying what you want to say, and it will work. Of course it won't. You should be thinking not what you're going to tell them, but what you want these people to feel and think after they've seen the advertising. Instead of writing propositions in briefs, you really should be writing *key responses.*"

HOW ADVERTISING *DOES* WORK

The most lucid explanation you will ever find is in Mackay's book *The Good Listener.*

"We're engaged in a lifelong process of constructing personal '*cages*' around ourselves. The bars of our cages are all the things that life has taught us: our knowledge, our attitudes, our values, our beliefs, our convictions. As the cage becomes stronger and more complex, we feel increasingly comfortable inside it and increasingly confident in our ability to cope with the world beyond the cage.

"The cage is the most powerful element in the communication process. It acts as a *filter* in the process of interpretation. Because we look at the world through the bars of the cage, the bars impose their own pattern on what we see."

Suddenly we have a very clear picture of what advertising has to do. Our creativity has to find ways to penetrate the bars of the cage.

Armed with Mackay's Cage Metaphor, we can see why people interpret messages in ways that make them feel comfortable and secure. It lets us see why empowerment advertising has a better chance of working than confrontational advertising. If we attack people's attitudes head-on, the bars will simply filter out what we are saying. In fact, in the process, the bars could even be reinforced.

We can also understand why Mackay, like Tim Delaney, believes ads should be relevant, not gratuitous. "Relevance ensures that messages will find a ready point of entry to the cage," Mackay explains. "People pay most attention to messages which are relevant to their own circumstances and point of view."

Fortunately for communicators, cage-building never ends. New experiences add new bars, or *modify* existing bars. Travel is one experience which can produce new attitudes, new bars. Marriage, childbirth, divorce, bereavement, retirement, life-threatening illnesses also cause people to reassess their values and reconstruct their bars.

So how do we slip our advertising through the bars of the cage?

Mackay suggests we can send messages which act as **signposts**. Advertising can signpost a social change, or a change in behaviour by our peer group.

A good example of the cage at work: when Pepsi challenged Coke on taste, it challenged the beliefs of Coke drinkers head-on. But when Michael Jackson became Pepsi's icon, he signposted that times had changed, that Pepsi was now 'cool', and loyal Coke drinkers *gave themselves permission* to change brands.

Another form of signpost is **sending a piece of news**. News about a price drop can change behaviour. So, too, can offering something new; it is news which people have never heard before. Stow cites a pot noodle which actually contained fibre. "It was an extraordinary message because nobody thought a pot noodle had any nutritional value whatsoever. It was news and it fundamentally changed behaviour."

Advertising can send messages of **support and encouragement**. One scenario: people buying expensive cars might be feeling dissonant about their extravagance. They will actively seek out messages which help justify their action and bring their attitudes into line with their behaviour.

We can base our message on some **existing part of the cage**, so the audience can see how the brand is consistent with what they already believe. At the Campaign Palace, writer Lionel Hunt and art

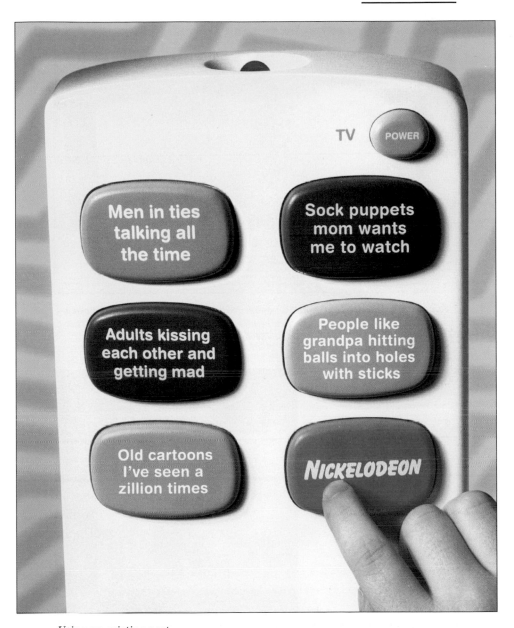

Using an existing part of the cage: Mad Dogs & Englishmen show kids how Nickelodeon is consistent with what they already believe.

Support and encouragement for dissonant readers: a Mercedes-Benz might be a tad expensive, but at least you'll survive to enjoy the view should it ever overturn. Springer & Jacoby, Hamburg.

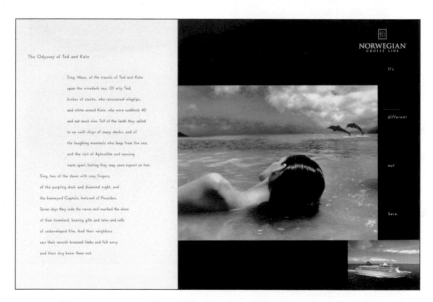

Not your average slice of life. Readers share the cruise experience of stockbroker Ted and his wife Kate, "who wore sunblock 40 and not much else". There is nothing formulaic in this treatment by Goodby, Silverstein & Partners, San Francisco. Readers can relate to Ted and Kate, who returned to the envy of their neighbours and their dog who "knew them not".

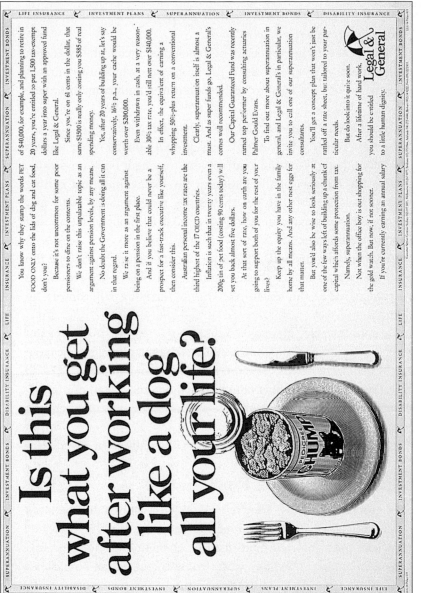

A great print ad will reach into the cage and put an arm around the reader's shoulder. Jack Vaughan crafted this famous ad around the horrifying truth that some Australian pensioners can only afford to eat pet food. (Note the campaign branding: Legal & General's full range of insurance products frames the ad.) The Campaign Palace, Australia.

director Gordon Trembath did that for Footrest Shoes. Footrest was making sensible shoes designed, unusually, by women for women. The photograph showed a pair of extreme stiletto heels going over on their sides with the headline: *Most women's shoes are designed by men who never have to wear them.*

We can **share experiences**. The consumer inside the cage can live a moment of someone else's life, someone whose life mirrors their own. It does not have to be executed in a mundane, formulaic way.

As Nick Cohen observes: "The best advertising, in a lot of ways, is like the best comedy. If you look at stand-up comics, what they're very good at doing is getting a mirror and turning it back on people, capturing the mindset of the nation at the exact time, just getting people to look at how they live their lives, making us all smile and laugh at it. It's very human stuff. A lot of it is about intuition and observational humour."

We can **answer dreams**. This does not involve us in rattling the bars of the cage, trying to change attitudes or beliefs. Research will have told us what the dream is. The advertising will simply be fulfilling it.

As a general rule, Mackay counsels, we should focus on behaviour, not attitudes. And we should seek small changes, not large ones. "Erosion," he states, "is more effective than explosion."

If everything thus far has penetrated *your* cage, well and good. The bars of your cutting edge value system should strengthen and prosper.

The next subject, however, may well evoke a different response.

RESEARCH: FRIEND OR FOE?

"Focus groups are bogus. They're broken." Bill Oberlander believes the more he knows about his target audience, the more he can craft the work to push the right buttons. But conventional focus groups are not the solution. "Anybody who's going to cut out an hour and a half of their time on a Thursday night to go to a very small, fluorescently lit, stale cookied, bad coffee'd room to talk about how they consume mosquito-bite ointment in their lives, I should think those people are losers."

The people who really make a difference to how brands succeed in the marketplace are what Oberlander calls opinion leaders. "They're very intelligent, very stylish, very together, and trust me, they're not going to focus groups."

John Salmon is equally sceptical. "If you think about the people who are prepared to go out and spend the evening talking about advertising, who *are* these people? If they are people who are fanatically keen on advertising and they're not in the advertising business, they should be eliminated from the sample. People who leave their homes and go out for fifteen quid, sit down with similar people and talk about advertising, these people have to be a subgroup like trainspotters. Otherwise, why else would they do it?"

"A lot of research in the advertising process is misguided," explains Mackay. "It asks people rational-sounding questions that create the expectation that there will be a rational explanation. If you ask people for a rational explanation, they'll give you one. *But it may have nothing to do with the truth.* How do you know that you wouldn't have got a different answer if you'd asked them a different question? How do you know that the thing the person said mightn't actually exist *unless* you asked the question? It was only an answer to a question. It had no roots in their psyche at all."

Asking a question and getting an answer is the great pitfall of all social, marketing and advertising research. Asking questions, warns Mackay, almost guarantees that we have put a barrier between ourselves and the consumers.

There *are* rational aspects of behaviour which are appropriate for formal questions and rational analysis: How many brands of chocolate can you name? When did you last visit a supermarket? How much did you spend?

But when dealing with the process of connecting people to brands and responses to advertising, the problem is to create a research method which will allow people to reveal the nuances of their feelings about a certain category, to reveal to us the dreams they are dreaming that they would like to come true.

"When we've heard all that, we respond to it. And if we do, *they* in turn will respond to *us*."

Connections made between consumers and brands, and the

passions aroused by certain propositions, are rarely a rational process, advises Mackay. "Of course there are rational elements in it, and the more money you're asking people to spend, the more you've got to provide them with rational things to support the process of falling in love."

The best way of understanding the advertising process, suggests Mackay, is to use the analogy of personal relationships. "Everything we need to know about how advertising works, we can learn from seeing how people fall in love, and how friendships evolve and prosper or break down. What you find when you look at why people connect with some people, and not with others, is rarely rational. If you said to someone, 'Why did you fall in love with her?', they'd look at you and say, 'How do you mean, *why?* I just did.' Suppose you asked me that question and I said, 'Well, she had this many dollars in her bank account, and I tested her IQ and it was this much, and I made some quantitative assessment of her physique, so I thought I might as well fall in love with her.' It never works like that, and neither does advertising."

Advertising, Mackay reminds us, should be a process where people respond to each other. "We've got to get away from this idea that we want people to respond to the ad. The overwhelming thought in any agency has got to be: *the ad must be a response to the people.*"

"Research is the first thing we do," Cohen reveals. "Qualitative research to find out how people relate to a brand, what people think of it. You need three bits of information: what's good about it; what the culture of the company behind it is, in a very honest way, because you can't misrepresent the client and you can't misinform the consumer; and you need to know what people think of it, what baggage comes with it." Cohen quotes the example of Exxon. "There are some realities you've got to face. They're an oil company, they're out to make tons of money, and they're selling something we need to put in our cars, but it's pollutive, it's mishandled, et cetera, et cetera. So you have to take on board all of that before you do an ad. With Exxon, one of our problems is that there's a distrust towards them, people think that they're evil, so you can't ignore that. You have to address that. So our usual starting point is: how people relate to the brand, what people think of the brand, balanced up with what the brand truly is."

Attitudes to research vary, according to experience. Some call research a tool, others a crutch. The question is, has the crutch turned the industry into a cripple?

"You can ask some people in the target audience about how they feel about a brand," suggests Tim Delaney. "You can ask them how they feel about language in a category. If I'm writing an ad about a tampon, which I don't use, I may want to understand as a writer what women feel about the tampon category, what language they're prepared to accept, what they're not prepared to accept. That doesn't make me a cripple when I get the information. The issue then, about writing an ad, is that I can do it because I'm armed with the right kind of knowledge. From then on in, it's about my intuitive ability to use that information and make an ad out of it. What research *can't* do is take that ad away and confirm with six women down the road that I've done absolutely the right thing. All you'll get are different opinions and I'm not really interested in the lowest common denominator."

It is a sentiment echoed by John Hegarty. "We like to use research at BBH because it's another opinion. It's a way of finding out what is going on in the world, what consumers are doing, and testing out theories. But when it comes to *predictive* research, researching an ad to see if people like it, then I think it's seriously flawed."

CONCEPT TESTING

Mackay is adamant: *"The best advertising research never, at any stage, mentions advertising."*

Not surprisingly, he is opposed to concept testing. "Don't fall for it," he warns. "The best advertising research is the journey around the consumer's head. What we really want to know is what dreams the consumer is dreaming, and how we can position our brand in such a way that will help those dreams come true. It's a technique borrowed from therapeutic counselling: tell me about your life, and in that story I'll find *a point of connection.*"

Besides, argues Mackay, the classic concept test is not a concept test. It is a *primitive* ad test.

"Concepts are mental constructs. They only exist in people's heads. As soon as you write some words on a piece of paper and draw a picture, it's not a concept. It's an expression. If you show someone an ad and get them to talk about it as if they are on some kind of consumer jury, almost certainly what you'll get is a spurious art director's or amateur copywriter's assessment. You're inviting them to be judgemental and you *don't* want consumers to be judgemental when they see your ad."

Pre-testing of rough executions and ads, in Mackay's view, is the refuge of the insecure. It also puts a little fence around what you can talk about with consumers. "All you can talk about is what is in the material. It might trigger some of the broader issues, but it's a big risk because you've already flagged what *you* think. The real challenge is to establish what concepts exist in the consumer's mind. If you can do that, you don't need to test. If you have taken the journey through the psyche of your target audience, and responded to that, you're going to have effective advertising. If you have really good people creating that advertising, it will also be brilliant as well as effective."

When Doyle Dane Bernbach's famous Avis campaign was pre-tested, half the people who saw the ads did not like them. "But half the people did," said Bill Bernbach, "and that's the half we want. Let's go with it." Fortunately, the Avis president Bob Townsend, himself a maverick, backed Bernbach's judgement.

Hunt is concerned that clients will deny themselves the creative breakthroughs they need to build their brands. After all, creativity is the opposite of conformity. "The more research that goes into providing the brief the better, up to a point, but after that I really think you should leave it up to the creators of the ad. If they are genuine, and talented, and students of human nature, you are better off leaving it to them than to any focus group. Of course, the creative team needs to be really good and really intuitive, but if they aren't, no amount of research is going to save them."

Because advertising is intuitive, Delaney believes we cannot research our way to a solution. "Intuition, by definition, is something which is without a kind of absolutism. There isn't anything absolute about what we do. The problem that I have with research is that it tries to prove *objectively* that we are right, when the essence of what we do is *subjective*. Because agencies won't own up to the fact that what we do is subjective, they're happier dealing with objectivity which they know to be spurious. But because it's got a logic to it, they follow that instead of just saying that we're like footballers, or cellists, or ballerinas. We're as good as our born, innate talents and that's it. There's no point trying to prove that one footballer is better than another by using research; there are no absolutes in that sense."

"Everybody knows predictive research doesn't work, but it's convenient for them to believe in it." Hegarty paints a familiar scenario: "If you're in a corporation, you go along to your boss and show him something really provocative and different, and there's a sharp intake of breath. So you say, 'Oh, but I researched it, and the research said it was fine'. In other words, I'm not to blame if it goes wrong, it was the research."

"It's dangerous, extremely dangerous," says Ian Batey. "We all know it's been a security blanket for advertisers and, I might add, for a lot of agencies. We've become such disciples of these practices, they've obsessed us. It's a disease that's getting worse as the years go by; that without the appropriate research, no one does anything. By and large, we're talking about brand managers and commercial managers, whose jobs rely on them achieving certain results every year, and they follow formulas, they follow a process. If you don't follow that process, they actually can't relate to you." Batey admires the businessmen who can trust their own judgement and marketing skills. "There are clients who can say, now listen, we've been around our business long enough that if *we* can't feel it, if *we* can't smell it, if *we* don't know what is going on, what the hell are we doing in this business?"

If people are insecure about their advertising, Mackay believes they should admit it. If the planner, the writer, the art director, the account director and the client are in *genuine* disagreement, or experiencing *genuine* doubt about whether they have caught the dream, testing ads would be appropriate. "But the testing should be as naturalistic as possible," he cautions, "and always done in homes. If it's a print ad, don't get a group discussion and hold it up. Give it to them in the context of a magazine or paper, ask them to look at it overnight and come back tomorrow for a chat."

A DIFFERENT DRUMMER

There are no rules, and Britain's Howell Henry Chaldecott Lury has developed an unusual approach to research.

Stow explains: "We tend to avoid doing research early on in the process. We would not start by doing focus groups so we could understand attitudes to the product. We think by using observation and intelligence, we can get to that quite easily. Focus groups can so easily hold you back. People can only tell you what is *now*, not what might be possible." Instead, the agency concentrates on understanding the client organisation and the competition. "Usually when people do a competitive review, it means getting the graduate trainee to put together a little reel of ads. We take the competitive review really seriously. We deconstruct the ads and try to see exactly what the competition is doing."

The basic learning from one such review, coupled with an understanding of the client, provided the breakthrough for the agency's famous Orange Tango campaign. "Everyone else in the soft drink category was rushing headlong into the area of glorious American youth, bright teeth, very smiley-wonderful-happy-healthy-people-having-good-clean-fun. That's the obvious place to go and a lot of people would think if those are the rules of the market, we'd better follow them. But we thought there was a great opportunity for someone to push youth on the streets, urban and gritty. That was where the tonality came from. Real life, *British* real life. There's a real resistance to Americana; in some ways we love it, in some ways we hate it. The tonality led us to the orange man, to the slap on the face." Stow says the message, *The hit of real oranges*, came straight out of product delivery. "We could have gone the fresh orange route, but it wouldn't have been credible because Tango has a taste that hits you in the mouth."

The agency uses research for creative development and always produces more than one idea. "We tend to use research to find out what is possible, rather than just what is. It's very easy to think these are the rules of the market, we can't break them, we can't go any further than that. But by researching creative work which takes a brand in a different direction, we can discover what *is* possible."

Possibly the most controversial aspect of the agency's approach is the way it treats *likeability*. "In a lot of focus groups that are being watched from behind the mirror, everybody's looking for the 'that's nice' reaction, 'that's lovely', because the client behind the mirror will feel good. We actually have an allergic reaction to that response," explains Stow. "People can say 'that's nice', then file it away and ignore it. We're looking for the ideas that *worry* people a bit."

The agency believes that if it is going to change behaviour, any behaviour, the first step is to be noticed, to let people know that something is happening. It has an effect on people because it starts them questioning things. "After the groups, we try to eavesdrop on people as they leave. We try to find out which idea they're still talking about. It's an indication that it stayed in their mind, registered enough, did enough. That kind of reaction means the shock value is not just shock value; it's got something intrinsic to it that's both shocking and interesting to people, but not irrelevantly so."

RISK AND RESPONSIBILITY

With so many fundamental beliefs under siege, conservative voices urge caution. The pursuit of creativity, they say, has lost its perspective. We risk ignoring our basic responsibility to our clients to produce what is called "effective" advertising. Certain rules, certain beliefs, certain methodologies have served the business well, and restraint is called for.

Most of the rules and methodologies have indeed served business. They have provided the cardiovascular systems of conventional agency structures. They have stifled evolution and innovation. They have proliferated mediocrity and made it respectable. The greatest risk in not taking risks is that advertisers will abandon the advertising industry and go in search of creativity elsewhere.

Oscar Wilde said: "An idea that does not involve risk does not deserve to be an idea."

If you agree that taking risks is a legitimate part of your responsibility, what specific risks should you be taking?

"The agency's responsibility is to go way *beyond* where the client could get to himself," asserts Simon Sherwood of Bartle Bogle Hegarty. "Clients can buy media, source production, do the analysis and strategy, but they can't take the creative step. If agencies don't take creative leaps, they're not doing the thing they can best do. We believe at BBH that we are manufacturing advertising properties which have a value to clients. We've always believed we should come to a very firm view about what the right kind of advertising is for a client. We never present clients with alternatives. If you do, it's an abdication of responsibility."

"An idea that hasn't been done before might, on the surface, look really risky," argues Bob Isherwood, worldwide creative director of Saatchi & Saatchi. "It's an area where no one has been before. There is no precedent. But usually the biggest risk lies in ideas that are predictable, because ideas that are predictable don't get noticed. You can't sell anything to anyone unless they notice you. To get a boring ad noticed, you've got to run it lots and lots of times. If you've got a really original message, you only need to run it a few times. People retain the message longer and it costs the client less."

"Safe advertising is the riskiest advertising of all," Graham Warsop believes, "because it runs the risk of not being seen. It's just too easy to create advertising that lets you tick the boxes showing all the strategic requirements have been met, but doesn't allow you to tick the boxes marked 'fresh', 'distinctive' for the category, and 'rewarding' for the consumer. Invariably, in such cases, the work just washes over the people who are exposed to it."

Interestingly, Warsop has observed that most marketers wear a consumer's hat when it comes to choosing their own favourite advertising. "It comes as no surprise when prospective clients reveal their favourite ads are amongst the most creative and distinctive in a category. It's quite helpful to remind them of this just before presenting the creative work for their brand."

"A lot of creative people think creative risk-taking means doing stuff that scares the life out of you," says Singapore creative director Garry Abbott. "The leaders of the industry, the Tim Delaneys and people like that, come up with things that are completely new which come out of nowhere; certainly not from last year's award books. They don't rely on borrowed ideas. Risk is about *freshness*. Ideas you haven't seen before. They give everyone a buzz, and they give the consumers a buzz because they're regaled with the sameness of advertising. Risk is about breaking rules." Abbott believes advertising should not have many rules. "We are supposed to be on the cutting edge of communications, yet we keep falling back on the same old things."

Risks must be taken at two levels, advises Mackay. "One is the risk of listening to the consumer, because when we hear what the consumer is thinking and feeling and dreaming, it might not coincide with our preconceptions. Going to the consumer and saying, tell me your story so I can really see what it's like to be you so I can respond to that, is a risk that creative people and clients are rarely prepared to take fully." The second risk? "I would define creativity as taking a set of familiar elements and rearranging them in an unfamiliar way so that the audience recognises both the familiarity and the *un*familiarity. In other words, present something the audience will recognise as themselves, their lives, their dreams, but with a twist, so they're actually a bit startled by it, or will get an extra insight from it. So it's not just a mirror, it's a mirror that's *cracked*. The safe thing is to say, 'Well, the consumer said I like X, Y and Z, so let's show them X, Y and Z'. But that's not creativity; that's journalism. Creativity is saying that's what the consumer feels, that's the dream, that's the aspiration, that's the *raw material* we're working with. Now we have to be creative with it, or we'll just be part of the bland advertising landscape and not be noticed."

CUTTING EDGE VOICES

As you begin to find your voice, it might help to hear some other voices: those agencies which not only do different work, but do their work differently.

Britain's **Howell Henry Chaldecott Lury** does unconventional work within an unconventional structure. Dedicated project teams are assigned to each account. Each team comprises an account director, a planner, a writer and an art director. There are no briefs as such; each close-knit team lives and breathes its account, literally writing its own brief as it burrows into its assignment.

As Steve Henry explains: "They work together more closely than would be allowed or encouraged in conventional agencies. They also have quasi-autonomy; for instance, the account director and planner will look at cuts of TV commercials *before* the creative director."

The system has produced some of the most electrifying work Britain has seen in two decades. It is not a cosmetic attachment to a conventional agency structure; it grew out of a belief that everybody should have a shared goal and a share in creating great work.

"In the early days of the agency, there were just the founding partners of the agency sitting together in one room, as it is when most agencies start from scratch," recalls Henry. "But the point about it for us was that we really enjoyed that method of working. We loved the kicks we got out of having three disciplines working so closely together, trying to solve problems as a genuine team, sharing responsibility and working towards a shared goal. As we grew and hired more people, we could have gone the conventional way and split up into different departments. But we wanted to preserve the magic, the chemistry, that happened when you mixed the different disciplines together."

Henry believes the agency has developed a more positive work environment as well as achieved work which hits its dual target of being surprising and effective. He admits that imposing a system of shared responsibility on people can take some getting used to. "But cynics who join the agency soon find that they couldn't possibly work any other way."

The Jupiter Drawing Room of South Africa is ranked among the world's top five creative agencies. With clients including Nike, Fiat and The Coca-Cola Company, it describes itself as a through-the-line agency delivering "integrated communications that transcend advertising solutions". Its multi-disciplinary approach is reflected in its awards. For example, it won the first Silver Pencil at D&AD for ambient media in 2000. At the One Show in 2001 and 2002 it won a Gold Pencil for mixed media, Silver Pencils for interactive mixed media and package design, and Bronze Pencils for corporate identity work, a newspaper campaign and ambient media.

Chairman and executive creative director Graham Warsop says the agency is not big on one-off executions, no matter how creative. "We tend to focus on integrated campaigns. In our experience, the 'creative risks' appear less 'risky' when a client sees the strategic rollout of the campaign across a number of disciplines."

Warsop believes agencies will find it easier to persuade their clients to take creative risks when they have built up case studies of how creative risks taken in the past for others have worked successfully for those brands. He cites his client, retail music chain Musica. "Its owners had given it six months to either perform or be closed down. With the blessing of the National Society for the Deaf, we took the creative risk of using a deaf girl to re-launch the chain. Today, Musica's market share has increased from eight percent to in excess of forty-two percent, by far the country's largest CD retailer."

In December 2002, the agency launched the world's first global creative independent – a virtual agency operating borderlessly on the Web called The Dukes of Urbino.Com. The Jupiter Drawing Room is its primary creative and strategic service provider. Its business model offers through-the-line creativity to marketers, design companies, media specialists, management consultancies, and other advertising agencies. Not only will The Dukes of Urbino.Com work for any brand owner in any country, it will also source creative input from an international pool of talent.

Meanwhile, years ago in Hamburg, **Springer & Jacoby** hived itself off into six totally independent agency units located within a 500-metre radius of each other. Each unit can call on support from media, research, planning and other agency departments.

Springer & Jacoby has consistently retained its position as Germany's premier creative agency. Guido Heffels elaborates: "Our unit system was created to keep our agency flexible. After all these years, it's made us multi-cultured."

Heffels stresses that each unit is free to work on its own style of advertising. "Each one has developed its own very special way of seeing things. Each has a totally different working process, from a virtual office like Chiat/Day to an eight-person unit with no account guys."

It may sound like a recipe for anarchy, but very pragmatic controls are in place. "Each unit is continually screened; its performance is measured against our 4 K's: Kunde, Kasse, Kreation, Kultur (Client, Income, Creativity and Culture). They *all* have to be in balance. So a lot of awards and happy clients are not enough if your billings volume is low and your crew is not satisfied."

How have major clients like Mercedes-Benz reacted to working with six-agencies-in-one? "It's an important advantage for them. They only have to deal with a small bunch of people: those that really count. There's no account managing senior supervisor, no supervising creative director, no copy north/west, no nonsense like that! If they wish, a client may work with several units which always leads to new ideas and a little bit of competition, too."

Keeping the work fresh is a key objective. "After a few years, it might be advisable to change the unit on the account," explains Heffels. "Which is, of course, much better than the client changing the agency."

Santa Monica agency **Ground Zero** has removed boundaries and created autonomous cells called brand teams.

Kirk Souder describes his agency as a *community*. "Each brand team consists of strategic people, media people, creative people and the client, and is responsible for uncovering the soul of the brand. Each member's perspective is deemed integral to the development of the brand's planning and positioning. For the brand team to function fully, it must exist for the continued growth and success of the brand, not for any departmental or company agendas." Souder points to the fact that Ground Zero has dispensed with the antiquated Us-and-Them client-agency relationship. "Not surprisingly, many Ground Zero client contacts end up actually moving themselves, either sporadically or permanently, into the Ground Zero environment to be closer to their brand team. In spirit, and in reality, this is one manifestation of what we mean by a community."

While Ground Zero's work is frequently described by the industry as "fresh and edgy", Souder sees a more fundamental issue. "We set out to first uncover the souls of our brands, and then communicate that essence in a clear way to the world. Inevitably, if we do that job well, the work will be new and different because every soul is new and different. The face of the brand must emanate and express the soul of the brand. If we do that, the work will be something more powerful than 'fresh and edgy'. It will be *true*."

It is delusional, Souder believes, for a company to exist for anything other than its people. "When people come to Ground Zero, both clients and employees alike, we ask them to be selfish with their time here. We ask them to look at every task as an opportunity to fulfil their own personal growth, their own personal journey to the truth, and to try what they've never tried before. We ask that in the knowledge that if they do that, inevitably the work will feel fresh, innovative and important. And, more importantly, that *they* will feel fresh, innovative and important."

At another West Coast agency, **Goodby, Silverstein & Partners**, San Francisco, art is the *raison d'être*.

"A lot of advertising people are afraid to even think about art, of course," says chairman Jeff Goodby. "They're proud to say they've got nothing to do with it. In our case, however, art is why we're here."

The word *art*, Goodby reminds us, has the same roots as *artifice*, something created to achieve a certain end, purpose or effect. He recalls: "We started the agency, frankly, because we believed advertising could be an interesting conjunction between art and commerce. We thought art could serve business in a powerful way."

Art, and a respect for the intelligence of the consumer, distinguish the agency's print work. "Have we proven what we wanted to prove?" Goodby ponders. "I'm not sure you ever quite *prove* art. We certainly have gotten it to serve our clients in a business sense on a number of occasions."

Art aside, Goodby talks about the agency's environment. "There's an element of fun here, which we deeply believe in. Contrary to a lot of Western thinking throughout history, we don't think good things only come about as a result of pain, introspection and torture. Study instead your freedom and exuberance each day," he suggests.

The agency's structure, he believes, is not all that different from other agencies utilising an account planning approach. "The key is to hire incredibly intelligent people and create an environment in which they treat each other, and each other's ideas, with respect. People have to feel free and secure to be as smart as they can be," he emphasises. "The rest is just procedure."

Goodby stresses that clients are a fundamental part of this equation. "We look for smart clients who want to bring their best to this process as well."

Democracy, energy and madness are at the heart of New York's **Mad Dogs & Englishmen**. Cohen calls it an inside-out environment. "In most agencies, all the senior people with all the experience have fancy offices with sofas and plants. It looks like they're there forever. All the young people are in lousy offices in the peripheral part of it. What we did was turned it around and made it all much more democratic."

As a result, says Cohen, the energy flows all around the agency. "Young people, and people without experience, are full of ideas. They're naïve. They're not cynical. They're very open so they're actually an amazing source of energy. As you get along in the business, you get a lot more experience and a lot more knowledge, but you also become jaded and cynical. All of a sudden, things become less possible and not more possible. By opening it up, we get a really good mixture of energy, vitality and hope, mixed with experience, knowledge and focus."

Cohen is English. He has worked in America for over fifteen years. He admires Chiat/Day, Goodby Silverstein, BBH, Howell Henry, GGT and Abbott Mead Vickers. "I like agencies that do work that changes my mind about things, makes me think about things in a different way. I don't like agencies that stick to the same thing. I like agencies that challenge. I always thought that the British ad scene was becoming very formulaic; it was always a double page spread with some nice body copy, a well-crafted argument. What the business needed was a good kick. GGT was like what the Sex Pistols were to rock-and-roll. When BBH came along and did some of their early Levi's work, I thought that they injected something deeply missing from British advertising: sex and sexuality. They were really clever; they made you really lust for things."

Mad Dogs & Englishmen started in 1991. "There was a recession. Nobody was starting ad agencies, they were downsizing them." Why the name? "We didn't want to sound like a law firm. Mad Dogs & Englishmen fitted our combination of maverick madness and British charm. It seemed like a good oxymoron."

Another New York agency synonymous with different thinking is **Kirshenbaum Bond & Partners**. Richard Kirshenbaum and Jonathan Bond believe cynical consumers have developed marketing radar as a form of self-defence. Their response is to produce advertising which gets under the radar. One of their most famous ideas actually ran underfoot, stencilled onto city sidewalks in washable paint. The message, for Bamboo Lingerie, read: *From here, it looks like you could use some new underwear*. It was under the radar before anyone realised it was an ad.

Oberlander says the agency has gone out of its way to hire a diverse range of people and personalities. "We look for *different*. Different kinds of thinking minds. Different nationalities. Different religions. Different genders. The ways that different kinds of people approach problems result in very different kinds of solutions."

Not all cutting edge agencies have conventional, big city addresses. Some prefer to do different work in some very different places. Jim Mountjoy, of **Loeffler Ketchum Mountjoy**, Charlotte, North Carolina, believes geography does not determine your fate.

"It begins with self-imposed standards and disciplines. Harry Jacobs in Richmond, Ron Andersen and Tom McElligott in Minneapolis, Stan Richards in Dallas, Dan Wieden in Portland, all believed first in themselves. All have proved it's not where your body's at, it's where your head's at."

Quality of life has become another issue, argues Mountjoy. "An environment is defined by far more than the office. Maybe that's why more young people today, still passionate about work, want a life outside the office. For some it's not The Big Apple. It's mountains, lakes and outdoor adventure just outside their office windows."

PREPARING TO LEAVE THE COMFORT ZONE

Cutting edge creativity asks a lot of you. Questioning conventional methodologies is just one aspect of it.

There has to be a personal commitment to risk-taking as well. Taking risks means you could fail.

"You've got to be willing to fail," insists Roy Grace. "It's a very important requirement. You've got to be willing to be embarrassed, humiliated, feel stupid. Believe me, I've had those moments. How do you know if an idea is a breakthrough or if it's rubbish? Sometimes it's breakthrough rubbish! I've done things I know have never been

done before, and they were awful. They should *never* have been done! At the time I was taking a big chance and they were terrible, really dreadful. Fortunately, we live in a business that forgives. It's interesting that the stuff you do that is recognised as breakthrough somehow sticks to you, and the really bad stuff just sort of vanishes into your closet."

"*Never be afraid of having ideas.* They're the most wonderful things in the world," says Hegarty. If they fail? "Failure is fantastic. You learn so much more from it. But it's a double-edged sword; it can instil caution into you. If it does, you begin to recede and draw back from having daring ideas. You've *got* to dare to be different. That is the thing you *must* be! If you let failure control you, you'll walk away from daring ideas and that will be the end of you as a creative person."

It is odd. Most people prefer to take the line of least resistance. As Shakespeare said, "All the voyage of their life will be bound in shallows."

So those who dare to be different, those who dare to take risks and create landmarks and become the figureheads of the future, will find the field surprisingly uncrowded.

3

THE EIGHT GREATEST LIES YOU'LL EVER BE TOLD

In advertising, the world is flat. Agencies are structured on a linear basis. Campaigns are created in linear formats. There are all kinds of rails and fences and obstacles to keep creative thinking linear, too.

Agencies preach change to their clients, without pursuing it themselves. Generations of creative people have been taught to obey certain rules. Despite social change, technological change and audiences which have become highly media literate, the rules have remained the same. In some agencies, they are mandatory.

The danger with any rule is its rigidity. When it ceases to be a positive influence, when it impedes our development, it deserves to be called a lie. Such lies are counter-productive. They spawn two evils: mediocre work and gratuitous work. They make us behave unprofessionally: on one hand, we impose restrictions on ourselves; on the other, we congratulate ourselves for thinking outside the box of our own making. Clients, observing such behaviour, must question our industry's relevance.

The rules, of course, had their roots in experience. In their day, they were applicable. They were the gospel. Even now, cutting edge creatives can still detect grains of truth in each lie.

So see them in perspective, not as rules carved in stone, but merely as considerations in the creative process.

LIE NO. 1:
YOU MUST HAVE A UNIQUE SELLING PROPOSITION

When this rule was written, products did have genuine, tangible differences. It made good sense to make those unique differences the central focus of the advertising. But, as John Hegarty tells us, those times have changed.

"We've gone from a time when products had genuine unique selling propositions, when you could genuinely manufacture a difference. Electronics firms now share research, Chrysler has joined with Mercedes, big brands come together to manufacture more economically. Products are reaching a fantastic level of quality, but their differences are fewer and fewer. We are now at such a competitive level that it's very difficult for brands to maintain a conventional u.s.p."

Now, Hegarty says, there are perceived differences, *emotional* differences. The u.s.p. has been replaced by the e.s.p., the *emotional selling proposition.* "There's nothing wrong with that. We shouldn't be ashamed of that. How one *feels* about something is incredibly important. Why do I wear a purple shirt as opposed to a white shirt? It's only a colour, but it makes me *feel* different."

As a result, Hegarty's agency sees itself as a manufacturing company. "BBH is not a service company. In a way, we are part of the manufacturing process. We make ideas that make the difference between one brand and another. We help make a brand really different. Not because we're selling something that's got an extra widget on it that no other product has, but because we make you feel differently about this product. You can feel more certain about it, more assured about it, more in love with it, more passionate about it. The emotional differences become the *real* differences."

Bill Oberlander believes in the u.e.p., the *unique emotional proposition.* "Product attributes are small fry and generic and totally vulnerable. Your competitor can duplicate whatever product attributes you have, especially in packaged goods. You have to come up with much bigger emotional propositions for the consumer to stay."

As Fallon Minneapolis art director Bob Barrie asks: "What is the u.s.p. for Coke or Pepsi? Their advertising has become their u.s.p."

Perhaps, then, the term u.s.p. is really a question of interpretation. Lionel Hunt elaborates: "I'm not sure the u.s.p. is dead at all. With the ever increasing number of messages competing for attention, it's more important than ever to be unique. The thing is, *it doesn't necessarily have to be a unique feature of the product itself.*" Hunt provides a charming example: "My favourite brand of all is Baxters Soups of Scotland. I learned recently, in print of course, that Baxters had rejected one hundred and eighty-seven takeover offers. The Chairman of Baxters said, 'No one will ever be asked to sit on our board who does not *fish*'. Now there's a unique selling proposition and the brief for a fabulous advertising campaign."

John Salmon maintains that some kind of brand property is still needed to imply superiority. "It's not always possible today to develop a u.s.p. of the type advocated by Rosser Reeves. I like that other idea of Rosser Reeves', that everybody's got little boxes in their head, and in each little category box they have a few brand names, two or maybe three. If you want to get your brand name in, you've probably got to kick another one out, because there isn't an infinite limit to the number of names that people can contain in their boxes. So you have to provide some kind of memorable element that they can attach to the brand name, some reason for putting it in there." Salmon stresses that the manner of expressing a u.s.p. has moved on. "One doesn't have to be dogmatic. You should try to make your product unique either in style, flavour, attitude, the way you talk about it, even if you can't bring to bear matters of fact, which was what Bates did, to deliver unique benefits."

"In an effort to make account executives realise they're in advertising, because most of them wish they weren't," recounts Neil French, "we wanted to get them to write briefs. So I wrote a very short book with very short words and big print. It was called *How To Do Ads*. It said that every ad had to have a button, something you press, that changes the consumer's mind. So their job was to find the button."

According to French, the button could be a u.s.p. or something else: "The button could be contained in the tone of voice. Because it's the personality of the brand speaking, it must have a definite character. 'Warm and friendly' will not do. What is the alternative? 'Cold and unfriendly'? And anyway, used car salesmen are, on the surface, warm and friendly, and who believes anything they say?"

Finding the button presents unlimited cutting edge opportunities. Brands can be *reframed*, so people see them differently. Like Hugh Mackay's analogy of the cracked mirror, the familiar can be made *unfamiliar*, so people's interest is *renewed*. Advertising can bring to light what was hidden, overlooked or forgotten.

Mary Stow talks about reframing the AA, Britain's automobile breakdown organisation: "When you don't have the luxury of having something new to say, you have to find a new spin on it, find a new way of talking about it, a new emotional territory. The AA had been doing all this advertising about the patrolmen being very nice men. The patrolmen were deeply patronised by motorists. The mindshift we got to on that was referring to them as *The Fourth Emergency Service*."

When you cannot be unique, be the *first*: the first to express a certain thought, the first to look at something from a particular perspective. For the consumer in a cage, the first information received about any subject becomes part of the filter through which all subsequent information on the same subject must pass. Mackay quotes Hitler's propagandist Goebbels: "Whoever says the first word to the world is always right." Not always the case, says Mackay, but quite often. "A great advantage which the first brand into a market always has is that the message of its advertising is new. The fewer reference points which are available to the audience for evaluating the advertising, the more they are likely to accept what the new advertising says."

Advertising's function has changed, explains Ron Mather, former national creative director of The Campaign Palace and now executive creative director of Grey Worldwide, Australia. "I don't believe you sell anyone anything any more; instead, you make them want to buy. Most of the time there isn't a u.s.p., so giving brands a personality is extremely important now. If you like the personality, you're more likely to like the brand. It's a bit the same with people."

LIE NO. 2:
YOU MUST OFFER A RATIONAL BENEFIT

Saint Augustine said: "I have encountered many people who wish to deceive, but no one who wishes to be deceived."

Somehow, over the years, rationality has come to be equated with substance. If the advertising offers a rational proposition, it will be more believable and effective.

"An absolute lie," says Bruce Bildsten, group creative director at Fallon Minneapolis. "Some of the best ads are totally *irrational*. One that leaps to my brain is the British campaign for Stella Artois, where they had fun with the fact it was overpriced. What a wonderful proposition. It's something that's as far from rational as can possibly be!"

Bildsten cites his agency's work for **Porsche**. One ad listed such irrational product benefits as *Too fast, Doesn't blend in, People will talk*. "It was a campaign that really resonated. We got so many letters from people and they said, yes, that's why I buy this car. There's nothing practical about it. I live in the United States where the law says I have to drive fifty-five miles an hour. It doesn't have room for my kids and my luggage. And that's exactly why I love it!"

Also citing Porsche is Salmon. "I think benefits can be purely emotional. There are all kinds of subrational benefits that people are quite prepared to pay large sums of money for. Take the case of somebody who buys a Porsche to drive on the Los Angeles freeways. There's no specific benefit to a Porsche other than you feel better about yourself sitting in one."

Hegarty quotes the classic VW campaign. "**Volkswagen** built itself on the proposition *it's ugly but it works*. The fact that a product has flaws is wonderful. Don't knock it. It's like a human being. Do you like someone who is perfect? You don't. You'd actually rather *dislike* him. Do you like somebody who comes into a room and starts knocking somebody else? Not really. Frailty is a wonderful thing in human beings. I love somebody who comes into a room and makes a joke about themselves. They seem like an interesting person, they seem *confident*."

Fallon Minneapolis at work for Porsche: irrationality that resonated.

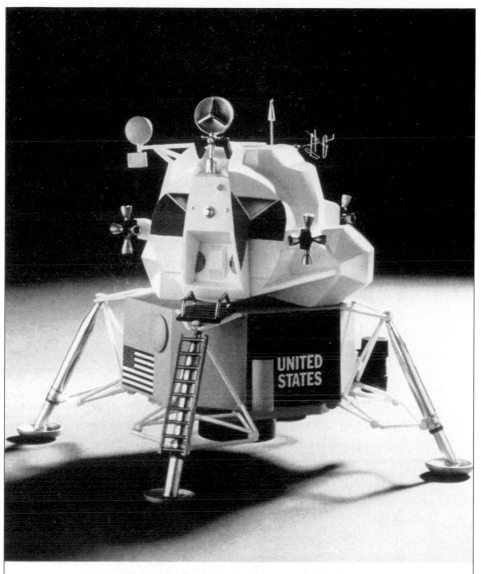

It's ugly, but it gets you there.

*Hardly a rational benefit on which to build a brand. But, as John Hegarty
reminds us, don't we love people who can make a joke about themselves?
Doyle Dane Bernbach, New York.*

Mackay provides a perspective from philosopher Bertrand Russell: "For scientific purposes, I suggest the following experiment. Let two soaps, A and B, be manufactured, of which A is excellent and B abominable; let A be advertised by stating its chemical composition and by testimonials from eminent chemists; let B be advertised by the bare statement that it's the best, accompanied by the portraits of famous Hollywood beauties. If man is a rational animal, more of A will be sold than B. Does anyone, in fact, believe that this would be the result?"

French certainly does not. "Anyone who thinks you need a rational benefit is ignoring ninety percent of the human psyche which is irrational. There's no rational benefit to Pepsi and Coke." However, says French, *the irrational can sometimes be made to seem rational.* "People like to rationalise fun. For instance, it's irrational, on the face of it, to go out and get drunk. It's easy to rationalise things, it's like people who buy *Playboy* for the articles."

Stow believes that sometimes people need an excuse or a pretext to change their behaviour. "I think ads have to either be rational, or *seem* to be rational, because people are smart enough, marketing-literate enough these days not just to buy the fluffy stuff around the edges. They have to feel something substantial in there. The question is, how real is that difference? *The hit of real oranges* is the functional heart of Tango. It talked about something functional which almost gives people an excuse to say, 'I like Tango because it's got the hit of real oranges'. In fact, what they were probably buying into was the giant orange man, the sense of fun, the fact it was real, British, and not American."

While most key decisions we make are emotional, says Simon Sherwood, strong emotional propositions often need rational underpinning. "All brands are a mix of rational and emotional credentials. You have to be strong in both. Our Levi's advertising talks about youthfulness, rebelliousness and sex, underpinned by rational product features like strength."

"You've got to have a balance between rational and emotional arguments," counsels Ian Batey. "There have to be core values providing rational support for the emotional proposition." He quotes his agency's campaign for Singapore Airlines. The *Singapore Girl* is

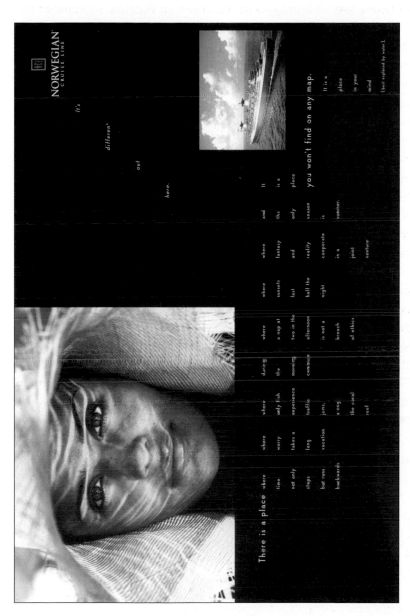

Inaudible whispers of the human soul, amplified by San Francisco's Goodby, Silverstein & Partners.

the emotional icon, says Batey. "*Inflight service even other airlines talk about* becomes the rational argument."

Making love at four in the afternoon on a Tuesday, or being naked more, or putting first things last are not exactly rational. But they are intensely human. If we listen to what people are dreaming about, and respond, consumers will respond to us. Describing Hitler's powerful effect on audiences, Carl Jung said: "He is the loudspeaker which amplifies the inaudible whispers of the German soul." Advertising can do precisely the same. Goodby Silverstein's campaign for the **Norwegian Cruise Line** amplified many inaudible whispers:

"I will be naked more."

"I will memorise clouds."

"There is no law that says you shall not study a sunset."

"Beyond heavy woollens, beyond the Nightly News, beyond the reach of what hurts you, beyond politics (national, local, sexual), beyond *beyond*."

There was nothing rational in the advertising about the ships, the friendly crew, the quality of the cabins and the cuisine, the amenities on board, or getting more ports of call for your dollar. There did not have to be. The emotional aura created by the words and execution made cruising with the Norwegians seem a perfectly legitimate and rational decision.

As Gary Goldsmith sums up: "I don't think you need to offer a rational benefit. I think you need to offer a benefit that a rational person can understand."

LIE NO. 3: HUMOUR DOESN'T SELL

"Humour was one of the phobias of the Rosser Reeves approach to advertising, which was always so absolutely stony-faced humour-less," observes Salmon. "Humour makes friends, but it's very difficult to use." Not everybody will laugh at the same things, he cautions, advocating that humour works best in a campaign format. "Within an overall campaign, you'll make them all laugh, sooner or later."

"There's always been a great debate over whether humorous ads work. There's a million case histories that they do," says Bob Barrie, who describes his own creative style as minimalist with a sense of

JOHN PLAYER SPECIAL.
WAHRSCHEINLICH IRGENDWIE ANDERS.

Who said the Germans don't have a sense of humour?
The proposition is: "Somehow different". Springer & Jacoby, Hamburg.

humour. "Brands are like people. The most important questions you have to ask: what is the personality of your brand, what is the most appropriate personality to project to a consumer audience, and which personality will they most readily accept? If IBM came out with the funniest campaign in the world, I don't think it would feel right to people. If Miller Lite Beer does, then it's acceptable."

"Of course humour sells," says French. "Look at the great salesmen in real life, like the guys in the markets in London selling crockery. They juggle the crockery. They have audiences in stitches. The funniest men sell the most crockery because they get the biggest audiences. Humour crosses all boundaries, financial boundaries, national boundaries. You'd rather buy something from someone you like than someone you don't like."

Graham Warsop believes humour in print involves a more intimate relationship. "I don't think it's possible to achieve the same level of hilarity in print that's possible in TV. The best print humour, in my experience, is understated and often 'dry'. It gets someone to smile inwardly rather than laugh outwardly."

In Singapore, there are many quaint abuses of the English language. Someone with a good command of English is likely to be told: "Wah, your England damn powderful." Ogilvy & Mather's campaign for **British Council** language courses did not have to look far for inspiration; malaprops and assorted howlers abounded. The use of signage was a tactful device. Nobody felt personally insulted. Humour helped people to laugh at themselves, while gently reminding them it was time to brush up their "England".

"You've got to entertain people," advises Garry Abbott. "Their lives are faster, more complicated. Advertising works best on an entertainment level. It stimulates them, amuses them for a nanosecond, sufficient for them to retain the message. Collett Dickenson Pearce did that so well. They were constantly entertaining the consumer and the brands didn't suffer. Quite the reverse."

The most unlikely products can benefit from humour. Even in Stuttgart, which is hardly the world capital of comedy, the makers of Mercedes-Benz applaud wit in their headlines. The brand becomes more accessible, less imposing.

Death, however, is another matter entirely. Defying conventional wisdom, humour has proved appropriate for **Chippers Funerals** of Perth, Australia. At agency Vinten Browning, writer Steve Browning explains: "Our brief for the Chippers campaign was unusual. The client, Kim Chipper, had seen some of our work and asked us if we could do a few ads for him. He briefed us on the finer points of his profession; the importance of grief, the various customs people observe, what a funeral director actually does, and the pros and cons of cremation vs. burial. Thankfully, he spared us the factory tour." Each ad in the campaign tackles one interesting aspect of death and funerals, and then turns the subject to Chippers. According to Browning, "Writing the turnaround at the end of each ad is often the most difficult bit. That, and getting the tone of voice right. I try and remember that some people reading the ads will have lost a close friend or partner that day, so you can't be irreverent or flippant. But an injection of gentle humour into the series seems to have done no harm."

Shelter Clothing broke advertising conventions in the skateboarding market. Agency Mad Dogs & Englishmen believes humour can look at faults and vices as well as virtues. Skateboarders were no

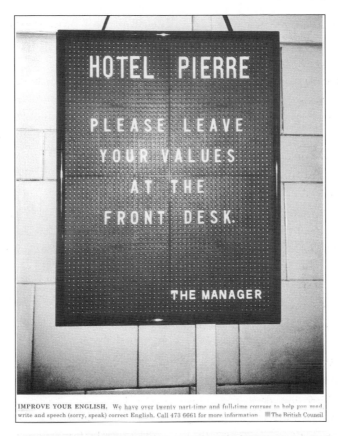

IMPROVE YOUR ENGLISH. We have over twenty part-time and full-time courses to help you read, write and speech (sorry, speak) correct English. Call 473 6661 for more information. ■ The British Council

A tactful use of humour: no one lost face, but the point was made.
Ogilvy & Mather Singapore for British Council English-language courses.

WHEN UTTERING YOUR LAST WORDS,
PLEASE SPEAK SLOWLY AND CLEARLY.

When Albert Einstein died in 1955, a group of friends gathered around his bedside. The most brilliant scientific mind of this century uttered his final words and then gently slipped away. With what thought did the great man leave us? A new theory? The answer to a tricky time-space conundrum?

We will never know, as none of his friends spoke German.

So becomes apparent one of the problems with last words. Another is timing. Given the fickle nature of death, few people are lucky enough to have their final utterings recorded and inscribed into history because often no one's there to hear them.

Even when someone is close enough to hear your well-chosen words, nature can still be unpredictable, as General Sedgewick found out. The American Civil War troop commander gave us a moment of unintentional humour when he peered over a parapet towards the enemy and boasted 'They couldn't hit an elephant at this dist.... '.

Some of our finest artists have given us great works but rather lame last words.

'Now let me sleep', said English poet Lord Byron. And the best Felix Mendelssohn, the composer, could manage was 'I'm very weary'.

But others left us with gems. Novelist W. Somerset Maugham commented 'Dying is a dull and dreary affair. My advice to you is to have nothing whatsoever to do with it'. And Oscar Wilde observed 'Either this wallpaper goes, or I do'.

Prima ballerina, Anna Pavlova, was famous for her sensitive portrayal of the dying swan in Swan Lake. How apt then her parting words; 'Get my swan costume ready'.

Stan Laurel, it appears, was the consummate comedian to the very last. 'I'd rather be skiing than doing this', he said to his bedside nurse.

'Do you ski, Mr Laurel?', she asked.

'No, but I'd rather be doing that than this', Stan whispered before he left us.

Closer to home, outlaw Ned Kelly departed with the short observation, 'Such is life'.

But the most positive outlook on the final journey comes from the English poet Gerard Manley Hopkins. Rather than a clever or gloomy quote, he simply said 'I am so happy, so very happy'.

At Chippers, we're seldom privy to a person's last words; our duty is to carry out their last wishes. A task we're proud to say we follow to the very last letter.

However simple or unusual the request, their wish is our command.

Which is why, in Western Australia, we at Chippers are often referred to as the last word in funeral directors.

CHIPPERS
The Family Funeral Director

Vinten Browning HBR21

© Chippers is a Western Australian family-owned company.

Will Australians die laughing? An appropriate use of gentle humour by Vinten Browning, Perth, for Chippers Funerals.

IT IS NOT UNCOMMON TO SEE ELEPHANTS WEEP OPENLY AT FUNERALS.

Some people refuse to go to a funeral. 'I'll deal with it in my own way', they say. 'And besides, it's not natural.'

With respect, we disagree. A funeral and the healing processes of grief are two of the most natural things in the world.

And if you don't believe us, take a close look at one of nature's biggest-hearted beasts; the elephant.

Elephants show a range of emotions that are uncannily similar to ours. When they meet each other, they touch trunks and rub shoulders. When a young elephant is in danger, its mother will go to extraordinary lengths to save it, even if she has to risk her own life. And when an elephant dies, its friends give it a funeral. Yes, honestly, a funeral.

The death ritual starts when an elephant is close to dying. A wounded or sick animal is soon surrounded by members of its herd who try and help it back on its feet. Two healthy elephants stand either side of their patient and use their trunks and tusks to lift, and then their whole bodies to support the animal.

Some observers have even seen young elephants bring food and water to a dying mother to help her recover.

When the beast finally breathes its last, the extended family circles it. Very slowly and with heads hanging gloomily, they walk around the body several times before standing still.

The assembled circle then turns away one by one until the body is surrounded by elephants all facing outwards. Their trunks hang limply on the ground, and they look as if they are mourning the loss of a loved one. (We'd like to believe that they are.) Maybe they find the sight of death too painful, or perhaps this

ritual has another meaning. Only an elephant can tell you.

And then, there's a simple funeral ceremony. The bereaved beasts gather branches, leaves and clumps of grass from the surrounding area and gently lay them on the body of their dead relative to form a simple grave.

Occasionally, elephants also weep. Big, salty tears roll down their wrinkles in a river of sadness. They weep because they are lonely or hurt, just as we do.

The family stands quietly at the graveside for several hours before moving on. Elephants have clearly not forgotten how to grieve. And we should follow nature's example. Next time you are invited to a funeral, please go. You may find the experience sad, but it's a natural start to the healing process.

And next time you are in need of a funeral director, we trust you will remember us; Chippers.

CHIPPERS
The Family Funeral Director

Very, very, very unconventional humour for Shelter Clothing from
Mad Dogs & Englishmen, New York.

exception. Nick Cohen describes the creative leap: "If you look at how skateboarders are marketed to, and how they see themselves, it's all about being tough, being out there, on the edge. The reality is, they're just people having fun. Skateboarding magazines are full of photographs of people doing really dangerous things. Everyone's trying to top each other. We wanted skateboarders to laugh at themselves a bit, so we chose things that were very *un*dangerous." Tripping up the blind and stealing from children provided irreverent scenarios which turned the joke on the skateboarders. The cynical strapline reads: *Very, Very, Very Tough Clothing.* Simple, black-and-white on-the-street photography was a stark contrast to the complex graphics and typographically-driven ads for competitors. "The art director, John Soto, did the ads when he'd just turned thirty. It was an honest look at his sport. Blatantly honest. It came from his heart."

Cohen is convinced humour endears, providing you are honest about your negatives as well as your positives. "Advertising is about building relationships, so if you forget about advertising and just think about *socialising*. If you get two Heads of State meeting, usually it's all laughs and smiles. Breaking the ice. Finding something they can laugh at. When you see Clinton with the Chinese Premier, the magic is when something funny happens, when the two of them are laughing and smiling."

Advertising that takes the consumer seriously does not itself have to be serious, Mackay assures us. "It's the classic combination of heart and mind, as opposed to being simplistic, patronising and insulting. Think of the brand as friend, as potential lover, talking to the consumer in a way that will nurture their relationship. You can be funny, vulgar if you have to be. You can send yourself up. But at the heart of it, the consumer has got to recognise that I, the brand, understand you, I like you the way you are, I'm not trying to change you, I'm trying to relate to you."

LIE NO. 4:
YOU MUST HAVE A MEMORABLE SLOGAN

"It seems like there's a locker someplace in the Advertising Hall of Fame with fifteen different words," observes Oberlander, "and they keep on shifting them around. Words like *experience*, and *thrill*."

Traditionally, straplines sat beneath the logo, down in the bottom right-hand corner, just above the address and telephone number. They were intended to deliver the final convincing clincher in the ad, or to make some meaningful statement about the advertiser or the brand. Mostly, they have become either shallow wordplays or meaningless phrases like *Progress is our most important product.* Technology companies promise *Tomorrow's Technology Today.* Telephone companies are invariably *In Touch With Tomorrow.* Should we persist with such nonsense?

"There are lines that come right out of the vernacular," says Oberlander. "They feel familiar to your brain. A friend could have said them the other day. Like the line for New York Lotto: *Hey, you never know.* Lines are good for wrapping your head around what the idea is, and talking about it. They're more of a convenience than something that's necessary. At the end of the day we always ask ourselves, does it really need a tagline? Because the truth is," Oberlander warns, "consumers hate advertising, and taglines and jingles are the biggest *clichés* within the parameters of advertising."

Roy Grace believes there is no fixed rule, either way. "I think they're good and I think they're bad. Avis had one, Volkswagen didn't. My basic instinct is *not* to do them. They're usually a waste of time."

French takes a harsher view. "I think we've all been failing for the last fifty years. When clients say they want a tagline, I write down half a dozen from large companies. When I ask the clients which companies they apply to, they can never remember. Pick up any magazine on your desk and read out the taglines," suggests French, "they're a complete waste of time and energy."

Salmon raises a similar eyebrow. "There's an endline which is greatly treasured on Lexus advertising in the States, *The relentless pursuit of perfection*, tucked away under the logo. I'm sure that everybody involved feels very warm that they've got that there, it touches on their corporate aims, and I'm sure they are relentlessly pursuing perfection. But whether it has any active value as far as people reading the ad is concerned, I'm not very sure." Salmon believes endlines have a different purpose in television: "Very often the endline is the scaffold on which television commercials are constructed. They are enigmatic and inexplicable, until the moment of *denouement*, when everything becomes clear and you discover, ah, that's what they meant."

Warsop's advice would be to only use a strapline if it makes a powerful, distinctive brand statement. "For every *Just do it*, there are a thousand instantly forgettable, irrelevant straplines which serve no useful purpose at all. I get the impression that sometimes straplines, which normally appear under the logo, are seen by agencies and clients as an expedient way to promote a brand positioning line. If you always place *Engineered like no other car in the world* under the Mercedes-Benz logo, presumably consumers who are asked in focus groups 'What does the brand stand for?' will recite: 'Mercedes-Benz are engineered like no other cars in the world'. The agency and client can then nod sagely that they have found a position in the consumer's mind."

Warsop believes there is a danger that over time straplines can lose their relevance and impact, or worse still, can end up defeating the original purpose for which they were conceived. "We recently started work on a bank which had used the strapline *It makes you think, doesn't it?* for some twenty years. In the early days, the line worked well, but after ten years advertising was being created where the obvious retort to *It makes you think, doesn't it?* was 'No, actually, it doesn't make me think at all'."

He points to a hybrid that works very effectively: a strapline *and* a brand proposition line together. "A good example was Tag Heuer's excellent *Success. It's a mind game.* Every piece of communication demonstrated this proposition. A swimmer imagining sharks pursuing him, a gymnast imagining the beam is high above a city, a hurdler imagining the hurdles are razor blades. What was brilliant about this campaign was its freshness in the category, avoiding all clichés and puns about time. It also created a fantastic positioning and pedigree for a sports watch. There was no other strapline detracting from the proposition or deflecting one's attention. For some reason, Tag Heuer abandoned this campaign and went with a predictable, non-compelling celebrity endorsement route. To my dismay, I recently saw a new Tag Heuer campaign with a line that read *100% style. 100% elegance. What are you made of?*"

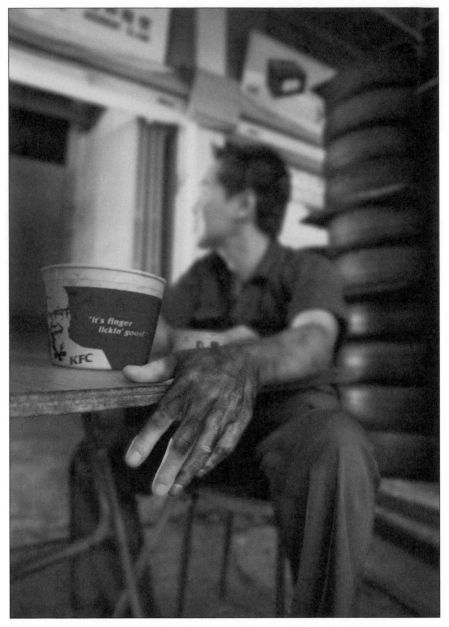

Giving KFC's world famous slogan a fresh, contemporary interpretation.
BBDO Singapore.

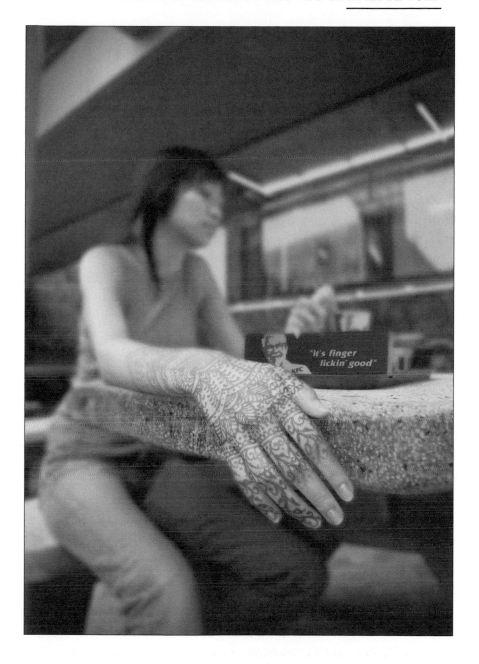

"Slogans now are becoming less and less important," considers Bildsten. "Some of the best slogans in current use are old ones that are used for their retro effect. I don't think anyone even feels compelled to write a slogan these days. It feels so tacked on, so forced. It becomes almost a crutch more than an aid to anything. It's usually reinforcing something that you weren't able to get across in the rest of the work, or for the benefit of a corporation's ego. But it's still possible to write ones that really reinforce the message," he concedes, "*Got milk?* for example."

"Great lines are great lines," says Sherwood, quoting BMW's *The ultimate driving machine*. "But they must have something interesting to say, not just corporate waffle."

At cutting edge Sydney agency Brown Melhuish Fishlock, Warren Brown argues: "The cleverness of your campaign resides with being able to come up with a lateral idea, not assembling a catchy line. Straplines and slogans are no longer valid. Any words that accompany a logo should express a simple thought or emotion." He cites lines like *If only everything in life was as reliable as Volkswagen* and Budweiser's *True*.

His former agency partner Paul Fishlock believes great lines like these can sum up a product idea, benefit or identity, lodge in the consumer's brain and influence behaviour for years. "Why would you not have them in your armoury? The current fashion in print advertising that regards wordless pages as the Holy Grail can be brilliant on occasions, but should never be considered the only road to great ads."

Many cutting edge print ads still carry straplines, but more as the *campaign thought* than a traditional slogan. Often they function as headlines. Some have become more organic, appearing as part of the visual texture. They run everywhere: top, bottom, sides.

"I think the best taglines are great headlines," Barrie argues. "If it's the right slogan, or a really great summarising thought, they still have a place. The worst tagline I've ever read in my life was for a company called TRW. It ran underneath the logo, which was a sans-serif TRW, and it said: *A company called TRW*. TRW, *A company called TRW*. I wonder what the strategy was there? Don't let 'em forget we're a company?"

"I think some of them do a lot of harm," cautions Goldsmith. "I hate using them, and almost never do. I can't think of too many that are very good. They're just stuck on to please the client or someone in the agency. I've always thought that if the ad does what it's supposed to do, then you don't need them. If the ad doesn't do what it's supposed to do, a strapline is not going to save it." He shares the view that most slogans are talking to themselves. "*Just do it is* actually very good because it's about the attitude of the people reading the ad. It's not about the company, it's not *Making better shoes for the people who do it.*"

There are no rules, but the consensus is clear. Unless your line is as powerful as *Just Do It*, don't do it.

LIE NO. 5:
YOU MUST HAVE A LOGO IN THE AD

"It's a lie that you *must* have a logo in the ad," reasons French. "If you write a letter to someone and the most interesting thing in the letter is your signature, you've wasted your time. You ought to be able to write a letter, not sign it, and everybody ought to know who it comes from because it's written in your tone of voice, your handwriting, and about the things in which you're interested. Most people could write a letter without signing it and the recipient would know who it came from. If nobody knows you, then you need to sign it."

"Some logos shouldn't be anywhere, of course, they're so horrible," argues Salmon. "If the logo is there in the bottom right-hand corner, in one sweeping glance the reader can know who is talking; it colours the way an ad is perceived." For copywriters, at least, Salmon acknowledges one benefit of a logo being in an ad: "It enables them to write headlines that don't have the product name in them."

The usual argument for removing the logo runs like this: Why advertise the fact that the ad is an ad? The less an ad looks like an ad, the more it is likely to be noticed.

It sounds logical. In most agencies, however, excluding the logo from an ad is akin to heresy. It is pure creative self-indulgence. The logo is essential for branding the campaign.

"The ad in itself, corner to corner, should look like the brand," stresses Oberlander. "The whole page is acting like a logo. If you're doing an ad for Coke, you know there's going to be a lot of red, some really beautiful script typography, and certain elements that are intrinsic to the Coke brand are going to be in the visual presentation. I would try to design a page so that the logo didn't appear in any *traditional* fashion. Because consumers hate advertising, once they see a page with a logo in the corner, it doesn't look like editorial, it doesn't look like the reason why they bought the magazine in the first place. It's a trigger that makes them turn the page faster."

If Oberlander is right, the plot has changed. It is not the logo that brands the ad, it is the *brand* that brands the ad.

"People are finding more organic ways to put a mark on an ad," Bildsten advises. "More and more, *products* are being used as logos. By making the logo more invisible, people feel they aren't seeing it. As Neil French says, the more elements you take away from an ad, the better it works, and I think logos are one of them."

Perhaps it is a question of being less literal with logos, and more lateral. Does making it the size of a pea in the lower right corner really achieve anything? In Fallon's *Time* campaign, the magazine's masthead is an integral part of every ad. In the same agency's famous Hush Puppies campaign, the actual Hush Puppies dog was the creative idea.

Barrie art directed both. "In Hush Puppies, the dog brought the company logo to life. It involved you and it was impossible not to remember who the ads were for."

Sherwood agrees. "If it's possible, make the logo part of the idea."

In themselves, logos can have incredible power. Some are more than just design forms or corporate devices. Some have a history. The BMW logo, for example, is actually a white propellor against a blue sky, symbolising the company's origins as an aircraft engine maker. The Levi's logo harks back to indestructibility in the Old West. If logos can convey so much, why bury them?

"I have never seen a brilliant ad rendered less effective by the inclusion of a logo," observes Warsop. "One should not forget that the purpose of a print ad is to communicate a brand message and in most instances the logo is the visual manifestation of the brand. So,

ALWAYS CARRY SPARE CAMERA.

DURACELL ULTRA. LASTS 50% LONGER THAN ORDINARY ALKALINE BATTERIES.

DISPOSE OF FLASHLIGHT PROPERLY AFTER USE.

DURACELL ULTRA. LASTS 50% LONGER THAN ORDINARY ALKALINE BATTERIES.

FOR BETTER PERFORMANCE CHANGE TOY FREQUENTLY.

DURACELL ULTRA. LASTS 50% LONGER THAN ORDINARY ALKALINE BATTERIES.

No logo. No product. But from corner to corner, these ads are unmistakably branded Duracell. Ogilvy & Mather, Malaysia.

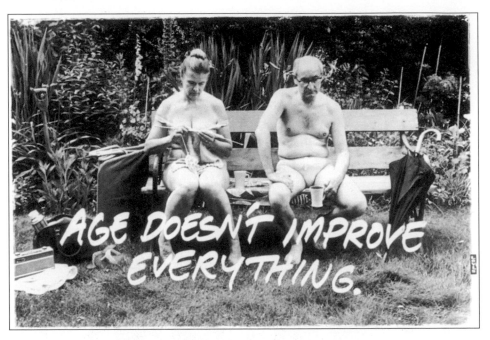

Making the logo more organic, less obnoxious.
Bartle Bogle Hegarty, London.

In The Jupiter Drawing Room's house ads, the agency's leather sofa was the branding device, not its logo.

undoubtedly, there is a place for logos. However, this does not mean logos should always be put in the bottom right-hand corner of the page. Nor, as importantly, should they appear at the embarrassingly large size many clients deem appropriate. I think it all comes back to the power of the execution." As Warsop points out, other visuals can sometimes serve the purpose of a logo. "We have produced five house ads for The Jupiter Drawing Room featuring our leather chesterfield sofa. We have never once used our logo."

Barrie recalls an Everlast campaign created by Goldsmith. "This obnoxiously huge Everlast logo filled the spread, with wonderfully thought-provoking lines underneath. It was great advertising, almost *anti*-advertising. It was like every rule you had ever learned about tucking the logo in the right-hand corner was just laughed at."

French returns to his analogy of writing a letter. "Sometimes the best ad is just a big logo. Everybody knows what the letter would say. Just put a tick on the page and I'll go and buy the sodding shoes. But don't try to tell a story, then put a big logo on it. That's really depressing. If the logo is so important that it's the whole point of the ad, don't try to write an important ad around it. Do one thing or the other. If you can write an ad and cover up the logo and it still makes sense, you've done a good ad. If you can throw the logo away and make people think this might not be an ad, I'd better read it, it looks interesting, *you've done your job*."

By definition, therefore, if you put a big logo on a bad ad, it will only increase the client's embarrassment, and yours.

LIE NO. 6:
YOU MUST SHOW THE PRODUCT IN THE AD

Neil Godfrey reflects on the famous surrealistic campaign for Benson & Hedges, which became the best-selling cigarette in its category. "We always had problems with the censorship authorities. I think they realised how powerful, how strong something could be that doesn't *overtly* show a piece of advertising, but is image-making based on the power the images can have." One execution showed a rainstorm of cigarettes beating down on umbrellas. It was the first time the pack did not appear. "We had gold umbrellas. Everyone knew it was Benson & Hedges just by the style."

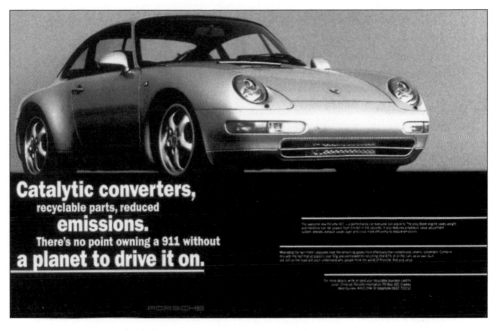

Two car makers saving the environment.
Porsche, through Leagas Delaney, London, shows the product in the ad.
Mercedes-Benz, from Batey Ads, Singapore, doesn't.

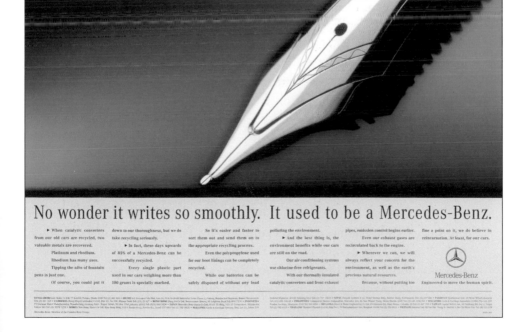

"We are not paid to put a product in an ad, but in the consumer's mind," says Guido Heffels. "Sometimes a colour or a special location can create an *image* of the product. It's the biggest pack shot you can put into your ad because it involves the consumer. It's like a *riddle* that the consumer will be proud to have solved. And that creates a much deeper impression than anything else."

"If you take something away," Bildsten contends, "you leave something more to the imagination. A beer with a head is a beer with a head. A can is a can. A bottle is a bottle. There are other ways you can *represent* the product."

"It's a lie that you must show the product," asserts Sherwood. "Consumers can picture in their minds what things look like. Lots of Levi's ads don't show jeans. People can visualise them."

"Ads should be based on what the product can *do* for the reader," Salmon reminds us. Other than that, "I think there are no rules that are unbreakable in advertising."

Grace believes showing products can impact negatively on the advertising. "Communication is far more participatory when it isn't an overt sell, when the sell is more internal. In the early days of DDB, one of the unspoken, guiding forces was that the product and the logo should never be in the ad, because it'll be an ad and nobody will read it."

The question is, what will work best for the strategy, the brand and the idea?

Generally speaking, says French, if the product has to be bought off a shelf, if pack recognition is important, you must show the product in the ad. Sometimes the name itself will be adequate. In French's own work, campaigns for Chivas Regal and XO Beer showed the pack and made it part of the idea; Kaminomoto did not, for legal reasons.

"One exception," says French, "is when you're selling something that's *so* different to anything else in its category and you really need the story to stick home. A new shampoo, say. Putting the product in the ad might stop people reading the story because they'd think it's just another boring ad for shampoo. Maybe then you shouldn't."

Strategic reasons could also preclude putting the product in the ad. Oberlander quotes Kenneth Cole Shoes as an example. "The shoes were actually changing styles so quickly that if we showed them in the ad, it would date the brand. So we just promoted the brand itself." One such ad was a simple typeset message regretting the fact that Imelda Marcos hadn't had the courtesy to buy a pair of Kenneth Cole shoes.

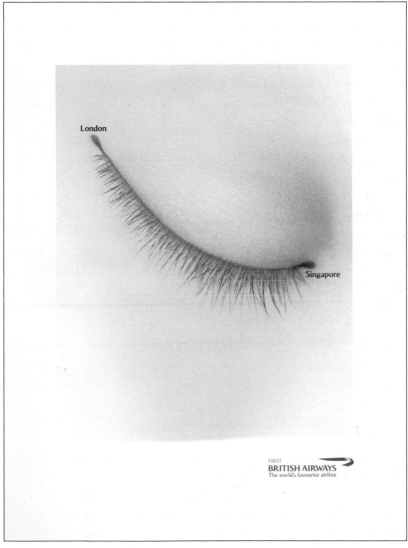

M&C Saatchi Singapore communicated the new First Class sleeper bed for British Airways using two words and one photo – but not of the product.

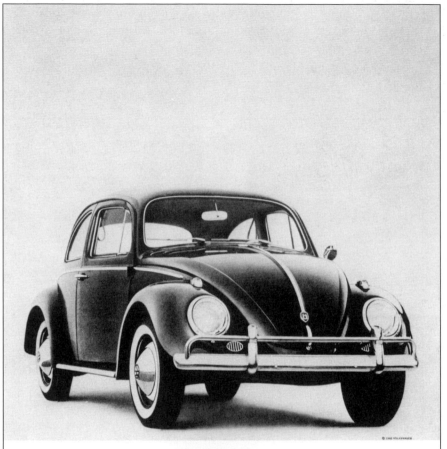

Lemon.

This Volkswagen missed the boat.

The chrome strip on the glove compartment is blemished and must be replaced. Chances are you wouldn't have noticed it; Inspector Kurt Kroner did.

There are 3,389 men at our Wolfsburg factory with only one job: to inspect Volkswagens at each stage of production. (3000 Volkswagens are produced daily; there are more inspectors than cars.)

Every shock absorber is tested (spot checking won't do), every windshield is scanned. VWs have been rejected for surface scratches barely visible to the eye.

Final inspection is really something! VW inspectors run each car off the line onto the Funktionsprüfstand (car test stand), tote up 189 check points, gun ahead to the automatic brake stand, and say "no" to one VW out of fifty.

This preoccupation with detail means the VW lasts longer and requires less maintenance, by and large, than other cars. (It also means a used VW depreciates less than any other car.)

We pluck the lemons; you get the plums.

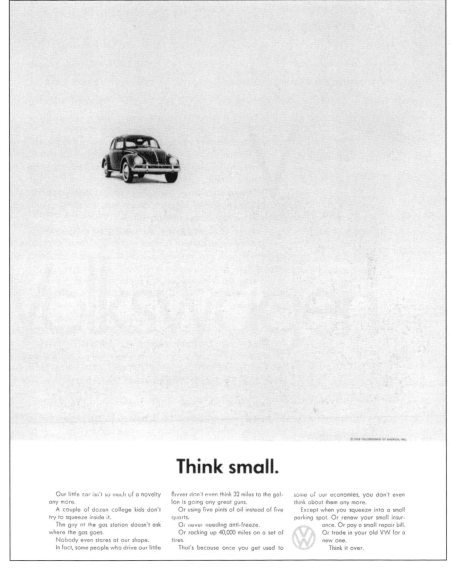

Think small.

Our little car isn't so much of a novelty any more.

A couple of dozen college kids don't try to squeeze inside it.

The guy at the gas station doesn't ask where the gas goes.

Nobody even stares at our shape.

In fact, some people who drive our little flivver don't even think 32 miles to the gallon is going any great guns.

Or using five pints of oil instead of five quarts.

Or never needing anti-freeze.

Or racking up 40,000 miles on a set of tires.

That's because once you get used to some of our economies, you don't even think about them any more.

Except when you squeeze into a small parking spot. Or renew your small insurance. Or pay a small repair bill. Or trade in your old VW for a new one.

Think it over.

Bill Bernbach told Roy Grace: "Either make the Volkswagen very big or very, very small." Doyle Dane Bernbach, New York.

Each category presents its own set of decisions. The car category is one of the most contentious.

"We've all got an idea of what a car looks like," says French. "It's got a wheel on each corner. If you've got a brilliant looking car, show it. If you're selling a Datsun, probably don't." French had the task of relaunching a famous Japanese car; one look at the current model convinced him not to show it in the ads. "It was a toilet on wheels, a terrible old nail, something your granny would drive." He made the advertising exciting instead.

"Sometimes you're selling a promise, you're not selling a product *per se.*" Bildsten talks about his agency's work for BMW. "With BMW, it's so difficult not to show the product. What we've done is show bits of it, very small details of it, because those details reveal the greater whole."

Grace remembers working on the classic Volkswagen campaign with Bill Bernbach. "I was twenty-seven when I took it on. Bill was already in his fifties, already a legend. Bill said to me, 'Whenever you portray a Volkswagen in an ad, Roy, I want you to do this: either make the Volkswagen very big or very, very small'. And I said, 'Why?' Well, he just gave me a look. He just *looked* at me. So for ever and ever, I never said 'Why?' to Bill Bernbach again."

In the computer category, the products look basically the same. Therefore, Salmon questions why every ad shows a picture of a computer. "Obviously the people who manufacture them can detect the finer points of difference. But if you look at the ads, it's hard to tell one from another."

So, why do it?

The hotel category has French baffled. "I can never understand why people show hotels in their ads. Nobody ever sees the hotel! You arrive in a taxi, that's the first idea you have that you've actually got to the place. Then you see the room. I find hotel advertising hilarious because they've all got these photographs of big, concrete block-houses. It's like they're saying, please come and stay in our prison!"

LIE NO. 7:
EVERY AD IN A CAMPAIGN MUST LOOK THE SAME

"Rather than look the same," muses Fishlock, "it's more important that ads in a campaign feel the same, that you hear the same voice talking to you, that it knows you and knows what you know, and builds on what you know. Rigorous corporate guidelines of 'picture goes here', 'this colour headline', 'this size copy', are not the way to achieve this. They're more likely to produce ads you ignore because you think you've seen them before."

Nobody in their right mind wears the same clothes day after day. Yet who we are, and what we stand for, remains constant. If brands are the same as people, a similar logic should apply. If a brand wears exactly the same look every time you see it, if its advertising conforms to a rigid layout grid, won't that defeat freshness and surprise? Won't that stifle the brand's personality?

"When they measure advertising recall, rigid formats are statistically the most effective," says Salmon. "But I believe in *repetition without monotony*. I think you have to change print ads frequently. Once you've looked at an ad, you'll recognise it subliminally as you go through a publication but you won't look at it again. You could argue that a second insertion will get the people you missed the first time, and maybe it takes three exposures for everybody to see it, but after that you start to show people something they're not going to look at again with fresh attention." Salmon prefers campaigns with elastic formats. "It's important to have a campaign look, with enough characteristics in common for there to be some synergy between one ad and the next." This could be achieved by some visual device which links them.

"There should be some variables which are consistent," recommends Oberlander, "so consumers know there's that guy again, trying to talk to me; there's that brand, trying to strike up a conversation with me. We should put together what we call the *visual turf* of a brand: the kind of photography, the kind of colour panels, the kind of typography. But the format should be kept flexible, so that each ad in a campaign is like a step-brother to the ad before it, rather than a perfect twin."

Brown agrees. "A tone of voice or look should be established for your client, but within that you should retain the flexibility to make each idea strong and appear fresh."

While a common visual family identity will help the branding in an ad, it can be quite loose – a typeface or border, for instance. "But the trick is not to allow it to become a straitjacket," cautions Gerard Stamp.

"Great campaigns change the rules, change the landscape totally, in whatever category they're competing in," considers Mark Tutssel. "Art direction should portray the look and feel of a brand – the brand's DNA. It has to be exactly right for the brand, giving you an emotional feeling about the brand and separating it from its competition." While every ad in a print campaign doesn't necessarily have to look the same, Tutssel says, "they do have to *feel* they are from the same family."

Warsop recalls David Ogilvy's ads for Hathaway Shirts. "The deliberate intention was, over time, to provide consistency and recognition. If you were to cover the logo you would still know which brand the advertising was for. If each execution is excellent in its own right, this can work very well for the client. However, when the creative is anything less than exceptional, the danger is that the consumer will recognise the look of the ad, make the response 'Oh, it's one of those ads for X brand', and simply gloss over the content. The other school of thought says each execution should be produced to an outstanding standard with no prerequisites other than the client's logo. Whilst this may sound as if it would produce advertising with inconsistent branding, the reality is that the freedom to create a series of unexpected executions, all art directed to suit the concept, may nevertheless give a distinctive brand personality. Many of the executions we have done for Nike in the last few years have no consistent look, and yet the freedom to create truly distinctive layouts gives the *totality of the work* a strong tone and personality for the Nike brand."

"Every ad in a campaign *must* have the same tone of voice," says French. "Which means, in the same campaign, you could produce an ad which is entirely copy and one which is entirely a picture, and they would both work." French did precisely that in his XO Beer campaign.

"You can have a *framework* for consistency," suggests Sherwood. BBH's Boddingtons campaign was designed to work as posters on magazine back covers. Within that framework, every execution contained a new interpretation of creaminess.

Done well enough, a campaign can become a series of surprises, rather than a series of ads. A diversity of executions and formats can invite comparisons and provoke public debate. When consumers talk about the advertising, every media dollar will be doing the work of three or four.

As David Abbott argues: "There's no reason why you can't mix visual and long copy ads within one campaign or one client's advertising. I think it's quite a good idea so you can surprise people. If you look back at classic Volkswagen ads, once the campaign had been established they often surprised you with format. There were occasional long copy ads and there was a lot of talk about it. It gave the campaign a great *spontaneity*."

What makes a campaign, for Heffels, is a great *overall thought*. "Everything you create for the brand should be driven by the same thought, the same idea. A few constant design elements may be helpful for a major brand to build up a global presence, but if that's all you've got, you will end up with a series of ads, not a campaign. See what Nike did over the last few years? There was no special look, no corporate design grid. Everyone had the freedom to go for the maximum in art and copy. What kept all the hundreds of different ads together, all over the world, was having the same overall mission."

Global advertising campaigns, in fact, frequently impose the most rigid formats of all. The worst excesses can be found in the hotel category. "Some genius works out a grid that every ad must follow," observes French. "Fortunately they only last for a couple of years. They become so tired that even the most rabid client cannot seriously keep running them any more."

It seems the real issue is the degree of flexibility, and knowing just how far to go. While there are no rules, there are commonsense guidelines.

"If you've a *small media budget*, if you're not as ubiquitous as Nike or Miller Lite, it would be a mistake to go off with too many different looks and voices," cautions Barrie. "You'd lose the synergy that you develop by having a unified look."

"If you're talking to a very *advertising-literate market* that's more hip, you can't be predictable," Sherwood advises. "That's why Levi's talks about the same things, but doesn't look the same."

In Tim Delaney's view, the *relationship with the consumer* should always be the deciding factor. "I don't like things in advertising being non-strategic. Campaigns are things which are aimed at consumers by advertisers on the basis they're looking for a cumulative effect. Is the relationship you want, from the brand's point of view, one that requires a tidy uniformity in order to get a cumulative effect? There are markets which are so crowded that unless you get a look, you are going to be lost. In that sense, a distinctive look can give you something back. However, there are other accounts where you want to have a different kind of relationship. Someone like Adidas has all different kinds of categories. You may want to change the flavour of the relationship depending on the category, and that's acceptable."

But as Lionel Hunt laments: "Most print ads are so appalling it would be criminal if the ones that followed them looked the same."

Lie No. 8:
Creative Ads Don't Sell

"The redoubtable Donald Gunn has proved they do, beyond any doubt," French reminds us. Gunn's research was conducted when he was the international creative guru at Leo Burnett, Chicago. "Donald also proved that ads which won Gold awards worked better than ads which won Silver, and that Silver worked better than Bronze."

The problem, as French points out, is that the word *creative* has achieved its own demise. "To most people, creative has come to mean self-serving and pointless. A form of self-abuse. Which isn't, of course, what being creative really is. Creativity is merely sugar-coating the pill. That's all you're doing. At the base of it, creativity is finding an interesting thing to say about a boring thing. And the more interesting it is, the more creative it is."

"To say creative ads don't sell is definitely a lie, no question about it," asserts Sherwood. "This is something that gets talked about a lot, particularly when the industry gets attacked for awarding itself too often." Sherwood quotes a correlation drawn between advertising which won creative awards and advertising which won effectiveness awards. "In Britain, the IPA run effectiveness awards every two years. The IPA awards are taken very seriously by clients. By going back over the years, it was shown that the campaigns which were deemed to be the most effective had also picked up large numbers of creative awards."

Sherwood also believes a correlation exists between the ads which consumers like and the ads which award juries like. He quoted the fact that BBH's Levi's Claymation commercial had not only been covered in creative awards, but was also voted the best ad on TV by a viewers' poll in Singapore. "There is definitely a relationship between creativity and effectiveness."

Cutting edge creativity impacts as successfully on consumers as it does on award show judges. Reaching the standard involves risk, but no rules. Having cleared away The Eight Greatest Lies, we have arrived at The One Creative Truth.

THE ONE CREATIVE TRUTH: EVERY AD MUST HAVE AN IDEA IN IT

Nothing in life, nor advertising, is easy. The value of the great single minded idea is under siege, or so it seems. Executionally-driven work, where the idea is secondary or even non-existent, appears to have become a respectable creative form.

While execution can act as a brand separator, can it ever substitute for a genuine idea?

"Of course every ad should have an idea," affirms Heffels, "otherwise it's not necessary to run it. An execution can't be an idea. It's only the vehicle to transport the idea."

"In my opinion, execution is never more important than the content," states Ron Mather.

Goldsmith recounts the joke about the art director who jumps up and says: "I've got an idea ... Herb Ritts!"

"It's a laziness," shrugs Goldsmith. "There's this illusion that if you use people who have shot good work, you will have good work, too. Execution is becoming such an equal playing field. Everyone can go out and buy all these computers. People are pretty hard to shock with execution." In Goldsmith's view, creating an idea still has the edge. "You tend to remember execution for a short while. You tend to remember ideas for a long time."

"I'm always suspicious of technique," Cohen confides. "I always feel it's a little bit self-conscious. It gets into smoke-and-mirrors land. It's shallow and gets very samey. There are agencies that do a lot of very executional, stylistic work. I like it to a degree, but I don't love it like I love a bit of work that makes me look at myself, that makes me smile." Cohen points to the great landmark ads which are still talked about in the industry. More often than not, he says, they were not that expensive to make. They didn't rely on technique or execution. They relied simply on putting a great premise in front of people. "There was nothing executional or flashy about the old Volkswagen work. It was presenting an underdog and talking honestly about it."

Ironically, it was the great Bernbach himself who said: *"Execution becomes content in a work of genius."* His words have haunted the idea-driven purists ever since. They have been quoted and misquoted in support of countless executionally-led campaigns, the last word being conveniently overlooked.

Grace was closer to Bernbach than most. The way he reads it: "There's nothing wrong with accepting it as an axiom, but like other truths, sometimes they're Big Truths and sometimes they're Little Truths. I think he was right, but I don't think it's formulaic. Sometimes, a simple photograph and no words at all can convey enormous amounts of information in a very profound way. Sometimes the presentation of a picture or graphics has some sort of emotional content that *can* be the message. But it has to be brilliant execution to work that way. It isn't something that's going to work as a formula all the time. Unfortunately, or fortunately, the majority of things that are done that way are just empty, meaningless and transparent. A lot of it is just surface decoration with no emotional content. Obviously, a lot of stuff comes out of computers. Many things are so overly designed, they interfere with the basic communication."

Grace ponders whether the famous Volkswagen *Lemon* ad would look the same if it was executed today. "I would hope that whoever came up with *Lemon* now would have enough sense to understand what it is they're doing and keep it stark and lean and powerful."

French believes execution defines the tone of voice, but warns against relying on it to replace an idea. "There are occasions when the execution is so original, and so powerful, it becomes the idea. In our Bank of China work there wasn't the ghost of an idea, unless you said the Bank of China is Chinese, therefore that's the idea. But it's very difficult to be that original, because there are only so many ways of doing something. It's much easier to take the tough way and have an idea."

"I think the execution has got to build up to something, or mean something," says Stow. "It's not enough just to have pretty pictures. People are smart enough to see through that."

Hegarty sees execution in terms of ambience, *adding depth to an idea*. "Our advertising is very, very simple, incredibly simple, in its thought process. Good advertising has to be that because people aren't prepared to give it a huge amount of time. People want simple things from the brand; what you can put *around* it is an ambience and an attitude that has a depth and complexity to it, a series of layers." BBH work demonstrates a textured, layered approach to simple strategies and ideas; as each layer is peeled off, another level of intelligence is revealed. But it's not about making things complex, says Hegarty. "Great pieces of communication work on a number of levels. They work on a very simple level; you get the idea straight away. But then they have a repetitive factor to them, so when you come back to them you see more things. I think that's very important when ads are repeated again and again. You can see something else in the way it was put down, a greater depth, something else is going on there." Hegarty believes the way you communicate should have a poignancy and power to it. He draws a parallel with movies. "For me, great movies are ones which are populist, but have a depth to them. On one level you can look at *One Flew Over the Cuckoo's Nest* and say it's all about Jack Nicholson, a bit of a wacky guy who can't get on in society; there are some good jokes in it, and in the end he dies, fine, that's the way life is sometimes. Or, on another level, you can look upon it as a very moving observation of society; how it excludes people who are different. It has a lot of depth and meaning to it. It approaches its audiences at all stages and at all levels, and I do like communication that does that. The more you get into it, the more it *includes*."

"Execution can be fifty percent of the ad, sometimes even more," David Droga believes, "but there is always a danger of things being overexecuted, and when you dig below the surface there's nothing. The bigger shame is when you see a great idea that's hidden below something."

David Abbott recognises the influence of a new generation. "A commonplace truism now is that we're talking to a generation bred on television and video. They have visual rather than verbal minds. They react to imagery more than the written word. I think there's some truth in that, you can't just discount that. I think that imagery is playing a bigger part in UK advertising. It's always been a strong tradition in Europe and especially on the West Coast of America. I think that's something to do with the sunshine," he quips, "and as we're getting warmer here, maybe it's got nothing to do with art directors at all."

Not surprisingly, Abbott confesses he is a purist. "I don't think I'm necessarily right, but I just do what I do as well as I can do it. I try and change, I try and embrace some of these things, but even if it's a non-verbal communication I still like to find an idea at the root of it. I think in the best execution routes there's an idea. In a lot of it there isn't, and unless the image is truly outstanding, it isn't as *memorable* somehow as a phrase, or a thought, or an insight. What happens, it seems to me, in the sports shoe market, you get your very, very quick imitators. You get everybody merging into everybody else. If that's all you've got, a panoply of images, it's easier to imitate and confuse one with the other. Whereas a statement is a statement, and it is allied to a brand and a proposition. There's more chance, long term, of being unique and individual."

The sports shoe market is at the forefront of the debate. Some argue that Nike print ads do not have ideas in them, merely an attitude. Others believe the attitude *is* the idea.

"It's okay to have attitude in an ad," concedes Barrie, "but not insincere attitude, phony attitude. Probably what I hate most is the kind of advertising that insincerely says, we know who you are. It tries to get into your head. Nike has done stuff in that vein, but done it really well and so poetically that it doesn't feel like advertising at all."

"I think Nike print ads are pretty crappy," asserts French, "and have become more crappy as time has gone on. Their line, *Just do it*, said to an extent that the end justifies the means. It was inherently baaaaaad, which was what was so good about it, which is why large black people who play netball wear Nike shoes because they're baaaaaad. 'It is easier to obtain forgiveness than permission' would have been a nicer way of saying it, but *Just do it* was snappier. Nike forgot the plot. It's supposed to be a rebellious brand that doesn't take notice of authority figures, but at one point in their lives they forgot that. Michael Jordan is one of the richest men in America, so how can he be a rebel? The seeds of their own destruction were sown at the moment they bought the very thing that made them. Almost a Greek tragedy in the making."

Delaney believes it is not a matter of saying that execution-based work is purely superficial and idea-based work is somehow deep and meaningful. "Advertising is there to capture people's imagination in the first instance, then to help them enjoy a relationship with the brand. In that sense, there isn't just idea-based or execution-based advertising; it's the kind of relationship you want. You may *want* to have a superficial relationship. Most fashion advertising doesn't have any idea in it, but it's highly successful. If you look at a brand like Prada, it's come from nowhere. It does advertising which is skilfully shot, with a beautiful model, with just a logo. That is an execution. There's no idea that I can see in it, but the brand is vastly successful. It plainly has an advertising relationship with its audience. The same can be said over the years for Calvin Klein and Tommy Hilfiger. They don't have advertising relationships that I would relate to, but they do have advertising relationships that their audience relates to, and it's *only* execution. Inside the execution, there are things that can be decoded and, on that basis, it is *more* than just a superficial execution. It's got depth to it."

Delaney says an idea should be used when the product itself does not necessarily grab people's imagination in a very crowded category. "If you're talking about a bath cleaner, or a rather ordinary, utilitarian product, that's the time when you can capture someone's imagination and delineate that product from its competitors by using an idea." As a preference, though, Delaney would try to build ideas into fashion ads as well. "You want something which is a little deeper than a photograph."

Execution, however, serves another purpose in Delaney's view. "Execution signals to people a kind of craft, which then goes on to signal that you have some conviction about the product. There's a direct correlation between the degree of craft in the execution and the fact that the advertiser really has some sense of belief and care, and even craft, within his product."

While the One Creative Truth is open to interpretation, French's logic is irresistible: "I'm trying desperately to think of anyone famous who has actually produced great advertising using only an execution. I can't, therefore it doesn't work."

4

THE CREATIVE WORK
BEFORE
THE CREATIVE WORK

C utting edge creativity does not happen in a
vacuum. As you will see, breakthroughs in
creativity are often the result of breakthroughs in
strategic thinking. Strategic leaps produce creative
leaps.

In the same way that people are questioning the
Eight Greatest Lies of print creativity, people are
also questioning the conventional ways of building
brands. New marketing paradigms are being
adopted. Single minded thinking is shifting to
open-minded thinking. Marketing strategists are
not just thinking outside the box; they have
discarded the box altogether.

These changes are not superficial. They are
fundamental. Not only will they disrupt the cosy
rules of the marketplace, they will challenge the
whole process of writing strategies and briefs in
advertising agencies.

Mary Stow says, "A brief is only good if it
produces good work." Yet the system used for
producing briefs is based on conventional agency
methodologies which have remained the same for
decades.

As a cutting edge communicator, you need to

know what is happening. You need to understand the changes. You need to see how they will impact on your own creative thinking process, because they will.

STRATEGIES AND BRIEFS

The joke goes something like this: a copywriter and an account director were visiting a client in Paris. The copywriter asked the account director how to get to the client's office, and the account director handed him a map of Europe.

Too often, conventional agency methodologies produce strategies and briefs which are meaningless. *Strategy* is probably the most abused word in advertising.

A strategy is not a request to produce a campaign. It should be the blueprint for the campaign, the path through the minefield.

What is a strategy? Simply put, if the objective is to get to New York, the strategic options are (a) take a plane, (b) take a bus, (c) take a train, or (d) drive there. If the client, the account director, the planner and the creative director all agree that taking a bus would be the best way to achieve the objective, that is the strategy. If the writer and art director decide to take a plane instead, they are *off*-strategy.

The analogy is crude, perhaps, but it makes the point. And a lot of creative work has to happen before the actual creative work can begin.

Simon Sherwood defines a strategy as *the single starting point for the creative process.* "Good strategies are very liberating, as opposed to very constraining. They should have a very clearly framed proposition from which the advertising can leap and a very clear direction in which the advertising can move."

Providing that single starting point is a very distinct skill. The account director and planner, often in consultation with the client, must make a series of decisions before reaching a judgement about what the advertising has to say. All too frequently, their thinking process will have been governed by logic and the rules of the category. Unless there is room for intuitive thinking, and lateral thinking, chances are their strategy will be a cookie-cutter replica of everyone else in the category.

"The trouble with logic, process and analysis," explains Sherwood, "is that everyone tends to end up in the same place. In the last ten years, our industry has been too concerned with things that can be measured. Too much value has been placed on research and getting consumer approval. People are frightened of making mistakes. With intuition goes risk." Sherwood hopes that clients and agencies can become less reliant on data, less reliant on analysis. "They must become more confident of their own ability to make judgements."

Intuitive, entrepreneurial judgements still drive the most successful marketing exercises, believes Ian Batey, from building an airline around a girl to something as bizarre as turning miners' boots into disco clogs. "We've got so much information at our fingertips, so much data, and we get driven along by it, that we forget that marketing and strategies are still esoteric things. Marketing is not a science, marketing is an *art*."

If the strategy is a mirror image of everyone else in the category, the creativity will suffer a similar fate.

If the strategy breaks new ground in the category, the creativity will, too.

As Ezra Pound said, "Make it new for me."

BRAND BUILDING

The ways brands are built, and the ways their personalities are defined and developed, are changing. In some quarters, the changes are radical; in other companies, imperceptible. Without question, though, their impact on creativity will be substantial.

According to conventional wisdom, companies used to work with a statement of the brand. It was carved in stone. This is what the brand is now. This is what it will be forever.

Some marketers would identify the single point of product difference. It, too, would be carved in stone. It would be the pillar on which all advertising was built. Now and forever, amen.

In recent years, the first cracks in the matrix appeared.

"It was amazingly constraining," argues Rod Wright of TBWA. "You cannot live on simple product differences in today's world. You cannot be so dogmatic about a brand and hope to stay relevant. As the consumer changes, how do you then shift your relationship?"

According to convention, the brand's personality is also carved in stone, and usually in an arbitrary way.

Stow has a horror of briefs which connect a list of adjectives to the brand personality. "They're meaningless," she says. The most commonly used include: Warm, Friendly, Innovative, Stylish, Caring, Contemporary, Dynamic. Pick any three or use them all.

"People are trying to establish a personality, but what they can't get their heads around is change." Stow draws an analogy with a human being. "You can't write down and fix in time that this person will always be X, Y and Z. A much more useful way of thinking about a brand is giving the sense of a living person, how they will grow and develop." She cites Tango as an example: "Tango can stay real-life, urban, young, streetwise, a bit of a lad. These quintessential characteristics can continue. The brand might dress slightly differently, and behave slightly differently, but fundamentally it will always be the young lad on the street."

Obviously a brand cannot keep changing, otherwise nothing will be built for the long term. It has to have some kind of structure. The question is, what kind?

"It should not be rigid. You have to build *elasticity* into a brand," Wright advocates. "You have to know what you can stretch with the consumer, and what is unstretchable."

As Wright points out, all successful companies and brands have core values. The task is to identify other values, other things, which the consumer would give you permission to change.

Wright likens the ideal consumer relationship to a rope. "Once, the convention was to build a rigid brand structure, with a rigid connection to the consumer. But in today's marketplace, the consumer is exposed to a constant stream of different stimuli. Their view will be moving. The brand will need to respond. So you have to allow for movement in the relationship. The consumer can move, the brand can move, but a rope keeps them connected."

Wright believes ropes are made when marketers communicate not so much what they make, but what they believe in. "Mercedes-Benz stands for brilliant product. Volvo says safety. What do other car makers stand for? There are blanks behind their brands. Brands should have points of view to which consumers are sympathetic."

Author Will Self once spoke of a *coinage of sympathy*: "I completely identify with that sentiment or that idea or that experience and I've never heard it articulated to me in exactly that way." By residing its brand in the soul of the athlete, Nike commanded such sympathies. When consumers discovered that sports shoes were allegedly made in offensive Asian sweatshops, the coinage was devalued.

Richard Kirshenbaum and Jonathan Bond describe brands as *communities of users*. Great brands, they argue, have a cultish quality, bonding consumers to the brand through a sense of belonging. A perfect example is Harley-Davidson, which has engendered a sense of community beyond its physical products, a virtual blood brotherhood where users are members.

Brand elasticity, ropes, communities of users, coinages of sympathy: dangerous talk indeed, and certainly not the way things are supposed to be. But if we reject the old brand building models, and all their conventional baggage, what lies ahead? More heresy?

What you will find is a return to the days when marketers trusted their innate intelligence. New brand building methodologies are pragmatic. Certainly, intuition and risk-taking are at their heart. But so, too, are the painful lessons derived from propping up antiquated brand structures.

Two examples demonstrate the leap from logic to ideas, promising more scope for creativity rather than less.

"DISRUPTION"

Jean-Marie Dru, co-founder and chairman of France's BDDP agency, and now president and CEO of TBWA, uses the term *Disruption* for his revolutionary approach to marketing.

"If you don't create change," explains Wright, "change will create you. The Disruption Theory starts from the premise that every company exists in a world where things are constantly changing in the context of the company, the brand, the marketplace and the consumer. Every company builds up a set of conventions about the way it operates, about the way its culture works. If a company is to move forward, it has to be able to break through its own way of looking at things; it has to disrupt its own conventions."

There are four spheres of conventions. "Corporate conventions are about how a company sees itself and how it works. Marketing conventions are the way companies in a category go to market, like banks offering friendly, personal service. Communication conventions are the way companies in a category advertise their products; shampoos always show silky hair, pizza ads always show melty cheese. Consumer conventions are the way consumers see products in a category. Using Disruption methodology, you can plan for different scenarios," suggests Wright. "If a company wanted to disrupt its marketing conventions, if it wanted to go to market in a different way, it may need to change its corporate conventions, too. A disruption in one sphere may well be the *vision* which drives changes in the other spheres."

The real challenge is for companies to make sure that the external brand and the internal brand meet. "You can't offer a brand relationship unless you have connected all the spheres. The corporate culture has to want to deliver the marketing. The marketing culture has to want to deliver the communications. And the consumer has to see the consistency."

In Dru's new book, *Beyond Disruption*, this point is neatly articulated. Perceptions about service brands, for example, primarily stem from customer experience. "Who cares about a brilliant 30-second commercial if you have to wait thirty minutes in the customer service line?"

According to Wright, Sony has achieved this consistency. As a result, it continues to offer credible brand relationships. But for many other companies, the dream has soured.

"They start off brilliantly," says TBWA planner Fiona Clancy, "but lose their edge, their motivation, their specialness. They get themselves into a stagnant or even vicious circle. Often they try to rectify it through communication, in the hope that a better, brighter advertising campaign will revitalise the relationship with the consumer. And sometimes it works; communication can have an extraordinary effect on all aspects of a business. But it's rarely the communication alone. Behind such breakthrough communication, there's usually a new evangelist, a visionary, changing the energy in the company."

But "just saying something", Clancy believes, will not transcend the turbulence of the marketplace. Companies must identify where key brand relationships lie, what makes them solid, and who and what can sustain them. Advertising must help build *sustainable* brand equities.

To help bring advertising disruptions into focus, Clancy uses a tool called the *Ladder*, offering six different areas called registers in which campaigns can be developed: Top of Mind, Attribute, Benefit, Territory, Value and Role. Shifting the advertising message from one register to another can be highly disruptive, as when Pepsi abandoned Benefit (taste) in favour of Territory (*The Choice of a New Generation*). The ladder provides a clear picture of advertising activity in any category. If the brand's competitors have situated their advertising in the Attribute and Benefit registers, the strategist can disrupt the category by claiming a Role or upholding a Value.

Once the fear of change is removed, companies gain a new sense of control. "Disruption is all about brands in permanent transition, all about control in permanent turbulence," says Wright. "In this context," he adds, "we don't talk about share of market, but share of the future."

"Disruption," as TBWA creative guru Lee Clow sums up, "means dismantling the status quo and replacing it with something bold and new."

"The Unthought Known"

At Howell Henry Chaldecott Lury, over twenty dedicated multi-disciplined project teams search for the *Unthought Known*, a key principle in the agency's brand building methodology.

"A lot of people produce communications which play so obviously to the rules of the market," observes Stow. "If they were talking about cars, for instance, they'd have lots of shots of the car, and sex would be a subtext. We'd say, hang on a minute, that might be the perceived wisdom, the rules of the market, but let's see if we can break one or two of those rules and see if that makes us stand out, which it usually does."

According to Stow, the agency has done away with the typical agency relay race. The account director, planner, writer and art director work as a team the whole way through. They do the research together, they set the strategy together, they develop the creative work together. "Because the teams work so closely, you don't have that awful ownership issue," says Stow.

The agency's methodology defies both conventional and *unconventional* wisdom. Brand building begins with research, but not with consumers.

"We tend to do a lot of research into the client organisation which is either behind the brand or is itself the brand," Stow elaborates. "That's where the point of difference will be. It will be in the cultural values of the organisation, or in the beliefs of the people working there."

Stow describes the process which led to the creative leap in the agency's campaign for the AA. "We did a lot of research into the way the Automobile Association worked. We interviewed the patrolmen, talked to them about their jobs, their lives. What we were looking for was the Unthought Known. We found it in some of the things the patrolmen said. They told us things like, 'Often we get to the scene of an accident before the other emergency services'. Just off-the-cuff comments like that. The team was throwing around what the patrolmen had said. It was the art director who was the first person to articulate the idea of *The Fourth Emergency Service*. It was a great strategic thought!"

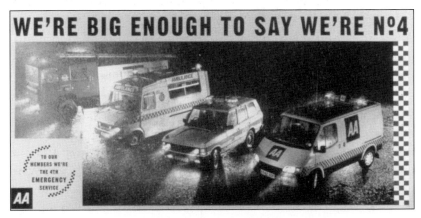

Howell Henry Chaldecott Lury, London, discovered the Unthought Known for the AA.

It was not just a reframing of the AA in advertising terms; it required the organisation to change fundamentally.

As Stow points out: "If your car does break down, it's a genuine emergency for you. But the AA had to ask itself if it was prepared to stand up and compare itself to the police."

What had been a traditional breakdown service with nice, friendly patrolmen completely restructured and rebranded itself. "They changed all the old vans; they now look like police cars. They answer the phones and say, 'AA Emergency Service'. They give priority to lone women motorists in certain cases. In every sense, they became *The Fourth Emergency Service*."

From a declining membership of seven and a half million, the AA achieved nine and a half million members and growing. Membership retention was running at an all-time high of eighty-nine percent.

STRATEGIC INSIGHTS

Reading about brand building is only a start. Strategic thinking must become the subtext to your creative thinking. It must become instinctive. It helps to be what Lionel Hunt calls a student of human nature. The best creatives have this quality, as you are about to see. Their work is unconventional; so is their thinking. Yet, in the final analysis, their creative processes are disciplined. And they all share one thing in common: the ability to produce what in retrospect seems so clearly obvious, but somehow was not in the first place.

Outward Bound. Jim Mountjoy of Loeffler Ketchum Mountjoy, North Carolina, puts his creative leaps down to disciplined chaos. "Discipline means being an advocate for the consumer versus a mouth for the client. It means listening to and understanding the consumer's nuances, emotions and desires not readily apparent on the surface. It means steeping yourself in the product and the consumer to find the common ground. Once you've disciplined yourself, then you're free to create with intelligence and purpose. You let the chaos happen. A bare wall gets papered with ideas. You attempt to do more than meet the strategy. You try to top it. Make it smarter. Go a little crazy. Fire at will."

CHAPTER 4

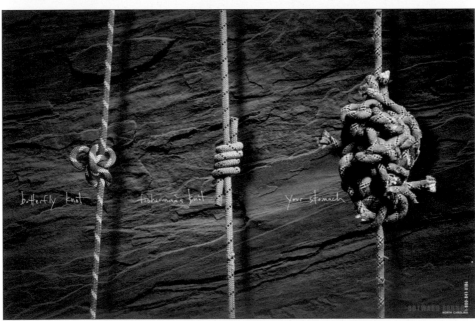

*A strategic, unconventional solution to a perception-reality problem.
Loeffler Ketchum Mountjoy's campaign for Outward Bound
was inspired by first-hand consumer experiences.*

The North Carolina chapter of Outward Bound faced a classic perception-reality problem. Their previous advertising had convinced teenagers, the core audience, that Outward Bound was a cosy summer camp which their parents would like. The kids craved adventure and challenge, precisely what Outward Bound really offered. When Mountjoy's agency researched the under-20s, it unearthed diaries and journals written by young people who had endured the programme.

The agency had found "the common ground". As the creative team riffed through the accounts of the wilderness-from-hell, they started making connections for stark, simple visuals. Kids told how they had answered the call of nature whilst being surrounded by it. How they had become incredibly resourceful. How scared they had felt on rock climbs.

The images of the hand and knots symbolise the soul of an Outward Bound adventure. The art direction preserves the rugged honesty of the woods and the handwritten experiences in those diaries. The brown sepia tone conveys a taste of roughing it.

Visa Gold. When Antony Redman was creative director at Batey Ads, Singapore, a pan-Asian campaign for the Visa Gold credit card presented both strategic and creative opportunities. "In Asia, there was burgeoning wealth," recalls Redman. "There was an almost wanton look on people's faces which you don't see in the West. Their idea of success was to amass all material possessions possible, to have it bigger, faster, stronger, shinier than anyone else. When it came to the credit card product category, those kinds of people wanted American Express Gold. It was the epitome of everything, the equivalent of a Rolex or a Mercedes-Benz. Yet within that environment of the *nouveau riche*, there was a younger group aged from twenty to thirty-five, maybe forty; in amongst all the uniformity and respect for authority that you have in Asia, they were trying to assert their individuality. They still wanted the same things, but they wanted to be seen as more individualistic, more international. They'd been educated in America or Europe or Australia, they had a more worldly outlook. The brief was to reach them, to get them to switch from Amex Gold to Visa Gold."

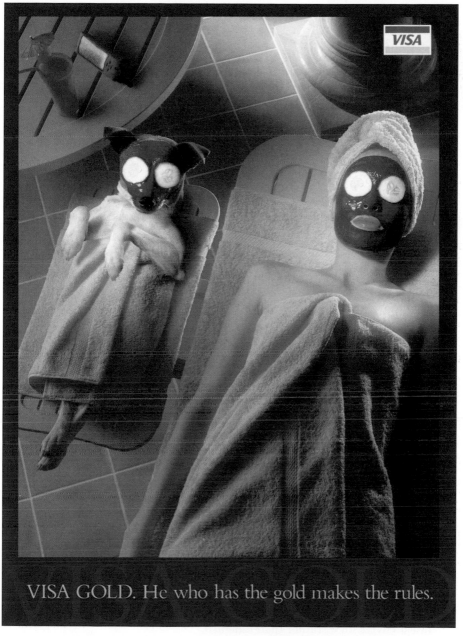

VISA GOLD. He who has the gold makes the rules.

Visa Gold subverted the conventions of wealth when it targeted wealthy young Asians keen to assert their individuality. Batey Ads, Singapore.

Redman knew that Visa Gold would have to break the convention in its category. "All those gold credit card *clichés* of people in restaurants, or driving a Porsche, wouldn't talk to our target audience."

His first decision was to make the campaign visually-led. "It had to work regionally. Also, the audience we wanted didn't have time to read. And because everyone knows what a credit card is for, what it does, there was nothing truly interesting to say. Instead, we asked ourselves, what is truly interesting about the people we're going to advertise to?"

Two creative teams explored four different directions. Ultimately, one campaign led through its originality, tonality and strategic appropriateness.

"It took the conventions of wealth and *subverted* them. When you're in the luxury market and you want to say something different, you need to subvert, to flip it on its head a bit. Some ideas were funny, but didn't show the wealth. The people we were talking to still wanted to be told they were wealthy and successful. What this campaign also tells them is that they have a sense of individuality, as well as a sense of humour."

Over sixty different concepts were tabled; five ultimately ran. The first ad which set the tone for the series was an impeccably shot bottle of rare vintage wine. It was, in itself, a parody of classic wine advertisements. On second glance, however, the reader discovered a cheeky straw poking out of the bottle. "It totally subverted the imagery associated with gold credit cards," says Redman.

The *cliché* of the facial was another target. "Someone who is wealthy goes to a spa. They lie down, and they've got all their fluffy towels, and they get a facial. So we subverted that. We said if someone is wealthy enough, and individual enough, they could treat their dog to a facial as well. Then we went the other way. We took a cheesy bit of popular culture, the hot dog. We said someone who is wealthy enough, and individual enough, could decide to put the finest caviar on it, rather than mustard."

Another ad showed pigeons wearing diapers sitting on a branch above a collection of luxury cars. In another, the owner has put his pet dog on the treadmill. Ideas which did not see the light of day included a mansion with Beavis and Butthead statues outside and a wealthy estate where all the bushes had been trimmed fastidiously into the shapes of famous cartoon characters.

"Originally, the line we had was *Whatever*, meaning whatever you want to buy, whatever you're into, whatever. But in Asia, whatever is also used in another way. If someone is lecturing you, ticking you off, and you want to annoy them, you say 'Whatever'. So we had a campaign, but no line."

Eventually the strapline came from the agency chairman, Rick Scott-Blackhall. "Rick had a passion for the product and the campaign, and it's integral to have that in an agency, from the top down. One morning he came in with a list of anonymous quotes. When I saw the line, the play on gold, I knew it said everything we wanted to say. *He who has the gold makes the rules* said you've got the money, you've got the power, you can do whatever you like, you can break the rules and make new ones, and damn anyone else who says otherwise."

Redman believes great ideas do not just come from the creative department. "I think it's important to have your ears out, to listen. You should open up to opinions. Some are damaging and boring, but some are worth listening to. Take it in, suck it all up, then edit out what you don't need."

The campaign was shot by Mike Skelton in Australia and art directed by Redman. "The visuals had to tell the story, deliver the humour. I kept the rest simple. The line was set in plain, boring Bembo. You need a simple, classic face for the luxury category."

As the full colour pages rolled out across Asia, eyebrows were raised from Taiwan to Thailand. Ultimately, though, the healthy dose of subversion left an indelible, highly successful footprint in Asia's conservative financial services category.

The Village Voice. What, on the surface, might appear an extremely outrageous campaign was created to address two strategic issues. Both were critical to the newspaper's survival.

"*The Village Voice* was about to change its business structure," explains Nick Cohen of Mad Dogs & Englishmen. "After being sold by subscription for years, the *Voice* was about to be given away free. From a business standpoint, they wanted to increase circulation. If they got more copies out there, they'd get a new audience. But there was a concern on the part of the client that it would be a real negative. Like, suddenly the paper wasn't worth anything any more, it was free because it wasn't worth paying for any more."

The agency had to grapple with a second strategic issue. The *Voice* wanted to attract a younger audience. "The problem the *Voice* faced was that they'd been around since the late 1950s. The kind of people who had co-opted the *Voice* when it first came out were the hippie generation. Young people thought, well, that's *their* paper, it isn't *our* paper. So we wanted young people in New York to realise how important the *Voice* was to them. The *Voice* was a pioneer. It was a newspaper that made it very possible for young people to live a kind of lifestyle that wouldn't be acceptable in other parts of America. If you're gay, for example, it's very hard to practise, to be open about the fact in most parts of America. But you can in New York, you can in the Village, that's what it was all about. It was about people being allowed to be themselves. Young people had forgotten that. They were all too ready to slag off the *Voice* rather than give it credit for what it had made possible."

In order to win that credit from younger people, as well as retain the paper's credibility among existing readers, the campaign focused on prejudice and hostility. Rather than turn the mirror on the target audience, the agency turned it the other way: on those most opposed to the paper and all it stood for. In so doing, the interests of both younger and older readers were unified.

"We reminded them that it's *Not America's favourite paper*," says Cohen. "The kind of people who live in Idaho, or wherever, are not going to accept the *Voice* at all. They're going to reject it, and reject anyone who reads it. So what the campaign was saying was, Thank God for *The Village Voice*. *The Village Voice* has made it possible for you to live the kind of lifestyle that you want to live. Give them credit. Support them. Don't forget that this paper is for you, and if it went away, it would be a worse world for you to live in than if it's around."

The campaign worked, paving the way for the *Voice* to go free without losing any credibility. The message also resonated for younger readers. As Cohen muses: "Everyone who's young, even-

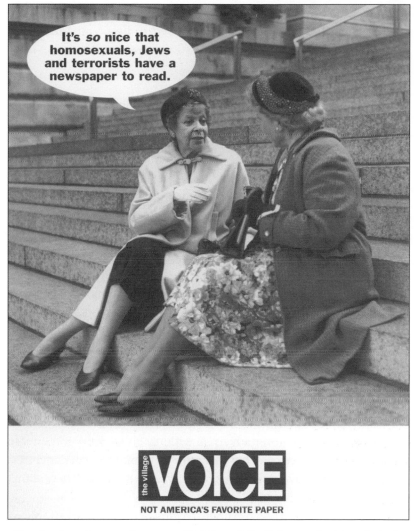

Turning the mirror on the enemy, Mad Dogs & Englishmen solved two strategic problems for The Village Voice.

tually they're all going to become fifty, but is our spirit going to be alive? The *Voice* is for people who are free spirits."

XO Beer. When Singapore Press Holdings briefed Neil French to promote its newspapers to the local advertising industry, they little realised the train of events they were setting in motion. XO Beer is essentially a study in lateral thinking. An unconventional strategy evolved, leap by leap, eventually reaching a highly unconventional creative solution. In the process, the need to be creator-and-critic emerges clearly. A schizophrenic function, it separates cutting edge communicators from the rest.

The XO story began routinely enough.

"The first thing I did was produce a campaign based on all the facts that said newspapers are as powerful, maybe more powerful, than television," recalls French. "I wrote it and sold it and they thought it was jolly good. But the next day I called up and said, look, we can't do that because I've just realised that those facts are totally available to everybody, and the fact they're ignoring the facts means there's no point in telling them again. That'd be silly. So I apologised very much and said I'd do some new ads.

"They said they wanted to get the FMCG business, detergents, shampoos, beer, that kind of stuff. So I said, let's pick one for a start. Beer seemed like the more relevant to me than shampoo, because I don't have any hair. What we'll do, I said, is go out and find a small, unadvertised brand of beer, do some great ads for it, put them in a newspaper, sell lots of beer, thereby proving print to the big beer advertisers. The clients said, right, okay, and off they went.

"The next day I rang them up and said, sorry about this, I've changed my mind again. We can't do that because if we do it success-fully, the big brands will say we've been taking the rice out of their ricebowls and they'll never advertise with us. So we were forced into the position that if we can't tell them the facts, and we can't advertise a real beer, we'll advertise a fake beer. It was that easy. There didn't seem to be another way to do it."

French believed it was crucial to make things as difficult as possible for the new beer to succeed. "If we gave ourselves an easy trot, everyone would say, yeah, well, of course, anybody could have done that. We looked at the research which said that all beer must be light in colour these days, so we decided we'd make ours *black*. It must be light in alcohol, so we decided we'd make ours, toss a coin, *12% alcohol*. The ads must have photographs of girls, so we decided *not* to have any photographs of girls. They must have status symbols, so we said *no* status symbols. They must have crowds of blokes having a jolly time in a pub, slapping each other on the back and pouring beer down their necks, as though people don't know what beer is for, do they rub it in their hair or something? Really, it's pathetic. Anyhow, we said we'd have *none* of that, either. Every rule we could find about beer advertising, we decided to *break*."

However, before he could do the ads, French had to name the product and design the packaging. "In naming it, in saying this beer was going to be powerful and expensive, I just ripped off the idea of the cognac which is XO," French explains. "I found out that XO wasn't ownable because it was a degree of cognac, so we could use it and no cognac company could sue us. I also found out I couldn't register it for beer as such, but that I could register the trademark. Which I did, in my own name."

French designed the XO logo so that it could be read on its side or the right way up. "There was a purpose in that. Most beer clients I've worked for are the most reactionary people one could ever come into contact with. They tend to forget that beer drinking is a rather jolly thing to be doing and they all get very serious about it and follow the rulebooks. It struck me that if you're selling a very strong beer that makes you fall over, then the bottle should have fallen over already."

The fallen bottle became a powerful campaign mnemonic. "If you look at the ads, there's no cap on it and it's dripping rather sadly. It's a drunken bottle, as well as a beer that makes you drunk. It seemed to me to be an important part of the message. It says this gets you very, very drunk."

The campaign was a celebration of inebriation. Singaporeans opened their morning papers and stared in disbelief at the ravages of alcohol. Collapsed drinkers, blood-flecked floors, a man about to drink XO with a pillow tied to the back of his head. In one execution, a barroom floor was sketched with coroner's chalk, showing where the bodies had fallen. In another, a naked man stared morosely down at his diminished manhood, thoughtfully framed out of shot. Beneath the visual, the little neck of the XO bottle was also drooping, "as things tend to do in my experience", observes French.

Another flight of ads were simple cryptic captions, set in Munich Beerhall Bold. They became so popular that readers could recite them word-for-word.

The campaign which Singapore breweries could not take lying down.
Neil French, for Singapore Press Holdings.

To experience the effect of our beer without buying one, stand behind a policeman's horse, lift its tail, and insert an ice-cube.

In absence of horse, policeman also can.

Like being struck behind the ear with a sockful of wet sand, only nicer. Slightly.

In research, consumers could recite the copy-led ads word-for-word.

As one half page colour ad followed another, barmen and waiters found themselves harangued and abused. "It was getting a tad violent out there. People were saying, 'Give me some of that XO Beer', and the barman'd say, 'We haven't got any', and he'd be called a bloody idiot, 'Of course you've got it, *I saw it advertised!*' It was really very funny."

It was not so funny for the major breweries as they tried to trace their newest competitor. The newspapers, naturally enough, refused to disclose who was placing the ads. "We really covered our tracks," French confides. "We'd started a company called Xerxes & Osborn, which purported to be the importers. We knew some smart guy would get onto it, hey, there's a new importer, Xerxes & Osborn, *XO*, I reckon it's *them!* So we got a phone number and put a girl on to answer it. If anyone asked for Mr. Xerxes or Mr. Osborn in the morning, she was instructed to say that they had very bad hangovers and would not be coming in. If anyone rang after lunch, she would say, sorry, but they've had a very large lunch, they've gone home to sleep it off. So the company was apparently run by two alcoholics who were never in the office and that really annoyed the breweries."

The campaign climaxed on the night of 31 March when a big party was held, ostensibly to launch the beer. Brewery executives and the advertising fraternity were invited. However, when they arrived, there was not a drop of XO to be had. They were told it had been held up at the docks. There were plenty of other beers to drink while they waited.

"At midnight, the boss of the newspaper got up and said, 'April Fool!' The breweries were very, very grumpy, but we'd proven our case. You *could* create demand for a beer in newspapers."

There was a postscript to the story. "When the beer people got stroppy, the newspaper people got stroppy back. The beer people said it was a product that didn't exist so it was easy, which is of course nonsense, so the newspaper people said in that case, we'll make the damn stuff. We got a microbrewery to start making XO, ran two more ads, and they were sold out in three days. They could see they were going to have to make a lot more, but they were having to pay me a dollar a glass, which was very nice, thank you very much, because I owned the brand. But they didn't want to pay me any more, so they took down all the XO posters and when people turned up they said, sorry, we haven't got any XO, but we've got this other stuff which is exactly the same. They were quite right, of course, it was the same, same recipe, same barrels, but people didn't want it and the place went broke. *Which is the power of the brand.*"

YES, VIRGINIA, THERE ARE *RETAIL* STRATEGIES, TOO

Hurry – Last Days is not an idea. Neither are *Giant Birthday Sale* nor *Special Offer – Save up to 25%.* Retail print is one of the world's biggest advertising categories, and creatively one of the most predictable.

Most retailers perceive themselves as outlets, a good plumbing term which says a lot about the advertising they pump into our daily papers. If you think of yourself as an outlet, you will simply run defensive price-led ads with stamp album layouts crammed with merchandise. You will never strike up relationships with customers and build something for the future.

In reality, retail stores are *brands*. Like any other brands, they can either follow convention or develop a real point of difference. A retailer who has nurtured strong brand relationships can override transient price differentials and survive a crisis. No brand, no image, means no loyalty, no visibility.

The same strategy applies to dealerships and service providers. As technology makes everything the same, the *dealer* becomes the difference. Smart dealers who build brand relationships cut the cost of generating leads. They come to own their categories.

Building brands in the retail sector does *not* mean abandoning sale ads or never showing merchandise and prices. It just means making a more conscious effort to communicate the flavour of the relationship, to surround the retail offer with some long-term substance. Retailers are actually in a luckier position than other brand builders: they can measure response instantly, and fine-tune their art direction and tonality accordingly.

Retailers will find many case histories to support their shift from price-led to brand-led advertising. Many guidelines exist to help them, as well as much good advice from people like David Mattingly, founder and chairman of Y & R Mattingly, Melbourne. Mattingly is Australia's retail advertising guru, the first Australian, in fact, to win an International Lifetime Achievement Award from the Retail Advertising and Marketing Association of the United States.

Mattingly believes a good retail ad should have four elements: a simple headline, an attractive visual, good copy and an effective layout. He argues that one great visual will hold a reader's attention, compelling him to read the headline and copy, whereas nobody will read a page crammed full of merchandise. Ads set the image, he says. The future direction of retail advertising, he predicts, would reflect that of retailing itself, where stores which are quick to pick up on trends will dominate.

Of course, it does not help improve retail advertising when so many people in creative circles look down with scorn on the category, or when agencies assign retail work to the juniors. The truth is that some of the world's best-known cutting edge creatives have happily turned their talents to retail print with exceptional results.

Launching Pizza Hut's new online pizza service.
BBDO Bangkok.

5 YEAR OLDS. 8 YEAR OLDS. 10 YEAR OLDS. HARRODS IS OVERRUN WITH THEM AT THIS TIME OF YEAR.

Cashing in on Christmas wine sales, while remaining consistent with the Harrods image. Leagas Delaney, London.

*Striking up a relationship
with consumers,
with a smile, and making it easy
for them to respond.
Abbott Mead Vickers, London.*

Read the Parker Knoll brochure in the discomfort of your own armchair.

Are you sitting uncomfortably?

Then we'll begin. The Parker Knoll brochure has 40 full-colour pages of contemporary and traditional suites, chairs and sofa-beds. And it's free.

To reserve your copy (together with price list and stockist list) send the coupon now.

- - - - - - - - - - - - - - - - - -

Please send me your colour brochure, stockist list and price list. To Sue Black, Parker Knoll Ltd., P.O. Box 22, Frogmoor, High Wycombe, Bucks HP13 5DJ.

Name

Address

Parker Knoll
A CORNWELL PARKER COMPANY

Postcode

PAY HALF NOW AND NOTHING LATER.

A range of five fitted kitchens with every unit at half price.

TEXAS HOMECARE

*Most people would have said "Save 50%", but not Leagas Delaney.
Shoppers respond to propositions they haven't seen before.*

WWW@@t.the:FCK
duz-it/@ll/me@n?

Damn, the internet! It comes barging into my life while I'm still figuring out how to set the clock on my VCR. Relax. Take an hour off work this week and come down to dx.com Internet Business Center. Let our very human staff sit you down on the latest equipment, take a deep breath and test drive the net until it all makes sense.

dx.com Internet Business Center
1 West 20th Street
New York, NY 10011
212-929-0566
outside new york:
800-472-dxdx

$12 per hour
net station rentals *
e-mail *
dial-up service *
web site design *
consulting *
web site hosting *
ftp service *
web site debugging *
lovely lamps *

dx.com

Sponsors:
UUNET Technologies
Mecklermedia
Apple Computer, Inc.

*As technology makes everything the same, the dealer is the difference.
Here, dx.com promises sanity and value-added service in human terms.
Internet-style art direction makes sense of the copy, service listing and address.
Mad Dogs & Englishmen, New York.*

The Tangs
Anniversary Sale
starts today

✂

APPLICATION
FOR URGENT LEAVE

SUBMITTED BY _____

DEPARTMENT _____

NO. OF DAY(S) APPLIED _____

FROM _____ TO _____

LEAVE BALANCE _____

SIGNATURE _____ DATE _____

APPROVED / NOT APPROVED

DEPARTMENT HEAD _____ DATE _____

HR DEPARTMENT _____ DATE _____

REMARKS _____

This sale ad ran as a broadsheet full page. Says Tangs vice-president group marketing and communications Gerry Rezel: "We have to challenge ourselves, and you get a little scared every day, but you have to try. The realisation of your goals is not over just one campaign, it's over time before it sinks in. The worst thing is to underestimate your customers, both intellectually and in their sense of aesthetics." WORK Singapore for Tangs.

Contemporary illustration techniques build store branding as well as sell merchandise. Tangs believe the smartness and intelligence of their advertising must be reflected in their merchandise presentation and the shopping experience they offer. WORK Singapore for Tangs Studio.

CHAPTER ONE

Trailing clouds of glory, Captain Corelli shimmered into the room. "Gaul is divided into three parts," he announced. "And for the really alert, and more literary among us, there were three clues in that first sentence, and four altogether, so far. Stay awake, please; for today we have naming of parts!"

The dormouse fell into the teapot.

The soldier glared at the offending rodent with a look that could warp walnut. "Shut up," he explained.

"The riddle of the sands is written on the subway walls. But this entire ad is a riddle, got up to look like a page from a book. Within this page are twenty clues, hidden references by title, quotation, or well-known passage, to famous literary figures of all sorts.

Next Tuesday morning, when Borders opens its doors, on the corner of Scotts and Orchard Roads, the first ten people to turn-up with a correct, (even if incomplete) list of these names will get as many free books of their choice as they have correct answers. In other words, get three names right, and choose three free books... up to a maximum of twenty." He sat down.

Suddenly, in walked a blonde. A blonde to make a bishop kick a hole in a stained-glass window. She walked in beauty, like the night.

"What contemptible scoundrel stole the cork from my lunch?" she mumbled, and joined the dormouse in the crockery.

"Certain women should be struck regularly, like gongs," said the highwayman to his coy mistress. "I must arise, and go now; I must go down to the seas again, the lonely sea and the sky. A year in Provence, or merely on the road, will suffice."

The Prince had found the last tycoon in "The Raven", drinking cider with Rosie. He was…well, if not actually disgruntled, he was far from gruntled.

"It requires a surgical operation to get a joke well into a Scotch understanding," he grouched. "Journalism is basically people who can't write, interviewing people who can't talk, for people who can't read. The editorial board is a parliament of whores."

"Not staying on, then?" ventured the little Prince.

"An idea that is not dangerous is not worthy of being called an idea at all!" he yelled, slamming the door behind him.

The silence hung in the air like a housebrick doesn't.

"Assassination is the extreme form of censorship," she said. "Maybe the board should have tried that?"

"He's a modest little man, with a lot to be modest about," he replied. "Standards are always out of date. That's what makes them standards."

He stood up.

"Ah, yes, Virginia, such is life." He gathered his papers. "All animals are equal, but some animals are more equal than others. It's been a funny old year; a winter of discontent, a silent spring, a dangerous summer, and now, the fall of the House of Usher."

"Actually, I'm Rosie, not Virginia," she said. "Fancy a walk in the woods?"

"A dance might be better?"

So over the blue remembered hills, and far away, they danced to the music of time.

THE END

"There are twenty-five clues to the authors of books, poems, or merely quotations on this page. The clues can be titles, well-known lines or passages…or even just 'clues'. The Borders store, on the corner of Orchard and Scotts Roads opens at nine in the morning. Next Friday, the first ten customers who give us a list of these authors can choose as many free books from our stock as they got correct answers. In other words, get three authors correct; get three free books. Up to the maximum of twenty-five books per customer. Good luck.

[125]

Ogilvy & Mather Singapore launched Borders with a challenge to book lovers. If all the great books of the world come together at the store, the agency reasoned, they could also come together in one intriguing story that gave readers the chance to win prizes for identifying the authors. It was the first time a newspaper page had been printed white-on-white to replicate the experience of opening a pristine new book. Neil French and regional creative director Tham Khai Meng led the creative team of Jaume Mones, Francesc Talamino and Alfred Wee with French taking 20 full days of research to find the appropriate clues.

DEFYING CONVENTION

Strategic disciplines are arduous. We cannot rely on logic, because real life is not logical. Nor can we be disruptive just for the sake of being different. Stepping beyond the accepted conventions could well mean suffering a little time in the wilderness. But then, most of our advertising heroes were heretics once.

If you believe that most advertising today is still formulaic, superficial and transparent, take heart from Neil Godfrey.

"What I hated about advertising when I first started was that advertising was *advertising*. What we helped it become was something that slipped into your life, *an elbow touching you.* I tend to have chosen writers, or maybe they chose me, who really weren't advertising people as such. David Abbott, Tony Brignull, Indra Sinha. They were writers outside of advertising, who wanted to move away from the kind of *brashness* that advertising has. Somehow, if you're in advertising, you're a commercial person. It was the last thing I ever wanted to be. My mother used to introduce me to friends as a commercial artist, and it was the biggest insult I ever had."

By learning how to think strategically, by understanding more about human nature than brash formulae, by being your own creative self, you can respond to the new cutting edge disciplines. The industry will need your contribution if it is to stay relevant to its clients.

As Hugh Mackay says: "The rate of public sophistication and technological change is speeding up. Anyone under thirty knows what the advertising tricks are. Many have done media studies so they know all about propaganda, the impact of quick editing. They're very comfortable with it. From the point of view of the advertising industry, this is a very good thing. One of the myths about advertising is that it has some kind of mysterious power, that it can influence people without them knowing. The more people are educated, the more they understand the advertising process, they won't be scared of advertising. They won't think it's manipulating them in a secret way. They will be more *confident* as consumers. That should mean, if we do our job properly, they will enter the relationship with us more confidently. We should not fear the media-literate young. Quite the reverse. We can be more daring with the young. We can actually take *more* risks."

5

HOW TO GET AN IDEA

We have some notions how advertising does and does not work. We have accepted that a lot of advertising truths, for the most part, are lies. We have seen new brand building methodologies replacing the old. We have a deeper appreciation of strategic thinking.

Having consciously prepared ourselves to understand the advertising process, we can now enter the creative process.

Creativity, according to Dorothy Parker, is a disciplined eye and a wild mind. The question is, *how* disciplined and *how* wild?

Creativity is supposed to rely on inspiration. But as any author, artist, actor or composer will tell you, inspiration is unreliable. We cannot wait for inspiration. We have deadlines. We have to deliver. We have to reach our creative peaks *without* it.

We have to develop our own personal creative methodology. Rather like slipping on a comfortable old jacket every morning, our methodology will become second nature. It will be a reassuring series of steps, a mental checklist. Nothing formulaic, just a few things we can do to get ideas happening, to generate concepts. While we are focused and working, the inspired ideas will invariably surface.

The alternative is to stare into space.

Is There an Idea in the Product Name or Logo?

Some of the world's greatest campaigns have kicked off from this point. When the product name or logo becomes the idea, there is less risk of creating a generic campaign. The brand will brand the advertising from the centre out. And if the campaign thought contains an alliterative device, so much the better.

Ariston. You want to communicate that Ariston appliances are more durable. In fact, you want to own the word durability in the appliance category. The idea: *Ariston and on and on.*

DHL. You want to position DHL as the world's most reliable courier. You want to communicate the risks of packages ending up in the wrong hands. The idea: *DHL or else.*

Silk Cut. If you cannot talk about smoking, at least you can get people to talk about your advertising. The idea: *cut silk.*

Cow & Gate. Baby food advertising is riddled with generics. How can you make your ads unique when you cannot avoid showing a happy, gurgling baby? The idea: behind every happy, gurgling baby *show a cow and gate.*

Castlemaine XXXX Beer. How do you convince the British that XXXX is the beer Aussies would die for? XXXX, easy, mate! Everyone knows Australians swear a lot. And XXXX is often used to replace the four-letter word. The idea: *Australians wouldn't give a XXXX for anything else.*

The Independent. You want to differentiate the newspaper's beliefs. You want readers to identify with them. The idea: *The Independent. It is, are you?*

Time. Fallon's campaign for *Time* has been running for years. Art director Bob Barrie has chalked up over fifty executions.

"The truth is, it was the third campaign that we'd shown *Time*. We'd liked the first two quite a bit. In retrospect, they killed them for very appropriate reasons; they were tonally wrong, and they couldn't have been owned as well by *Time* as the one we eventually ended up with."

After the first two ideas were killed, Barrie recalls how he went back to his drawing board quite depressed. "I don't know exactly what happened, but I think that the *Time* red border was just emblazoned into my brain. I'd actually grown up with the magazine; my parents subscribed to it when I was a child in Green Bay, Wisconsin, and I'd subscribed to it all the way through college. I just started playing around with it on some photographs from the magazine, using it to isolate different parts of the image. It became the look of the ads. Then with some fine copywriting by Dean Buckhorn, the campaign kind of sprang to life."

Barrie believes the writing in *Time* magazine is as big a part of the product as the photography. "We tried to come up with a way to fuse the two in the advertising. When you're dealing with a product like *Time*, where you have access to what are basically some of the world's greatest photographs on a weekly basis, it would be idiotic not to use them. You can use a killer photograph of a man like Bill Clinton that ran in *Time*, without getting permission from Bill Clinton, because it's the product."

Having established the campaign based on the magazine's border and masthead, Barrie then looked into the craft details. "Rather than have big, bold headlines in the traditional Minneapolis look, I actually borrowed the typography from the editorial itself. If you look at it, it's spaced and set in the same point size as actual copy written in *Time* magazine."

Over the years, Barrie says, the campaign continued to evolve strategically. "While there's been no change in the look of the ads, the tagline has changed. It was originally *Understanding comes with Time* and the ads tended to be competitive against other media like television and newspapers. Then they wanted to take more of a high road and they positioned it as *The world's most interesting magazine*."

Creatively, Barrie sees the campaign has become more playful. "We've isolated ears, and a hand that took kickbacks, and we used double borders when cloning was a big debate. The Bill Clinton ad came out at the height of Zippergate. It was the first *Time* ad we did that has no headline. We approached them with a couple of ideas, but they said they didn't want to do an ad about Zippergate, they didn't want to pass judgement. Then we saw this photo which had run in *Time* where he's perspiring profusely. So we simply framed the perspiration on his forehead and said, here's an ad you can run because you're putting the onus on the reader."

Back to the drawing board for Bob Barrie.

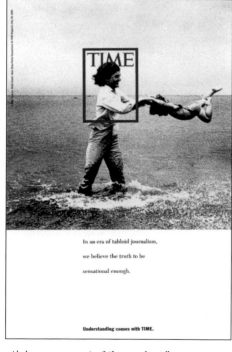

"I love it when the design of the advertising comes out of the product,"
says Fallon Minneapolis art director Bob Barrie.

How a campaign can keep evolving and keep fresh.

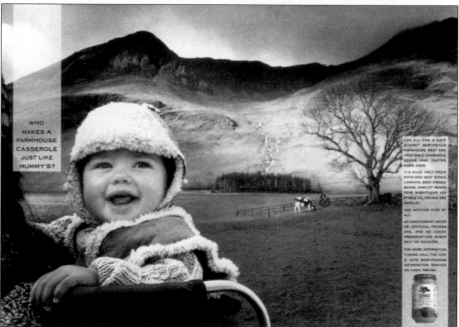

Abbott Mead Vickers, London, can always find a cow and gate.

*Branding the beer that Aussies swear by. Saatchi & Saatchi, London, for
Castlemaine XXXX Beer.*

M&C Saatchi achieved 100% branding by using the shape of
New Zealand to form a percentage sign.

The all new Hot Dog £1.39

香蕉奶昔新鮮上市

Filet-O-Fish. £1.39

The Golden Arches have inspired many instantly branded ideas from Leo Burnett creatives around the world.

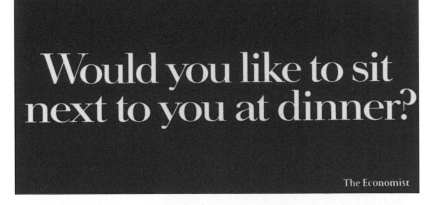

The Economist

The Economist. One of the great British campaigns, with its hallmark white on red, had its genesis when David Abbott, lost for an idea, sat staring at the magazine's masthead.

"I had a notion that you couldn't really spell out what we needed to say in long copy. It would be banal, and even rather offensive, to actually seriously try and say, read this and you'll be successful. Whereas you could probably get away with it with the kind of lateral, funny, witty lines that in themselves didn't take the notion too seriously, but would leave a kind of trace element of the idea in people's minds so, over a period of time, this would become a club that you wanted to belong to."

"I was sitting, wondering what to do, with the magazine in front of me," Abbott reflects, "with no real media direction, against a

"I never read The Economist."

Management trainee. Aged 42.

One of Britain's greatest, most enduring campaigns began when David Abbott sat staring at The Economist *masthead. Abbott Mead Vickers, London.*

background where we'd done quite nice ads for *The Economist* over the years but nothing that really hung together as a campaign, and against a background where it was almost impossible to get body copy through *The Economist*. They had a great list of people who had to see all written words of advertising, and they were all journalists, and they all felt they were better writers than the copywriters at the agency. So getting ads through with philosophy statements or even comments on the contents was always a laborious, heart-breaking business; so there was part of me trying not to write body copy."

It suddenly dawned on Abbott that the white-on-red masthead of the magazine happened to be the same shape as an outdoor poster.

"I was just looking, and I thought, well, why not outdoor? And I was prompted absolutely by staring at the logo, and thinking, yeah, maybe. And I wrote the first one, *Management trainee, aged 42*, very, very quickly. They all came very quickly after that and we presented a raft of them to David Gordon, who was the client, and he bought it. That typeface, and that white on red, have become great branding. It was just using the livery of the magazine in a way they'd never really done wholeheartedly before. I think it *is* often about going at something with gusto, and being single-minded."

Posters and print ads proliferated. Occasionally, the words vanish; once they were replaced by a white keyhole on the familiar red ground.

"They've got harder to do as the years have gone by," confesses Abbott, "simply because we've been in most areas. Now in the agency, everyone has a go at them. I collect a big pile of maybe sixty or seventy, and I choose the ones that either haven't been done before or that tickle my fancy. We end up with five or six a season. The terrain is so tightly defined, whether it's irony or whatever, and some people can do it, then they use up their supply of ads and they need a rest from it before they come back. Maybe people have only got so many *Economist* ads in them."

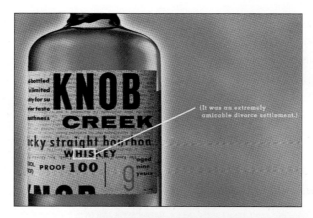

(It was an extremely amicable divorce settlement.)

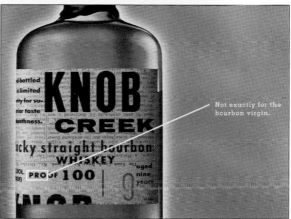

Not exactly for the bourbon virgin.

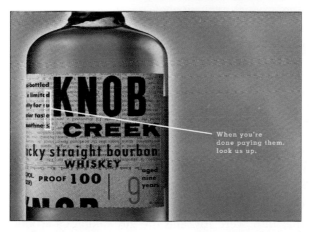

When you're done paying them, look us up.

Fallon Minneapolis positioned a new whiskey by touring its label. When product logos or packaging are central to the advertising idea, the brand becomes more visible in store.

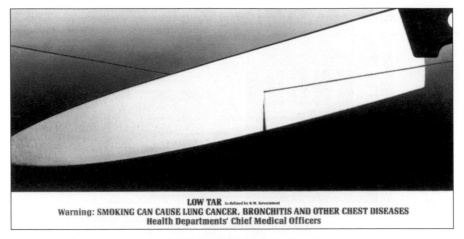

LOW TAR As defined by H.M. Government
Warning: SMOKING CAN CAUSE LUNG CANCER, BRONCHITIS AND OTHER CHEST DISEASES
Health Departments' Chief Medical Officers

Cutting silk and owning the colour purple.
Saatchi & Saatchi, London.

IS THERE AN IDEA IN THE PACKAGING?

It could be the shape. It could be the colour. It could be the material it is made from; how it feels when you hold it or use it. It could be the way it opens or reseals. It could be something on the label: a phrase, a list of awards or gold medals, somebody's signature, maybe something as bizarre as the factory address or telephone number.

For that matter, it could be the label itself. In which case, your idea will belong to the product exclusively.

IS THERE AN IDEA IN HOW THE PRODUCT IS MADE?

Is it handmade by robots? After they paint the car, does somebody paint the paint? Is there a tough man behind all those tender chickens? As Britain's Robin Wight says, "Interrogate the product until it confesses its strengths."

Bob Isherwood agrees. "Every time we had to do a Parker Pen ad, we would go down to the factory and walk around and we would see things there that would just write the ads for us," he recalls. "For instance, one day when we were there, we saw a big pile of walnut shells. We asked what they were for, and the guy taking us around said, well, we use them to polish the gold. We asked why walnut shells and the guy said, dunno really, we just put them in a barrel, the shells with the gold, and we roll them round and they polish it better than anything else, must be something to do with the walnut oil. There was a fantastic ad in that and you could never make it up sitting in your office. Offices are the worst places to write ads." For his trouble, Isherwood received a Gold Pencil at Britain's Design and Art Direction Awards.

Nine times out of ten, manufacturers will take their own manufacturing processes for granted. It takes the disciplined eye and wild mind of a writer or art director to find the stories. And if you find them, and they excite *you*, your excitement will convey itself to the reader.

The Volvo 460 is cocooned in a multi-layered shell of anti-corrosive material. No wonder Abbott Mead Vickers could shower it with 6-inch nails.

INSTEAD OF A COAT OF PAINT, WE GIVE IT A SUIT OF ARMOUR.

IS THERE AN IDEA IN WHERE THE PRODUCT IS MADE?

Very often there is. It could be something unique in the air, a special property in the water, found nowhere else. Do the grapes grow better there? Do the tomatoes grow fatter there? Is it the only place on earth where they craft that kind of steel or blow that kind of glass?

In the north of England, for example, the bitters are very creamy. Boddingtons is no exception. It is the kind of beer you drink through the cream. John Hegarty recalls the brief.

"It was the idea of making a beer from Manchester famous, staying true to its roots, in a way that would talk to a younger audience. We believe you've got to find something in the brand which elevates it. It doesn't necessarily have to be a unique thing within the brand. It might also elevate other products as well. You find that one thing, and you build your advertising around it."

That one thing for Boddingtons was its *creaminess*. "People described Boddingtons as a creamy pint," says Hegarty. "They liked it. But the creaminess is much the same as Guinness and the other Northern bitters, so it wasn't unique."

The solution was to present the creaminess in a very unique way. "We put beer into an ice cream cone, photographed it against black, made it very graphic. It demands attention, but the message in it, the thought in it, is very simple. Creaminess."

By presenting the familiar in an unfamiliar way, Boddingtons owns creaminess in its category. In terms of perceptions, cream now equals creme. The strapline, *The cream of Manchester*, became so well entrenched that it no longer appears in every execution.

Bartle Bogle Hegarty, London, making a beer from Manchester famous.
Creaminess is not unique, but the advertising is.

Is There an Idea in the Product's History?

Stuck for an idea in the present? Go back to the past for a solution. (Or, thinking laterally, if the product has no past, you can always invent one.)

The Royal Peacock Hotel. Advertising for this charming boutique hotel celebrates its days, or, more precisely, nights of infamy. Singapore's historic red light district is now an exotic memory, which Saatchi & Saatchi deploys to differentiate the Royal Peacock from its competitors. Wisely, Rowan Chanen's copy exercises restraint; style and elegance are communicated. Each execution, art directed by Ted Royer, pays tribute to Chinese posters of a bygone era, preserving mellow illustrations and quaint borders. The choice of typeface avoids the Chinese Checkers look; it is complementary, without being *clichéd*.

Lee Dungarees. Seaminess of another kind was celebrated by Fallon Minneapolis. There is no rule that says product heritage must always be presented in long copy, nor that it should always be treated with reverence. Miners minus their Lee Carpenter Pants make history more accessible, more engaging.

History revealed by Fallon Minneapolis.

You'll rest comfortably all night at the Royal Peacock Hotel. My, how times have changed.

THOUGH A GENTLEMAN never tells, it was not long ago that a night spent at the Royal Peacock meant forgoing only one thing. Sleep.

Enticed by the red lanterns that hung from the innocuous shophouses, many a lonely sailor and weary traveller would often find themselves wandering along Keong Saik Road.

Far from home, they would take comfort in the arms of an "Ah Ku"; politely known as a lady of the evening. No doubt leaving a good deal happier than when they arrived.

SO IT MAY RAISE MORE than an eyebrow to learn that ten of those very shophouses have now been artfully restored to create one of Singapore's most elegant boutique hotels.

Though the Ah Ku no longer grace the sidewalks, resplendent in their delicate silk Cheong Sam, the Royal Peacock offers much to keep the modern traveller entirely satisfied.

A EUROPEAN SLEIGH BED adorns every room, certainly a fitting inducement for a restful night's sleep. Voice-mail allows one to deal with the telephone when

it suits; a choice of newspapers is delivered directly to your door every day.

You may prefer to while away a few hours with a movie (perhaps "THE WORLD OF SUZIE WONG"). Then again, a book from our modest library may do. Suffice to say, these are the comforts one expects to find in a small, luxury hotel.

AND WHEN MORNING COMES and you fling open the cherry-red shutters to greet the day, it may cross your mind to explore the curious lanes below.

For the fragrant medicine shops, exotic spice emporiums and colourful provision stores will surely beckon. But not before a splendid complimentary breakfast, European or Asian, served in the restaurant downstairs.

AS YOU BID the front desk staff a hearty good morning (by now they will already know you by name) you will set off from the Royal Peacock as happy as those many travellers who called there long before you.

Of course, you will be rather considerably better rested.

For that is the charm of the Royal Peacock. A BROTHEL BEFORE, A HOTEL NOW. GOOD SERVICE ALWAYS.

小樓雕欄依舊在

夜深高枕入夢鄉

THE ROYAL PEACOCK

55 KEONG SAIK ROAD SINGAPORE 089158 TELEPHONE: (65) 2233522

Exotic memories building the brand for a boutique hotel.
Saatchi & Saatchi, Singapore.

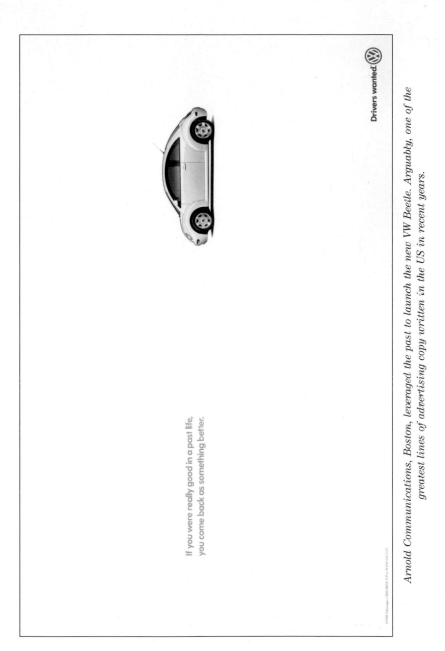

If you were really good in a past life,
you come back as something better.

Drivers wanted.

Arnold Communications, Boston, leveraged the past to launch the new VW Beetle. Arguably, one of the greatest lines of advertising copy written in the US in recent years.

IT ONLY TAKES
A COUPLE OF DRINKS
TO BRING OUT
THE COWARD IN YOU.

It was in March 1930 that Noel Coward and a friend quietly slipped into Singapore Harbour aboard an old Danish freighter from Siam. His friend was promptly rushed to the nearest hospital to spend a month recovering from dysentery.

NOEL, ON THE other hand, was rushed to the Raffles Hotel where he was to recover from a badly creased tuxedo.

Sitting on the verandah on his first night, the poor chap thought that he would die from the stifling humidity.

He should have been grateful.

After all, it was this weather that would eventually lead to him writing 'MAD DOGS AND ENGLISHMEN.'

Besides, the humidity eventually broke and was replaced by a light shower.

Coward, unused to the Singapore weather, thought it the most thorough-going rainstorm he'd ever seen.

The hotel's marble-floored verandah faced a brooding South China Sea and Coward was convinced that it was about to become part of the boiling, murky waters.

Proven wrong, he retired to the luxury of his suite, completely dry, but utterly miserable.

Fortunately, it didn't take him long to discover the few basic necessities that would make an Englishman's life bearable in Singapore.

The first being the Raffles Hotel's Bar and Billiard Room.

The second, the perfect gin sling.

The third, was some generous if not gullible sorts to finance the second.

(Apparently, a perfect gin sling can only be improved if paid for by someone other than the recipient.)

A couple of those and he was soon feeling himself again, offering some wonderful observations of the place and its expatriate inhabitants.

"SINGAPORE IS A FIRST RATE PLACE FOR SECOND RATE PEOPLE," he blithely proclaimed, to a far from appreciative audience.

The Bar and Billiard Room was a splendidly, civilised place, where white-jacketed patrons would casually commune under high ceilings and lazy fans, cosetted by attentive serving staff. And in keeping with etiquette, a strict dress-code was stringently adhered to.

Coward, taking no chances, stated, "I TAKE STOCK OF MYSELF IN THE MIRROR BEFORE GOING OUT; AN UNFORTUNATE TIE EXPOSES ONE TO DANGER."

His fortunes further improved when introduced to the Quaints, a local theatrical

group with a frighteningly varied, if somewhat dubious repertoire.

They would spend evenings collectively singing dance hall numbers around the Bar and Billiard Room's Piano. (Dance hall music, of all things.)

Spurred on by his brilliant performances at the piano, it wasn't long before Coward found himself on stage, "TAKING A PERFECTLY GOOD ROLE AND THROWING IT IN THE ALLEY."

Unfortunately, he also threw it into the waiting hands of critics.

The show closed after three days.

Well, at least it paid for his drinks.

The Bar and Billiard Room has long been synonymous with the famous and infamous, who would, and still do, wax lyrical over the finest cognacs, champagnes, single malt whiskies, vintage beers and, of course, Singapore Slings.

Because, in the right surroundings, with the right stimulation, there's a little Coward in all of us just waiting to be coaxed out.

BAR

FOR YEARS THE BAR AND BILLIARD ROOM WAS PATRONISED BY SOMERSET MAUGHAM.

AS WAS EVERYONE ELSE.

"Observing these people, I am no longer surprised there is a scarcity of domestic servants back in England."

SUCH COMMENTS did not endear him to Singapore's colonial elite.

Yet he strongly believed the world's best stories were to be found in the East.

Which consequently led to many of his stories starting the same way.

Or to be more precise, in the same place. The Bar and Billiard Room.

At least two of his books, "A MOON AND SIXPENCE" and "OF HUMAN BONDAGE" were written in the hotel.

He was often found reclined in a leather armchair beneath a blue Havana haze spiralling up to lazy ceiling fans, absorbing the atmosphere, the alcohol and the lives of the expatriate planters.

Busily recording notes to be used, incriminatingly, later.

At other times, he'd be surrounded by an appreciative crowd. All laughing a little too loudly at his scything repartee.

But Maugham was also a great listener; patiently sitting and inquiring of your life as if you were the most interesting person he'd ever met.

Queues of adoring expatriate wives would divulge their personal stories to his attentive ear.

Like lambs to slaughter.

Not surprisingly, many of them were far from happy on finding their thinly-disguised lives, graphically mocked in the pages of his books.

There's no pleasing some people.

After all, he couldn't be expected to insult everyone in person.

"AMERICAN WOMEN EXPECT TO FIND IN THEIR HUSBANDS A PERFECTION THAT ENGLISH WOMEN ONLY HOPE TO FIND IN THEIR BUTLERS", he once penned.

When accused of rudeness, he retorted in a fittingly Maugham-esque manner: "THE RIGHT PEOPLE ARE RUDE, THEY CAN AFFORD TO BE."

Not that Maugham was completely misunderstood. Aleister Crowley once stated, "THOUGH MANY MAY RESENT THE CURIOUS TRICK HE HAS OF SAYING SPITEFUL THINGS ABOUT EVERYBODY, I HAVE ALWAYS FELT THAT LIKE MYSELF, HE MAKES SUCH REMARKS WITHOUT MALICE, FOR THE SAKE OF CLEVERNESS."

A fine testimonial which may not have been helped by Crowley's own notoriety, for being voted the wickedest man alive.

Whatever his faults, Maugham was undoubtedly a charming character who only added to the legend that is this graceful old hotel in the tropics.

The Raffles Bar and Billiard Room has long been synonymous with the famous and infamous.

And with its history come the finest cognacs, champagnes, single malt whiskies, vintage beers, connoisseur coffees and chocolates.

Along with some of the legendary conversation, to which many have been attracted and some subjected.

Batey Ads Singapore leveraged the romantic history of Raffles Hotel and famous eccentric guests Noel Coward and Somerset Maugham. Copywriter: Kash Sree. Art director: Andy Fackrell.

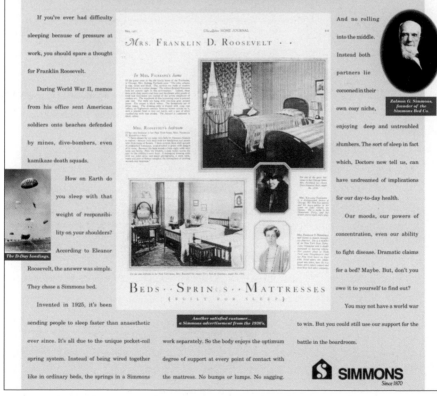

FOR PRESIDENT ROOSEVELT, A DAY AT THE OFFICE INVOLVED SENDING 750,000 MEN INTO A MINEFIELD. EVER WONDERED HOW HE SLEPT AT NIGHT?

If you've ever had difficulty sleeping because of pressure at work, you should spare a thought for Franklin Roosevelt.

During World War II, memos from his office sent American soldiers onto beaches defended by mines, dive-bombers, even kamikaze death squads.

How on Earth do you sleep with that weight of responsibility on your shoulders?

According to Eleanor Roosevelt, the answer was simple. They chose a Simmons bed.

Invented in 1925, it's been sending people to sleep faster than anaesthetic ever since. It's all due to the unique pocket-coil spring system. Instead of being wired together like in ordinary beds, the springs in a Simmons work separately. So the body enjoys the optimum degree of support at every point of contact with the mattress. No bumps or lumps. No sagging.

And no rolling into the middle. Instead both partners lie cocooned in their own cosy niche, enjoying deep and untroubled slumbers. The sort of sleep in fact which, Doctors now tell us, can have undreamed of implications for our day-to-day health.

Our moods, our powers of concentration, even our ability to fight disease. Dramatic claims for a bed? Maybe. But, don't you owe it to yourself to find out?

You may not have a world war to win. But you could still use our support for the battle in the boardroom.

SIMMONS
Since 1870

Malcolm Pryce's favourite ad from the Simmons campaign.
"It was like finding Rembrandts in the attic," he says.
McCann-Erickson, Singapore.

Is There an Idea in the Product's Old Advertising?

Robin Wight is a strong advocate of resurrecting old advertising icons and slogans. He calls it *advertising archaeology*. In a world of rapid change, the deeply familiar can be deeply reassuring. There are, of course, no rules. Retro campaigns can preserve the original, or parody it.

Simmons Beds. When McCann-Erickson, Singapore, explored Simmons advertising archaeology, they struck gold, literally, at America's One Show awards. Writer Malcolm Pryce describes how he resisted doing the campaign at first.

"We'd been briefed to do very practical demonstration ads. The traditional sort of ads, show me a wine glass balancing on the mattress with somebody lying next to it. We dutifully started work on that because the bed was based on this unique pocket-coil spring and we did a lot of ads with elephants, and trampolinists, and all that sort of stuff. Then the client changed his mind and said he wanted to do some ads on heritage. I'm ashamed to admit it," says Pryce, "but me and my art director just burst out laughing. How can you do heritage ads for a bed? We just ridiculed the idea with the arrogance which creatives quite often have."

Fortunately the client stuck to his guns. "To underline his passion, he sent over what was basically a corporate brochure," recalls Pryce. "I read it, and I was so blinkered by my derision for the fact that you could do heritage ads for a bed, that I failed to notice all the nuggets of gold in it. Ironically, it was my art director, Marc Schattner, who was also the creative director, who came back and said, look at *this!*"

In the 1930s, the Simmons Bed Company had run ads which were testimonials to the product from some of the greatest people in the twentieth century: President Roosevelt, Marconi, Henry Ford. As Pryce would later write in one of his headlines, *They all slept in the same bed*. The corporate brochure which the client had sent reproduced one of these ads, a testimonial by Eleanor Roosevelt.

"It was like finding Rembrandts in the attic," declares Pryce. "It was unbelievable, because when you're creating ads, you're always looking for a great hook to hang your hat on. When I saw that ad with Eleanor Roosevelt, the bell just went off in my head. In the 1930s, having President Roosevelt's wife talking about what bed they used was quite normal behaviour, but these days the idea of getting the President of the United States to advertise your bed would be just unheard of."

Because the testimonials were matters of historical record, Pryce and Schattner knew they could resurrect them freely. Once they had reached that point, says Pryce, the headlines came quite easily. "They seem so obvious when you think about it. I think the best ads you see are always like that."

IS THERE AN IDEA IN SOMETHING THAT'S HAPPENING AROUND YOU?

"Ideas are all around you," believes Hegarty. "They're *everywhere*. If you spend your time looking at award annuals, all you'll ever do is repeat what other people have done. But if you open your eyes and observe what's going on around you all the time, the humour and the charm and the fun of things, then you will get ideas that really do surprise, and charm, and are fresh. You can't invent some of the things that happen."

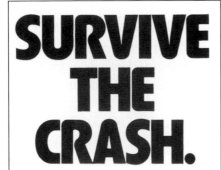

When the 1987 stock market crash first made headline news, this ad appeared overnight.
Saatchi & Saatchi, Sydney.

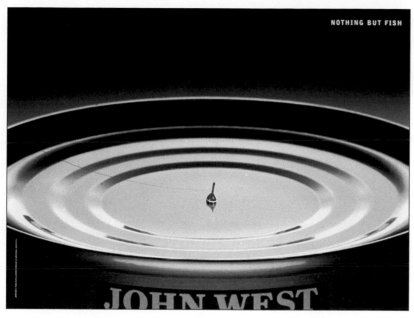

*Ideas are all around you, especially when you can see things the way
nobody has ever seen them before: such as the top of a can
(John West from Leo Burnett, London) and the Japanese flag
(Toshiba air conditioning from O&M's Results, Bangkok).*

AN IMPORTANT MASSAGE FOR LAMB LOVERS

Remarkable new activities published for the first time today shows how massaging a leg of lamb before roasting can greatly improve its flavour.

It's the result of a yearlong study by the Department of Lamb at the Waddaloddo Food Institute working in collaboration with the Bull College of Physiotherapy.

Professor Hans Allflavor, one of the study's authors, has proven how a brisk rubdown of a lamb leg just prior to roasting releases natural taste-enhancing enzymes called 'flavourons', which are up to three times more powerful than any herbs or spices available at your supermarket.

Co-author, Mary Hodliddle, added that by changing the type of massage you can alter the character of the flavourons. "A deep two-handed rub gives the meat added pepperiness, while a chopping motion brings out a hint of rosemary".

Although the full Waddaloddo-Bull Report is yet to be released, the initial findings are published today to give you the chance to maximise the flavour of your traditional Sunday lunch.

Follow the simple diagrams shown on the left for a Shiatsu-enhanced rosemary roast or a Swedish-enriched garlic flavour. But whatever you choose be sure to start before midday and begin by giving your leg a good pull.

We love our Lamb

GIANT CHOP BONE DISCOVERED

A remarkable find in the outback has experts convinced that the giant woolly dinosaur, *Aurumdoon Sutitubitytto* – popularly known as Lamb-o-saurus – once grazed the now plains Australian sheep, do today.

The massive rib revealed for the first time this morning by Professor Hugh Folders-Haff was unearthed in a remote area where a rosemary-like shrub is known to have grown 35 million years ago. Could this chop bone be the remains of a caveman's feast? Its discovery next to what is believed to be a fossilised BBQ suggests yes. A single Lamb-o-saurus chop would easily have fed a family of ten and a leg as many as 75-80).

We know the giant herbivore was hunted for food (particularly at this time of year when it pulled the wool over its eyes) and primitive man may well have regularly swallowed Lamb-o-saurus bolt.

Just as we love our Lamb today it now appears that 35 million years ago they loved their Lamb-o-saurus.

We love our Lamb

NICOLE HEADS HOME

Maybe Mum's doing a Lamb Roast

We love our Lamb

Use the news that happens around you. Brown Melhuish Fishlock, Sydney, has created a raft of topical ads for Australian Lamb. Topics have included April Fools' Day and Nicole Kidman's split with Tom Cruise.

Hegarty talks about the way you can put two seemingly random thoughts together. "One of my best TV commercials came out of a personal experience, an incident I observed. I saw two people walking along in the rain. They only had one umbrella. So one got immediately behind the other, and walked along completely in unison, as though they were glued together, so they wouldn't get wet. I thought at the time, what a wonderful image that is. It just stuck in my mind. Then, much later, I used it for Audi, the commercial about the designers who follow each other around." Hegarty does not recommend keeping such thoughts in a notebook. "Your brain is the most fantastic place to keep things. You put all these things into your brain, because what your brain is brilliant at doing is suddenly putting them together. Something you saw six months ago can be put with something you saw yesterday, and together they make something incredible. In a notebook you can't do that. One thought is on page 17, the other is on page 217."

Benson & Hedges. Neil Godfrey also believes that observation is a great source of ideas. His famous Pyramids ad, in the Benson & Hedges surrealistic campaign, happened as a result of something he saw on a plane. As Godfrey explains, his agency, Collett Dickenson Pearce, had originated the surrealistic images to overcome the banality of cigarette advertising.

"It was a case of what do you do when you're faced with a product where there was nothing you could say, except that it might kill you in so many years. They had done the mousehole at ground level, and Stonehenge, and the one with the pack transposed into a bird cage, but the shadow was still in the shape of the bird. Then one day, I was flying to Italy with Frank Lowe. I was reading a magazine and there was a picture of the Pyramids in it. Just at that moment, I looked up and I saw someone smoking a pack of Benson & Hedges, and I just *happened* to notice the angle that the pack was at, and I thought when you turn the pack on its side like that, it makes the shape of a pyramid. It was as *simple* as that."

Godfrey had been to the pyramids and knew how dramatic they were. "For the ad, though, I had to put together an amalgam of several pictures, because the pyramids don't actually look as pretty as that at sunset. On the day the ad ran, I had a call from the

Egyptian Tourist Board. This official congratulated me on my beautiful photograph of the pyramids. He said he'd never seen anything like it before and he asked if they could use it on their tourism brochures. I asked him what he was going to do with the Benson & Hedges pack, and he said, 'What pack, *effendi?*' He hadn't even noticed it."

A chance observation on a plane gave Neil Godfrey the idea for his famous Benson & Hedges Pyramids ad.

IS THERE AN IDEA IN SHOWING WHAT HAPPENS *WITH* THE PRODUCT?

This route is a bit like showing the "After" without first having shown the "Before".

It is a far cry from those old-style product demonstration ads. It means asking yourself, what will happen when somebody uses the product? What effect will it have on them? How will it change things? As you explore this territory, your ideas could well become more and more outrageous. But at least you will be having ideas, and as creator-and-critic, you can revisit them later and cull out the least relevant.

Mitsubishi Spacewagon. The brief Antony Redman received asked him to communicate that the Spacewagon was a people-mover. It could comfortably seat seven people. The conventional approach would have been to show a big family of seven, with lots of luggage, all piling inside. Or seven fat people. Or, for a quick executional thrill, seven nuns or other supposedly quirky people. Redman's mind worked a different way.

"I started from the point that Mitsubishi had gone into the public bus realm. It was a Spacewagon. It was about space. A lot of space in the interior. Enough for seven people. So my process was, not who is comfortable in a big space, but who is uncomfortable in a *small* space? That got me to claustrophobics. A claustrophobic fears being caught in an elevator. You could say, therefore, that a claustrophobic would fear sitting in a car with six other people. So that was it. Claustrophobics are fearful of small spaces, so what do we do? We throw seven claustrophobics into a Spacewagon with big smiles on their faces. It was very straightforward, really."

The next problem was to identify them. How would the reader know they were claustrophobics? Would the headline tell him?

"I wanted to keep the ad visual. I wanted to make people think a bit about the ad. So we stuck this big sign on the outside of the Spacewagon: *Society of Claustrophobics.* It was like they were all members of this society, all happy and gleeful, driving around. So the sign became the headline. I didn't need copy, either."

Redman hastens to add that the society is entirely fictitious. "I happen to know because the account executive was worried about it, so I asked him to check it out."

Showing what happens when seven claustrophobics go for a ride in a Mitsubishi Spacewagon. Euro RSCG Partnership (The Ball Partnership), Singapore.

Showing what happens when you own a Sony Playstation.
Whybin Lawrence TBWA, Sydney.

Showing what happens when you drive a Mercedes-Benz with ESP.
Springer & Jacoby, Hamburg.

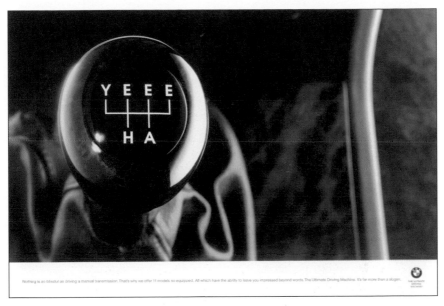

Showing what happens when you drive a BMW (Fallon Minneapolis) and what might happen to John Hegarty and David Abbott with Electric Art Retouching (George Patterson Bates, Sydney).

Showing what happens with Nike Shox.
The Jupiter Drawing Room, South Africa.

Showing what happens
with Max Factor's
Waterproof Mascara.
Leo Burnett, Hong Kong.

Actal Anti-Flatulent Antacid. "So often you get very fuzzy propositions," laments Steve Elrick, formerly creative director at Ogilvy & Mather Singapore. "This brief came in two parts. There was the main antacid product, then there was the anti-flatulent antacid. Antacid is just another me-too product, but anti-flatulent was a very distinct proposition and, to be honest, we latched onto it straight away."

The first issue Elrick tackled was the term anti-flatulence. "It isn't a colloquial term for the problem, so what do we refer to it as? Do we call it wind, or gas, or the devil's bad breath? The answer was actually on the packet. There was a very small line that said, 'No wind'. So 'wind' was the colloquial, homey way to say flatulence, if in fact 'wind' could ever be described as homey."

Elrick talks about the process that led to the creative leap: "The first stage was knocking out all the cheap schoolboy gags about wind, and embarrassed faces in lifts, and so on. They wouldn't have done the product justice and they wouldn't have got past the client. After we'd been round the houses a few times, we went back to a couple of sketches we had on the pad earlier on, which were just very simple visual expressions of no wind, meaning wind as in weather. That was the leap, from saying no wind as in gas, to no wind as in no wind blowing. Once we got to that, it worked for itself."

The thought, an absence of wind, led to a complicated variety of executions. "One idea was windmills," says Elrick. "We had Don Quixote sitting down because there's no wind, so he doesn't have to attack the windmills, how weird is that? Then there were kites just lying on the ground. Then we had stock images where wind was a part of the picture; the flag going up on Iwo Jima, and all the guys were looking up but the flag wasn't blowing. So we stepped back from it and got some images that everyone would instantly recognise, the more simplistic ones like the wind-sock and the weather-vane, and then the famous image of Marilyn Monroe standing on the grate with her skirt blowing up. It was a very recognisable icon that said wind and it was the one that made everyone laugh. I think it's because everyone has seen this image of Marilyn Monroe a few thousand times in their lives. It was the twist of seeing something

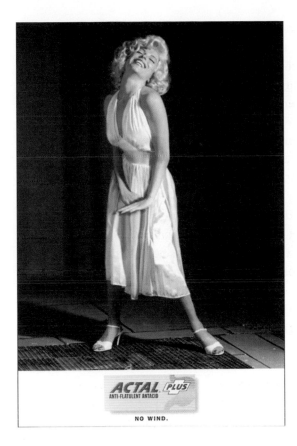

Showing what happens
when you take Actal
Anti-Flatulent Antacid.
Ogilvy & Mather,
Singapore.

which you've always seen one way, to suddenly seeing it slightly different."

The famous Monroe picture had to be completely reshot to get around the copyright problems. "Our shot is actually *three* transparencies comp'd together. We just couldn't get quite the perfect pose on the day. Sometimes the legs would be fine, sometimes the arms would be fine, sometimes the tilt of the neck was just right, but we couldn't get the perfect pose in one shot. If you look at ours and the original, you will see differences. In the original, the pavement is stretching back to some brownstones in the background. But even in the genuine one, your attention is so much focused on what she's doing."

Other layouts were considered. "At one stage we thought it looked too simple. So we tried some with copy, and some where the visual was in a circle like a tablet. We tried some with the pack offset. We even had the pack on the ground inside the shot. But we thought it was too tricky. So we came back to basics and decided that the visual was strong enough by itself."

Elrick experimented with other typefaces, too. He always imagines how a headline or tagline might sound if read aloud. He believes the typeface should reflect the way you would want the line spoken. For the Actal campaign, the statement was very simple, very matter-of-fact. "So it had to be set in a very simple, very plain typeface."

At one point they debated whether the line *No Wind* was even necessary. "I think it would have been asking too much of the audience to read anti-flatulence on the pack and then get the joke. We were trying to involve and reward them, not give them a test."

Is There an Idea in Showing What Happens *Without* the Product?

This route is a bit like showing the "Before" without ever showing the "After".

Some people call it the negative sell, yet ironically enough it has produced some of the funniest and best-loved ads in the world. Many ads from *The Economist* campaign belong in this territory. Abbott's *Management trainee, aged 42* conveys what happens without *The Economist*; in itself, it is not a happy thought, but it brings a positive smile.

Why is this genre so popular? Is it because the most penetrating human insights have been always inspired by adversity? Or simply that it leaves the reader to close the circle?

Nature's Course Dog Food. At Fallon Minneapolis, Dean Hanson remembers thinking that an all-natural dog food was a kind of silly idea. "The incongruity of it, going to that length to make sure your dog has pure, natural food, seemed ridiculous."

Hanson's thinking process began with a very simple proposition. "It was a natural dog food. So it meant putting down all the fundamental truths I knew about additives and artificial ingredients and how they apply to *human* food, then taking them in the context of a *dog*." Connections were made between pesticides and a dog wearing

Showing what happens without Nature's Course Dog Food.
Fallon Minneapolis.

a mask; between artificial colours and a Dalmatian with multi-coloured spots. "It wasn't a complex proposition to put forward. We wanted to make the statement clearly, hopefully in a humorous way. When you're talking about dogs, people want to smile."

Hanson's art direction was minimalist. The visual occupied well over eighty percent of the ad. The product neatly integrated with the copy. The layout was clean and spare.

"There wasn't a lot of information to put across and I wanted to use the dog to full advantage. Dogs are entertainment in themselves. There's an old *cliché*, dogs and babies. Norman Rockwell, the American illustrator, once said if a thing is not going well, put a dog in it; if it's *really* not going well, put a dog with a bandage on its foot in it. If you're lucky enough to have dogs as a subject matter, you sure as hell should take advantage of it. If you can't do a great ad with a dog, you should be horsewhipped."

Preparation H. "It was all about being close to the product," contends Elrick, discussing the campaign for a haemorrhoidal ointment which he and art director Phil Marchington created at Bates, Hong Kong. "It was a case of one of us asking the other about the affliction."

The product eases discomfort in the early stages of haemorrhoids. Previous ads had used lengthy, medical copy, but Elrick and Marchington wanted to reach sufferers in a more direct way. It was a question of finding a visual means to express the problem and the pain. The creative leap came when they talked about how the most innocuous objects hold special terrors for haemorrhoid victims.

The bicycle seat was the first execution. "We wanted to get inside the heads of the sufferers, *to see what they saw*. A bike seat doesn't look threatening at all," says Elrick, "but to someone suffering from piles, the idea of sitting on a bike seat is horrific. It's one of the most extreme situations a piles sufferer would try and avoid. So we asked ourselves, how would the sufferer see a bike seat? It would be something very sharp, excruciatingly painful."

The connection was made by transposing a razor sharp saw in place of the seat. "It was like doing a crossfade on television, only doing it in print."

Showing what happens without Preparation H haemorrhoidal ointment. Bates, Hong Kong.

*Showing what happens
without Epilady depilatory,
using the Chinese
characters for woman,
arm and leg.
Bates, Hong Kong.*

There are better places to stash your money.
ANZ Access Advantage.

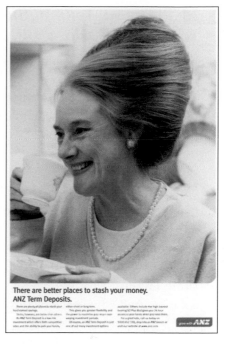

There are better places to stash your money.
ANZ Term Deposits.

There are better places to stash your money.
ANZ Cash Management Account.

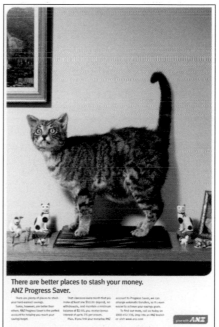

There are better places to stash your money.
ANZ Progress Saver.

Showing what happens without an ANZ Bank investment account.
M&C Saatchi, Melbourne.

Is There an Idea in Showing What Happens With and Without the Product in the *Same* Ad?

In this route, "Before" and "After" are shown side by side, for easy comparison.

It is the modern manifestation of that great old advertising formula called the "Problem-Solution" ad. The convention is to show the "Before" (or the "Problem") on the left, and the "After" (or the "Solution") on the right.

The tackier version, of course, emerged in the bad old days of hard sell advertising. The "Villain Product", better known as Brand X, failed on the left, while the "Hero Product" triumphed on the right.

Nothing much has changed. It is still a valid concept ground. Sometimes two separate pictures are used, left and right, or even above and below. Sometimes both scenarios are contained within the *same* picture, with the headline statement positioned under the solution. And who needs pictures? Typographical devices can represent both sides of the story.

There is only one rule which appears unbreakable: the problem must always *precede* the solution.

The genre continues to evolve. There are endless new variants, many of them narrative by nature. What happens when someone has the product and someone else does not? What happens when the product works so well that other things go wrong? At its heart, though, one truth remains: it is still one of the most effective ways to signpost a message to the consumer in a cage.

Kaminomoto Hair Restorer. As Neil French explains, the creative process behind his classic campaign was fraught with complications.

"Kaminomoto was close to my own heart, or possibly close to my own head, because I'm also as bald as a badger. I know, from honest experience, that when you open a paper and there's a big headline screaming 'BALD?' at you, you might read it if you're at home. You say to yourself, yes, here we go, come on, what have you got to sell me, and you *never* believe it. But if you're out and about, the last thing you're going to be seen doing is reading an ad that says 'BALD?' because it's embarrassing! You may be bald, but you don't want everybody else to know that it bothers you, and it *does* bother you,

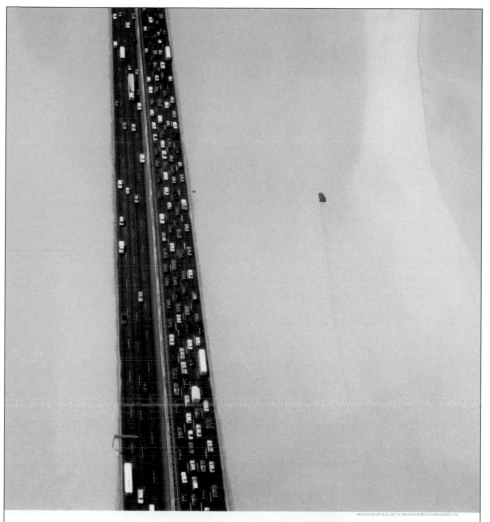

Can you spot the Range Rover in this picture?

Goodbye road. Goodbye traffic. Goodbye 5 m.p.h.

A Range Rover does something far more impressive than get you through a traffic jam in air-conditioned, arm-chaired, stereo-surrounded comfort.

A Range Rover takes you where there are no jams. Because there is no traffic.

Through the woods. Along the beach. Across the desert. Range Rovers, after all, are so extraordinary, they drive for years in places ordinary cars couldn't drive a quarter of a mile.

So it's not surprising that to many a Range Rover's most luxurious feature isn't its elegant interior, optional sunroof, or the

RANGE ROVER

security of 24 hour roadside assistance.

Its most luxurious feature is its ability to provide an experience a bit more exhilarating than a highway to the suburbs at six p.m.

Why not call 1-800-FINE 4WD for the Range Rover dealer nearest you?

We won't deny that at somewhat above $34,000 a Range Rover is hardly inexpensive.

But after all the time you've spent in trafficlikethis, what could be nicer than going off on your   own?

The problem on the left, the solution on the right, with two
brilliantly subtle typographical effects in the last two lines of the body copy.
Grace & Rothschild, New York.

no matter what anybody says. I was lucky; I went bald when I was twenty-one, so I've had plenty of time to get used to it. Those poor blokes who go bald at about thirty-five are constantly worrying about it, and it's really tragic. So the one thing we couldn't do in our ads was shout 'BALD?'

"The other thing we couldn't do is show the bottle, because the laws in Singapore don't let you say hair restorer, and that's what it says on the top of the bottle. So that was the pack shot gone, and that was the basic product description gone!"

The further French investigated, the more restrictions he found. "We weren't allowed to show bald men, because that was against the law, because it might indicate that this was a baldness cure, which you can't advertise. And we weren't allowed to show blokes *with* hair, because that was also against the law, because it might indicate that you'd actually grown hair on them. So if we weren't allowed to mention what the product did, and we weren't allowed to show it, we were up against it somewhat, really."

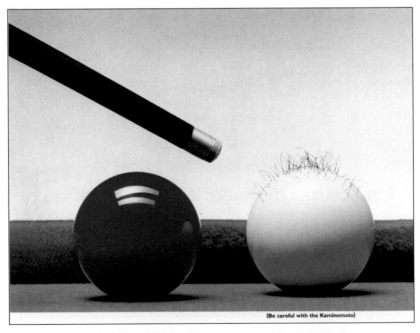

(Be careful with the Kaminomoto)

Neil French's classic Kaminomoto campaign demonstrates the
potency of visual suggestions. Nudge, nudge, note the use of brackets.
Euro RSCG Partnership (The Ball Partnership), Singapore.

(Be careful with the Kaminomoto)

(Be careful with the Kaminomoto)

French's creative solution was visual. "We had to indicate what had happened by *suggestion*. The first thought that came into our head was bald as a billiard ball. So that was easy. We just put two billiard balls down on a table, stuck hair on one of them, and said *Be careful with the Kaminomoto* underneath. Which indicates to a bald person that if you spill this stuff on a billiard ball, it might grow hair. To anybody else, of course, it doesn't mean anything at all; but we're not talking to anybody else, so it doesn't matter. It's not a threatening ad, it's a funny ad. If you're seen reading it on the train you're not seen as some poor, desperate bloke trying to find some way to grow some fluff on his head; you're seen as a normal person trying to decipher a completely indecipherable ad. But of course to a bald person it speaks loudly, and you can tuck away that little piece of information about Kaminomoto and trot into a pharmacy and buy it along with all those other things you buy in the hope that no one will ever notice you bought."

The billiard balls execution was followed by two eggs, one of which had also sprouted hair. "The photographer's wife plucked out his assistant's eyebrows, one by one," recalls French, "dipped them into superglue, and stuck them onto the billiard ball and the egg with tweezers. By the end of it, the poor bloke had only got one eyebrow."

The most significant detail of crafting was in French's treatment of the headline. He located it outside the picture, in small type, between brackets.

"You can make a person read an ad in the way that you art direct it," says French. "So if you want something to be shouted, it's big. 'BALD', in really big letters. But if you want something to be a kind of nudge, I like brackets. I think brackets indicate a nudge, an afterthought. Small type is quiet, but smaller than small between brackets, is a nudge. It's like saying, nudge, nudge, *be careful with the Kaminomoto*, out of the corner of your mouth. It makes it more of a whisper, more of a joke. It makes it become less important. The fact that the whole point of the ad is apparently the *least* important thing on the page makes me laugh."

While French was amused, an advertising watchdog committee was not. They descended on the agency, demanding the campaign be stopped forthwith.

"They said the ads would make people buy a baldness cure. We said, yes, well, that's what we're paid for. They said, it's against the law. So we said, here's the law, where have we broken it? Then there was a long silence while they went away to have a little think about it. When they came back they said, well, you haven't broken any laws, but the fact of the matter is, you can't run the ads any more. And in future, they said, in addition to no bald men and no hairy men, you can't show *anything* that didn't used to have hair that now has hair, therefore no eggs, no billiard balls, and they thought they'd got us. So the next ad that came out showed a chihuahua looking at a little Skye Terrier. The chihuahua's got no hair at all; the terrier's a very hairy little dog. Well, of course, the committee went completely ape and we said, no, they're both in their original state, neither has been changed. But they said, people will remember the *other* campaign! So we said, what to do?"

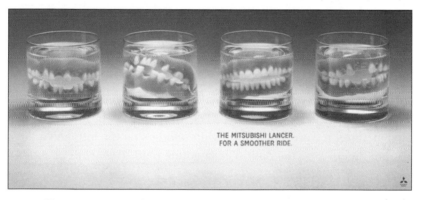

There are no rules. Comparisons can be made in one picture or two.
Euro RSCG Partnership
(The Ball Partnership), Singapore.

Crisan Shampoo. Hair was obviously a growing concern at The Ball Partnership, Singapore. The agency's next challenge was an anti-dandruff shampoo, and once more, the side-by-side comparison formula resurfaced.

The category convention is to show silky clean hair of the feminine variety; men, according to convention, do not have dandruff. If Crisan was to have any hope of standing out in the category, the last thing the ad could show was hair. The solution had to be lateral.

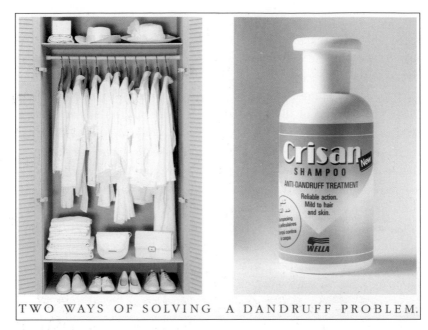

TWO WAYS OF SOLVING A DANDRUFF PROBLEM.

Breaking the category convention within a classic advertising format.
Euro RSCG Partnership (The Ball Partnership), Singapore.

According to writer Danny Higgins, the worst-case scenario for any dandruff sufferer, male or female, would be having to wear white clothes to conceal the evidence. The Crisan concept emerged with two pictures: a wardrobe full of white clothes on the left, and a huge shot of the pack on the right. The headline read, *Two ways of solving a dandruff problem.*

The problem-and-solution were clearly demonstrated for dandruff sufferers of either sex.

The moral of the story is, never be afraid to show the product, as big as possible, if it is part of the idea. By doing so, all the text on the label could be read, so there was no need for additional body copy. And because the manufacturer's logo was also prominent, there was no need to repeat it somewhere else. So that the brand could brand the ad, the blue from the Crisan pack was replicated in a blue headline and the toning of the wardrobe shot.

Mitsubishi Spacewagon. Everybody knew what the Spacewagon looked like; besides which, the newspapers were full of car ads, crammed with colour and black-and-white photographs. Could the

Who needs pictures? Anger and abuse in a crowded car,
compared with space and calm in a Spacewagon.
Euro RSCG Partnership (The Ball Partnership), Singapore.

medium be used in some other way to communicate the feeling of private space and comfort which Spacewagon offered?

Chinese readers opened their morning paper to find full page ads shouting abuse, curses and insults, courtesy of copywriter Peter Soh. The dense, angry typography occupied half the page, recreating what happens when too many people are squeezed into an ordinary car. The other half of the page remained white and empty, except for a strip of copy communicating the space and calm of the Spacewagon.

For diversity, one ad presented the contrast left and right; another, top and bottom.

Because every language has its own treasury of insults, the concept would work just as well in English, French or Swahili.

Is There Even an Idea in *Where* the Ad Will Run?

Let the medium become the message.

The newspaper page has a smooth vertical edge, with jagged trims top and bottom. What better place to demonstrate the superior cutting power of a lawnmower, let alone a hairdresser?

Clemenger Advertising, Melbourne, showed how a full page could be cut into twelve pieces and used as toilet paper. *Life's harsh when you run out of Sorbent*, said the message in the corner.

Butterfield Day Devito Hockney turned the bulk of a newspaper into a demonstration of how deeply the sun's UV rays can damage skin. The headline, for Uvistat sun cream, jolted complacent readers: *If your skin was this newspaper, the sun's rays would have reached the sports page.*

The way a magazine is opened and closed might suggest how other things can be joined or separated. Euro RSCG Partnership, Singapore, used a centre spread in *Reader's Digest* to demonstrate how Crisan repaired split ends.

As always, there are no limits.

Everlast. Gary Goldsmith's famous Everlast ad came out of very pragmatic concerns.

"The brief was probably worse than many of the briefs young people get," he recalls. Everlast was in a bleak position. "They were being outspent by all their competitors by a ton, so we knew we had

IF YOUR SKIN WAS THIS NEWSPAPER, THE SUN'S RAYS WOULD HAVE REACHED THE SPORTS PAGE.

Don't underestimate the power of the sun's UVA rays. Unlike UVB which burns, UVA passes right through the outer layers of your skin into the deeper living tissue.

The collagen (which gives the skin its elasticity) breaks down, eventually causing it to sag, wrinkle and age.

Help is at hand. Uvistat sun-creams and lotions filter out a wider range of harmful UV rays than most other products on the market. The protection starts at Factor 6 and goes up to Factor 30 Ultrablock. (There's also an aftersun and lipscreen.) Naturally, we care for all skin types.

Uvistat is hypo-allergenic, lanolin free and non-greasy.

So the good news is you can let through some of the rays that help you tan and stop the ageing rays at page one.

If you'd like to know more, send the coupon to Uvistat, Windsor Healthcare Ltd, Bracknell, Berks. RG12 4YS.

Name

Address

Postcode

● UVISTAT
THE GENTLE ART OF SUN CONTROL.

Using the bulk of a newspaper to demonstrate how UV rays damage the skin.
Butterfield Day Devito Hockney, London, for Uvistat sun cream.

to be kamikazes and go after those other people. We knew we had to do with *one* ad what Ralph Lauren or Perry Ellis could afford to do with twenty ads. In a media sense, we had to be able to place one ad amidst twenty of their ads and have people talk about our ad. We had to place them as an enemy, and trade off of them. That gave us a start."

Goldsmith studied the media environment. Kamikaze thinking led to the idea of trading off a scratch-and-sniff concept.

"Knowing that everybody was saying the same thing in there, everybody was showing beautiful clothing, perfectly photographed, we said let's show some sweaty old T-shirt and make a comment that's against all the fashion correctness." The line that disrupted the category: *This is not one of those scented ads. Good thing.*

When you are being outspent 20-to-1, you can disrupt your category by disrupting the media environment. Goldsmith/Jeffrey, New York.

How to Get Better Ideas

The concept grounds will always be there. What will determine success or failure, greatness or mediocrity, are individual creative processes.

Are great advertising people born great, or can individual creative processes be shaped, honed and perfected? If great advertising people are like great athletes, there is a good chance they can be.

"We all pay less attention to the process than we should," observes Goldsmith. "If doctors and scientists operated in the same manner that we do, it'd be a scary world. What they do is creative, too, in its own way. They've devoted a lot of thought to the way in which they arrive at a diagnosis, and the way in which they treat it. But with us, it's almost like we have this thing in our head, we don't need to do that, we should just sit down and come up with ideas."

Goldsmith believes the best creative people do have their own processes, whether they call them such or not, that they work by. He thinks there are certain learnings which can help every writer and art director improve their individual process. "After an assignment is over, stop and think about it. What happened when you did good ads? What did you do *differently* than the times when you did bad ads? Then think about how you've got to do those things more often than not, like an athlete. If great athletes could only perform that way occasionally, it'd be terrible."

Goldsmith is right; the best creative people do have their own personal methodologies. For many, they are a defence mechanism against the panic factor.

"I think you discover, over the years, ways to get yourself going. For me, the discipline is to pick up a pencil," says Abbott. "Before I really start scribbling, I've absorbed all the information I can get hold of, though that's not always true. I find I have to start scribbling or drawing. I always think on the pad. I always draw the outline of the ad, usually quite small, whether it's a double page spread or a 24-sheet poster, so I know the boundaries that I'm working within. Generally speaking, I get a kind of mixture of tone of voice, a feel of the ad, I often see the ad in my mind before I actually know the details, a feel for the way the ad should be. I very often think of the picture before the words, if there are going to be words. But there isn't a set rule really. If I'm stuck, I change the tactics. I might work backwards on something. I might start from a new endline, though I don't always accept that you need an endline, but I might just start there. If that's not working, I might start with a picture, or go back to the strategy and rewrite the strategy. One of the ways of getting going is to walk away from it, to go and think about something else. Over the years, you learn not to panic."

Abbott likens his creative process to playing tennis. "I was always very relaxed, but as soon as the points began to matter, I seized up. I was less interested in winning a tennis game than hitting a great shot that I could remember, which is part of my personality I suppose. I now don't panic really, and I don't seize up with ads, because I sort of think that I may not get it out on time, but I will get it out."

Bruce Bildsten also starts by scribbling ideas. "I do these little drawings which only make sense to myself. Even though I'm a writer, I like to think very visually. I know I can always write a line later. Sometimes, I'll often think of ads in terms of a layout as much as what the visual is. It helps me to do a little layout of something so it's a complete idea. Sometimes, I'll just write lines." Bildsten never shows his layouts to the art director. "I'm a terrible artist. I end up explaining them. It might be talking about something as simple as the style in which something is photographed, or the size of the headline, because the size of the line is as important as the line itself."

Ron Mather works with a small notepad and pen. "Layout pads are a bit difficult to fit on restaurant tables. Very rarely does the big idea pop up first." Mather goes through a few ideas that are developed or rejected totally before something comes out that he is really happy with. "A great visual might prompt the idea, or it might be a great line that inspires a great visual. There aren't really any rules." Mather believes you are more likely to come up with a great idea in a great agency than in a mediocre agency. "I think it's the atmosphere, being around very good people in an environment that promotes great creative thinking. I think experience plays a big part, too. *Good* experience, not just lots of years in the business."

Graham Warsop relishes the discipline of starting with a piece of white paper, knowing there are only so many square centimetres to fill and that only a handful of other people will be involved in whatever finally appears. "When I was first employed in advertising, I fell in love with the print work of Tim Delaney and Steve Dunn, circa 1990. So, curiously, whenever I conceive a print ad, I have in the back of my mind a hypothetical broadsheet ad of theirs. My first question is, how might they have approached this task? Once I've come up with an answer that satisfies me, but admittedly may not have satisfied them, I relax a little. Then it's time to start exploring other options. I have a preference for ads with copy over ads that are purely visual, but it amazes me how often one ends up producing advertising with little or no copy at all."

Before Tim Delaney starts thinking, he has to believe in the strategy. "The strategy comes first. I can't think of anything until I know the area in which I'm writing. The premise has got to be right. If the issue seems muddled or plain wrong, then I can't start. So the first thing I do is sort out what I'm going to say, and check on it, and *believe* in it, and make sure that it's what everybody wants me to say." Inevitably, Delaney says, if you are worried about it, somebody else back along the line will be worried about it, too. By the time the strategy is sorted, his first thoughts are forming. "They could be visual or verbal thoughts, it doesn't really matter. If it's television, I'll be thinking of storylines, narratives, a way a thing can unfold."

Goldsmith also begins analytically. "I was an architecture student before I got into this crazy business. So I tend to break the problem down in terms of who we are talking to, what we want to say, what's the tone of the company. I'm very conscious of *tone*, because I work on a lot of big corporate stuff. The company might tell you, well, we're customer-focused, our company is about integrity, honesty, trust for the consumer. And you realise there's nothing you can say that's very different, it's all going to be tone. What's a great ad for IBM may be a terrible ad for Everlast. The tone is like a piece of clothing; it has got to fit the client. If it doesn't, they're not going to feel comfortable in it." Goldsmith's first thoughts are generally *rational*. "I don't work like some people do; they tend to start purely intuitively. I can't do that. I try to build *outwards* from the rational. Once I have a rational thought, then I ask how can I add some spice, how can I make it more intuitive?" Goldsmith advocates finding out where the ads will run. "Maybe there's an idea there, like the Everlast scratch-and-sniff ad. But one thing has never gone away," he adds. *"The panic."*

"I think it's good to feel scared," says British art director John

Messum, "otherwise I think you're going to fall into the trap of doing something that's too easy."

At Saatchi & Saatchi, London, art director Bill Gallacher says the panic begins at the execution stage. "I don't panic when I first get the brief. I think, this is going to be great, like another journey to go on. There are just so many things you can do. You find out about yourself, what you're capable of. I always start with *words*. Sometimes I'll write the sense of the headline first. If I get really frustrated, I'll sit down and draw loads of visuals. The hard part starts when you see the words, when you see how they're going to make sense to a lot of people. You see a kind of hazy vision of what you're after. You start to panic, because you think this is a really good idea, how am I going to do it, if I screw this up I'm never going to forgive myself. Once you're over the panic bit, which doesn't last long, you start working your way into the idea and try about twenty different ways of doing it. But without the panic, I don't think you'd be working as well. If you just sat back and said, well, that's easy, I know what to do ... I couldn't work that way."

"A lot of times, briefs are just laundry lists of things they'd like to do," says Dean Hanson. "Isolating the key ideas is critical for me. It's the very first step." Hanson starts by collecting his thoughts. "I put down all the basic truths that I know. Then I try and put down in a sentence what it is we're trying to communicate. I'll put it up on the wall in its flattest, most mundane way; a sentence on the wall that says exactly what I'm going to say. And then I'll break it down. I'll think about the personality I want to project, the chemistry of the ad that I want, if it has to have dignity, if it has to be broad and humorous."

Hanson believes it is easier to get ideas for products on which you haven't worked before. "There's always baggage that comes with something you're familiar with. If it's something you've worked on for a long time, you know all the tricks, you stop yourself making connections. But if it's new you're learning, you're just like the people you're talking to. If you have a bit of ignorance, just partial knowledge, you're like young people, new people, you have the advantage."

Hanson describes the creative process in terms of jumping over a wall. "You run up to the wall, try to jump over it. If you don't get there, you try another tack. If you get stumped, you go to a bookstore. Bookstores are fabulous places to get ideas. You look up the subject, just immerse yourself in it a little bit, to get off that roadblock you've hit. Or get a *Shots* reel, or *Archive*, sit down and see how other people have attacked problems. I never just sit there and look at the wall. You either talk to somebody, or you try to get stimulus from something to break through."

French often finds inspiration from the product itself. "I always try to put the product on the table in front of me and look at the thing. You don't actually get that much information off products these days, but somehow you have to understand what it's all about. You have to suck in the essence of it so your ads can't contradict it. If you try to turn something nice and reliable into something frightfully hip and trendy, of course it doesn't work. When people turn up with their money at the moment of truth and it has all been a lie, they will never come back to you. You should look at the product from every angle. If it's going to be sold on a shelf, look at it on a shelf. See how it reacts to light and different angles, until you really *know* the thing. Then put it to one side, and never look at it again. Write your ads, and remember you're writing to a person who's going to pass hundreds of other products on a shelf."

Barrie agrees. "Hold the product. Stare at it. Imagine situations where you'd use it. Enjoy the product yourself. If you're working on Miller Lite, it doesn't hurt to have a Miller Lite in your hand."

Barrie's former colleague, writer Mike Lescarbeau, believes writers and art directors should often start work in isolation. "The first thing I really like to do is sit down and say, if I was working on this thing by myself, what would I do? I ask the art director to do the same. Then when we come together, our ideas have come from completely *different* places. We haven't influenced each other. We haven't thought about it only one way." At Fallon, writers and art directors work in separate offices, rather than shared ones. Teams do not work as married couples. Everybody moves around, works with everybody else. "We think that's healthy. It keeps you fresh, keeps you from getting into ruts." Getting stuck for an idea, though, is an occupational hazard, and Lescarbeau suggests talking it over with colleagues. "We'll show each other what we have in terms of ads. *Why* is this not going anywhere? *What* is it we're missing about this brief? Honestly, a lot of times it's just twenty more minutes until you get something you really like. It's not like you have to work another two days."

John Bevins, of Sydney's John Bevins Advertising, describes himself as a loner. Bevins, the doyen of Australian copywriters, is wary of writing naïve advertising. "A lot of the briefs now aren't for things you automatically know about. They're in whole new categories like technology or financial services. You suddenly have to become an instant expert in order to write about the subject. You have to quickly scramble up the learning curve and you can only do that yourself, I think. I don't believe you can sit back and expect other people to distil it for you." Bevins relies on the Internet to become knowledgeable. "You can't just sit around and brainstorm with an art director. You have to have the confidence that you know what you're writing about. But I don't worry it to death, though, because I've learned that if you don't enjoy writing it, nobody will enjoy reading it. It will come across as grudge copy."

For Godfrey, it was often a process of elimination. "Sometimes, there isn't an obvious direction to go in. You can sit there for a couple of nights and feel completely panic-stricken. There doesn't seem to be anything. You dig a little borehole into every aspect of the problem. You look at little tiny details. If you can't think of anything to do for your product, turn to the competition. Look at a product that's not as good a product as yours. Find out *why* it's not as good. Ours is a stage better *because* ... and that might give you a clue." Godfrey is a firm believer in the investigative process. "Talking to the client in detail, going to factories, even talking to other companies who make similiar products. I always found I related their view of the product to my view of it, and immediately you would start thinking of things. You try to hone what you think is the personality of the client into something you can use as a statement. This would be a kind of starting point."

Godfrey was art director to two of Britain's most accomplished writers, Tony Brignull and Indra Sinha. Invariably, the ads would come out of conversations. "It was not just me putting a picture to a line. We used to talk, not do ads, and we'd realise that one of the lines in our conversation was actually a headline. We didn't desperately think an ad has to have a headline. We would sit in a room and talk. Once we had something really interesting, then I would see if I could tip the balance and make it look great just by doing one or two things."

Godfrey believes that what distinguished Brignull and Sinha was their understanding of people's motivations. "As writers, Tony and Indra were very human people, not advertising people overtly. Tony would write a line of copy, and it would seem like nothing, unless you'd been sitting with him for days talking about the problem. Then you'd realise he'd captured something that was very *essential*. Someone walking into the room wouldn't understand it, so people were never allowed in our office while we did ads. Tony wrote lines that weren't spectacular, but were *right*. We worked on a campaign for Dunne & Company. They were gentlemen's outfitters that were a bit behind the times. The sales people were very restrained. Some of Tony's headlines didn't seem like headlines at all: *We train our salesmen not to sell you anything* and *Are you old enough to buy a suit at Dunne & Company?* Indra and I would sit in a room and just talk, too. Indra liked being sparked. He always scribbled on a pad, he'd listen to everyone's conversations."

Listening and observing are a critical part of Isherwood's creative process. "Ads actually write themselves. It might be something a client says without realising it." He remembers working on a campaign for a finance company that was lending money to small businesses. "We got a group of small businessmen together and we asked them what the issues were. They came out with lines like, the trouble with banks is I can only get a bank loan when I don't need it. That's a great ad. *How come I can only get a bank loan when I don't need one?* Then another guy said, yeah, my employees make more money than I do, and that was another great ad. If you just listen, and you take the trouble to actually get yourself into that environment, into that understanding of the product and the market, the ads actually do themselves for you."

Like Delaney, Isherwood insists on having a clearly defined strategy, a defined problem. "I have to know what the problem is that

I have to solve. And, this is a personal thing, I find I have actually done my best work when I've had a lot more mandatories put on me; you know, you can't do this and you can't do that, and we have to keep this, and you've got to keep that. I take all those elements and actually work through them, each one is a problem that has to be solved." Sometimes your first idea is best, Isherwood says, but you often have to go through a long process to realise it. Not getting bogged down, keeping yourself a bit free in your mind, is essential. As Isherwood admits: "Sometimes it's easier to solve a problem as a creative director. You don't take the problem so personally, the pressure isn't on you as much. You can walk in, take a short look at the issues, and you often get a very quick flash of the whole thing."

Flashes are how Hegarty gets his ideas. "I get a vision of the finished ad. That's how ideas have always come to me. And I know this will sound very plonky and pretentious, but I see an idea as a *person*." Hegarty thinks having ideas is the closest a man will ever come to giving birth. "When you've had an idea, and it's a really good idea and you know it, it has a *life*. You can see what's right for it, you can see what's wrong for it, you can see what it should be, what school it should go to, what kind of street it should live in, what clothes it should wear."

The first things that enter Bill Oberlander's mind are positions, angles and propositions. "I don't think about what I'm thinking in. I'm just thinking. I'm just trying to come up with some conceptual way to have the brand be more hip, cool and urgent in the consumer's mind."

Nick Cohen's ideas usually arrive as funny juxtapositions. "Sometimes it's words, sometimes it's pictures."

The tonality comes first for French, the detail later. "I tend to see the look of the ad, before I see a picture or any copy. I know more or less what the thing should look like. Then, I tend to think in pictures first. Afterwards I might think that's a rather wimpy picture, what it needs is a much better line, and then I'll let the line take over. If I can do it with a picture, I prefer to. Although I have this reputation of being a long copy freak, I'm really not. Only if I'm forced into a corner."

How to Know When Your Ideas Are Great

Developing a personal creative methodology is one matter; being your own critic is another. Is there an infallible way to tell when you have come up with a good idea, maybe even a great idea?

Some creatives become jubilant; others, uncomfortable and uncertain. Godfrey thinks you can *never* be sure. "We all have that problem. You see some ads and you think that they're never going to be anything else but great. But when the people were doing them, they were completely unsure. If there's somebody alive who thinks that once they do an ad it's going to be fabulous, I think they're probably not very long in the business."

Lescarbeau believes it is easier to tell if you have done a good ad. If you have to wonder about it too much, it is probably *not* good.

Goldsmith takes an equally pragmatic view. "If you still like it two or three days later, once the tiredness has gone away and you're feeling more detached. A lot of times, when you first come up with an idea, you're just so happy to be out of that state of worry and overimmersion."

Bildsten relies on experience to tell him. "But I always have this fear that there's somebody else, somewhere in the world, doing exactly the same idea. The more I judge shows, the more I realise that people do come up with similar ideas. That's why the presentation of an idea can make such a difference. Because people are thinking in similar ways, it's more and more incumbent on you to execute everything to the finest detail."

Gerard Stamp judges ideas on their ability to prompt interaction with readers. "A great print ad will usually need the reader to 'complete the circle'. If somebody has to engage a little brain power to understand and appreciate an ad, the effect will be more enduring."

Mark Tutssel judges ideas on their campaignability. "A great idea should instantly suggest lots of words and pictures. Only then do you know if you have an enduring idea."

Some creatives talk about physical symptoms. For Guido Heffels, sweaty hands and insomnia. For Redman, butterflies in the stomach.

"It's the one thing you can still truly enjoy in advertising," Redman elaborates. "When you've come up with an idea, and you look at it, and through its simplicity, or its uniqueness, or its vitality, you know you've come up with something special. It's not something you can teach. Sometimes, you just know it's great. Sometimes, though, you're not sure if it's too far ahead of its time, if it's too weird, and whether it's good to push those boundaries. It's good to be unsure. If you surround yourself with people you respect and admire, you can use them as a sounding board. And sometimes, *they* won't know either."

Barrie values the opinions of peers. "Like most creatives, I'm one of the most insecure fellows you'll ever meet. I only *perhaps* begin to think I've done a great ad when a number of people tell me so, or when it wins an award. Even then, I'm still filled with self-doubt, that's the honest-to-God truth. I always look back and imagine how I would have done things differently." As Barrie confesses, he rather likes the feeling of uncertainty. "The times I thought campaigns were the best things I'd ever done, people would be very polite and say, 'that's interesting'. If somebody says something is 'interesting', then you know it's lousy."

Cohen sticks ads on the wall and waits for reactions. "That's the only way I can tell. That's one of the reasons we opened up our environment. So many agencies operate in a closed door environment where everyone's competing with each other. People are too scared to show their ideas to other people, in case they don't like them. Actually that's pretty important information: if people don't like them is just as important if people do like them. It's all about seeing how people respond. And you don't have to be an expert to respond, just a human being. It could be the receptionist or the cleaner, it doesn't matter. If they walk straight past it, don't look at it, don't respond to it, it's probably not a very good ad."

For Oberlander, there is a sense of irony; for Abbott, a little smile in his head.

"It's what mathematicians talk about, the elegance of a solution. You know when you've got the bits working together. And you've used an insight." Abbott recalls working on a pitch for a holiday company. "I wrote an ad based on the fact that the sign of a great holiday for a woman is that her nail polish lasts for a fortnight. After I'd written it down I realised it was an observation my wife had made; that when she's at home, her nail polish lasts three or four days, but when she's on holiday, and not washing up and cleaning, it lasts a long time. And so I felt this was a nice way of talking about what women get out of holidays, the absence of routine. I was conscious that I hadn't read that thought anywhere else and I got a little kind of buzz that I was saying something that maybe hadn't been said before, and something that was also likely to be persuasive and work."

French describes what he calls a moment of epiphany: "There's a moment at which you suddenly realise you've done something as near-original as you ever will. Of course, nothing is ever original, but there's an indefinable moment when you sit back and look at something and think that's it, *that's* the one. I can't write any better than that. The art direction is about as good as it gets. The moment you realise it's not only a great ad, but it's going to work. And it doesn't happen very often in your life. I *knew* XO was going to work. I *knew* Kaminomoto was going to work. I *knew* Chivas Regal was going to work. There's a moment when you say, that *can't* fail. You just know it in your heart. I don't know if I knew it when I was younger, perhaps I didn't; but with experience, you just *know*. Other stuff you do which you know is going to work, but isn't great, is funnily enough less obvious than the creative highpoints. You can look at some stuff you've done which worked, and which a lot of people liked, but it's not one of the ads that's going to be shown in history books in fifty years' time, whereas XO and Kaminomoto might be." As French observes ironically: "It's kind of tragic that you can spend an entire lifetime turning out four great pieces of work, and they're all ads. Nurses and ambulance drivers do something a thousand times as important, five times a day."

6

THE FIVE CRITICAL CHOICES

A concept ground is selected. A campaign idea is taking shape. The next question is: what kind of print ad should be done?

There are really only five choices. Creatives will make them intuitively, with little conscious debate. In many cases, the ideas themselves dictate the choices. There are some executional rules, though, if the cutting edge is to be achieved.

WILL YOU SEND A POSTCARD OR A LETTER?

It is all a question of words, and whether you want to be more visual than verbal.

Mostly, a postcard is a *visually-led* ad. Not always, but mostly. Certainly, by definition, postcards always have very few words; *very, very* few.

On the other hand, a letter is always a *copy-led* ad. Letters have hundreds, even thousands of words.

Oddly enough, some of the world's best-known postcards and letters have been sent in the footwear category: Fallon's Hush Puppies campaign (*postcards*) and Leagas Delaney's Timberland campaign (*letters*).

As Neil French defines the choice: "A postcard is something you send from a holiday; a letter is something you might send when you are on your deathbed. Somewhere between those two extremes of human experience are the answers to your ad. Something that's jolly and light and not terribly important can be a postcard. The more serious it gets, the more like a letter it has to be. It's that simple."

David Abbott has sent both postcards and letters. "It's mostly guided by what would work. But it's also tied up with trying to do it differently. A kind of competitive thing comes into it as well. If I were pitching for *The Economist* now, and some other agency had done the poster campaign, part of me might be saying, well, they've done it short, now we'll try and do it long."

But hasn't advertising become more visual and less verbal? Surely sending a postcard would be a wiser decision?

"For as long as I've been in the business, this discussion has been going on," says John Salmon. "Art directors have always said copy is finished; it's all going to be visual from here on. I think the fact of the matter is that certain propositions demand words, while certain propositions demand pictures, and you have to make the decision based on the product, the market, *and* the proposition."

There is also no reason why postcards and letters cannot coexist in the same campaign. Attitude, tone of voice, typeface and campaign branding can all contribute a sense of continuity.

Fortunately, there is only one rule. postcard or letter, *be single-minded*. It must be one or the other. Either the visual must dominate or the words must. There is no room for compromise; for example, if a lot of copy is shoe-horned into the base of a visually-led ad, the effect will be totally lost.

As we are about to see, the best postcards are simple and focused.

Hush Puppies. This classic Fallon Minneapolis postcard campaign started life as a stopgap measure. As art director Bob Barrie tells us: "We had gotten the Hush Puppies account with a campaign called Match the Faces to the Hush Puppies. It had celebrities on top, with their legs and shoes on the bottom, and it was all mixed up. It was meant to show a range of shoes, and the fact that cool people wore them, and get readers involved in the ad. But before this campaign could be executed, there was a small problem of some media space which their previous agency had bought. Because the celebrities campaign couldn't be turned around in time,

Jarl Olsen the copywriter and I were called in to execute some quick ads."

The idea seems really obvious in retrospect, says Barrie. "We took the Hush Puppies dog as an icon, and used it as a vehicle to show the variety of shoes by doing little visual puns with the dog. It was a very easy-to-produce campaign."

Famous postcards from Fallon Minneapolis. Dominant visuals, minimal copy.
The logo came to life and branded the ads.

Easy to produce, but not so easy to sell. "It was *not* something they wanted to do. The company wasn't doing very well at the time and they associated their mascot with their perceived dowdy image. The *last* thing they wanted to do was ads with a basset hound in them. Primarily because deadlines were looming, and because we could produce the dog campaign fast, they said they'd try it. The ads ran nationally in *USA Today*, big colour pages. When floods of requests for reprints came in they thought, maybe we have something on our hands here. Then one of the celebrity ads ran, and one of the stars, as is often the case, got into a bit of trouble with the law. So it had to be pulled and the dog campaign just took over."

Barrie continued executing dog ads for two years. Then came television. "They weren't used to spending a lot of money, so I went to the stills photographer here in town, Rick Dublin, and we ended up shooting six 15-second spots for about US$125,000 I think, which is nothing. They were the print ads, coming to life, which I don't always recommend, but this was one case where it was very charming, very filmic. The very first commercial we shot, and the very first commercial Rick ever shot, *Ventilated Hush Puppies*, won a Gold Lion at the Cannes Advertising Festival."

American adman George Lois had advocated the idea of moving print ads; the Hush Puppies commercials are often upheld as the perfect example of his technique. Barrie cautions: "When people try to turn or extend print ideas into television, often they make the mistake of just literally doing that; putting a print visual on TV and making something move. They forget that it has to be filmic and interesting."

Burger King. A French fry that looks like a match was the creation of Andrew Clarke at Saatchi & Saatchi, Singapore, for Burger King's spicy Mexican promotion. Now that it has been done, it looks so easy.

"The connection came when I was just doodling a French fry," says Clarke. "I had it dipped into a bit of ketchup and I thought, that looks vaguely like a match, and I knew instantly it *would* look like a match if I did it properly, and that was that!"

It was a first thought, an obvious first thought, and one which many creatives would have dismissed as too simple, too *un*complicated. And therein lies a big lesson: Clarke's minimalist ad has won a Gold Lion at Cannes, a Silver at the One Show, and acceptance into D&AD. As Clarke explains, it was a case of Love and Protection.

"I could have put a black background behind it, I could have put an orange background behind it, I could have put it in a matchbox, I could have had a hand holding it. I could have done a million things, but at the end of the day, I have this thing I call Love and Protection. Obviously, if you love an ad, you want to art direct it to the nines; you want to play with borders, different typefaces, and that's called the Love. Then, there's the Protection. And that's where you protect the idea from all the stuff you *shouldn't* be throwing at it, and that's what I based my decisions on. When I had it up on the Mac at the agency, there was a lot of *umm*ing and *ahh*ing. Shouldn't there be something else? Somebody wanted to change the typeface, it was far too simple for them. Somebody said, put a red border around it, and I said, why? *Why?* I knew instinctively it was right, but I could also see that it was tough, really tough, for some people to actually do it this way."

Clarke talks about the typeface, Cooper Black, and why the caption and logo are tucked together into the lower right corner. "It was a face I've always wanted to use, because it's really ugly, and it's a bit trendy. By putting *Fiery Fries* near the logo, it reduces the ad to two elements. I did try *Fiery Fries* just below the picture, and I also tried it centralised under the picture at the bottom, and both times

Fiery Fries. BURGER KING

Resisting the temptation to complicate a great, simple idea. A postcard from Saatchi & Saatchi, Singapore.

the logo was in the corner. So there were three elements, picture and caption and logo, and what it did was break up the pureness of the white, so I just tucked it all into the corner. That's the thing about the white background, you have to be very careful with it. If you start putting little bits all over it, it suddenly doesn't become a white background; it becomes a background with a lot of bits on it. So you have to let the white do its job, and put everything else neatly where it belongs. Don't try and complicate it."

Adelar Pet Training and Grooming. As Simon Mainwaring explains, "animals acting like humans" is the thought behind the Adelar campaign which he created with Dean Mortenson.

Obedience training was the first execution. "We started out by wondering that if you could teach a dog to, say, catch a ball, what else could you get it to do? That eventually led us to the thought of humanising their skills. Animals acting like humans have always made people laugh and it seemed like a good way to dramatise the benefit. And that's where the toilet training ad came from." Once they had the dog at the urinal, they had the basis for a campaign. "It was just a matter of pushing each subsequent idea until we had the funniest and most relevant execution for the subject."

Humanised pets in a layout which carefully balances the logic of the ad.
Postcards from DDB, Sydney.

Placement of captions and logos will always tip the balance in cutting edge work. One element was removed by not having a headline as such. Once you read *Obedience training* or *Pet grooming*, you get the idea. The issue was, how big should it be, and where should it be?

"We gave it prominence by reversing it out of black," explains Mainwaring. "We tried putting it top left, then top right. We even tried putting it in a dog tag at the bottom. But as soon as we strayed from the basic bottom-right-hand-corner solution, the logo started to overwhelm the picture and ruin the logic of the ad."

An unusual circular edge around the logo panel helps distinguish Adelar ads. "Dean and I felt that a black corner jutting out into the image lessened the impact of the picture. So we softened it by rounding the edge." As Mainwaring admits: "We did try several things, but in the end, staying simple proved to be the best."

UTA French Airlines. This ad, from Euro RSCG Partnership (The Ball Partnership), Singapore, breaks conventions in the airline category. There are no planes, no smiling stewardesses, no happy passengers; there is nothing, at first glance, which suggests it might be an airline ad.

The brief was to communicate that UTA offered more non-stop flights to Paris from Singapore than any other airline. The creative thinking was to find a French visual which demonstrated either something uninterrupted, or something which had been deliberately interrupted. The idea was a first thought. A French baguette, sliced four times, would symbolise a flight with four stops.

Many art directors would have added "some nice atmosphere": a checked tablecloth, perhaps, or a nice wine glass, or a French newspaper, or all three. Art director Norman Alcuri shot the sliced baguette without adornment: "Nothing could get in the way of the reader's mind latching onto the *cuts*; we were demonstrating cuts; we had to focus the reader on the cuts; then they had to follow that little headline running down the right-hand side of the baguette. We allowed ourselves a few crumbs, that was all. It was such a weird idea, just cutting a baguette, that anything you put into the picture would have got in the way of the idea. We had to pare it down, which was its strength."

Minimalist art direction lets the mind latch on to a weird idea.
The baguette was life-sized on the broadsheet page. A postcard from
Euro RSCG Partnership (The Ball Partnership), Singapore.

Alcuri's art direction was minimalist. The ad ran in full colour, on a broadsheet full page. The picture occupied ninety-five percent of the page; the minimal body copy and logos were tucked away at the base. Why? "Having the baguette life-sized on the page added another dimension," says Alcuri. "You opened your paper and saw this full-sized bread. Yes, it could have been done in a half-page vertical, but it would have lost its boldness, the slight cheekiness of it all. I struggled with the headline typeface; it had to be pared down, too. The logic was to focus on the cuts; then the headline, also cut into four pieces; then the copy."

How did Alcuri determine the way the baguette should be sliced? "Normally, you cut a baguette into smaller pieces. But that would have pushed credibility. Cutting it four times was more acceptable; like Singapore to Bangkok, Bangkok to Delhi, and so on. If you go too over the top, people won't believe you. The credibility factor evaporates."

Institute of Mental Health, Singapore. When writer Ben Hunt was looking at a picture of a brain one day, he suddenly saw that it could make the shape of a crouching man. "I just looked at it, and I saw the visual of the man," recalls Hunt. "I got an art director to draw it up, and I stuck it on my wall and left it there for two months. I often think the best things are accidents. You're thinking of an idea for something, and your subconscious is working. As soon as I got the image of the man and the brain, I knew I could use it one day, even if it was just for the cover of a book of lousy poetry."

As luck would have it, Hunt was commissioned privately to write a brochure on clinical depression. "I was going to do something quite straight. Then I saw the picture on the wall and I thought, hang on, this would be a great ad for depression." Sadly, Hunt's client could not afford the production costs. The picture was about to go back up on the wall when his client put him in contact with the IMH Clinic for Anxiety and Mood Disorders.

"I later found out that IMH stood for the Institute of Mental Health, but they don't call it that because of the stigma involved. The Institute loved it."

Photographer John Clang took two shots. "We had to experiment with lots of different models of brains before we got exactly the right image," explains Hunt. The man huddled over in a position of torment proved easier. "He was an account guy from another agency."

Cutting edge digital imaging, so often squandered to layer technique over weak ideas, added a new dimension to Hunt's concept. "Art director Francis Tan put the two shots together. He made them come alive. He had the vision that it should be very dark, so the first time you look at it you only see the brain. Then the second time you look, you see the man."

Hunt quotes a famous novelist who once wrote that the pain of depression could be so intense it was beyond description. "People who see this image have told me that it's exactly how they're feeling. What you can't express in words, you can express visually."

And, having expressed it visually, and with such power, Hunt and his team had the good sense to minimalise copy and position it sensitively.

IF YOU SUFFER FROM CLINICAL DEPRESSION, WE CAN HELP.

A postcard from DMB&B, Singapore. A powerful message about clinical depression which happened by accident.

After Doyle Dane Bernbach's Volkswagen and Avis work, this is arguably America's most famous campaign. Created by Fallon McElligott in Minneapolis, it is a classic postcard concept. Minimalist art direction locates the copy and logo beneath the "Reality" picture.

A postcard from Abbott Mead Vickers, London, an agency traditionally known for its love of copy. On this occasion, only three words and a logo relate the cage-like construction of a Volvo to protection from danger.

Making the postcard visual work harder by challenging readers to find lost pets in each picture. Leo Burnett, Singapore, for the Society for the Prevention of Cruelty to Animals.

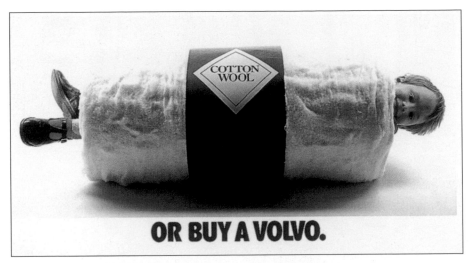

The postcard genre is ideal for creating unusual juxtapositions.
Abbott Mead Vickers, London, used cotton wool for Volvo.
O&M Malaysia used chopsticks for Maggi.

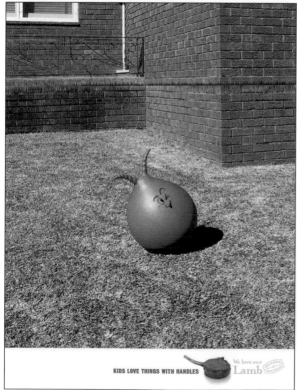

Postcards for Australian Lamb from Brown Melhuish Fishlock, Sydney. Says Warren Brown: "I think people are time poor and they respond more to fast ideas than long copy. The channels available to people now to seek out more information are many, so the need for print advertising to carry lengthy copy no longer exists."

Compelling, intelligent postcards from The Jupiter Drawing Room, celebrating client Nike's sponsorship of South Africa's Paralympics team and (below) the South African Wheelchair Marathon.

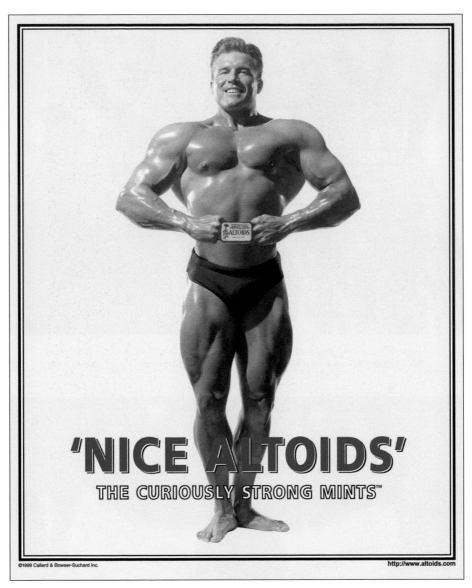

A postcard for Altoids from Leo Burnett USA.
"The life of a press ad is brief, so let it be brilliant," says
Mark Tutssel, deputy chief creative director and
Cannes Grand Prix winner. "Think visually – ask someone
to describe a spiral staircase and they'll use their hands
as well as words. Sometimes the best copy is no copy.
Edit, edit, edit. Less is more."

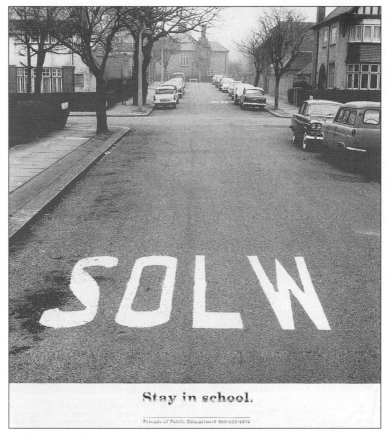

A public service postcard from Fallon Minneapolis. Further proof that strong visual ideas work best when supporting elements like captions and logos are treated simply. Nothing should distract from the idea.

BEFORE sending a letter, two questions have to be answered with brutal honesty.

Is the product story interesting enough to warrant long copy?

And if it is, can it be written well enough?

Three masters of the genre elaborate.

"The quick hit of the picture has always been the first line of attack," reflects French. "If you can find a great picture, it may not say a thousand words, but it will say the important ones quickly. Long copy came in as a reaction against just a rather naff picture. There was a slew of heavy copy ads in the 1960s and 1970s, and to a lesser extent in the 1980s, caused by the fact that there were suddenly a lot of great copywriters around. Unfortunately, an awful lot of people who shouldn't be allowed near a pen also started writing long copy, which actually brought the genre into disrepute. But long copy will always work if the occasion calls for it. Long copy isn't dead any more than the book is dead, and the book is actually growing; you're reading one now."

"I don't think there's a hard and fast rule that nobody reads it or everybody reads it," considers Mike Lescarbeau, "although I think it's closer to nobody. But even as a visual, long copy, whether it's read or not, gives a strong implication that the product has a lot to be said for it. We're writing less long copy at Fallon's these days, but if we felt we had a relevant story, and that the specific market for the product would read it, we'd write it."

"There are two reasons to use long copy," observes Paul Fishlock. "When you've got a lot to say, and when you want to look like you've got a lot to say. The second can be as powerful as the first. People can still read, do still read, and enjoy reading, but they only read what they are interested in. Looking beyond what I can only hope is a passing trend, the fact we see very little long copy these days is more a function of how at least half of the people with 'writer' on their business cards these days can't write. Visual ideas are brilliant at grabbing attention, but in the majority of cases, you need well crafted words to close the sale."

Timberland. One of the world's most admired long copy campaigns was penned at Leagas Delaney, London. The Red Indian ad has been singled out universally as one of the half dozen classics of the genre. As Lionel Hunt says, "It's one of the best print ads I wish I had done. It's rightly famous. Outrageously, wonderfully, politically incorrect."

Ironically, the headline started life as a throwaway line in some body copy. Tim Delaney recalls: "I wrote that headline in the first bit of copy for another ad, and it was in parenthesis. I'd got to the Indians and I'd written this short thing that literally just went, *We stole their land, their buffalo and their women, then we went back for their shoes.* Then I went along to my art director, Steve Dunn, and I said, look, I've written this thing, I think it's a headline. He put it out and we had it there in two minutes and we just liked it. It was a headline that just popped out."

The whole campaign, in fact, originated with an ad for the Timberland department in Harrods. At the time, Delaney and Dunn would sit down and work on ads together.

"What was important about that first ad, we wrote it in a certain way, with lots of little silly puns in it. It talked a certain language. The big leap for us was when I started to create a little world in New Hampshire which is completely obsessed by boots, and cold, and extreme conditions, and Red Indians, and moccasins, and all that sort of stuff. This world sort of evolved and I could keep writing about it till the cows came home. It wasn't easy, but I could do it, and then I had America on top of that. I found out there were more miles of water on the inland coasts than there were on the outside of America. I also found out there are seventy-five thousand nerve ends in the foot. I'm a mine of useless information on all things to do with boots, feet, America, Red Indians, all kinds of stuff. That's where you find yourself. You've got to have an inquisitive mind. It's one of those things about a creative guy, you've got to be a bit of a Nosy Parker. You've got to be curious about how everything works around you, how people work. Out of that comes a sense of being able to connect and pull things together."

Delaney's little world of New Hampshire also set the tone for the art direction. "Out of that world came the look, black and white, it was more honest. The essential honesty of the product was definitely reflected in the honesty of the medium and the treatment, which I didn't get from the colour magazine ads in the States, like the guy lighting a fire. He looked immaculate, yet he was supposed to be in the wilderness."

What draws people to the Timberland campaign? Why has it become an international icon for copywriters? For its clever headline structures, the copy and art skills working so deftly in unison, most certainly; but there is something more – a lesson for anyone attempting a similar standard.

"How much can you write about a boot?" Delaney muses. "I wrote two thousand words an ad, or whatever it was. We wrote about things that people *never* used to write about boots. *We pushed the conviction we had about the product.*"

WE STOLE THEIR LAND, THEIR BUFFALO AND THEIR WOMEN. THEN WE WENT BACK FOR THEIR SHOES.

The Red Indians were an ungrateful lot.

Far from thanking the whiteman for bringing them civilisation (guns, whisky, disease, that kind of thing), they spent years making very bad medicine.

Naturally, during the course of their disputes, the whiteman found it necessary to relieve the Red Indians of certain items.

Thousands of square miles of land, for instance, which they didn't seem to be using.

The odd buffalo, which provided some interesting culinary experiences for the folks heading West.

And of course the squaws, who were often invited along to soothe the fevered brows of conscience-stricken gun-runners and bounty hunters.

But perhaps the most lasting testament to this cultural exchange programme is the humble moccasin.

A shoe of quite ingenious construction. And remarkably comfortable to boot.

Even now, nearly two centuries after the first whiteman tried a pair on, they have yet to be bettered.

Which is why at Timberland, all of our loafers, boat shoes and walking shoes are based on the original Red Indian design.

How is this possible? Surely a shoemaker of our standing is capable of showing a clean pair of heels to a few pesky injuns?

Not really.

Although over the years, we have managed to make some modest improvements.

Rather than use any old buffalo hide, we always insist on premium full-grain leathers. And when we find a tannery that can supply them, we buy its entire output.

We then dye the leathers all the way through so you can't scuff the colour off and impregnate them with silicone oils to prevent the leather going dry.

It is at this point that we employ the wraparound construction of the moccasin to create the classic Timberland shoe.

Using a single piece of softened leather, our craftsmen mould and stretch the upper

around a specially-developed geometric last.

This has the effect of breaking the shoes in before you've even set foot in them.

It also extends the life of the shoe for many, many moons.

Our hand sewn shoes also hark back to the days before the whiteman came.

No machines. No mass production. No deadlines.

Just a pair of nimble hands making shoes in the time-honoured way.

With just a little help from the twentieth century.

Like the high-strength nylon thread, double-knotted and pearl stitched to prevent it coming undone even if it's cut or in the unlikely event that it breaks.

The two coats of latex sealant, added to stop even tiny droplets of water sneaking in through the needle holes.

And the patented process which permanently bonds the uppers to the soles.

(If the Indians had only known how to cobble soles onto their moccasins, we probably wouldn't be in business today.)

As you would expect, the result of all our

labours is a shoe which comes with a heap big price tag.

For which we make absolutely no excuses.

After all, who else uses solid brass eyelets? Or self-oiling rawhide laces? Or glove leather linings?

Come to that, what other shoemaker shows such concern for your feet when big rains come?

For example, as well as utilising all our traditional methods, our new Ultra Light range uses new technology to keep your feet dry.

They're lined with Gore-Tex to make them completely waterproof while allowing your feet to breathe. (Gore-Tex has 9 billion holes per square inch. We didn't believe it either but it works, so now we believe it.)

The soles are made from an incredibly lightweight and highly resistant, dual-density polyurethane.

And, in an uncharacteristic concession to fashion, some models even sport tightly woven waxed cotton cloth.

LEFT: TIMBERLAND UPPERS. RIGHT: THE ORIGINAL MOCCASIN.

A far cry from the Red Indian moccasin?

We certainly hope not.

Because if we ever forget our origins, or change our old-fashioned way of making boots and shoes, one thing's for sure.

A lot of people are going to be on the warpath.

Timberland Shoes and Boots, 23 Pembridge Square, London W2 4DR. Telephone 01:727 2519.

Timberland ®

Breaking convention,
pushing conviction.
Letters from
Leagas Delaney,
London.

"I know bourbon gets better with age, because the older I get, the more I like it."

~ *Booker Noe*

BOOKER NOE grew to love BOURBON in his home state of Kentucky.

BOOKER NOE *will never forget* THE FIRST TIME HE sampled *the legendary* bourbon from his grandfather Jim Beam's distillery. Even as he tells the story today, his face twists into a grimace, his head shakes slowly back and forth and his big hand swats at the air in front of him.

"I didn't like it at all," he says, without apologies.

Now, if that confession sounds a bit strange coming from a man who's devoted his life to making fine whiskey, there is a perfectly reasonable explanation.

Booker Noe, perhaps better than anyone else, understands that an appreciation for bourbon isn't something people are born with.

You see, in his time as Master Distiller at the Clermont, Kentucky home of Jim Beam Bourbon, Booker has come to cherish the subtle flavors found in the world's finest whiskey.

And he's discovered he's especially fond of bourbon in its

*"*LIKE MOST PEOPLE, *learning to love fine bourbon took me a certain amount of time. But as the years have gone by, I've decided there is just nothing better than the taste of whiskey aged in charred white oak to the peak of its flavor. It's uncut, unfiltered and straight from the barrel. This is the bourbon I've chosen to put my name on."*

purest form, taken straight from the barrel, at its natural proof.

It is this bourbon, Booker Noe believes, with all of its rich, oaky body intact, that is the very best of the best.

Until recently, uncut, unfiltered bourbon like this was the domain of the Master Distiller alone. And while he's no doubt appreciated having the privilege, Booker has always wished that other people, people who truly love fine spirits, could taste this whiskey for themselves.

Which is why Booker Noe recently began bottling his unique bourbon and making it available to the few connoisseurs who can appreciate it.

Considering the special pride he takes in his favorite whiskey, it's not surprising that Booker has put his own name on the label. Nor should it come as any shock that he personally approves every batch of Booker's Bourbon before he allows it to be sent along to you. Fact is, only someone of Booker's experience can determine whether a straight-from-the-barrel bourbon is at the very peak of its flavor.

Depending on the temperament of the seasons in the Bluegrass State, Booker's Bourbon reaches that peak anywhere from six to eight years into the aging process. And since every barrel of whiskey ages differently, each batch of Booker's has a different proof, which can measure anywhere between 121 and 127.

Once selected, the bourbon is painstakingly hand-sealed in a hand-labeled bottle and marked with a tag showing its unique proof and age.

With any luck, you'll find Booker's Bourbon at your local liquor retailer. But since, by its nature, this is not a mass produced bourbon, you may have to look further.

If you should find Booker's impossible to locate,

BOOKER'S BOURBON comes straight from the barrel, UNCUT and UNFILTERED.

we suggest you call the toll-free number listed at the bottom of the page, and see about obtaining your Booker's Bourbon that way.

Regardless how you obtain it, Booker Noe believes you'll find his bourbon well worth the time and effort you spend searching.

Especially if, like Booker himself, the years have done for your taste what they do for a bourbon's.

Booker's™ Kentucky Straight Bourbon Whiskey, 60.3%-63.5% Alc./Vol. Bottled by James B. Beam Distilling Co., Clermont KY ©1992 James B. Beam Distilling Co.

At $50 a bottle, Fallon Minneapolis thought letters were appropriate.

Booker's Bourbon. Before joining Fallon Minneapolis, Mike Lescarbeau worked at Leagas Delaney. With Tim Delaney, he co-authored the award-winning long copy campaign for Ordnance Survey Maps. He shares French's view that the genre is a victim of abuse.

"It's on a decline because products that didn't necessarily need long copy were getting it. But it still works when you have products like Booker's Bourbon, because people need to know why it costs $50 a bottle."

Lescarbeau describes how the long copy strategy was formulated. "We imagined, and it turned out we were correct, that men would want to pour this for a guest in their home and impress them with it." Booker's Bourbon comes in a hand-labelled bottle with a tag certifying its proof and age, signed by master distiller Booker Noe, grandson of Jim Beam. "They needed the lore that went with it, in order to have something to converse over, because unless you're an absolute maniac, you're going to take a little time to drink it."

According to Lescarbeau, it was a given that the ads would have a big bottle in them. "We fought it for a while. Then we said, what if the bottle was the hero, and we put in some secondary visuals of Booker Noe?"

The anecdotal ads scored Gold and Silver at the One Show. They disavow pretension and favour Kentucky folksiness. *I know bourbon gets better with age, because the older I get, the more I like it* begins one.

Lexus. In Singapore, one car in every ten is a Mercedes-Benz. Elbowing Lexus into that market required Dentsu Young & Rubicam to break several conventions.

"Mercedes-Benz had years to build its reputation," explains writer Mark Fong. "We had literally a few months. We had to show that Lexus stood for something."

Mercedes-Benz and arch-rival BMW owned engineering. "We had to sell engineering, too, but we wanted to show all the small things, all the small details, that make a car great," elaborates creative director Patrick Low. "So we decided to marry the high standards of the owners with the high stardards of the car, to show how the driver's values are reflected in the car. We took the positioning, *For perfectionists, by perfectionists.*"

Before we subjected the Lexus to the mercy of the critics, we first exposed it to the mercy of the elements.

For Perfectionists. By Perfectionists.

Selling a US$200,000 Japanese car to a country in love with Mercedes-Benz.
Letters from Dentsu Young & Rubicam, Singapore.

The decision to use long copy print ads defied the conventional wisdom that Singaporeans do not read them. "We ran the ads in English and Chinese on Sundays, when businessmen had more time," says Fong. "The mass of information presumes high quality. The Chinese-educated reader assumes that because there is so much to write about, it must be a good product."

The campaign's tonality was more Western than Asian. As Fong recalls: "Toyota had many of the same features in other models, so we had to sound different. We had to couch the features in a very different tone and manner, one which would appeal to the kind of people with money, who were at a stage in life to drive a Lexus." There was no shortage of subject matter. "The product manager was very passionate, he kept feeding us nuggets of information, all kinds of trivia, and we soaked it up like a sponge. Every headline was a point of entry to the key subjects like power, silence, safety, ageing well. My copy ran one third over length on average," he laments. "Every cut was painful."

Low crafted the visuals so all seven ads shared a campaign look, without being exactly the same. "Some pictures were bigger, some were smaller. I wanted to create little pockets of interest with sidebars. People always read captions and quotations."

The new marque captured both market share and consumer imagination. The salesmen were surprised when customers could quote facts and figures from the ads. For the agency, there was a bonus: a Silver at the One Show.

Have you ever wondered why one newspaper advertisement works better than another?

Why, for instance, has *this* particular advertisement attracted your attention?

Is it because the headline offers you an intriguing benefit?

And speaks to you in a personal way?

Or could it be the typestyle that is deliberately inviting and easy to read?

In truth, every single element in this advertisement is carefully calculated to attract your interest and keep it.

It is, in effect, an ideal ad, created entirely to demonstrate some proven principles of newspaper advertising.

Many more are contained within the copy below.

All you have to do is read on.

We'll simply swap a few minutes of your time for 80 solid years of well-researched wisdom.

Higher potential readers.

To start with, the very fact this advertisement is even *in* a newspaper gives it a head start.

Almost 90% of readers see every page of their newspaper, excluding the classified sections. And spend, on average, some 40 minutes with their favourite daily paper.

In addition, newspaper readers are more receptive to advertising.

According to Starch readership surveys, they actually give *equal value* to the information received via ads as they do editorial.

The same can't be said of television, where advertising content is viewed as an intrusion. (A phenomenon known in the trade as the "flush factor.")

Nor does it apply to radio, often referred to unkindly but perhaps accurately as "wallpaper sound".

Listeners aren't standing with one ear cocked for the commercials.

Given the unique advantage of the newspaper medium, it's up to you to capitalise on this natural curiosity.

Strong headlines lead to strong bottom lines.

The key to being noticed is to target the message by means of the headline.

A good headline should say "this message is for you, read on".

Such an effect is most often achieved when a headline promises or infers a benefit.

You see an example above.

A headline should also involve the prospect personally. It doesn't have to use the word "you" or "your" but it's amazing how often these words can help.

David Ogilvy maintains the reader must be "flagged down" in the headline.

Bill Bernbach argued that headlines "go to the essence of the product".

Headlines then, are crucial to capturing prospects.

Lose them there and the rest of the advertisement is academic.

The laws of gravity.

Once having gained a reader's attention, layout and typography take over to help guide it through safely.

Some age-old maxims are borne out in recent research conducted by Colin Wheildon, Publications Editor for the NRMA.

In the Western World, reading is done from top left of the page to bottom right.

Figure 1. Gutenberg diagram charts basic reading eye movement. Picture-captions like this, by the way, also help make your advertisement more information-rich.

The same applies to eye travel through an advertisement (See Fig. 1).

The eye falls initially on the top left, the Primary Optical Area (POA) and leaves the page at the bottom right, the Terminal Area (TA)

Crosses indicate dead corners, and wavy lines track "backward" movement which the reading eye resists.

(You may have noticed this advertisement adheres closely to these dynamics.)

This is known as reading gravity, the laws of which are broken with grave results.

For example, test layouts complying with the principles of reading gravity (Fig 2) score 73% good comprehension.

Figure 2. An example of a layout which complies with the principles of reading gravity.

But turn the page – and the diagram – upside down, and you see an example of a layout which completely opposes these principles.

And causes the comprehension scores to become totally reversed; 37% as against 73%.

How long is a piece of copy?

If good layout guides readers through an advertisement, it is body copy which holds them.

The extent to which body copy is read has always been a vital question, even a hotly contested issue, for advertisers.

But the amount of copy which prospects are willing to read is often completely underestimated.

Ogilvy's own research shows that "although readership falls off rapidly up to 50 words, it drops off little between 50 and 500 words".

(As a matter of interest, this ad contains over 1000 words.)

Long copy can often convey the impression that you have something important to say, whether it is read or not.

Copy length ultimately depends on the fascination of the subject matter.

If you were to be handed six tightly spaced pages someone had written about you, you'd probably read every word.

	%
1. Roman old style lower case	92
2. Sans serif lower case	90
3. Roman modern lower case	89
4. Roman old style italic lower case	86
5. Roman modern italic lower case	86
6. Sans serif italic lower case	86
7. Optima lower case	86
8. Optima italic lower case	80
9. ROMAN MODERN CAPS	71
10. ROMAN OLD STYLE CAPITALS	69
11. *Square serif lower case*	64
12. *ROMAN MODERN ITALIC CAPITALS*	63
13. ROMAN OLD STYLE ITALIC CAPITALS	63
14. *SANS SERIF ITALIC CAPITALS*	59
15. OPTIMA ITALIC CAPITALS	57
16. SANS SERIF CAPITALS	57
17. OPTIMA CAPITALS	56
18. SQUARE SERIF CAPITALS	44
19. *Cursive or script lower case*	37
20. **Fragmented lower case**	32
21. FRAGMENTED CAPITALS	26
22. **ORNAMENTED CAPITALS**	19
23. *Black letter lower case*	10
24. BLACK LETTER CAPITALS	3

Figure 3. Legibility of headline styles comprehension scores.

It takes all types to make a world. But not an ad.

The most common and legible newspaper typefaces are serif styles, such as we've employed on this page.

(Serifs are the little "feet" on the extremities of the characters.)

Sans serif type – such as you see in this example paragraph – is demonstrably less readable, especially when the copy runs to any sort of length.

One school of thought argues that capital letters in headlines achieve more impact. But the eye is presented with A SERIES OF SOLID RECTANGLES AND RECOGNISING WORDS BECOMES A TASK INSTEAD OF A NATURAL PROCESS.

The argument for lower case headlines has human physiology on its side.

When a person reads a line of type the eye recognises the letters by the shape of their upper half.

In fact, a line of lower case type with the bottom half completely missing is still quite legible, as you can see.

This is because the top half of lower case letters are quite distinctive, and, when framed by the white space around them, permit easy recognition.

Again, various other tests have shown conclusive – even brutal results – in favour of lower case letters.

With headlines set in Roman Old Style lower case scoring highest with 92% legibility, and black letter capitals coming in a bad 24th, with 3%. (See Fig. 3.)

The same principles apply to text.

Tests have shown serif type leads to 67% good comprehension and sans serif a mere 12%.

There are other, but equally important, principles worthy of note.

Justified body copy, such as you see here, where the text is lined up on the left and right-hand margins, tends to rate more highly in comprehension tests, scoring 62%.

Set it ragged, however, the way you see it in this example paragraph, and suddenly the comprehension level drops down to an alarming 10%.

Columns too, should be no wider than 40 characters or one-and-a-half alphabets. (The column width you are reading now averages 40 characters.)

But once a column width drops below a 20 character measure, so does the score.

Even the tightness of letterspacing, and kerning as it's called, can influence legibility.

Set it too tight, like this (where characters are kerned 4 units) and you get an almost total loss of comprehension.

The ideal is to kern around one unit, as demonstrated in this line.

Words of Caution.

Of course, you can't simply go great ads "by the numbers" as I have this fashion.

Otherwise every ad in this newspaper would look exactly the same.

Thus defying the very first principle of advertising – to stand out.

The skill comes in knowing the rules so you are able to break them creatively.

There are thousands of permutations of these guidelines and just as many success stories behind them.

So finally, let us give you one more guideline of good newspaper advertising.

Close the sale.

Further information can be obtained from The Newspaper Advertising Bureau of Australia, 77 Berry Street, North Sydney 2060. (02) 92 1044.

The Newspaper Advertising Bureau is a marketing organisation established by Australia's major metropolitan and regional newspaper publishers as a service to industry.

As such, the NABA is a non-profit organisation.

Which it can afford to be, given that so many of its advertisers aren't.

Newspapers work.

Incidentally, it has frequently been shown that the best place for your company logo or brand is down here. In the bottom right-hand corner. After all, where do you place the signature on a personal letter?

The creative partnership of Jack Vaughan and Rob Tomnay at the Campaign Palace, Sydney, has resulted in some of the most effective and memorable Australian advertising produced in the past few years. They created this ad for the Newspaper Advertising Bureau of Australia.

Jack Vaughan's masterpiece for the Newspaper Advertising Bureau of Australia. A superbly crafted letter from The Campaign Palace.

PUTTING A CROSS IN THE LABOUR BOX IS THE SAME AS SIGNING THIS PIECE OF PAPER.

1. I hereby give up the right to choose which school my children go to and agree to abide by any decision made by the State on my behalf.

2. I empower the Labour Party to take Britain out of Europe, even though my job may be one of the 2¼ million which depend on Britain's trade with Europe.

3. I am prepared to see the Police Force placed under political control even though it could undermine their capability to keep law and order.

4. I agree that Britain should now abandon the nuclear deterrent which has preserved peace in Europe for nearly forty years. I fully understand that the Russians are not likely to follow suit.

5. I agree to have the value of my savings reduced immediately in accordance with Labour's wishes to devalue the pound.

6. I empower the government to borrow as much money as they wish from other countries and I agree to let my children pay the debt.

7. I fully agree to a massive expansion of nationalisation, whatever the cost to me in higher taxation.

8. I do not mind if I am forced to join a union. I do not expect to vote for the leaders of that union and do not mind if I am not consulted by secret ballot before being told to strike.

9. I sign away the right to buy my own council house.

10. I do not mind paying higher rates.

11. I am prepared to allow my pension fund to be used by the government to invest in any scheme that they see fit whether or not this shows a good enough return on my investment.

12. I understand that Labour's plans could mean that prices will double once more, as they did under the last Labour government.

13. I realise that the tax cuts from which I will have benefited under a Conservative government may be withdrawn at once.

14. I waive my right to choose any form of private medicine for my family.

15. I understand that if I sign this now I will not be able to change my mind for at least five years.

SIGNED.

CONSERVATIVE ✗

Each word in this ad was as deep as this caption when it ran as a double-page spread in broadsheet newspapers during the 1983 British election campaign. Saatchi & Saatchi, London, for the Conservative Party.

A speed reading course from Castrol.

FLUID MOTION

Trace your finger along the line in this next passage in one fluid motion. It's important not to stop.

"In February 1899, Charles 'Cheers' Wakefield took what was perhaps the greatest decision of his working life: he resigned from the old company to which he had devoted his previous 15 years, and set himself up in competition. Thus founding one of the most innovative, successful and highly respected lubricants businesses in the world. A company that's been at the forefront of technology in every one of its 100-year history. Producing the oils to allow the world's drivers, riders and aviators run farther, faster and higher.

This exercise forces your eyes so continually scan new text. Preventing your eyes from stopping and repeatedly looking at unfamiliar phrases and words. A common cause of slow reading. When in fact, if you keep moving, your brain in most cases will comprehend the meaning. Try it again, but this time a little faster. Then move on.

FLOW FASTER

Another way to increase your speed is to reduce the number of words on a page. This next exercise does just that. Several words in the following passage are set in a boldface. These are the key facts of the subject matter. This is what the mind of a good speed reader sees. Try reading this next paragraph focusing on just the words in the boldface. Then tell to see if your comprehension suffered by reading all of the words.

On October 15th 1997, at Nevada's Black Rock Desert, RAF pilot Andy Green got behind the wheel of the Castrol sponsored Thrust SSC (Super Sonic Car). A 'car' powered by two Rolls-Royce engines lubricated with Castrol oil and generating 100,000 horsepower — the equivalent of

CASTROL HAS BEEN THE DRIVING FORCE behind some of the most famous achievements in speed of the 20th century. The Concorde's crossing of the Atlantic in just 3.5 hours. Malcolm and Donald Campbell's historic World Water and Land Speed records in their famous Bluebirds. And pilot Andy Green's unbelievable

541 Formula One race car engines. This 'car' didn't just break the World Land Speed Record. It broke the sound barrier. Streaking across the desert at an average speed of a truly amazing 828.1 km/h (763.035 mph). Making Andy Green the first man to drive a car faster than the speed of sound. Amazing isn't it?

breakthrough of the sound barrier in a jet-powered car (pictured above).

And now, to liven things up a little in this our 100th year in business, we'll now attempt to improve the speed of something completely new. The speed of your reading. So put your head down, take a grip of this magazine and let Castrol make you faster.

PORE OVER

Most of us read one word at a time, taking a short pause between each word. This of course slows you down.

But by eliminating the gaps and focusing on several words at once, you'll

8ars flowing at an incredible rate. Try it with this next passage.

Speed in the water has been just as keenly contested as the speed in the air and on land ever since the early part of the century, but perhaps enjoying a slightly lower profile. Nonetheless, Sir Charles Wakefield took an interest in water-borne achievements and a great many race-winning craft were lubricated by Castrol. In 1930 the World Water Speed Record first went to a Castrol-lubricated boat: Henry Segrave reaching 158.94 km/h (98.76 mph) in Miss England II on Lake Windermere, England. In 1937, American Malcolm Campbell took the Castrol lubricated Bluebird to Lake Maggiore in northern Italy, where in calm water he set a new record of 203.6 km/h (126.5 mph). Over the following years, Campbell continued to raise the record until 1939 he reached the tremendous speed of 228.1 km/h (141 mph).

That was quick.

This is a diagram of a poor reader's eye movement.

MOTOR SKILL

Well we hope you've learnt something about yourself and about us. As you can see, we love our oils. And we love to prove that oils is oils. Why just recently, Australian legend Victor Bray regained his position as the world's fastest drag racer at Willowbank Raceway in Queensland. Lubricated with Castrol GP50, Bray's blown alcohol Top Doorslammer Chevy reached a World Record Speed of 370.06 km/h (229.24 mph), matching his personal best of 6.55 seconds over a quarter mile.

That's some reading.

IN MARCH 1899,
Charles 'Cheers' Wakefield founded C.C. Wakefield & Co. later to become Castrol.

SIR HENRY SEGRAVE
in Miss England II breaks the World Water Speed Record.

FIRST semi-synthetic oil, Castrol R20, developed in partnership with Mercedes Benz.

THE CASTROL brand logo – 1946.

CASTROL lubricated Thrust SSC, the World's fastest car.

A 1927 poster celebrating Malcolm Campbell's World Land Speed Record.

WORLD'S fastest Chevy. Victor Bray's blown alcohol Top Doorslammer.

Proving that OILS AIN'T OILS for 100 years.

Let Castrol lubrication make you faster, on the page as well as on the road. Copywriter Tim Brown's speed reading course was superbly art directed by Steve Carlin and typographer Juliana Melhuish and moved the genre forward. Saatchi & Saatchi, Sydney.

The longest print ad in the history of advertising contains 11,000 words of body copy describing every step of a gruelling 96km road race. The sign-off: Pietermaritzburg. Challenging to read? Try running it. *The Jupiter Drawing Room, South Africa, for Nike. The walk to the stage was a lot shorter.*

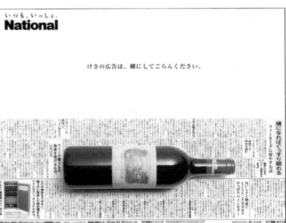

English is not the exclusive language of long copy, as Hakuhodo, Osaka, demonstrated in its campaign for National Wine Cellars. Each ad talked about how to care for your wine by keeping it out of the sun, not shaking the bottle, and maintaining the right temperature.

WILL YOU HAVE A BENT HEADLINE WITH A STRAIGHT PICTURE?
OR A STRAIGHT HEADLINE WITH A BENT PICTURE?

Again, there are only two choices. But this time, the choice is made consciously.

If the idea in the ad is being carried by the headline, it means the headline will contain a twist, a trick, a turn, a shock factor; it will be *bent*. Therefore, the accompanying visual must play a subservient or *straight* role.

And vice versa.

If the idea in the ad is being carried by some creative twist in the picture, the picture will be *bent*. Therefore, the headline must be absolutely *straight*. No puns, no wordplays, no embellishments. The words could even be taken from the product statement in the brief.

It is a truth in which Lionel Hunt absolutely believes. In fact, he coined the terminology. "It was to do with the importance of thinking about print ads as words and pictures that work in unison. If a copywriter only thinks about the copy, he will never write a straight line because, in isolation, it won't appear clever enough. However, in conjunction with the right picture, it might just be a brilliant ad. It's the same with the art direction."

John Hegarty agrees. "You're using words and pictures. What you don't want to do is make the picture do what the words are doing, and the words do what the picture is doing. So you've got to decide which is *leading*, which is taking you forward, and if it's the picture then almost certainly what you want is a very simple headline. Or it's the other way round: a very simple picture and you've got an intriguing headline. So there is a kind of juxtaposition. But you *can't* have both. Then it's bland, and they work against each other, one's fighting the other rather than complementing it."

The classic example is having a straight photograph of a car. If you write a straight headline, the ad will be boring and forgettable. If you write a bent headline like *Lemon*, everybody will sit up and take notice.

Every ad in this book conforms to this truth.

If you are sending a letter, by definition you must have a bent headline. The headline carries the idea which extends into the long copy. Delaney's Timberland is a campaign of bent headlines with straight pictures of boots, Red Indians and New Hampshire trivia.

If you are sending a postcard, however, you will have to make a conscious decision whether to bend the headline or the picture.

The cream of Manchester is a very straight headline; a beer in an ice cream cone is a very bent picture.

Two old ladies talking on the steps is a very straight picture; *It's so nice that homosexuals, Jews and terrorists have a newspaper to read* is a very bent headline.

Cutting silk is a bent picture; the brand name *Silk Cut* is the invisible straight headline.

Management trainee, aged 42 is a bent headline; the colour red is a straight picture.

For his Kaminomoto postcards, French bent the pictures and wrote a straight headline. For XO beer, sometimes he bent the pictures, other times he bent the headlines. But he never bent both in the same ad.

If both the headline and the picture are bent, the ad will lose its focus. Neither will work.

If both the headline and the picture are straight, the ad will be bland and lifeless.

All letters have bent headlines. Because the words are carrying the idea, the supporting pictures must be straight.

In 1092 William Rufus, angered that Carlisle was *proclaimed* part of Scotland, went north, drove the Scots out and ordered the building of a stronghold in the borderlands. Thus *Carlisle Castle* was constructed just half a mile outside the city. And ever since it has been the scene of numerous battles with different factions fighting for ownership. It was besieged by parliamentarians in the Civil War, then by Bonnie Prince Charlie during the Jacobite Rising. In order to repel such attacks, the castle defences have been extensively remodelled over the centuries. Perhaps the most notable 'guest' at Carlisle Castle was *Mary Queen of Scots*, a prisoner there back in 1568. You can see Queen Mary's Tower and take the very route she took during her daily walks around the grounds.

This year marks the 250th anniversary of the imprisonment of Jacobites inside Carlisle Castle following the 1745 Rising. Led by Bonnie Prince Charlie, they succeeded in taking Carlisle Castle before marching southwards to claim the throne for Charlie's father, James Stuart. An *exhibition* within the castle tells the dramatic story of the Jacobites' movements. How they returned north in defeat with the Duke of Cumberland's men hot on their heels. How they were captured and imprisoned, many of them later to be hanged, drawn and quartered on the nearby Gallows Hill. In a dungeon, you will see the famous Licking Stone. A permanently moist wall which provided a little water for the Jacobites in this overcrowded prison.

Located in the small village of Belsay, 14 miles north-west of Newcastle, *Belsay Hall* consists of a well-preserved fourteenth-century castle, the ruins of a seventeenth-century mansion and one of the most important neo-classical houses in Britain. But the real jewels in the crown are the 30 acres of magnificent formal gardens, exotic quarry gardens and woodland that surround the buildings. A stroll through the grounds at Belsay

reveals sycamore, oak and ash trees, the Magnolia Terrace, the Rhododendron Garden, the lovely Meadow Garden. Much of what you see there reflects the economic character of Sir Charles Monck. He returned from his 14-month European honeymoon, 1804-1806, full of ideas to build a *new home* at Belsay in beautiful neo-Greek style. And to have it set in an equally beautiful landscape.

To celebrate the 1996 Year of Visual Arts, Belsay Hall will come alive again from 4th May until 26th October. The 'Living at Belsay' exhibition will feature the work of selected craftsmen and artists who'll be refurbishing the entrance and the three main reception rooms. It's a novel idea which will see the normally bare rooms equipped with magnificent furniture, fine ceramics, glassware and wall hangings. A rare chance to see contemporary artistry in an historical setting.

WHEN

YOU BUILD A CASTLE FOR A KING WHO'S RENOWNED FOR CHOPPING PEOPLE'S HEADS OFF, YOU BUILD A REALLY NICE CASTLE.

Walmer Castle, Kent.

When Osborne House was completed in 1851 to provide a country residence for Queen Victoria, it was considered by Her Majesty to be 'small and snug'. However, to humble subjects such as you and I, it is anything but. *Osborne*, on the Isle of Wight, served as a peaceful seaside retreat where Queen Victoria and Prince Albert could escape the strict confines of ceremony. And a magnificent retreat it is too. Albert's passion for the Italian *Renaissance* is clearly evident, what with the Italianate terrace, the Andromeda fountain and the ornate copies of the fine Medici Lions from the *Loggia de' Lanzi, Florence*. Inside you will see a classical Roman statue, the *Marine Venus*, a lovely fresco painting by William Dyce and lots of extravagant grotesque decoration. In the Durbar Room there's a change of country, this state banqueting hall having been designed in the Indian style. Other rooms worth visiting are the Royal Apartments, the Billiards Room and the Nursery Suite. And the perfect way to *finish your day* at Osborne House is to take a Victorian horse and carriage ride from the main building to the delightful Swiss Cottage, a present from the Queen to her children in 1854.

Henry VIII aside, many other royals have spent time at *Walmer Castle*. Amongst them Queen Victoria and the current Lord Warden, HRH the *Queen Mother*. Indeed, this delightful residence, just a mile from Deal in Kent, boasts an extremely impressive list of distinguished visitors. Like William Pitt the Younger, who was Lord Warden until his death in 1806. He would try and visit whenever his official duties would allow. A later Lord Warden, the *Duke of Wellington*, was equally taken with his 'charming marine residence'. His room is arranged just as it was during his stay, its plain, modest furnishings bearing testimony to the Iron Duke's preference for unsophisticated surroundings. You can see the very armchair where he died in 1852, his campaign-bed which still retains its original horsehair mattress and, in the Wellington Museum just along the corridor, the boots worn by the celebrated British war hero.

D URABILITY, not beauty, was the main requirement in the construction of *Walmer Castle*. However, the architects, not wishing to take any chances with the notoriously hard to please Henry VIII, wisely decided to address both issues. One of a chain of coastal artillery forts, Walmer was built to thwart any invasions by Spain or France. This was a real possibility as Henry's split with the Roman Catholic Church and destruction of many monasteries had infuriated the papacy. The castle differed from earlier mediæval defences in that it had no high walls or lofty towers. In fact, so *attractive* was Walmer that only minor modifications were needed to make it the comfortable residence it is today. For more information on English Heritage and our role in preserving the nation's significant buildings please *call* 0171 973 3434 or *visit* any one of our 400 sites.

It's yours. Why not visit it.

ENGLISH HERITAGE

Leagas Delaney, London.

Warning.
This product can cause
blisters, aching
and shortness of breath.

The damp morning air wheezes in and out of your healthy lungs as if each breath might be your last. The hill you've been climbing seems to get steeper with every step. Was that a twig snapping? Or was it your knee creaking?

Congratulations.

You are enjoying the countryside with the help of an Ordnance Survey map.

Enjoying? Don't we really mean to say enduring? The truth is, with our maps you'll be able to do more than your share of each.

You see, at Ordnance Survey we believe when it comes to travelling through the wilds of Great Britain, the best route to take isn't always the easiest one.

That's why maps like our Landranger Series will not only show you quiet country roads, but also very quiet country pathways.

They'll help you to discover many little known public rights of way, which often lead to some even lesser known picnic spots.

And they'll point out the hill that's over

the hill, and has a better view of the lake.

All of which might induce you to expend a little more energy. But is sure to be well worth the effort.

*Fair Quiet have I found thee here,
And Innocence, thy sister dear,

Mistaken long, I sought you then, in busy companies of men.

Your sacred plants, if here below,
Only among the plants will grow.

Society is all but rude, to this delicious solitude.* - Andrew Marvell

Each weekend, thousands of people escape the crowded, noisy cities of Britain only in order to meet up with each other a few hours away at crowded, noisy tourist spots. [So much for finding delicious solitude.]

The problem, of course, is that everybody seems to go to the same few places.

Well, in addition to all the things an Ordnance Survey map can help you find, there are also some things it can help you avoid. Like other people.

With more details on your map, you'll have more places to choose from for a day away. Including many that aren't overrun with your fellow travellers.

Moreover, wherever you decide to go, you can always trust those details will be the most accurate available.

After all, at Ordnance Survey we've had exactly 200 years practice making maps.

The first Ordnance Survey maps were

commissioned in the late 18th century for one reason. To map the South Coast in case of attack from Napoleon.

Naturally, the job had to be done to an exacting standard. And we still create maps today — as if someone's life might depend on them.

Although nowadays people use our maps to plan peaceful weekends, instead of battles.

You finally reach the crest of the hill and look up from your aching feet. Suddenly, you find yourself staring out in utter awe across thirty miles of folding hills and valleys.

If you need an incentive to keep yourself striding boldly up a challenging hillside, nothing can beat the views you are bound to encounter when you go out rambling with an Ordnance Survey map. You can gaze down upon ancient stone monuments. Spy way off in the distance what might be the site of King Arthur's first court. Or perch high up above famous medieval battlefields, [seeing them from a safe distance, just as the generals did].

But even if the vista has no known historical significance, you will still be able to enjoy something the road-bound traveller rarely experiences. Nature.

Or what William Wordsworth called 'The anchor of my purest thoughts, the nurse, the guide, the guardian of my heart, and the soul of all my moral being'.

In Wordsworth's Lake District alone, Ordnance Survey maps can guide you to well over a hundred waterfalls, dozens of ancient earthworks and countless historic houses.

One of these houses, in fact, was lived in by a Mrs Heelis, a prosperous lady sheep farmer whose hobby was writing and illustrating stories under her maiden name, *Beatrix Potter.*

It seems Beatrix Potter Heelis enjoyed a quiet walk in the country as much, if not more, than sitting in her Lake District home and writing some of the world's most famous tales for children.

'I loved to wander the Troutbeck Fell,' said the much admired author in a 1942 interview. 'Sometimes I had with me an old sheepdog, more often, I went alone. But I was never lonely. There was company of gentle sheep, and wild flowers, and singing waters.'

Meanwhile, Beatrix had written in a letter to her publisher, 'These d......d little books... I am utterly tired of doing them, and my eyes are wearing out'.

Still, she did do them, and you can see the study she toiled in even today, as long as you know where to look.

You look down one last time at the green and yellow quilt of fields below, and stand to start your descent. This time, you're glad for the extra weight around your middle. Gravity will be doing most of the work.

There are three kinds of walking maps made by Ordnance Survey, and you can get one to cover every field, every wood, every lake and every stream in Britain.

In the more popular touring regions of the countryside, one of our Outdoor Leisure maps will help you know your way around as well as the locals, maybe even better.

If you're planning to travel to other areas, we suggest the Landranger Series or the larger scale Pathfinder Series maps.

Each has dozens of helpful symbols in its key that point out important features you might miss on your own.

For instance, you'll find three different symbols used just for marking churches, with tower, with spire, without tower or spire.

Are we going overboard? Does anyone really need this much detail in a map?

Well, considering that most of our customers are on foot, yes, we think they do.

Ramblers don't have motorway signs to go by, and need landmarks to find their way.

Landmarks that are mapped accurately, since getting lost on the moors is somewhat more unsettling than getting lost on the M6.

So if you're going to venture out to those places where there might not be anyone to ask for directions, we strongly suggest that

you take along a map from Ordnance Survey.

Because we wouldn't want you to suffer from any more blisters, aching and shortness of breath than you absolutely have to.

Ordnance Survey.
The most detailed maps in the land.

Leagas Delaney, London.

How to kill a baby.

It's easy. All you do is walk up to it. It won't run away.

Then, as it looks up at you trustingly, mistaking you for its mother, you smash in its skull with a baseball bat.

That's what happens to baby seals in Canada every year in a bloody ritual that lasts six weeks.

In Japan they do it a different way. They herd dolphins into the shallows, wait for the tide to leave them stranded, then go through the same grisly process.

Then there's the whales. You know what happens to them.

Doing it is dead easy if your mind is warped enough. Stopping it is a whole lot harder, but there is something you can do.

In this week's Woman's Day we're running a thought provoking article on what's happening to these beautiful creatures.

We're also running a simple competition that you and your children can enter. All you have to do is tell us in less than twenty words what the seals, the dolphins or the whales would say to us if they could speak.

There are cash prizes, but far more importantly, for every entry in the competition Woman's Day will donate 10 cents to Greenpeace to help their work in bringing this ghastly business to a halt.

Look for this week's Woman's Day. It's the one with the baby seal on the cover, seconds before it dies.

Woman's Day.

Bent headline, straight picture. This ad, written by Lionel Hunt,
first brought The Campaign Palace, Australia, to world fame.

The more you bend the picture, the straighter the headline should be. If both are bent, one will fight the other. Sometimes it is as simple as hanging a bent picture on the product statement in the brief.

Only three words appeared in this acclaimed postcard: "The new SLK". Even the brand logo ran without the words "Mercedes-Benz", and certainly without a slogan. ("I'm no great fan of straplines," said its creative director Gerard Stamp.) Art director Mark Tutssel, writer Nick Bell. Leo Burnett, London.

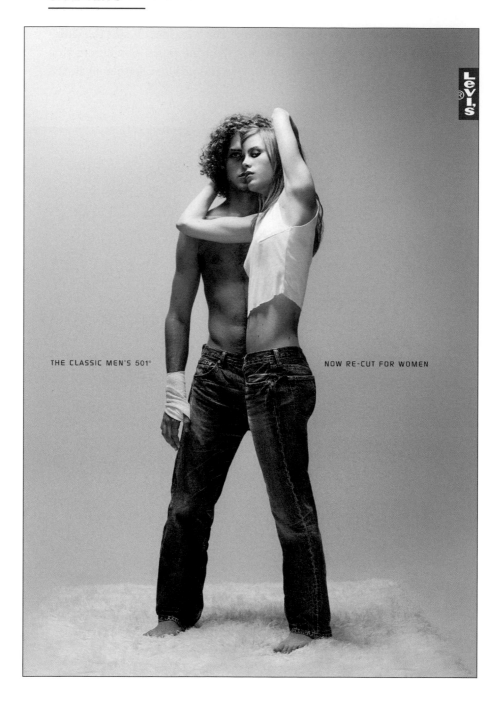

THE CLASSIC MEN'S 501®   NOW RE-CUT FOR WOMEN

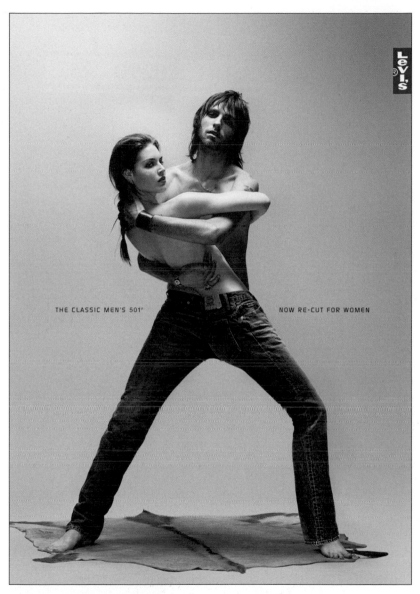

THE CLASSIC MEN'S 501®   NOW RE-CUT FOR WOMEN

The brief: communicate that Levi's 501 men's jeans had been re-cut for women.
Bent pictures (shot by Nadav Kander) showed two models intertwined as one,
with a straight product proposition line. Creative director: Steve Elrick.
Creative team: Alex Lim Thye Aun and Marthinus Strydom.
Bartle Bogle Hegarty Asia Pacific.

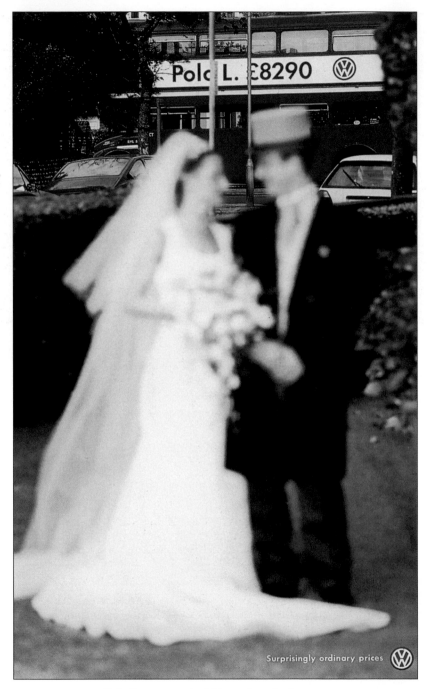

*Only three, very straight words and a logo ran
with this bent picture. BMP DDB, London.*

Two postcards with very bent pictures. Saatchi & Saatchi, Singapore, used four straight words ("Welcome to Animal Planet") while O&M's Bangkok hotshop Results used only a Ray-Ban logo.

A straight picture can always be liberated by a bent headline. If all you can afford is the product shot, you can still achieve the cutting edge.

Saatchi & Saatchi, London.

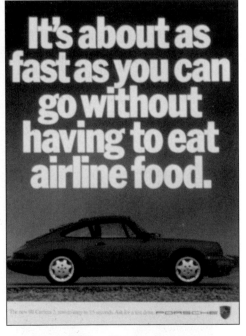

Fallon Minneapolis.

Having a beautiful picture is *not* an idea. Thousands of ads have beautiful pictures and become beautiful wallpaper. You will still need a bent headline for a cutting edge juxtaposition.

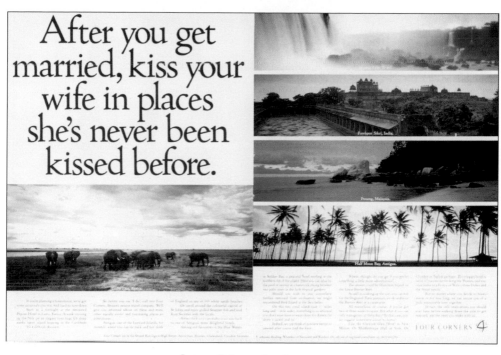

Leagas Delaney, London.

Not all postcards need words.

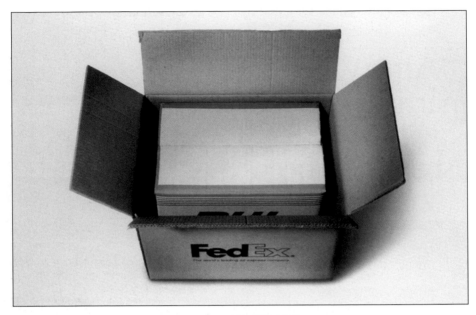

BBDO, Bangkok, for Federal Express.

Not all postcards have pictures.

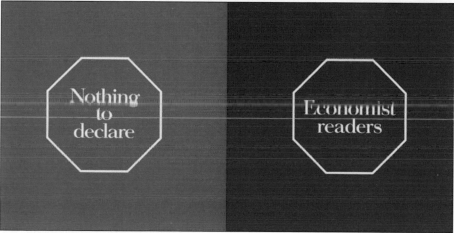

*Abbott Mead Vickers, London, proving five or six
words are all you need.*

Not all postcards have bent pictures.

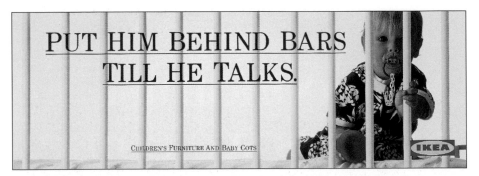

Dentsu Young & Rubicam, Singapore.

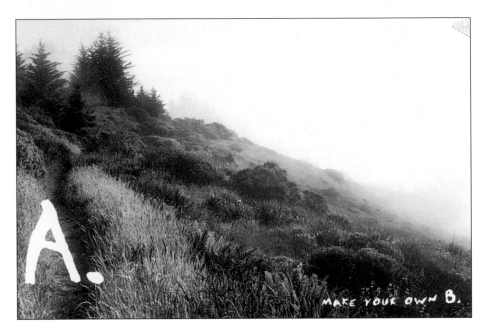

Leagas Delaney, London.

There is no law that says you cannot mix ads with bent headlines and ads with bent pictures in the same campaign. It is like mixing postcards and letters in the same campaign; it adds spontaneity. For WFLD-TV Chicago, Fallon bent their headlines whenever they used straight library pictures. When they could create their own pictures, they bent them and wrote straight headlines.

Fallon Minneapolis.

Or, Will You Use Typography Instead?

You can still send a postcard with a bent picture, even when there is no picture.

A typographical ad communicates the idea solely by typography. There are no other visuals whatsoever.

The two rules of the genre are simple. The headline or copy should be straight; the typography provides the bent picture. If the words are bent as well, it does not work. And, if a shape or an object has been formed typographically, there should always be enough space in the ad to frame it. If the shape runs edge to edge, there is a risk it will not be recognisable.

Typographical ads can communicate ideas which cannot be expressed in traditional ways. Agency Houston Herstek Favat of Boston formed a typographical message into the actual shape and size of a two-month-old baby's lungs. The copy described the effects of second-hand cigarette smoke on babies for the Massachusetts Department of Public Health.

When competitors all use visuals, a typographical campaign can disrupt the category. For example, the Mates Condoms campaign formed straight product statements into the shapes of copulating couples. For property consultants Jones Lang Wootton, Australian agency OMON constructed a headline in the shape of a skyscraper. It posed the question: *What happens to your new building if experts aren't handling the finance?* The answer appeared alongside; the headline had collapsed into a pathetic jumble of tangled letters.

Typographical ideas can turn low-budget print ads into highly visible cutting edge print ads.

Everything is possible.

Not all typographical ideas are based on making shapes out of words. Some communicate what might happen without the product by removing key letters or words. Others represent the product typographically as an intellectual challenge to sophisticated audiences.

At a time when people are debating whether print ads should be visual or verbal, the typographical genre comes into its own. As Guido Heffels says: "You can't make a distinction between words and pictures any more. Words have become pictures, pictures have become words. This is the rich language an art director or copywriter should use to express his ideas. The choice between words and pictures is only the search for the best expression, and the 'words' which express the idea best are the ones you should use."

If Heffels is right, the typographical option could well be where visual and verbal meet best.

What happens typographically with and without JLW. OMON, Sydney.

Charter Regional Medical Center. Scott Sheinberg, writer and executive creative director at Henderson Advertising, Greenville, South Carolina, discusses the strategy behind the breast cancer ad seen in Chapter 1 of this book.

"In concepting the ad, our goal was to force the involvement of the audience. Women typically don't read mammography ads or literature because it's something they would rather not think about. So we sought a solution that had a sufficiently provocative headline to lead the reader to the body copy."

The headline, *Can you find the lump in this breast?*, led readers into copy typographically shaped as a breast. The breast, however, served more than a visual function.

"The period (full stop) in line 17 is the same size as lumps which can be detected in a mammogram," explains Sheinberg.

The copy, which urged women readers to have a mammogram, concluded: "If you haven't found the lump by now, chances are, you're not going to. It was in the 17th line. The period at the end of the sentence was slightly larger than the others. So think about it, if you couldn't find it with your eyes, imagine how hard it would be to find it with your hands."

As Sheinberg says: "The only way to illustrate that concept was typography." The judges at Britain's D&AD agreed.

Levi's. The famous Levi's fingerprint ad demonstrates the rules of the genre. The words are straight, the picture is bent. The six words, *No two pairs are the same*, are repeated endlessly, typographically crafted into the whorls of a fingerprint. Adequate white space allows the fingerprint shape to be recognisable. The Levi's logo is the only other visual element in the ad.

Hegarty reviews the concept: "Jeans are unique as a product, and Levi's are the original, in that they are identified as your own by the way you wear them. They become a part of you. There are very few products that we ever own that actually have that quality, that as you wear them they become more of your personality. If you wear them at the knee more, they will show that. If you always put something in your back pocket, they will show that. The way you wear them becomes a part of you. The fingerprint was simply to say they're as individual as your fingerprint, and we thought it would be very nice to make the type work within the fingerprint as a way of pulling the two things together."

Singapore Ministry of Health. A low-interest subject and a low budget suggested typography for a dental health message. Creative director Garry Abbott recalls: "We didn't have any money for photography, and frankly what could we show anyhow? Decayed teeth would be a turn off, while perfect teeth would make us look like a toothpaste ad."

Abbott believes typographical ads cut through against traditional ones. "We took a very simple campaign statement and simply let the key word, *teeth*, drop from the headline. It communicated instantly and, just as importantly, worked as well in Chinese as it did in English."

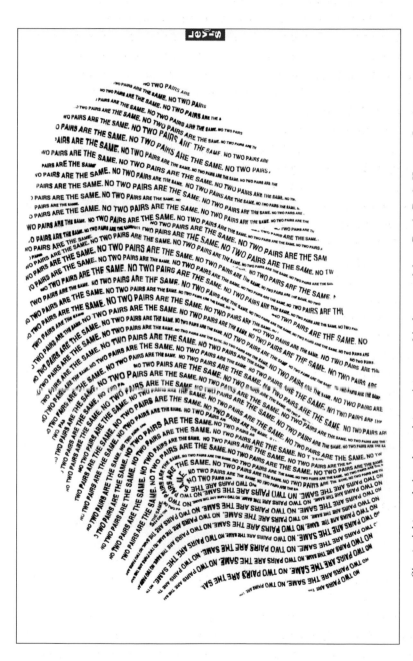

Six straight words in a bent picture. A typographical postcard from Bartle Bogle Hegarty, London.

Brushing, flossing and seeing your dentist keep your gums healthy and help stop your falling out.

*t*eeth

HEALTHY TEETH NEED HEALTHY GUMS. Ministry of Health

A low-interest subject on a low budget. Using a straight headline, bent typography worked by suggestion. Ketchum Advertising for the Singapore Ministry of Health.

Art director Heintje Moo and typographer Gordon Tan selected Ticonderoga as a sufficiently decayed typeface to convey the message. A Chinese typeface was modified to replicate it.

The work was selected by the Type Directors Club of New York for its Best of Ten Years Advertising Typography exhibition.

J&B Scotch Whisky. "Sometimes," says Roy Grace at Grace & Rothschild, New York, "when you're blessed, or cursed, with some horrible looking product, you make an asset of it."

With Volkswagen as his creative lodestar, Grace grappled with branding. "The typography of the J and the B was some sort of crushed Clarendon. So I had somebody create a typeface to match it, so we would have at least uniform ugliness."

The idea for a typographical campaign based on the J and B was an inspiration. In retrospect, as always, it looks so obvious.

"Sometimes you can pound your head into the wall and the most obvious solution eludes you. Some sort of electronic pulse occurs in the brain, based on assimilating as much information as you can," Grace believes. "I've always been a proponent of that old parable of the monkey sitting down at a typewriter. Given enough time, it will write every great novel. Given enough time, and enough information, you will come up with a great ad."

In fealty to Bill Bernbach, he kept the product out of the ads.

 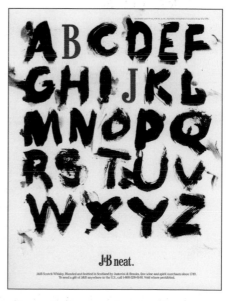

A classic typographical campaign where the product name drives the idea.
Postcards with bent pictures and straight headlines from
Grace & Rothschild, New York.

Strokes of genius from M&C Saatchi, Singapore.
Chinese, a pictographic language, is perfect for typographical ideas.

BMW. Chinese is a pictographic language. Certain combinations of strokes convey pictorial meanings. So not only can Chinese copywriters play with words, they can play with pictures within the words. Small wonder, then, that Chinese lends itself perfectly to typographical ideas.

The BMW campaign from M&C Saatchi, Singapore, broke convention by being originally conceived in Chinese. It proved so popular that an English version ran later. Usually in Singapore, campaigns are conceptualised in English first.

Typographically, it draws two contrasts: between the crowd and the individualist in one ad; between crudity and refinement in the other.

The first ad is based on the Chinese word *rén*, meaning a person. In fact, the Chinese character rather resembles a running man. The Chinese word for a crowd, *zhòng*, looks not unlike *rén* written three times. Taken together, *zhòng rén* means everybody. By contrasting a crowd, going around in circles, with the single individualist, the BMW owner is appropriately flattered. While the English subheads couch this thought in philosophical language, the Chinese original appears at first quite blunt. It reads, literally, *Everybody is befuddled; I alone am clear minded.* The Chinese subheads balance four characters on either side of the equation, a favourite linguistic gambit. But the fourth character, *zuì*, and the eighth character, *xǐng*, share the Chinese pictograph for alcohol, thereby conveying a meaning far deeper and more subtle than any two English words could ever achieve. *Zuì* expresses intoxication and stupefaction; *xǐng* implies a revival of conscious thought.

In the second ad, the character reversed out of black is *tǔ*, meaning soil or earth. Its long base stroke indicates a picture of the ground. By shortening the base stroke, and lengthening the cross stroke above, it becomes an entirely different word: *shì*, meaning a scholar or a refined, commendable person. So the reader has two choices: without the product, he is earthly bound; with the product, he will be one of the worldly elite.

The campaign was conceived and art directed by Yue Chee Guan. The Chinese copy was written by Linda Leong; the English by Paul Ruta.

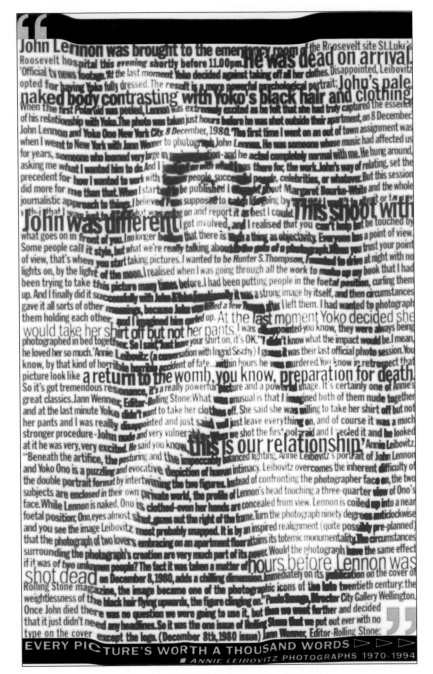

A postcard from Saatchi & Saatchi, Wellington.
A typographically bent picture with a straight headline,
turning Annie Leibovitz's words into one of her greatest photographs.

City Gallery. Saatchi & Saatchi, Wellington, broke conventions when advertising an exhibition of Annie Leibovitz photographs; firstly, by choosing not to show her work in the ads, and then by choosing a typographical idea to announce the event.

The concept uses Leibovitz's own words to replicate one of the world's most famous photographic icons: her shot of a naked John Lennon in the foetal position, embracing Yoko Ono, only hours before his murder. The image of John and Yoko emerges through a sepia sea of words. Typographer Len Cheeseman, formerly of Collett Dickenson Pearce, London, magnifies certain poignant phrases: *This shoot with John was different ... a return to the womb, preparation for death ... this is our relationship.*

CHOOSING whether to send a postcard or a letter, whether to bend the headline or the picture, or choosing to do a typographical ad instead, will help determine whether your ideas reach the cutting edge.

But beware of genre conventions. For example, the visual pun is becoming a formula in itself. As Nick Bell, executive creative director at Leo Burnett, London observes: "This type of ad does particularly well at Cannes where pure visuals break through language barriers. But it is becoming boring, and I think more innovation and intelligence needs to be brought to the medium. There is a difference between the visual pun and the purely visual ad. I am all for the latter if it is the simplest, purest way to communicate the message."

As the great Hollywood screenplay guru Robert McKee will tell you, genre conventions are not carved in stone. "They evolve, grow, adapt, modify, and break apace with the changes in society. As society enters each new phase, the genres transform with it. If a genre becomes inflexible and cannot bend with the changing world, it petrifies." His advice applies to advertising genres just as much as it does to movies.

What follows next is execution, perhaps the most perilous phase of all. The crafts of art direction and copywriting will determine whether everything is won or lost.

7

HOW TO CRAFT VISUALS

There is nothing more fragile than a great idea in the wrong hands.

"The problem is," says Bob Isherwood, "ideas have to be executed. Someone has to be able to art direct it, someone has to be able to write the copy, otherwise the idea doesn't end up looking very good. I think there is a lot missing in what are basic craft skills."

The strongest ideas in this book are the simplest. And, in every case, their art direction has kept them focused. To the unwary, the word *craft* can imply complexity; crafting an ad means complicating it, layering it with dozens of executional touches, decorating it to death.

Craft really means judgement. Craft can mean subtraction as well as addition. Craft means being appropriate. Craft means knowing when an extra detail can be added, when an extra layer of technique cannot. Craft is the watchdog of clarity.

In the same way you were asked to commit yourself to some new philosophies about advertising, brand building and generating ideas, cutting edge creativity asks you to commit yourself to a new perspective on craftwork.

"I'm not sure these days if people have the same crafting commitment," challenges Ian Batey. "We used to eliminate, eliminate, eliminate. We finessed ads right up to the time they went to press. Now I think we've lost the plot a bit. It's not important to people any more. You don't see the kind of print work that Neil French did any more, you don't see the startling stuff."

What do we see?

Roy Grace calls it high mediocrity. "Everything looks pleasant. There are so many people out there who are slick; they can make things look good. But it's sort of like cotton candy. Empty inside. What's happened, because of the present structure of the advertising business, the testing and research, the bottom of American advertising has been cut away and discarded. You don't see the real awful stuff as much. But so have the heights gone, too. You don't see that real great stuff, either. That's what's missing for me. We're too polished, we're too slick."

Grace recalls a conversation he used to have with Helmut Krone: "We used to talk about this, fifteen years ago. We were always striving for a way to articulate it. It was the need to be wrong, the need to be ugly, the need to take people off guard. Everything was so polished. There is a certain advantage in always going against the grain. We need to do stuff that's a little *raw*."

John Messum recalls Paul Arden saying a similar thing: "Paul would ask, what can we do that's *wrong*? What happens if we do it wrong?" Messum believes it can force you to break out. "You make rules for yourself. If you can break out of them, you'll find something more exciting. Doing things wrongly sometimes leads to a more surprising solution."

WHAT DOES ART DIRECTION HAVE TO DO?

"The number one requirement," stipulates Bill Oberlander, "is for an ad to captivate the heart and soul of the reader, and that basically comes from powerful art direction. A lot of agencies historically have presented art direction as kind of *decorative*. Art direction is considered an aesthetic that happens after the fact." Oberlander believes art direction should happen at the same time as the idea. "You have to find some kind of visual equity in the brand, and then activate it, and exponentially multiply it through all the communication levels. First and foremost is amazing art direction, relevant to the brand's emotional equity with consumers."

At Bates Dorland, creative director Jay Pond-Jones considers art direction can differentiate one brand from another. "The point is, how can the look and feel of an idea be most wholly differentiated from the competition, and from the media environment? Sometimes, with the best ads, the line is very hard to draw between art or advertising. Occasionally, you can get to communication that's like art in its originality, or naïvety, or simplicity. But that's very rare."

Simplicity will be a recurring theme.

In the hands of great art directors, great ideas are never obscured. They are strengthened by minute attention to craft details, including the craft of reduction.

For example, there is no rule that says strong ideas can only work on white backgrounds. It is not formulaic. But it is commonsense. *When in doubt, leave a great idea alone.*

As you will see, great art direction is about judgement, moving an idea in stages through a series of crafting decisions.

When to keep it simple

□ HEREDITY   □ ENVIRONMENT   □ JUBILAEUM
(CHOOSE ONE)

KEEP EVOLVING.

Why bury a breakthrough idea?
Besides which, a white
background lets the reader
tick the little boxes.
Fallon Minneapolis.

Keeping it simple at Dentsu Young & Rubicam Singapore for radio station Class 95 FM. Art directors: Tan Han Ming and Patrick Low. Writer: Mark Fong.

CHAPTER 7

*"Nobody was going to read
a letter about teeth," says
creative director Garry Abbott.
So writer Daniel Lim and
art director Heintje Moo crafted
postcards with bent pictures and
straight headlines. The background
was not taken for granted, either.
It was left stark and clean.
Ketchum Advertising for the
Singapore Ministry of Health.*

When to add another layer

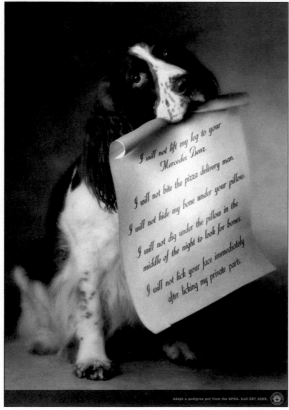

One compelling idea, flawlessly art directed by Edmund Choe. The visual elements have been reduced to two: the bent picture incorporating Jagdish Ramakrishnan's charming copy, and a straight headline at the base. Choe follows the rules of the postcard genre, letting the visual dominate ninety-five percent of the ad. Evidence of craft is everywhere, yet it upholds every tenet of cutting edge creativity. A Gold at Cannes was not surprising. Saatchi & Saatchi, Singapore, for the SPCA.

When to keep layering

When appropriate, a richer visual texture can convey atmosphere without burying the idea. Saatchi & Saatchi, London, for the Department of Health/COI.

When to craft a classic

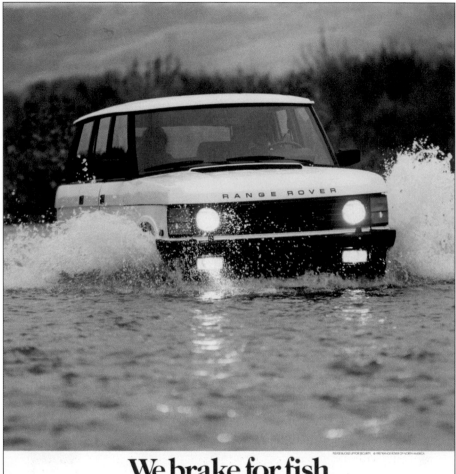

When in doubt, craft a classic. A classic layout, with classic typography.
A bent headline with a straight picture, from Grace & Rothschild, New York.

IS LESS MORE?

"I'm into very minimal art direction," Neil French declares. "I think it was Chet Baker who said, 'It takes a very, very good drummer to be better than no drummer at all'. I'm inclined to think that about art direction. It takes a very, very good art director to be better than no art director at all. So what I try to do is express things as simply as possible, and hope that because it's expressed so simply, the core idea will come across. Sometimes the art direction is a bit flat, and that's my fault, and sometimes the sparsity of it actually makes it work, which is also my fault."

Gary Goldsmith echoes his sentiment. "I'm from the school that thinks people should be able to understand the ad. There was a period where it was almost like if you can read it, and if you can get it, it must not be very good. I'm all for experimental type, and doing really quirky, unusual stuff. Just because a lot of my stuff tends to be more straight, does not mean I don't like work that's more experimental. I do. But," he stipulates, "it's still got to ultimately make sense."

Dean Hanson is another minimalist. "People are more bombarded with imagery every day and if you keep it simple, like a billboard, you will win. The odds of it breaking through are multiplied exponentially." Hanson recalls judging the Clios. "The ads that cut through like crazy were from Singapore and Hong Kong. I assume the reason they're so simple is because of the language barriers they have to jump over. They have to be visual. Most of the time, if it can be done visually, it should be done visually. If you can tell the story visually, with a minimum of copy, and reduce the elements, you're so far ahead of the game. In the award shows, those are the ones that score." One exception, Hanson considers, is when you have to educate people about a totally new product. "*Then* you have to tell the story. Sometimes, long copy ads in the Neil French school are a breath of fresh air because you're just not seeing long copy any more. Long copy has really taken a hit, so when you do see it, and if it's well written, it can be very effective."

"More often than not, when you see too much flimmery and flammery," David Abbott believes, "it's camouflage for a lack of a strong central idea. The art directors I've worked with have all come from the DDB tradition. They've all been interested in what I've been interested in, which is not ornamentation, but simplicity, and clarity, and strength. So I've never had that problem, but obviously one observes it in other people, where I think people put too much into the ad and lose the strength of the idea."

Norman Alcuri opposes art direction which gets in the way of the idea. Ideas never go out of fashion, Alcuri believes; ornamentation does. "I'd be a happy man if, for the rest of my life, I could just do ads with three-quarters picture, headline underneath, three columns of type, logo bottom right, with *brilliant* ideas in them," he confesses. "Who needs art direction?"

When Bill Gallacher art directs, he thinks about the amount of time the message will have to sink in. "People aren't waiting for your ad. They're seeing thousands of visual messages every day. You have to carve a way through that by the mere thought in the ad. So your level of art direction has to hit that point. If I want someone to think longer about it, I'll add more layers."

"My things tend to be real minimalistic," admits Bob Barrie. "I see other people doing the exact opposite and being successful, but I think, generally, as a rule, simpler is better."

Some would argue that simple means simplistic, minimalist means cold and devoid of emotion. If execution can help separate brands, why opt for sparsity?

"I am a fundamental believer that it is the idea which drives things," says John Hegarty. "On my wall, I have a little blown-up quote from the dictionary and it says, 'An idea is a thought or plan formed by mental effort'. In other words, the colour blue is *not* an idea. Wonky type is *not* an idea. It's a means of making your idea more profound, or of exaggerating it. Each idea determines if it should be minimalist or more adorned. You must listen to the vibrations that the idea is sending out to you. *You* have to decide what is right." Hegarty believes the debate between different styles of art direction is nothing new. "We think it's a new debate because of technology, because of the Mac, but the Renaissance painters had the same problem. We all know the story. Christ was born of the Virgin Mary, He died on the Cross, rose from the dead after three days, and went to Heaven. The Church kept saying to them, well, paint us these pictures so that people will believe, and they had to come up with different versions of it to make people think, wow, I didn't quite see it like that."

WHEN SHOULD YOU STOP ART DIRECTING AN AD?

"You just know," says Ron Mather. "You start to feel you should leave it alone. I hate overcrafted ads. In fact, I hate overcrafted anything. Great typography or exquisite photography will never save a bad idea."

"Once you've communicated the idea in the strongest possible way, then you quit," concurs Goldsmith. "Some people build a certain fussiness into a lot of their work. Unless the idea requires that type of art direction, I don't feel the need to put artifice all over it."

"When you know that it's communicating at its clearest," maintains Andrew Clarke, "and you're pretty sure that what you've done to the ad, in terms of art direction, isn't destroying the idea, that's when you stop."

"When it touches the nerve that runs right through the middle of you," says Gallacher. "There's no logical reason, you just look at it and think, that's close to the pattern of the idea you had in your head when you thought up the idea. When the art direction reaches that imaginary point in your head, you think, right, stop there."

"When is the moment to stop? Taste tells you," Hegarty believes. "There is no absolute moment. So much of what we do is about taste. I've observed that about the people who are more successful at this craft, or at any expression of creativity. It becomes more about taste than anything else. I'm increasingly getting to the point in life when I say most things are about taste. It's like a client buying a good strategy, it's like a client understanding why one particular ad is better than another. It comes down to taste. People are attracted to taste and style; they don't actually know why they are attracted to those things, but they are."

"When the art direction gets in the way of the communication, that's when you should definitely throw it out," says Antony Redman, who describes himself as an intuitive art director. "I never had any formal training as an art director. I've always worked by myself out of necessity; the best art directors at The Ball Partnership were always occupied, working with their writers, so I was more or less *forced* to art direct my own stuff. So I can only go with my gut. I can't sit and craft for weeks. I just go with what my heart says." Redman says he art directs quickly. "I tend to play with the layouts for one or two days, until I've got something I'm happy with, then I'll work it out properly. I think you know when you're over art directing something, when you're gilding the lily, because you start thinking about it way too much, it all gets too fancy."

Barrie, a confessed minimalist, recognises a new dichotomy in art direction. "Once, my answer used to be when the ad didn't suffer by removing an element. Neil French has that wonderful talk he gives about removing all the elements from an ad and getting it down into its purest form. I still think a lot of great work is done that way. But, the world's changing, and especially young people seem to be digesting things differently," he points out. "What I've seen in focus groups is that they really get into complicated things, packed with information. They like studying all the subtle little nuances. So my answer now is, I think it varies, depending on the audience. There are probably five hundred and sixty-two extraneous elements in our Miller Lite print ads, but they work. In the case of more youth-oriented advertising, young people would get bored by simplicity. They want to dig into some meat."

Barrie's colleague at Fallon Minneapolis, Tom Lichtenheld, who has won some of the most substantial awards in the industry, believes in tweaking things to death. "And then some," he adds. "My motto is, anything that's worth doing, is worth *over*doing. I don't think you can stop tweaking too late. I don't mean you should overproduce it or overembellish it, I just mean paying attention to detail. Making sure every element is in the right place. It's a matter of taking things out, especially in photography, until the idea is left with nothing superfluous."

Lichtenheld talks about the joys of crafting an ad at his computer. "It's that rare kind of quiet time, with me and my pencil and piece of paper. I do my sketches on paper, but my final tweaking is on the Mac. There are always the formulae that will work, but one of the challenges is to push beyond those, even when you're comfortable with them. I see work these days which has the classic elements, a great headline and an interesting visual, and then somebody has gone beyond any format I've ever seen and brought a completely new look to it. Usually it involves more integration of those things than I've seen before. In other words, there will be *less* difference between the visual and the headline; either the type is worked into the visual, or the type is designed in conjunction with the visual so there's a completely designed unit, no part of which is just laid on top of another. I think it's a real achievement to take classic elements and bring design on top of that, to make it a thing of beauty as well as a great concept."

"I'd infinitely rather fall into the trap of overcrafting an ad than undercrafting it," confesses Graham Warsop, "though clearly a healthy balance is preferable. To me, style is very important. If advertising looks cheap, people will assume the product is inferior. Whilst it may be true that no consumer looks at your ad and says, 'Nice use of Gill Sans, the 7-point type really does work a treat', I do believe that consumers today show more appreciation for aesthetics than ever before. A while ago, *Time* magazine devoted a cover story to Design – showing how consumers today don't simply want better, they also want better looking. So whether or not a consumer can rationalise why something that looks a certain way is appealing to them is less important than the fact that 'better designed', 'more stylish' and 'crafted' seem to influence their purchase decisions." Warsop spends many hours in bookshops, engrossed in studying the design and typography of book jackets. "My belief is that the aesthetics of a print ad are largely intuitive in that the art director or creative director can look at a piece of work and immediately know how it can be improved."

Oberlander reviews ads by looking at them upside down. "I don't care to read them until I know the art direction is telling a story," he explains. "The way an ad looks can actually say more than the words themselves. So you push the art direction, push it and push it and push it, until you don't know where to look on the page first. Then you can develop the sense of prioritisation, where you want them to look first, second, and third. Obviously, the ad must have some kind of intellectual proposition, too, that connects the brand to the consumer, something that makes them think: that brand thinks like

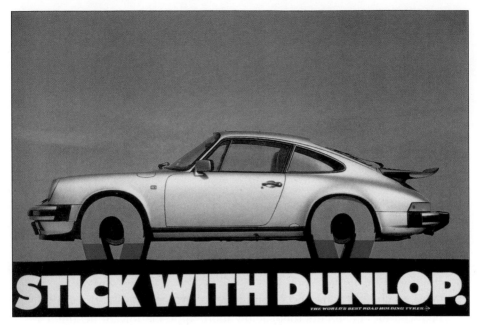

The Campaign Palace demonstrates how art direction can achieve simplicity
and clarity. For Dunlop (above), the idea was the only thing on the page.
For Australian Beef (opposite), a more complex communication,
layout elements were reduced by integration. With less difference between
the visual and the headline, readers were led to the copy argument faster.

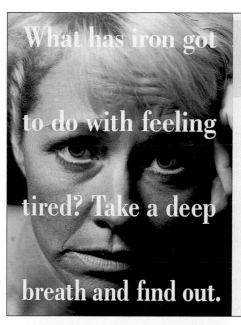

What has iron got to do with feeling tired? Take a deep breath and find out.

Your lungs are now full of air, the most important part of which is oxygen.

But it's not just your lungs that need oxygen, every cell in your body does.

So how do you get it to your toes, the tips of your fingers and your ear lobes?

By attaching it to the iron rich cells in your blood stream. Simple and efficient.

Unless, like seven out of ten Australian women aged 25-54, you're not getting your recommended intake of iron.

Or worse still, you're among the one in three running an increased risk of iron deficiency and quite possibly experiencing symptoms such as fatigue, lethargy and lack of concentration.

You may also find yourself more prone to illness and infections.

And in severe cases, become anaemic.

All because you haven't got enough iron to carry oxygen to where it's needed.

The early warning signs of a possible iron problem are so familiar that many women dismiss them as 'normal'.

Others blame their tiredness on another aspect of their life. Stress, raising a family or lack of sleep, for instance.

All of which may be contributing factors. But lack of iron could be another.

So how can you tell if you're not getting enough iron?

And what can you do about it if you aren't?

Firstly, if you recognise any of the symptoms we've described, ask your doctor to check your ferritin level (iron stores).

If it's particularly low your doctor may prescribe an iron supplement in the short term.

However, nutrition experts agree that for most women a change of diet to include iron rich foods is by far the more natural and effective long term solution.

(Especially for those who can barely remember the last time they weren't on some kind of fad diet.)

One of the best iron rich foods readily available is lean beef.

As part of a balanced diet, the Australian Nutrition Foundation recognises it as one of the richest sources of iron.

It also helps you absorb up to four times the iron from other foods, like vegetables.

If you'd like more information on iron and how to make sure you're getting enough, please write to Nutrition Communications, PO Box 4429, Sydney 2001.

The good news is that lack of iron is one women's problem that's, more often than not, very easily solved.

Doesn't that make you breathe easier?

Are you getting your essential daily iron?

SUPPORTED BY AUSTRALIAN NUTRITION FOUNDATION

Source: National Dietary Survey of Adults, 1983.

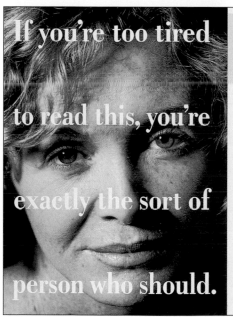

If you're too tired to read this, you're exactly the sort of person who should.

Do the words run down, listless, worn out, lethargic or sluggish ever describe you?

You are not alone.

A great many women feel exactly the same and lack of iron may be to blame.

Perhaps it's time you did something about it. Reading this could be your first step.

You may be wondering why everyone is suddenly talking about iron.

Is it misuse of the month? Another dietary fad that will disappear as miraculously as it came to light?

Unfortunately not. The iron issue is very much a fact of modern life.

Seven out of every ten Australian women aged between 25-54 years aren't getting their recommended intake of iron.

With at least one in three running an increased risk of iron deficiency which may eventually progress to anaemia.

Most of us always knew we needed iron. But no one ever told us why. So let's start right at the beginning.

Iron is important for several reasons. Maintaining a healthy immune system and energy production are two of them.

But by far its most vital function is carrying oxygen in our blood.

If we don't have enough iron, our muscles don't get enough oxygen and that's when we can start to feel tired and run down.

Unfortunately, this is so familiar to many women that they simply dismiss it as being, well, normal.

Others blame something else in their life. A busy schedule, stress, not sleeping well, sometimes even the weather.

All of which may be contributing factors, but lack of iron may well be another.

So what can you do about it?

What sort of things should you be eating to top up your iron stores?

Are iron supplements the answer?

According to the nutritional experts who agree that for most women it is much better to obtain nutrients from natural food sources.

The Australian Nutrition Foundation recommends a balanced diet including foods rich in the two types of iron.

Haem iron (found in red meat, poultry and seafood) and non-haem iron (found in breads, vegetables, cereals etc).

Of the two, haem iron foods contain iron in a form that is much more easily absorbed by the body.

For instance, a moderate 125g grilled lean rump steak has about three times more iron than a regular 70g serving of cooked spinach.

On top of which, twelve times as much of the iron present is absorbed.

As a general rule, the redder the meat, the higher the iron content.

Which is why lean beef is recognised as one of the best sources of daily iron.

If you think you might have an iron problem see your doctor and ask about your ferritin level (iron stores).

Or if you'd like more information why not call 008 675 892 right now.

And if you're too tired to pick up the phone? You guessed it.

You're exactly the sort of person who should.

Are you getting your essential daily iron?

AS CHOSEN BY AUSTRALIAN NUTRITION FOUNDATION

Source: National Dietary Survey of Adults, 1983.

me, I like that brand, that brand is a friend of mine, I will take it into my life."

Goldsmith reviews ads by putting them up on a wall and looking at them from ten feet away. "I don't want to know what product the ad's for. If it's a car ad, I don't want to know it's a car ad. I want to think, maybe that's a soup ad. If it's a soup ad, I want to think, maybe that's a liquor ad. I'm looking for that element of surprise." When Goldsmith is art directing his own work, he will often list all the *clichéd* visuals in the category. "If I'm doing an ad for a bank, I'll list all those things like guys in suits, a vault, handshakes, smiles, money. If I do end up using one of those visuals, I've done it *consciously*. I've chosen to use it because I'm going to defile it or something, or go against it in some way."

Clarke stands on a chair to review his own work. "If I stand a bit higher, I can see everything better. Not so much for magazine ads, but definitely for posters. If I stand eight feet away from it, I can see it in its entirety. I always believe in mapping out the ideas first on paper. But if I'm working on a Mac, believe me, I *don't* put my Mac on the floor," Clarke adds.

TYPOGRAPHY: A QUESTION OF CONTROVERSY

If print had music, it would be typography.

Typefaces are decoded as we read. The cut of each letter will transmit dozens of signals to the brain. Typography underscores words with emotional presence, creates atmosphere, colours the way we want our messages interpreted.

As Gerard Stamp explains, "A typeface can add colour to an ad. Some look serious, some look fun, some look feminine, some look aggressive. The sort of personality you want to convey about the brand should guide your choice of typeface. A word of warning, though: less is definitely more with typefaces. The fewer the better."

But with the advent of the Mac, thousands of new faces and typographical techniques have been spawned overnight. Type is being bashed, mutilated, distorted for effect, rather than for effective communication. The tyranny of the Mac enslaves; the mouse has become the umbilical cord of creativity. Anyone who can work a Mac can be an art director or, as Alcuri calls them, a "Mac hack". Even scarier is the fact that the new high-tech typographical weaponry is available to consumers at home. The mystique of print creativity is evaporating.

Two art directors have become the world's masters of typography: Neil Godfrey dominated the British industry; Neil French roamed the Asian stage. Their perspectives are sobering.

"Papert Koenig & Lois in New York, led by George Lois, one of the really all-time great designers, virtually did all their work with one typeface, Franklin Gothic," Godfrey recalls. "The discipline was that it was the ideas that counted, not the typeface. I probably haven't ever used more than about eight or ten typefaces; I tend to find the most legible ones."

Godfrey has received more coveted Pencils in Britain's Design and Art Direction awards than any other art director. "You're always safe using Franklin Gothic and Gill; they don't date very much. In serif faces, one of my favourites is Plantin. Type is about colour, as much as anything else, and when you do long copy ads, you find that maybe only half a dozen typefaces give you the right greyness on the page."

Legibility should be a prime concern. "When I worked with a copywriter who spent several days of his time writing a fabulous piece of copy, the first thing I would do was make it legible." Godfrey has seen dozens of fads come and go. "I hated that period when everyone put in bags of line spacing; you could drive a bus down it. If you tried to read it, you had to make a big jump down to the next line. As soon as somebody does something slightly different, everybody else wants to do it. And yet the reason it was different in the first place was completely appropriate. It may work again in a similar idea, but *why* do similar ideas?"

Godfrey introduced many techniques which today are commonplace. "Bill Bernbach got incredibly excited when I did a campaign with David Abbott. I dropped pieces of wheat into the copy, and ran the copy around them. Then everyone started running copy around things."

Godfrey was modifying typefaces long before the computer era. "A lot of people used to accept a typeface for what it was. But what I used to do was either cut the ascenders down, or lengthen them, to

"IT'S AN UNMITIGATED PIECE OF SHIT AND WE SHOULDN'T EVEN BE TALKING ABOUT IT!"

It was the tea-break. Outside, an excavator clawed disconsolately at the red mud.

Steve Dunn, checked shirt glowing like an inquisitor's brazier, his eyes burning with Jesuit certainty, gripped his polystyrene cup, and leant forward. His voice hissed, as steam from the fires of hell.

"And what's more, this is the most banal conversation I've ever had."

John 'Once-I-start-laughing-I-just-can't-stop' Curran eased his chair back. This was obviously not going to be an opportunity for non-stop hilarity.

"Couldn't we give it an award for lateral thinking?" Siimon Reynolds' fine, ascetic features a study in serious. His ensemble of stockbroker-striped shirt twinned with vivid lime-green Bermuda shorts belying the impression somewhat.

He switched to the smile. The sun came out. Birds sang.

Some were tempted. Not Dunn.

"That's like saying let's make a TV commercial really badly and expecting a prize for originality!" The knuckles whitened; the cup resigned itself to a non-biodegradable eternity.

Indra Sinha's Himalayan bulk was seen to shift one millimetre to the left. Totally overwhelmed, his chair leant with him. No choice. That or join the cup.

The voice, sonorous as the Ganges in flood, the eyes hawk-hooded, the face a temple mask:

"Jim..." a conciliatory rumble, "Can we give it anything at all?"

The adjudicator consulted the book of rules. Unnecessarily. "It's either in or out. Simple as that."

Silence.

The auditor, anxious, hovering like a nervous waiter. "We're ready for E22 to E30..."

"What's that?" snapped Dunn.

Siimon levitated, glowing. "English Language. Print Campaigns. Let's do it."

Like predators roaming a twilight jungle, the five figures passed softly among the serried sentinel display boards.

Tunes of Glory there were, in the background, if you listened hard. But you had to strain your ears through the cacophony of dreams crushed by the jackboot of logic. Hopes died quietly; an early night in a singles bar. Unloved. Unnoticed, even. Sad.

As much-vaunted reputations bluffed and blustered their way to the slaughter, uncaring ballpoints dispatched cherished brainchildren to cold oblivion.

Pages flicking, shuffling. The only sounds in the morgue.

Dour faces collecting the sheets. Compiling, computing, calculating: God bless the accountants.

♦

"I think it's terrific." David Fowler's eyes shone like the stars on Sunset.

"Well I think it's shit. Would you really, seriously trust your business to a bank that so blatantly tells lies in its own advertising?" Sinha was massively, and implacably, immovable.

He blinked, it is said. Once.

Fowler's gunslinger drawl gave the lie to his bank-clerk stature. "Well, my only question is what to give it, that's all."

"I know what I'd like to do with it. I'd like to set fire to the effing thing."

It was getting late.

♦

Tense. Coiled. Steve Dunn, a snake about to strangle a chicken: "It is an insult to bald people."

"It's not. I don't find it in the least bit insulting." Fowler. No chicken, he.

"You're an expert?"

"Well, yes. I'd consider myself an expert." Fowler smiled. His eyes didn't. A blood-red ribbon restrained his flowing pony-tail . But above it, skullwise, barely a suspicion of fuzz.

"He's trying to tell you he's bald; he'd buy the damn stuff," snorted Indra.

"That's not the point at all," Dunn persisted. "The ad is a bloody insult."

As silent as a snowdrift, five men sat and contemplated their criteria.

It was late. And getting later.

♦

Indra, prowling; an intellectual bear trapped in a cave of mere advertising, chubby Buddha-fingers clutching at a clipboard, relentlessly hunting for any piece of copy Neil French hadn't written:

"We've missed something. There's a great bit, somewhere in the stuff we threw out while we were looking for something else." If Sinha's syntax was slipping, his resolve certainly wasn't.

"Dammit, we can hardly penalise the man for being good." Dunn was in danger of becoming charitable.

Sinha wasn't.

Hollow-eyed, the helpers dragged a truckload of what had so nearly been scrap cardboard back across the floor.

Were there living among those who had been presumed dead?

It was going to be a very late night.

♦

From March 9th to the 12th, 1991, Singapore advertising stood accused of complacency, incest and self-indulgence.

Five men considered their verdict.

Those who were acquitted appear in the 1991 Gong Show Annual. S$190.

No, not an account executive. Another award-winning ad.

SOME FUNNY POSITIONS YOU CAN GET YOURSELF INTO.

Account Service

Account Service people: Commonly known as The Suits, bless 'em. They are the frontline troops of the agency; the intrepid people who advise, beg, cajole, and have lunch with, clients.

The pecking order in Client Service goes: Client Service Director, then Account Director, and Account Manager, after that come the Account Executive, Assistant Account Executive, Messenger, Tea-lady, Cleaner, and Trainee Account Executive.

Regardless of whether you are a Bachelor of Business Administration, or a Professor of Dental Surgery, or merely a taxi driver right now, you'll probably start in advertising as a Trainee Account Executive: The Lowest Form of Life.

(Frankly, a degree might help. But what will help more is a love of great advertising, and a burning passion to see it run. A free tip, here: some homework will stand you in good stead. Do some.)

A lot of people (namely, clients and creative staff) tend to dismiss the humble Account Executive as a mere bag-carrier.

Which, of course, makes your job doubly difficult, or doubly challenging. The latter, we hope.

What *does* makes it so fascinating is the vast job specification.

A good account service person builds up a strong rapport between the agency and its clients, getting the work through on time, on budget, and on brief.

A *great* account service person does more. He, or she, will be able to guide the client along the prickly path of marketing and communication by determining the *strategy* — the route map, if you like, to achieving the client's objectives.

He or she will then be able to brief the creative team, inspiring them with enthusiasm, not only to adhere to the single-minded strategy mapped out for them, but to excel themselves in doing so. It's a job for a master tactician.

Good account service people are able to counsel their clients, rather than just taking orders.

Great account service people are also able to perform incredible juggling feats,

harnessing all the agency's resources in order to support, execute and run the great advertising campaigns which come from great strategies.

In this way, they earn the respect of clients, creative people and agency managements.

Which is why they're as scarce as hens' teeth, frankly.

Copywriters

This, of course, does not refer to people who copy what other people write.

Nor should it refer to the poor bloke who fills up all the holes in the ads left by art directors. (Of whom, more, later.)

The copywriter is the backbone of the agency. (I'm one, after all.)

From his inspired and insecure, talented and tortured mind come the words, the ideas, the solutions. And while others may, later, craft the jewellery of a campaign, the fire in which it is born is the copywriter's domain.

Every line of this 12-page brochure was hand-printed to avoid
awkward settings and hyphenated breaks. If it didn't fit, it was rewritten.
A pleasant Sunday evening's work for Neil French.
Euro RSCG Partnership (The Ball Partnership), Singapore.

LIKE ALL GREAT ADVERTISING, IT'S SLIGHTLY INDULGENT, BRILLIANTLY PRODUCED, AND HORRIBLY EXPENSIVE.

Furthermore, it's quite possible that only half of it actually worked.

Luckily for creative people all over the world, that's not one of the criteria by which *creative* awards are bestowed. And since we've seen fit to open this particular can of snakes, we may as well strangle the buggers here and now.

Read our lips: The sine qua non of *all* advertising is its effectiveness.

If an ad doesn't work, it's a total waste of time, money, and perfectly good trees. There are no awards for doing your job right, — and neither *should* there be; that's what you're paid for. If it's *not* done right, then the client fires the agency, and both the creative people *and* the account handlers are at liberty to open little knitting-shops instead.

However many awards they've won. And quite right, too.

Creative awards are merely the end-of-term prizes handed out by our peers, for work we'd have been proud to have done ourselves.

No more than that. And no less.

Which brings us, by a somewhat tortuous process, to the matter of the Creative Circle Annual for 1989.

Remember 1989? Before it all went mad? Before Saddam Hussein, before the recession, and before the quota system? In those far-off and forgotten days, somehow it seemed the weather was nicer, food tasted nicer, in fact the entire world was suffused with niceness.

Naturally though, in the world of advertising, it was the same rat-eat-rat-smile-as-you-stab-your-best-pal-in-the-back-why-does-that-bald-old-sod-win-all-the-awards picnic that it is today.

And with an alacrity that would have put a paralytic tortoise on the winners rostrum, the Creative Circle committee has finally stumbled its way to producing the long-awaited 1989 Gong Show Annual.

It has some lovely stuff in it: The British Airways ads with the red dots; the white-space Chivas campaign of blessed memory; the wrinkly dog in the Payot ads, (sorry madam, not you); the rubbery-faced plea for a grin from yer average Singaporean . . . They're all there, reproduced in glowing colour, bound in an elegant black hard-backed cover, in a book as big and square as Gordon Tan.

It's a feast of bygone triumphs and it's all yours for the miserly sum of $160. Alright, then, $159 for cash. There is, of course, one little drawback. But isn't there always?

IT'S ALSO LATE.

Neil French at work. Every single word in these ads was originally hand-printed onto the layout, precisely replicating the font, weight and typesize. The light burning in Neil French's window at midnight became a regular landmark along Singapore's Beach Road. Small wonder. Euro RSCG Partnership (The Ball Partnership), Singapore.

"I will not have hyphenated words at the end of lines," says Neil French. Do so at your peril.

give shape and balance to the page. I chose Franklin once for a raincoat campaign, but I wanted the type to look a little bit watery, to have round edges instead of sharp corners. So I brought the complete alphabet home and Leila, my wife, who was a lettering artist at Doyle Dane when it was still hot metal type, cut off all the sharp corners and rounded them. So we were inventing our own typefaces in a way."

There is always the time when a new face or technique will work, Godfrey believes, providing it is appropriate to the ad. "I've had art directors come up to me and say, I've just found a fantastic new typeface and I'm going to use it in my next campaign. My answer to that was always, hang on a bit, will the campaign *want* that kind of face? The typeface can never take over from the words. You have to be able to say, it'd be great to use that face, but this is *not* the opportunity. You have to use restraint."

Like Godfrey, French also confesses to having a limited repertoire of typefaces.

"They're the only ones I learned to trace," he explains. "I learned to trace Franklin, and Times, and Palatino for some reason, I don't know why. Perhaps in those days, there wasn't an awful lot of typefaces, and frankly I chose them because I could read them easily, and then afterwards I didn't see any reason to set anything in a typeface that would make it more difficult to read."

One of the great French legends is the fact that all his copy is first laboriously printed onto his layouts by hand, before being sent for typesetting. Rumour has it that it was a firing offence at The Ball Partnership to remove a pen from French's desk.

"It's only because I'm completely inept," he says. "I can't handle a slide rule, and I don't understand any of the new machinery, and it never looks as nice on a computer as when I do it by hand. And I don't know why that is. I think it's because computers haven't quite got the hang of kerning yet, but my eye has. I realised a long time ago that because I was completely incapable of casting off copy, as we used to call it in those days, it would be easier for me to learn something that's painstaking, rather than actually figure out mathematics. That's how much of a complete twerp I am. So I spent many, many hours with type books, tracing over type. Then I found you could get all these Japanese pens in different widths, and therefore I could do my type in light, medium or heavy, so I learned how to do that, too."

All the typesetters have to do is follow French's layouts. "I can write you a piece of copy in 10-point, or 14-point, in bold, medium or light, and in *italics* if you wish, and it will always match a good piece of typesetting. These days, it will not match a piece of typesetting from a computer, but if you then add in kerning, it will almost always fit. It frightens young art directors quite a lot. I like to see my ad full size in front of me before I send it off to be finished, and this is the only way I can do it."

Another French legend concerns his hatred of hyphenated line breaks. Books, of course, are full of them; so are newspapers, magazines, and hundreds of award-winning print ads for that matter. The human eye is perfectly able to decode a hyphen and travel to the next line. As some writers might well say, a hyphen will even help the reader read on to the next line.

"You could argue that," shrugs French, "but you'd be wrong. I want the flow of my sentence to carry you on to the next line, not a little arrow in the form of a hyphen. The flow is better achieved if you can read a word *fully*, without having to flick your eye seven centimetres to the left. Whenever I do a piece of copy, if there is a word that needs hyphenating, I change the word, or change the sentence, or change the paragraph, but I will *not* have hyphenated words at the end of lines," he insists. "Also, I am a Virgo, I am so hopelessly anal retentive and breathtakingly tidy."

With new typefaces proliferating faster than you can say "Mac", it may be surprising to learn that the world's most accomplished and awarded art directors, for the most part, shun them. It is not a question of age, but judgement.

Three young Turks first:

"The problem with the Mac is that it's a great tool, but if you don't have a clear idea of what you want, you mess with your head," says Redman. "There are so many options, so many avenues, so many ways to make something look good, you just don't know what's good any more. You still need to sit down with a pad and work out what you're trying to get across. Broken up type has its place, but you've got to know where that place is."

"Macs are only tools," confirms Messum. "I think they're vital as long as they're not abused. They open up new veins for your inspiration. Where it falls down for a lot of young people, they rely too heavily on the machine to have all the answers. I still work with a pen and a layout pad. I still truly believe in presenting an art director's rough to a client. It's too easy to pick a bit of type, stick it on a stock shot with a logo in the corner, and think you've got an ad. It's *not* an ad. Clients need to buy the idea, not what it looks like."

"The Mac can do anything you want," agrees Clarke. "I don't mind bashed up type, I've done it myself, as long as it's relevant to your idea. If it's not, what's the point of doing it?" Clarke relies on the classic faces. "I use Garamond, Helvetica, Trade Gothic, Times, Univers, Franklin, and of course, Clarendon. The classic typefaces have so many families, there's so much scope. I try to make all my work simpler, the simpler the better." When it comes to setting body copy, Clarke quips, "I'm a justified person who's open to ragged right."

Grace, asked to choose six desert island typefaces, says: "I don't think I'd have six. I got tired of choosing typefaces twenty-five years ago. I used to use a typeface that was called Standard Medium, which comes from a Swiss type, and it's now called Helvetica. I don't really use it that much any more. When I go for type at my agency, they say, oh, here he comes, here's Futura. So at the top of my list, Futura, medium or demi. Then Caslon, a really great Caslon. Bauer Bodoni would be certainly up there, as would Baskerville. Then for fun, a good, fat Goudy. I think I've been using that same typography for 90 percent of everything I've done."

"The typeface," asserts Nick Bell, "should come seamlessly out of the idea, otherwise it runs the risk of getting in the way of the communication."

"There is nothing more frustrating than seeing an idea trapped in a typeface in which it doesn't belong," Warren Brown laments. "Call me old fashioned, but first of all a typeface has to be easy to read. It should be effortless, seamless, and in complete harmony with the words. Normally I try and view the type as a person. Sounds weird, but I need the words in my ads to talk, not just to be read. If you use your imagination *you can hear the type talk* and if it feels right for the idea then you have embellished the personality of your ad."

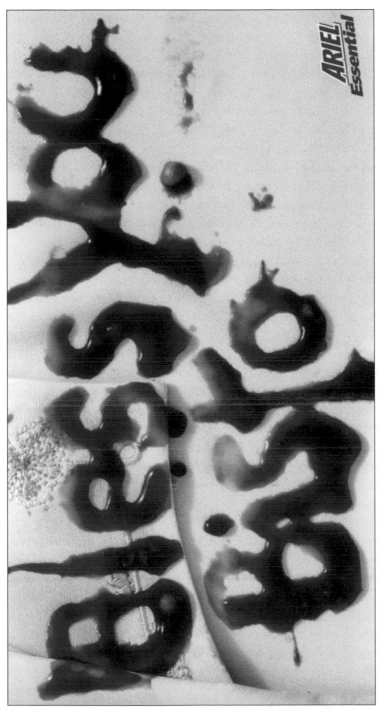

Typography that comes seamlessly out of the idea. Art director Andrew Clarke, typographers Peter Cole and Alex Normanton, for Procter & Gamble's Ariel. Saatchi & Saatchi, London.

"I hate gimmicky typefaces," asserts Barrie. "When I first started out in my career, there was this trend in the Southeast, that was picked up in Minneapolis, for condensing typefaces and setting everything real close. I look back at some of the ads I did in that period and I just cringe. As a result, I really tend to be like Neil French. I'm a classicist when it comes to typography. I want to be able to look at an ad in ten years' time and be able to celebrate the idea, and not get caught up in gimmicky typefaces. Right now, with the Mac, and distressed type, there's going to be a hell of a lot of ads people look back at in ten years and say, what was I thinking! The computer can be your own worst enemy simply because it allows you to do a lot more things, the majority of which are inappropriate."

Lichtenheld's love affair with typography began when he was a sign painter. "I was doing lettering that was five feet high. You really develop a nice sense for the nuances of typography when you're painting a serif that's thirty inches wide, and you know you've got to get that curve from the vertical stroke into the serif just right. In the past couple of years, though, working on BMW, I've been pretty much restricted to Helvetica." Lichtenheld's desert island typeface is Bembo. "I could work anything in all the fonts of Bembo."

He encourages young art directors to study typography. "In today's environment, a well done, classic piece of typography is really going to stand out. One of the things I admire a lot is when I see classic typography treated in a very current, contemporary way. That, to me, is pretty exciting because it's going to have some timelessness to it. It shows me that somebody knows the craft. When I say I admire something, it usually means I kick myself for not having done it."

Lichtenheld's priority is to make headlines less self-conscious. In that context, he believes bashed up type can make a contribution. "When it first came out, it looked like an art director had said, let's photocopy this a hundred times, then run over it with a beer truck and put it in the ad. Now I see it being used more appropriately." Citing Saatchi & Saatchi London's work for the British Army, he says: "I admire it when I see it done *invisibly*, when it doesn't feel like a technique layered onto something that didn't need it. I admire it when it's done in such a way that it works the type into the visual, so it's not type any more, it's just words, words that have an idea in them. Headlines should be part of the visual, then there are no limitations as to whether it's type, or whether you paint it on the side of a wall and photograph it. People have better and better filters for advertising these days," Lichtenheld stresses, "and you have to find techniques to get past their filters. One of them, obviously, is to make advertising that doesn't look like advertising."

"While I accept that there are some very *'interesting'* typefaces about," says French, "I've also noticed, over the years, how they come and go. I've seen two typefaces come and go in just eighteen months. One was a kind of blobby thing that looked as though it had come out of a computer. It had a very big vogue for about six months. Of course, nobody uses it now because it dated so quickly. There was another one with crosses and things all over it, it was very 'in' for a while, and I'll guarantee nobody's using it in six months' time. But everybody will always use Franklin and Palatino and Times, because they will *never* date." French lends qualified support for bashed up type. "I think it's a good thing if there's a point to it. There'd be absolutely no point doing it if it was just for the effect," he cautions. "For instance, when we did some ads about the destruction of Angkor Wat in Cambodia, it would have been crazy to have nice, tidy type. So the art director bashed it around, to make it look as though it had been destroyed, so it carried part of the message. That's perfectly acceptable; in fact, it would have been *un*acceptable not to have done so. But to muck around with a typeface, just for the sake of mucking around with it, is a waste of time. Why don't you go down to the pub instead?"

SHOULD HEADLINES BE SET IN CAPS
or should they be set in lower case?

"It should be whatever it has to be," acknowledges Grace. "I prefer upper and lower case, because it's the way you read books. I always believe that information should be assimilated as quickly as possible. When you read a book, it's a very comfortable process, and I think the eye is more used to it. I have used all caps, and I will use all caps again. I think the ideal is upper and lower *serif*; it's not necessarily my favourite, but I think it's the ideal."

Barrie agrees. "I prefer the understatement of upper and lower case. It's how you're used to reading."

"I don't have any criteria," says Clarke. "It's whatever feels right for the ad. I think I've used caps more often."

"There are no set rules," affirms Brown. "Whatever best captures the tone of voice of your ad is most important."

"I've seen great ads both ways," observes Redman. "I've also seen atrocious ads both ways. It's what works best."

While there are no rules, WAR IS DECLARED reads well as three words; but, the longer your headline is, the easier it will read in lower case.

Or, judged another way, how would you want your headline to sound if it were read aloud? If it is meant to scream, it is caps. If it is meant to be conversational, or laconic, or witty, it is lower case. (And, nudge, nudge, maybe even in brackets.)

Should Every Word In A Headline Start With A Capital Letter?

Barrie is implacable. "Never use initial caps on words!"

"Initial caps were an affectation that started in the 1980s," observes Lichtenheld. "There is no literary or grammatical precedent for them."

Should ALL the words in a headline be the same SIZE?

"The thing now that you see, that just defies logic, is various words in different sizes in the same headline," groans Grace. "It slows down the communication. It impacts negatively on the meaning of the headline because you're not reading it in a normal fashion; it changes the emphasis of the words. It doesn't make sense. It really is *stupid*."

"I call it the ransom note school of typography," says Lionel Hunt. "The sooner it dies, the better. Having each word in a different size or face is a fad which I particularly loathe. It makes lines very difficult, if not impossible to read, which is the opposite to what you are trying to achieve. No copywriter should ever allow it to happen to what he or she has written."

"Keep the point size of all the characters in your headline the same," urges Barrie. "I've seen headlines that literally gave me a headache trying to read them. It was like there were thirty-two different point sizes in the line. It's something that's done because the computer allows you to do it. You paid three grand for your Mac and you want to get your money's worth."

What Should Come First: The Headline or the Picture?

As French says, people read an ad by the way it is art directed. Invariably, a bent picture will precede a straight headline. And a bent headline will generally precede a straight picture. But it is not formulaic.

"If you want someone to look at the visual and wonder what it's about, and you want them to get it with the headline," advises Clarke, "then the headline goes underneath, to reveal the idea. In long copy ads, the headline goes at the top because you're leading people into the copy."

"The formula for me," says Lichtenheld, "is to determine which one is leading the idea, the headline or the visual. If the visual is a payoff to the headline, then theoretically you put the headline at the top and the visual below. If it's a visual concept, the headline is small and goes at the bottom. That said, I would always try it both ways and see which feels better."

"Rules are made to be broken," affirms Barrie. "It takes a lot for an ad to stop me. A headline, no matter how witty, is not going to suck me in. What will, is the visual look of the ad. The headline should work as an afterthought."

Should Headlines Always End With a Full Stop?

Newspaper headlines never end with a period. Editors want readers to read on.

So, of course, do art directors. Which does not explain why most advertising headlines end with a punctuation mark which signals readers to STOP.

The jury is still out.

Invariably, a bent picture precedes a straight headline.
Lowe & Partners Singapore for Mighty Dog.

There are better ways to save money.
ANZ Money Saver Home Loan.

Getting six months out of a pair of pantyhose might save you some dollars, but if you want to make big savings, talk to us about an ANZ Money Saver Home Loan.

It's a no frills home loan that offers a low variable rate for the life of the loan. Yet, it still gives you the flexibility to make additional payments whenever you choose.

So if you're serious about saving money, call ANZ, Personal Investor magazine's Home Lender of the Year on 1800 035 500, drop into any ANZ branch or visit www.anz.com

grow with **ANZ**

A straight headline goes under a bent visual to reveal the idea.
M&C Saatchi, Melbourne, for ANZ Bank.

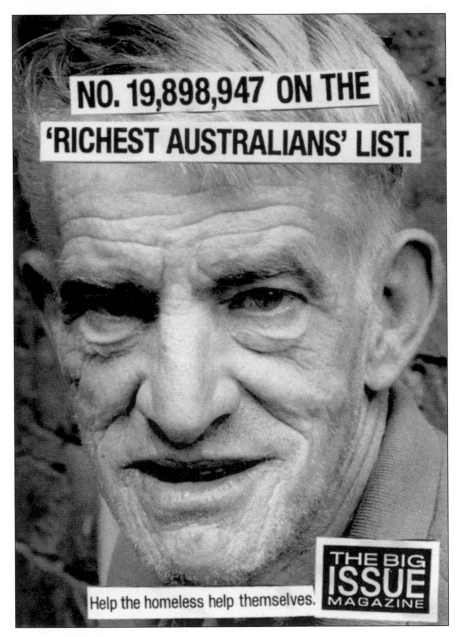

If the idea is in the headline, the headline should lead and be at the top.
The visual is the payoff. Whybin TBWA, Melbourne.

However, one writer resolved the issue happily. David Fowler's headlines once continued, unfinished, into the first line of his body copy.

It Takes All Types

There are really only two types of typography: appropriate and inappropriate.

The inappropriate is invariably derivative and shallow; technique for technique's sake.

The appropriate is invariably the result of cutting edge judgement and taste.

Welcome to the latter.

The Village Voice. Before the *Voice* circulated free, it was sold by subscription; not an easy task, as Nick Cohen explains.

"The *Voice* has an equity that's anti-establishment, trying to cut through and present a much more honest perspective of what's going on to its readers. The dilemma was, how do you sell the corporation, the *Voice*, while you try to flog subscriptions? So we wanted to take the opposite side; the *Voice* poking fun at itself, which they do in the newspaper a lot."

By representing the opposite viewpoint, Cohen hoped they could address those people who were opposed to the *Voice*. "A lot of people think the *Voice* is a bunch of whining, moaning types, so we wanted to create a more balanced view. By being able to laugh at yourself, and question yourself, and see your own faults, you can make a connection with people. We wanted people to come away from the ads thinking, I like the *Voice*, they're just really honest people, they're not full of themselves, they understand that there are pros and cons to everything."

What developed was a classic coupon campaign, but with a difference. "We didn't want to do anything that was slick, because that would have been the opposite to what the *Voice* is about. We didn't want to do anything that looked like they'd spent any money on." Commitment and dehumanisation provided fertile ground for creative concepts. "It was also about poverty," adds Cohen. "They didn't have any money, and I think the ads cost them only a few bucks to make."

(GULP)

You want me to commit to you for an entire year? I mean, we're talking big "S" subscription here. I don't understand why we can't just keep things the way they are. If I'm in a "Voice" mood, I pick up an issue. Why do you want to start complicating things, don't you trust me? This is a very serious step, I don't think we should just rush into it. I mean, I just got out of a really long subscription with National Geographic and it's been really hard for me. Maybe I just need a little space, a little time to myself, not tied down to any one paper. I just want what's best for both of us. Look, why don't we just stay really, really good friends?

☐ **YES,**
I WANT TO BUY A
YEAR SUBSCRIPTION
TO THE VILLAGE VOICE.

$47.95 (Just 92¢ per copy). To order, call toll-free 1-800-336-0686 (24 hours a day). Or mail this coupon to: The Village Voice Subscriptions, P.O. Box 8044, Syracuse, NY 13217.

Name_____
Address_____
City/State/Zip_____
Check enclosed_____ Bill me_____ Charge me_____
AmEx___M/C___Visa___ Card_____
Exp date_____ Signature_____

Rates and 'bill me' good in U.S. only. Canadian/foreign subscriptions $79.20/year, must have payment with order. Please allow 2-4 weeks for first issue to arrive.

VOICE

#31070

subscription holder, reporting for duty! Is that what you want, for me to become another faceless entity that you can anonymously slip your paper to? Maybe I'm an antique, but I don't mind going down to a real newsstand, paying with real money, flashing a real smile, and heck, maybe even slipping in a "Thanks, 'preciate it." What human contact do we have left? Computo-bank tellers, TV diplomas, "Personalized" bulk mail, blow-up dolls, push "1" for this - push "2" for that. How 'bout I come down there, push "3" and blow your whole operation to bits? Listen here, you... you...personality leeches, I'm a real person! I have a name. I am not, I repeat, NOT, a credit card number!

☐ **YES,** I WANT TO BUY
A ONE YEAR SUBSCRIPTION
TO THE VILLAGE VOICE.

$47.95 (92¢ per copy). To order, call 1-800-336-0686 (24 hrs/day). Or mail coupon to: The Village Voice Subscriptions, P.O. Box 8044, Syracuse, NY 13217.

Name_____
Address_____
City/State/Zip_____
Check enclosed_____ Bill me_____ Charge me_____
AmEx___M/C___Visa___Card #_____ Exp date_____
Signature_____

Rates and 'bill me' good in U.S. only. Canadian/foreign subscriptions $79.20/year, must have payment with order. Allow 2-4 weeks for delivery.

VOICE

0   17805   66604   2

Cheap type let The Village Voice *laugh at itself. Mad Dogs & Englishmen, New York.*

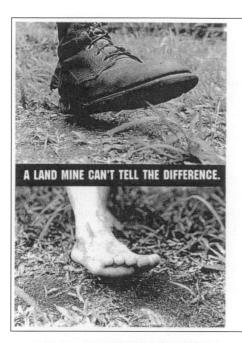

OFFICIALLY THE WAR in Cambodia is over. Unofficially the killing still goes on. And it will go on well into the next century.

The catch is, over the last 20 years Cambodian government and resistance soldiers have saturated the country with land mines.

They've sown them around villages, on footpaths, on riverbeds, in paddy fields - tens of thousands of them. These mines can't be deactivated.

There's no handy switch to turn them off. So they're there for ever.

Or until some day someone steps on them. The Cambodians have a word for land mines. They call them 'eternal sentinels'.

Because land mines never sleep.

They'll kill the children, even the grandchildren, of the soldiers who laid them in the first place. They just never, ever give up.

Recently hundreds of thousands of Cambodians have returned from refugee camps in Thailand, lured, ironically, by the promise of peace.

Many have literally walked into minefields.

The rural poor have been the worst hit - peasants gathering firewood, harvesting rice, herding animals, ploughing their fields or fishing for a meal for their families.

And tragically, their children.

Mines are blind weapons. They can't distinguish the footfall of a soldier from that of a young girl, or a boy herding cattle in a field.

Cambodian shepherds, teenagers mostly, have suffered out of all proportion. In their search for fresh pasture, they often have to stray on to untrodden land alone.

And far too often they die alone. Undiscovered, untreated - from blood loss and exposure.

Statistically, for every mine victim that makes it to hospital, another will die in the fields or on the way.

Even those who do reach medical facilities will find the dice loaded against them.

X-ray film, anaesthetics, surgical equipment, antibiotics, simple things like electricity and water, are all in chronically short supply.

And in many rural areas the doctor/patient ratio is as high as 30,000, or more.

On Route 5, the war-torn strip of highway that connects Phnom Penh with the north, a legless barber sits in a wheel chair shaving a customer under a tarp he's fashioned into a tent...

A little further on, a boy who can't be more than five years old stands by a bomb-blasted bridge with a homemade crutch under his arm...

In a Battambang market, a group of women amputees sit together on the remnants of a cardboard box. Unfit for the fields, they try to scrape a living selling odds and ends...

Cambodia has the highest percentage of physically disabled people in the world.

There are over 35,000 amputees out of a population of just eight and a half million.

One out of every 236 Cambodians has some sort of mine injury. A comparable figure in the United States would be over a million people.

Last year alone, over 6,000 Cambodians had to be amputated after stepping on land mines. And in an average month 500 new amputees join the line.

In Jane's Military Vehicles and Logistics, you'll find 76 pages devoted to land mines. (But of course not one devoted to their victims.)

The Claymore mine, for instance, projects 700 steel balls for more than 50 metres at a height of two metres. Made in Louisiana, it was sold to the KPNLF in Cambodia.

And the Valsella Valmara 69, an Italian land mine, scatters a thousand metal fragments for 25 metres at a height of half a metre.

(Depending on whether you're an adult or a child, that's roughly knee or groin height.)

Not all land mines are so sophisticated. Some are very simple, fiendishly so.

A PDM-6, for example, is nothing much more than a hinged wooden box containing TNT and a detonator.

And as a Chinese manual helpfully explains, a mousetrap and a few grenades will do - use plenty for the 'anti-morale' effect.

(The Khmer Rouge learned how to improvise such mines from the Chinese. And the KPLNF and the ANS had lessons from the British SAS.)

Nobody knows how many land mines there are in the world today.

But more than 250 million have been produced in the last twenty-five years.

And they continue to be manufactured at a rate of five to ten million a year.

Unlike chemical and biological weapons, land mines have never been banned.

On the contrary, international law permits the use of land mines to achieve 'military objectives'.

(Although what constitutes a 'military objective' has never been satisfactorily defined.)

What we want is an unconditional ban on the manufacture, possession, transfer, sale and use of land mines.

What we need is your support. Please speak out.

ASIA WATCH is a division of Human Rights Watch, established to monitor and promote observance of internationally recognized human rights in Asia. For more information, contact Asia Watch, Human Rights Watch, 485 Fifth Avenue, New York, NY 10017

A LAND MINE CAN'T TELL THE DIFFERENCE.

THERE'S ONLY ONE way to clear a minefield. Inch by inch. Make one false move and you're dead.

That's why in Cambodia the local mine sweepers are taught to wear a string on their conical hats.

If you're bending over and your hat falls off, it's a reflex action - you take a step forward and pick it up.

But it could be the last step you ever take.

In Somalia mothers tie toddlers to trees to keep them from crawling into minefields.

Because nobody is safe anymore.

In fact, people walk in fear in more than sixty countries around the world.

Over the last ten years, more than ten million mines have been scattered throughout Cambodia. There are more than a million in Somalia.

In Bosnia-Herzegovina more than three million land mines have been sown, unmarked and unmapped. And 50,000 more are planted every week.

In Egypt there are 23 million land mines scattered all over the country. In Iran there are 15 million more. Angola has as many again.

Afganistan, China and Iraq have ten million each. There are two million more in Mozambique, a million in Eritrea, a million in Sudan, a million in Ukraine...

What's more, the situation isn't getting any better. More than 250 million land mines have been produced over the past twenty-five years.

And land mines continue to be manufactured at an average rate of five to ten million per year.

While the resulting casualties beggar belief.

Last year alone, in Cambodia alone, over 6,000 men, women and children were amputated after stepping on land mines. And in an average month over 500 new amputees join the line.

Like Neas Pok.

Her dreams went up in smoke one hot and dusty afternoon in April.

She was gathering wood outside her village when her husband heard the bang (they were married six weeks before, when she turned twenty).

He carried her to the side of the road, flagged down a cyclo and took her to the nearest first aid post.

But they didn't know what to do.

And it was 7 hours later by the time she reached a hospital where surgeons amputated her right leg.

Chaing Song, a 38 year old fisherman and father of four, stepped on a mine just as he was tossing his net into the water.

He was horribly mangled and had to be amputated high above the knee.

Chok Chuon was 6 years old when she lost her right

leg to a land mine while she was playing near a railroad.

Loch Chem's family was literally torn apart. His eldest son, Chhim Pang Soun, was the first to lose his legs to a land mine. Then he fell victim to a land mine himself.

And to add insult to injury, when he was finally released from hospital, his younger son had to go in.

A typical hospital is the one at Mongol Borei. It's bursting at the seams.

Patients sleep outside in cots, or lie on bamboo mats in the corridors. New arrivals prop themselves up as best they can against the filthy walls.

I'ising Chhontrit, a grey-haired lady, sits stoically on a bamboo mat by the door. She still has some feeling in her left leg. It's one of those odd things.

The leg was amputated yesterday. But it takes time for the brain to get used to it.

She swats a fly buzzing round the base of her stump and explains how she was herding cows when it happened.

Certainly, she'd worried about stepping on mines. But the cattle had to be grazed, she says.

It took her 12 hours to get here. First she was carried on an oxcart, then on the flatbed of an old truck. And her troubles still aren't over. The doctor amputated well above the knee. But the stump has got infected badly.

There's a huge shock wave when you step on a mine and closing with the shrapnel, dirt and bacteria get driven deep inside.

In Praing Chhoeun's case, there's another serious complication: plastic shrapnel.

The frog-green fragments are very tough to find. They won't even show up on X-rays. But if you don't get them out, the wound will get infected.

The biggest danger is osteomyelitis. That can rot a bone right down to the marrow.

In Jane's Military Vehicles and Logistics, you'll find 76 pages devoted to land mines. (But of course not one devoted to their victims.)

The Claymore mine, for instance, projects 700 steel balls for more than 50 metres at a height of two metres. Made in Louisiana, it was sold to the KPNLF in Cambodia.

And the Valsella Valmara 69, an Italian land mine, scatters a thousand metal fragments for 25 metres at a height of half a metre.

Unlike chemical and biological weapons, mines like these have never been banned. But they must be.

What we want is an unconditional ban on the manufacture, possession, transfer, sale and use of land mines.

What we need is your support. Please speak out.

ASIA WATCH is a division of Human Rights Watch, established to monitor and promote observance of internationally recognized human rights in Asia. For more information, contact Asia Watch, Human Rights Watch, 485 Fifth Avenue, New York, NY 10017

IN A MINEFIELD YOUR LIFE CAN LITERALLY HANG BY A THREAD.

Restrained type in an editorial format. DMB&B, Singapore.

Asia Watch. While walking through rural Cambodia requires a certain vigilance, a campaign calling for an unconditional ban on land mines required even more.

"We were talking to people who were in a position to do something," recalls art director Norman Alcuri. "They wouldn't be taken in by a gimmicky bit of art direction."

The subject was serious; however, there were legitimate stylistic options. There always are when dealing with futility, death and horror. "We talked about distempered type, of course. We talked about the inclusion of little graphics. We talked about different backgrounds. But we pared it all the way. I even had a black border around the ads at one point, then I got rid of it. We decided to make it more like editorial than an ad."

Alcuri allowed himself one concession with the headline type. "We asked ourselves whether we should use a stencil effect, like you might see stamped on armoury cases. We modified the type a tad, to reflect that. It's not new, I know, but I reversed the headlines out of black panels for strength." He broke convention by setting the two columns of long copy in a sans serif face, rather than a traditional serif. "You're always asking yourself, should I break the mould or not? It's what Graham Fink said, if it's been done before, should you do it again?"

Unusually for a campaign of letters, some of the visuals and headlines could have worked alone as postcards. The juxtaposition of the soldier's boot and the peasant's foot, for example, would have worked just as well without all the copy. Another ad had two identical pictures of a rice field; one was captioned *Paddy Field*, the other *Mine Field*. It would have been a classic postcard ad.

"There was a need to tell the full story, the full horror," Alcuri acknowledges. "The writer, Andrew Bruck, had gone off and done all the research. He was very passionate about it. He'd dug up all these facts, like the peasants wearing a string on their hats to stop them falling off. If their hats fell off, they used to take a step forward to pick them up. Sometimes it was the last step they ever took."

Gun Control Network. After a mad gunman massacred young children, the British government decided to ban guns with the exception of .22 handguns. Singling out the .22 did not make sense to the anti-gun lobby, nor to the creative team at Saatchi & Saatchi, London. "The art direction had to look angry," recalls Gallacher. "Originally we just had big type, a black background, a small picture. It was very in your face. But the trouble is, a lot of people just turn away from that."

Gallacher decided to lure people in to the message instead. "We found a .22 shell, which reminds you that someone has already fired the bullet, and we thought we'd put the captions on that, like they'd been stamped into the metal."

To create a carved in look, the settings in News Gothic were degraded sufficiently, then merged with the photographic image of the shell. "Then we laid in the third visual, Kennedy and the grave,

Degraded type, necessary for a technical effect. Saatchi & Saatchi, London.

with a bit of show through. The show through makes it more like a *memory*, like your name is on the bullet. There is a certain kind of prettiness about it, to lure you in, and the message is the sting in the tail."

Gallacher believes good art direction never takes over from the idea. His decisions are guided by the fact that print is not a static medium, because the thought process is not static. "When I work on print, and an idea starts to form in my head, I look at it like a piece of film. It's never flat and lifeless, it's moving, and I have to ask myself *where* do I stop the film, which frame do I take out? Should I stop it slightly earlier, or add another layer, and stop it slightly later?"

FUR WEARERS:

WHACKING PEDESTRIANS ACROSS THE HEAD AND DRAGGING THEM AWAY FOR MATING IS NOT PERMITTED IN THIS AREA.

FUR IS A THING OF THE PAST. EVOLVE.
Friends of Animals

FUR WEARERS:

PLEASE REFRAIN FROM CLIMBING TRAFFIC LIGHTS, MARKING TERRITORY AND/OR SNIFFING OTHER PEDESTRIAN'S CROTCHES.
—BUREAU OF SANITATION

FUR IS A THING OF THE PAST. EVOLVE.
Friends of Animals

ATTENTION FUR WEARERS:

PLEASE HELP KEEP OUR STREETS CIVILIZED. AVOID SWINGING FROM DELI AWNINGS, HUMPING TAXI CABS OR THROWING FECES AT JOGGERS.

FUR IS A THING OF THE PAST. EVOLVE.
Friends of Animals

Conventional type, unconventional strategy. Fur wearers were targeted for public humiliation by what appeared to be municipal signage. Mad Dogs & Englishmen, New York.

*Classic type in a contemporary treatment by Len Cheeseman and Eric De Vries.
Saatchi & Saatchi, Wellington, for the Mary Potter Hospice.*

PERENNIAL NUMBER ELEVENS–HOW DOES NUMBER SEVEN SOUND?

HAVEN'T YOU LONGED TO HEAR THOSE WORDS FROM YOUR SUNDAY SUB–DISTRICT CAPTAIN? HAVEN'T YOU YEARNED TO SHOW THE WORLD THE STROKES YOU'VE BEEN SECRETLY PRACTISING IN FRONT OF YOUR BEDROOM MIRROR EVERY NIGHT? (NOT THOSE ONES.)

So you're the night watchman, only brought out to test the durability of the team's new perspex visors against the rabid onslaught of bouncers.

That doesn't mean you're not handy with a bat. That doesn't mean you can't do your country proud at Lords. A career in test cricket awaits you. A career playing for the country that invented the "gentleman's" game.

England.

We're more forgiving and far less demanding than the teams you might be used to playing for.

No one can understand the mental and physical traumas of the lean period more than us.

That's why, in our eyes, as long as both your batting and bowling averages are in double figures, you're an all–rounder.

An English all–rounder.

And you needn't have been born in England to play for the Old Country. Maybe one of your grandparents was.

If not, don't worry, we'll find a connection. We always have.

But just to make sure you're the cricketer we need, we've devised a bit of a screening test (see below).

Can't just have anyone turning up and playing for the Old Dart, can we now?

NAME THESE BATTING STROKES AND YOU COULD BE ON YOUR WAY!
Choose from: Forward Defensive Stroke, Hook Shot, Cover Drive, Sweep Shot, Square Cut.

1. _____ 2. _____ 3. _____ 4. _____ 5. _____

ENGLAND NEEDS YOU.

The typography in Kash Sree's ad for Nike Australia appropriately replicated a newspaper of 60 years ago. Wieden & Kennedy, Portland.

In 1881, the Raffles Museum was built to improve thousands of minds.

SADLY, THE MAN BUILDING IT LOST HIS.

Diverse type, within the context of long copy. Writer Antony Redman and art director Andrew Clarke chose pastel colour backgrounds often found on Singapore's heritage architecture. Euro RSCG Partnership (The Ball Partnership), Singapore, for The Little Island Enterprise.

The statues on this temple ward off dangers and evil influences.

THEY COULDN'T WARD OFF A FIVE LANE HIGHWAY AND SIXTEEN OFFICE BLOCKS.

This was the home of Singapore's most influential architect.

IT'S NOW OCCUPIED BY GIORGIO ARMANI, COCO CHANEL AND RONALD McDONALD.

ILLUSTRATION: WHEN SHOULD YOU USE IT?

Godfrey speaks for many art directors when he says: "I like to use something people can believe in. I rarely used illustration. Nine-tenths of the time, it just doesn't have the impact of a photograph."

Others have used it judiciously. French chose to illustrate his Martell campaign in the style of Impressionist painters. On an earlier occasion, illustration was appropriate for his Singapore Tourism Board work.

"Even though people are savvy to retouching, they still believe photographs don't lie," says Lichtenheld. "I would use illustration if it was a matter of style, a retro look, or if a certain illustrator's work brought something to the ad like whimsy. But," Lichtenheld warns, "you're really relying on execution which can be dangerous, because it has to be truly unique and something people haven't seen before."

Hegarty sees illustration serving a strategic, more competitive purpose. "We have a view that when the world zigs, you should zag," he explains. "This will sound hideously pretentious, and I don't wish it to do so, but when I have an idea, I get a kind of vision in my brain. It's like a flash. And in that flash I see the ad, I see it as photography, I see it as illustration, or without either. That's how ideas have always come to me. But then I apply a point of view. If everybody's using photography, why don't we use illustration? You apply that thinking, you try to be different, you try to do something that *isn't* like everybody else. You have to ask, is this going to stop somebody? Is this going to be challenging in some way or another? People are looking for that. So that's what you must try and do. Try and find a way of capturing a difference, understanding what the idea is about, understanding what the brand is about, and do things that *belong* to that idea and that brand. You must find a way to make it more unique. And if that means daring to be different, then dare to be different."

When used appropriately, illustration becomes more than just an executional option. It becomes intrinsic to the creative idea.

Use photography when you really want to tell THE TRUTH. *Award-winning photographer Allan Myles captured the essence of Russian life for Stolichnaya Vodka. Leo Burnett Connaghan & May, Sydney.*

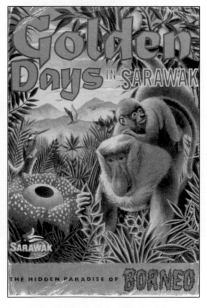

Making the rainforest less scary on a low budget. Batey Ads, Singapore.

Sarawak Tourism Authority. A low budget and a desire to make the Borneo rainforest less scary led to the choice of illustration for the Sarawak print campaign from Batey Ads, Singapore.

"Photography, to be any good these days, costs the earth," observes writer Malcolm Pryce. "But you can still get brilliant illustration comparatively cheaply and we had a very small budget."

Photography is the convention in the travel category. Illustration would be highly disruptive for a small, unknown advertiser. "Ian Batey has this genius for building brands. When you've got such a small budget, you need to create something which is instantly recognisable and distinctive, so it reinforces the brand every time you see it."

Illustration appealed for another reason. "Rainforests can be considered rather scary, full of dark places and frightening animals that do horrible things to you. Actually, the Borneo rainforest doesn't have the dangerous animals. It can be viewed as a botanic wonderland. We wanted to make it user friendly. We wanted people of all ages to go there, not just adventure travellers. So it had to be less threatening. We originally started off with an illustration style based on the work of a nineteenth century French painter who drew tigers in the grass and made them look quite sweet."

But Pryce and art director Tham Khai Meng felt something was missing. "The campaign had to look friendly, but there was still a sense of adventure, a cultural heritage to portray. It's always been a place where adventurers and smugglers and desperadoes have gone for centuries. It's always been an island of myth and mystery, most of it untrue. So we took a walk down to the Tower bookshop and we found this book which had the covers from 1950s American paperbacks."

Those quaint pulp fiction covers inspired the illustration and typography style of the campaign. Michael Lui was commissioned to illustrate a series of old-style book jackets which became posters and print ads.

From being simply a technique, illustration became inseparable from the idea and the brand.

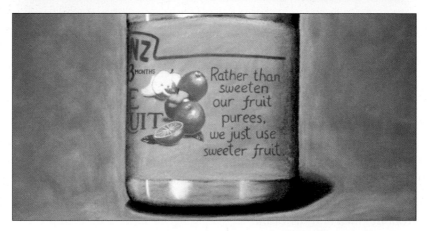

Somehow, photography would have been artificial. Robin Heighway-Bury's charming illustrations and hand-lettered captions convey the essence of Heinz natural ingredients. Bates Dorland, London.

Michael had agreed to a life of celibacy,
but like the Murphy's he wasn't bitter.

Declan misunderstood the shout of 'fore',
but like the Murphy's he wasn't bitter.

The tandem was running deeper than O'Brien realised,
but like the Murphy's he wasn't bitter.

Eamon's team lost 84-0,
but like the Murphy's he wasn't bitter.

*The ironies of Irish life, illustrated by Janet Woolley in a way that belongs to the brand.
Art directed by Graham Watson at Bartle Bogle Hegarty, London.*

David Chin captures anger and frustration which no photograph could ever express. Euro RSCG Partnership (The Ball Partnership), Singapore.

Chaos on the streets. Theseus Chan pumps adrenaline for Nike retailer D Corner,
combining illustration, hand-lettering, typography and typewriter.
WORK Singapore.

Retro illustration and typography appropriately combined for
City Gallery by Saatchi & Saatchi, Wellington.

M&C Saatchi Singapore subverted traditional Chinese paintings to communicate how the new BMW X5 off-road vehicle can go anywhere.

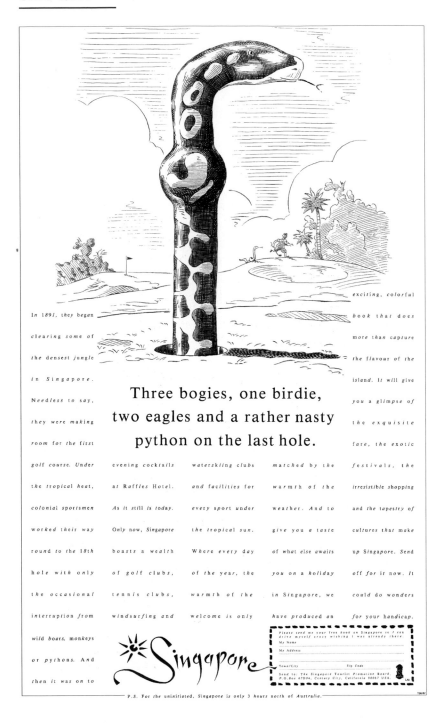

In 1891, they began clearing some of the densest jungle in Singapore. Needless to say, they were making room for the first golf course. Under the tropical heat, colonial sportsmen worked their way round to the 18th hole with only the occasional interruption from wild boars, monkeys or pythons. And then it was on to

Three bogies, one birdie, two eagles and a rather nasty python on the last hole.

evening cocktails at Raffles Hotel. As it still is today. Only now, Singapore boasts a wealth of golf clubs, tennis clubs, windsurfing and

waterskiing clubs and facilities for every sport under the tropical sun. Where every day of the year, the warmth of the welcome is only

matched by the warmth of the weather. And to give you a taste of what else awaits you on a holiday in Singapore, we have produced an

exciting, colorful book that does more than capture the flavour of the island. It will give you a glimpse of the exquisite fare, the exotic festivals, the irresistible shopping and the tapestry of cultures that make up Singapore. Send off for it now. It could do wonders for your handicap.

Singapore

Please send me your free book on Singapore so I can drive myself crazy wishing I was already there
My Name
My Address
Town/City   Zip Code
Send to: The Singapore Tourist Promotion Board, P.O.Box 470P4, Century City, California 90067 USA.

P.S. For the uninitiated, Singapore is only 3 hours north of Australia.

Looks like your dinner's in the drink again.

Who wouldn't be, after being drowned in half a bottle of brandy? Which is how you cook Drunken Prawns, one of Singapore's more flamboyant local delicacies. Or if that's not your tipple, why not try something a little more old-fashioned like Hundred Year Old Eggs, for instance? Then for the more adventurous, there's Fresh Sting Ray, or when you're

really hungry, there's nothing like sinking your teeth into a mouthwatering Fish Head Curry. Bacon and Eggs? No problem either. But why not go the whole hog? Roast Suckling Pig's a Singapore specialty too. In fact, there's very little here that

isn't a local favourite. Singaporeans love their food, and to prove it, boast some of the finest chefs in the world as well as the most tantalising array of Chinese, Indian, Indonesian, Thai, Malaysian, Japanese and Western

foods. Would you like to see the menus? No problem. Send off the coupon for our free colourful book that will whet

than whet your appetite for a holiday in Singapore. For starters, it shows you the scenery, the shopping, and the hotels, with the jungles, the wildlife and the festivals to follow. To say the least, it's somewhat intoxicating.

SINGAPORE

Please send me your free book on Singapore so I can drive myself crazy wishing I was already there.

My Name

My Address

Town/City   Zip Code

Send to: The Singapore Tourist Promotion Board, Suite 1804, Level 16, Westpac Plaza, 60 Margaret Street, Sydney 2000.

Scraperboard-style illustrations disrupted the convention that tourism ads must use colour photography. Disruptive typography italicised every second letter in the text. Batey Ads Singapore.

A patchwork of colour swatches lets us see new possibilities through the eyes of Prodec Paints. The Jupiter Drawing Room, South Africa.

These famous Volkswagen ads proved that illustration and photography can coexist in the same campaign, especially when the ideas themselves dictate it. Doyle Dane Bernbach, New York.

Out With Incest

Advertising art direction is incestuous. As Godfrey says, whenever somebody does something slightly different, everybody else wants to do it. Imitating ideas in award annuals is futile; they have been done already, and the same idea, done again, is unlikely to be awarded again. The distinctive styles of Neil Godfrey, Neil French and Steve Dunn have been aped *ad nauseum*; it is flattering but equally futile. If everybody copies everybody else, art direction will cease to evolve beyond its present stage.

Technique and technology have obscured the need to be original, or as near-original as possible. For example, when was the last time somebody actually invented a layout?

Arguably, only *two* advertising layouts have ever been invented. Forty years ago, Helmut Krone invented the famous VW format at Doyle Dane Bernbach, New York. More recently, Bob Barrie at Fallon Minneapolis invented a format in answer to a specific creative problem. It has been imitated, universally, ever since.

Jim Beam. "It was a period when spirits like whiskey, bourbon and vodka were losing market share to wine and beer," explains Barrie. "The campaign ran during the late 1980s when people were drinking a lot of faddish drinks. It was intended to show how people come back to their senses."

The idea was a time line which began and ended with the same object. Barrie's layout acknowledges the way an eye moves across the page.

"You'd start with white boxer shorts, and end with white boxer shorts, and show every aberration you wore in between. It reminded you that Jim Beam was a classic that you'd return to after you were through with all the fads." Modestly, Barrie admits to having seen fifteen different permutations of his Jim Beam layout. In reality, there have been many dozens.

Typically of Barrie's work, the campaign ran for five years. Over fifty different versions were produced, from handshakes to salt and pepper shakers, from sports to jeans. However, Barrie confesses that campaign longevity is never a conscious factor in his thinking.

"You can't be thinking that far down the road. Initially, you're just trying to get a campaign out there that works. Like Hush Puppies, all

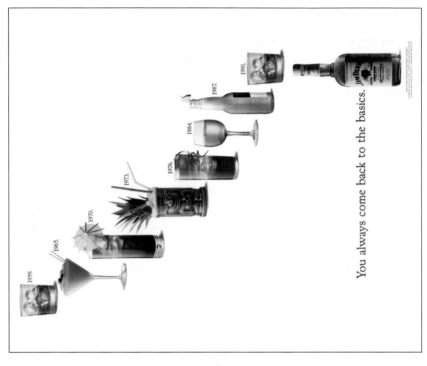

You always come back to the basics.

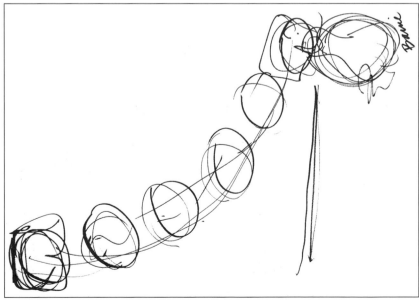

The layout invented by Bob Barrie acknowledges the way an eye travels across the page. An idea strong enough to inspire 50 different executions over five years. It's time advertising art direction got back to the basics, too. Fallon Minneapolis.

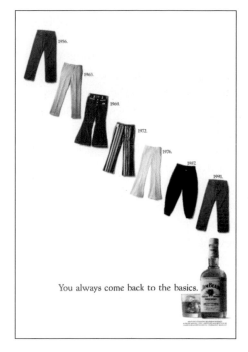

You always come back to the basics.

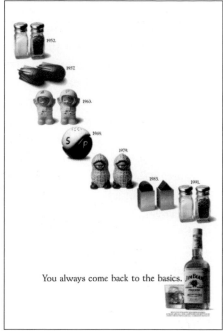

You always come back to the basics.

You always come back to the basics.

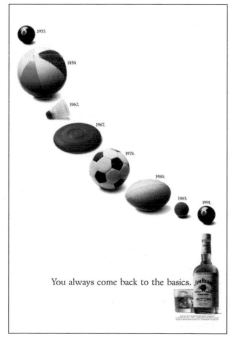

You always come back to the basics.

we wanted originally was to get five ads running in the spaces that the client had booked. We thought that was going to be it, so we tried to make them the best that they could be." Barrie believes longevity is inherent. "If a campaign strikes a chord with people, then it's usually the type of campaign that can be extended. *Time* was very extendable because it was playing off yesterday's news. Jim Beam was extendable because each year new things kept coming back into style, like penny loafers and Smiley buttons and all those classic things, so we could just play off culture and keep it fresh and relevant."

Inventing a new layout is not always possible, or even necessary. However, it is *always* possible to introduce something which gives the work an outstanding point of relevant difference.

New Zealand Red Cross. "Our Red Cross work started with a more traditional look," reports Kim Thorp, former executive creative director of Saatchi & Saatchi, Wellington. "The concepts and headlines were strong, so we always knew they would be good ads. But it was our typographer, Len Cheeseman, who pushed their visual power."

Cheeseman worked closely with the creative team, Ken Double and Steve Cooper, to create a startling new look.

"The idea was to make the whole campaign look more representative of the war-torn countries in which the Red Cross operates," says Thorp. "We selected several locations around Wellington where buildings were either about to be demolished, or were located in the seedier parts of town. We then erected scaffolding and our in-house illustrator, Evan Purdie, literally spent his summer holidays painting the headlines and graphics onto walls with house paint. Some of the sites were very large. It took an enormous amount of work and time."

The walls were the ads. Each was photographed and ran as the dominant element of an ad, above a small strip of red copy. By integrating visuals and headlines onto ravaged surfaces, the campaign became more evocative of the Red Cross and less like advertising.

When you think you've hit a brick wall, use a brick wall. Visuals and headlines integrated onto devastated buildings made the ads more harrowing, and less like ads. Saatchi & Saatchi, Wellington.

IN ADVERTISING, incest is a very public crime. Crafting print art direction leaves the art director alone on the page.

"I like feeling alone," volunteers Lichtenheld. "It's that rare opportunity to get back to the craft of myself and the writer and the blank page. Whenever I'm three-quarters into a TV shoot, I start to wish I was back in my office crafting a print ad. I wouldn't have thirty people around me, I'd have much more control, not as many variables." Lichtenheld, a realist, talks about the frustrations of executing ideas. "From the point I have the idea to the time it's done, it's downhill all the way. When you first imagine an ad, you see it as great as it can possibly be. From there on, it's a process of trying to keep it great and accepting the disappointments that come along the way." Lichtenheld gets his ideas when he is swimming. "I write headlines, too. It's fun because writing headlines is something I know I don't have to do, so it's easier. I have a beginner's mind when I write. I don't know what the bad ideas are."

Lichtenheld suggests one way to sidestep incestuous art direction. See the page beyond the terms of an advertising layout, he urges. "The page is a blank canvas and *anything* can be a layout, especially now that designers and art directors are working together more. If the brand is covered in some other way, the logo can be dispensed with. If the visual is the concept, you don't need a headline. So all of a sudden, you have just one visual that *is* the ad. That said," he puzzles, "we always seem to gravitate back to the elements, the same elements: the visual that gets across the concept; the headline; and then you usually need a few words of body copy, and the logo, and the phone number, and the slogan." Slogans, says Lichtenheld, are little security blankets. "They're okay if they relate to something in the reader, but mostly they're meaningless within people's lives."

Colleague Hanson says homework is the best defence against incest. "It's so tempting when you're doing an ad, and you're against the gun, to open a *CA* or *D&AD* and just say, okay, I'm going to rip that one." Hanson stores a treasure trove of typefaces, reference material, cuttings, videos and ideas in big metal files. If something strikes him, he squirrels it away. "You're the audience as much as anybody else," he believes. "I've got all kinds of things. When I hit a wall, I go and dig in there. I'm constantly refreshing my memory about what's in the files." It sounds an extremely complicated way to work, but Hanson swears by it. "It's not a question of whether I *have* to do it, I *want* to do it. If you want to do good work, you have to look at the world around you, at the stuff that stimulates you, and you have to write down ideas all the time, then you file it. Once I was watching Discovery Channel, and there was a Jacques Cousteau special on the Andaman Islands, and I saw this swimming elephant. I held on to that tape for three years, and then Coke came up." His swimming elephant commercial for Coca-Cola was lavished with recognition. "Everybody should have those gems stored away. Trouble is, there's nothing more devastating than if you turn on the television and someone else has got there before you."

Hanson says there is nothing more magical than to see your ad run for the first time. "There's something that happens when you pick up a magazine and fold it over. It's never going to go away." For Hanson, great print ads are the ones which are fresh in a well-worn category. "Anyone can do a condom ad. I like to see a great bank ad, because everyone has done bad ones. It means someone has persevered and *beaten* the category. Those are the ones I really love, that make me envious."

Gallacher believes self-confidence can overcome incest. "You've got to learn to trust your own beliefs and your own self. You've got to bring *yourself* to the industry, not what other people have done in the past." Gallacher maintains that advertising is not a sprint to the finish. "It's a marathon, and the more you learn, the better you become. You have to be able to art direct according to the product, and the copywriter's tone of voice, and the target audience, so you *can't* have just one style." Gallacher seeks his inspiration everywhere. "I go down to Zwemmers photographic book shop. I sit and watch TV. I watch how they do the programme titles. I soak it in like a sponge. All that award books can do is show you how to make things simple. You have to learn to use your own emotions."

Barrie often seeks his inspiration from editorial design, not advertising award annuals. "I once did a campaign for Continental Bank, long copy ads, and I chose an editorial look because there was a lot to say."

Let's say the foot is your company, the banana is a change in interest rates, and the floor is extremely hard.

The economy can be accused of many things. Predictability is probably not one of them.

This economic fickleness can place your company in a rather vulnerable position. As you charge boldly into the future, eyes on the horizon, even a fairly minor fluctuation in interest rates can sneak up on you and bring your company to its knees.

Or to some even humbler portion of its anatomy.

The same thing can happen, of course, if exchange rates or commodity costs decide to dance a little jig.

Clearly, some thing should be done to deal with this threat. At Continental Bank, we suggest financial risk management.

In brief, risk management allows your company to specify exactly how much rate variation you're willing to tolerate. If rates rise or fall beyond the limits you've specified, you're protected.

Whether the rate in question is the prime or Eurodollar, yen or deutschemark.

Beyond the obvious peace of mind it offers, financial risk management confers numerous other benefits.

It controls your cost of funds. It allows you to budget your interest expense with greater confidence. It prevents unforeseen depletion of your capital. On the whole, it permits you to do business in a much more orderly fashion.

Risk management is a relatively recent arrival on the financial scene, but it is already being heralded as the ideal mix of prudence and opportunity. It accords well with our philosophy—which is to bring our customers the most innovative, most effective financial tools we can find, develop or invent.

To learn more about how risk management can help your company, talk to a Continental banker at (312) 828-5799. There'll still be bananas in the world. But at least you won't be stepping on them. **Continental Bank** A new approach to business.

A lot of people are uninformed about the latest developments in business banking. (Unfortunately, many of them are bankers.)

The business-banking field is fairly exploding with new products and services these days. Just ask any banker.

Hmm. On second thought, maybe you shouldn't.

Now, understand, we don't mean to disparage our chosen profession. But most bankers have been brought up to be conservators of the status quo—as straight as the pinstripes they wear, as staunch and solid as the buildings they inhabit. And that's fine.

We're a little different here at Continental, though. We have this nagging feeling that a bank's job shouldn't be to resist change, but, rather, to help its clients deal with change.

So we've become quite preoccupied with the search for new ways to assist businesses like yours. Even to the point of shedding our retail banking interests entirely.

You'll discover what this means the first time you sit down with a Continental banker.

Instead of massaging, kneading and pummeling your problems until they fit the standard banking solutions, we study your situation as it really is, from every conceivable angle.

Instead of trotting out the same timeworn collection of financial tools, we're perfectly willing to head for the foundry and forge something new.

Instead of viewing orthodoxy as a thing to be worshipped, we prefer to look at it as a thing to be improved upon.

What's our problem? Can't we leave well enough alone?

Well, we could. But there are plenty of banks doing that already. And plenty of companies to keep them busy at it.

If your company is interested in not being one of them, it's time we talked. Just call (312) 828-5799 and ask us what's new. Although we should warn you: around here that's a leading question. **Continental Bank** A new approach to business.

Bob Barrie seeking inspiration from editorial design.
Fallon Minneapolis.

Simplicity is Barrie's answer to incest. "Usually, I'll start with the idea in its purest form, and from there I'll create a look for it that's unique to the product or the campaign. I'll keep it simple enough so it doesn't get in the way of the idea. And if the idea is strong enough to begin with, it will remain strong if you don't complicate the layout."

Godfrey has a similar view. "Every ad has its own way of being put together," he observes. "One of the most successful agencies has been Abbott Mead Vickers, and strangely enough they've rarely moved off the beaten track of what we call the old DDB way of doing it. The *Economist* campaign is just a straightforward line on a sheet of red paper. It's a perfect layout, based on the masthead of the magazine, and you do not have to move out of that."

Hegarty sees originality in terms of freshness. "We often have ideas, and we've seen that idea before," he explains. "But have you expressed it in a way that's different and fresh? I always like to use the word *fresh*, rather than the word *original*. I think *original* is an overused word and a dangerous word. When you sit on award shows and people say, we're only going to give awards to original ideas, I think, well, that's it, we might as well go home. God was the last person who had any original ideas. The rest of us are just imitators."

Hegarty talks about how freshness can be achieved. "The style with which you put something down adds to the freshness. It's the *voice* of the ad. Think about it in those terms. Should the voice be quiet? Does it need to shout? Does it need to reverberate with a thousand other voices behind it? There are so many ways of speaking to people. As somebody once said, you can give six people the same joke. One person makes it very funny, and the other five don't. Well, that's because that person has the technique. It's the same with art direction. You have to decide how best to tell the story."

8

How to Craft Copy

"To all those people who say that the word is dead," Indra Sinha challenges, "I say, if you take the words off your ads, what are you left with?"

"Generally in advertising," says David Abbott, "I think it's the words you remember."

"Words actually get deeper into the psyche than pictures," Neil French insists. "And they got in deeper even when I set them in that almost unreadable Germanic typeface for XO, because in research, people were able to parrot them perfectly. If something looks interesting, people will make the effort to read it."

Someone once asked Carl Ally if he thought people read ads. Ally's immortal reply: "People read what they *want* to read."

If Ally is right, the issue is not about whether the word is dead, but rather about supply and demand. If we can assume that the demand is still out there, *what* are we supplying to satisfy it?

"Writing, in certain markets, is stagnant," Tim Delaney observes. "If you look to some of the writing in America, which invented the whole vernacular, the whole fast-talking, off-the-cuff remark, the classic New York one-liner which a lot of copy is based on because it's very clipped and quite raunchy, I think they can still write brilliantly. You don't see a lot of it, I might add, but when they *do* do it, they do it really well. In the British market, I think it's almost non-existent. You've got the influence of those agencies which say copy is dead, the fact that people can't be bothered to write it, and when they do write it, it's not very well written."

Sinha agrees. "We're told nobody wants to read, therefore nobody wants to write. Kids who come out of art schools flip coins to see which one has the terrible task of being the copywriter. I wonder why they bother? Why call themselves copywriters? They should just call themselves ad creators, and share the horror of having to actually put words on a page."

Nor does it help when aspiring copywriters buy textbooks containing such spurious advice as, "Copywriting relies on the heavy use of *clichés*", and "*Clichés* provide impact and stimulate action". Lines like "For goodness sake" are upheld as shining examples of the copywriter's craft in food ads.

As we prepare to write cutting edge copy, none of these issues should really concern us. Instead, remember that the myths and lies about how advertising works are receding, brand building is changing fundamentally, and in the bigger context, words are an inseparable part of all that. Whether the copywriter has to write fifteen words for a postcard, or a letter of fifteen hundred words, the demands of the craft remain.

And they begin with style and the writing process itself.

M EN WANTED for Hazardous Journey. Small wages, bitter cold, long months of complete darkness, constant danger, safe return doubtful. Honor and recognition in case of success — Ernest Shackleton.

Arguably the best ad ever written.
Explorer Ernest Shackleton's copy is stark,
compelling and challenging.

SHOULD COPYWRITERS DEVELOP THEIR OWN STYLES?

It may sound pretentious to suggest that advertising copywriters have anything in common with authors and poets. They do, of course. Words are their tools of trade. Words are their only means of expression and persuasion. Copywriters should never pretend otherwise.

In Oakley Hall's *The Art & Craft of Novel Writing*, Jorge Luis Borges describes symptoms familiar to all young copywriters: "At the beginning of their careers many writers have a need to overwrite, to impress. By the excesses of their language, these young men and women try to hide their sense of inexperience. With maturity the writer becomes more secure in his ideas. He finds his real tone and develops a simple and effective style."

The argument can be made that the best style is one that appears to be no style at all, contends Hall. Perhaps the writer's true style begins to emerge when he makes no deliberate effort to produce one. As Ernest Hemingway said, "Prose is architecture, not interior decoration."

"I'm not a writer, I write copy, I write a kind of language that I understand is right for advertising," maintains Tim Delaney. Yet Delaney's style is one of the most imitated in the industry.

"A writer's style is more than his diction – word choice – or his rhetoric – his intention to persuade," explains Hall. "It is his use of sentence rhythms, short, long, simple, complex, or of compound sentences connected by *ands* that suggest the diction of the King James Bible. Style is reflected in the use and originality of metaphors, the form of the conditional, or the use of the present tense instead of the more conventional past; in differences of punctuation, the use of dashes, parentheses, and exclamation marks; in the use of dashes rather than quotation marks to set off dialogue; in the use of italics, the upper case, even semicolons; in fact, style emerges from all the author's quirks and mannerisms, weaknesses and strengths."

"I don't have a *conscious* style," says Abbott. "I suppose we all have a style, just in the way that we talk or shrug. I think I write like I am, whatever that means. It's not a very studied procedure. People tell me that they can recognise a piece of my copy, but it's not a game

I can play." Abbott illustrates a specific example of his style. "We were doing a pitch for a holidays company. We'd found this great photograph of a couple on a balcony in Paris looking over the roof-scapes, a very moody photograph. We were selling cheap weekends and city breaks, and I think the headline was *How can you possibly declare your love without a balcony?* In the body copy it said something like, 'You can have a weekend in Paris for £119'. I wrote the small print and it said, 'That's for two people, sharing a room'; then I added brackets and said, '(That shouldn't be a problem, should it?)'. I use brackets a lot, as it were, in conversation." Perhaps, then, he writes as he speaks? "I suspect that's true, but it's not something you can judge for yourself."

French believes style cannot be forced. "I wasn't aware that I had a style, until people told me I'd got one. It wasn't conscious. I think I probably write like I talk. I tend to put *um*s and *ah*s and dots and things like that in, because that's how I speak. When you're reading something, if you can hear the man's voice, it's far more appealing, if not more convincing. And I think everybody does that to an extent; Indra certainly speaks *exactly* the way he writes. But it's not the kind of thing you can give advice on. As soon as you tell a copywriter to write like he talks, he's going to think, how do I talk, how do I talk! Because it's unconscious, and the worst thing you can do is force anything. The best way of writing is to write, just sit down and keep churning it out, because the more bored you get with trying to force syntax, the less forcing you'll actually do. Just get it down on paper."

French suggests writing long letters and keeping a diary. "I used to when I went on holiday. I used to take a little book and write two or three pages every day. You can't keep putting 'Sat on beach, drank', 'Sat on beach, drank', 'Sat on beach, drank'; God, this is boring! In the end, you've *got* to write something else, so you just fill in. And then when you get home and you pick it up and read it, it is actually like you're talking to yourself because it's not important, it's just waffle. If you waffle interestingly, people will read it. And if you waffle boringly, like this, *nobody* will read it."

Paul Fishlock's view: "Unlike other writers such as novelists or journalists, who write with their own voice, a copywriter must be able to write in many voices – one for each client." Fishlock's work was celebrated in the D&AD *Copy Book*. He believes copywriters who use the same writing style in every ad, even a very elegant style, miss out on powerful ways to differentiate their clients. "It is a part of our job to create unique personalities for our clients. We do this not just in what we say, but also in the way that we say it – in the case of print advertising, how we write the copy. Copy for a skincare client should sound different from copy for a power tool client, which should be different from copy for baby food. Different vocabulary, different sentence construction, different language rhythms. Does this client talk about themselves in the first person or the third? Are they chest beating or understated? There's a right time and place for both. Then you must be consistent – the same writing style in the cinema commercial and on the poster as in the recruitment ad – the same unique voice. Move on to the next brief and you slip into a different voice. It's hard work, but it's what copywriters are supposed to do. Sadly, in an industry full of copywriters where it's often draft six before they get to something even grammatically correct, stylistic nuances have become an all too rare luxury."

Antony Redman also questions whether a writer can superimpose the same style across everything. "I think style is dictated by the subject or product. Sometimes you might want to write the twisty, turny stuff, other times not. What's more important to me, especially if I'm writing a long copy ad, is to have facts which *I* find interesting. It's the same if you're telling a story, if you're a novelist or a film maker. If something moves *you*, and you put that into an ad, or a novel, or a film, then it's going to move *other* people. If you're doing a serious ad, particularly a public service ad, you've got to make it sound reasonable to people. If you write long copy that sounds unreasonable, people are going to switch off. You can have anger in it, but it's got to be a quiet anger. Some people get angry and bang the table, whereas someone who's angry but speaks quietly, with some knowledge of the topic, you'd actually fear them more."

Rather than construct walls between themselves and their readers, Sinha argues that great copywriters allow their own personalities to come through in their work: "The difference between a great advertising writer and a good one is that the great one breaks through, his personality expresses itself. I'm not talking about just serious ads, it could be a frivolous thing. When someone's personal experience shines through, in the words, in the way they're used, it will always communicate in a more lively way, like one person talking to another, *instead of a set of ideas talking to a theoretical person*. Tony Brignull wrote an ad about Parker Pens, where he talked about the nib moving over the paper, 'leaving a trail of wet, shiny words'. Only someone who loved using a pen, and knew what it was like, could have written that. It immediately communicated the joy of writing with that instrument far more than clever phrases, or puns or wordplays about its balance or value. Tony is the greatest advertising copywriter that Britain has ever produced, and always in his ads you had his personal passion breaking through. That's what made his ads great."

Hugh Mackay concurs. The transmission of the writer's passion makes the reading experience potentially more intense than the viewing experience. "It's the magic, the power, the passion of the creative act in the words. And it sounds paradoxical; they're just words, they're just ink on paper, they're not a complex audio-visual experience. But the really creative, passionate writer does something with those words that the reader finds peculiarly engaging. John Bevins is fond of saying, if you enjoy writing the copy, the consumer will enjoy reading it. When there's real passion and intensity in the writing, there's likely to be the same intensity in the *reader*."

HOW *SHOULDN'T* COPY BE WRITTEN?

For generations, advertising copywriters have been taught that the most powerful words in the English language, or any language for that matter, are "new" and "you".

Sinha takes exception to "you". "I think I'm at odds with most of the advertising world on this. I actually don't like the way advertising is done. I think it's done in a way that's manipulative, which works against itself in the long run. More enlightened self-interest might be to stop being so obviously manipulative, and start trying to communicate," he suggests. "Copywriters always talk of 'we', and will always talk to 'you', and I question whether this is necessary. It's one of those conventions. *Who* are 'we'? 'We' becomes a faceless corporation. 'We' are always benevolent and wise, and have 'your' best interests at heart. There are three places where the second person, talking directly to '*you*', is commonly used. One is advertising. Another is a certain sort of pornographic sexual fantasy where 'you' are in a room with a beautiful blonde, blah, blah, blah. And the third is multi-user reality in cyberspace where you are constantly told 'you' are standing on the corner of a road, or 'you' are this, or 'you' are that. These are the three sleazy uses of the word 'you'." Sinha believes copywriters should break the mould. "By saying 'we' all the time, it just encourages the writer to feel part of a community of copywriters. No one actually feels as though they're writing on behalf of the client. What they're really doing is saying, 'we', me and my fellow copywriters, and the 'you', half the time, are the award jury judges. It's a very incestuous kind of world in which ads are often written just to win awards."

"Writers should see themselves as not the client's representative, but the reader's representative." John Bevins never writes copy from a first person plural perspective. His work is addressed to "you", talking about "*them*". "I think 'we' worked for a while when writers first started using it. It looked like the advertiser was talking. But it's become such a *cliché*."

Good writers wage a daily battle against *clichés* and formulaic copy. Of greater danger, however, are their own *unconscious writing habits*, the little affectations which are often mistaken for style. They can take the form of favourite linking phrases, or (wait for it) the use of bracketed phrases in the middle of sentences, or the use of capitalised letters to Really Make A Point, or sentences starting with "Time was when ..." and "Truth is ..."

"You have to beat those affectations out of yourself," warns Bevins. "You have to be constantly vigilant. They can very quickly become a habit, and you read back over your copy and really cringe."

"Writers definitely slip into an easy groove," agrees Bruce Bildsten. "More so in the United States, where young people's books all look the same. There's a certain attitude, a kind of smart aleck attitude. There aren't enough different styles, and different ways of coming at it."

The conventional agency environment does not help. Copywriting becomes a very commercial process, a very *conscious* process. The writer's real emotions are suppressed. The work becomes very external, restricted, lacking warmth and wholeness. The text is thin, not textured, not layered. There is no emotional resonance.

According to Hall, the conscious mind must be persuaded or tricked into getting out of the act. The creative mind must be rescued from the "dead hand of the conscious". Hall quotes John Hersey's description of the Censor of the Mind. The censor, near the surface of the mind, selects and filters and gives form. It is the arbiter of taste. But it is also an interrupter, an inhibitor, conservative and repressive. If we can paralyse our censors during the writing process, we will have free access to the "rich deep-brain source of primary feelings". Once we have trawled our subconscious, the sensor can handle the verification process later.

Advertising copywriters are well aware of those feelings when something wants to come out and do something completely different from the conventional. Some stifle those urges, either through self-consciousness or shame, and resort to the familiar and formulaic. It is safer.

Sinha says: "Just let what comes out, come out. There's this little critical thing that sits on your shoulder and says, no, that adjective isn't good enough, or don't use adjectives at all, and if you listen to it too much, it's going to stop you from getting very far in. Superficially, when the critic tells you that you haven't said something well enough, you've got to say, shut up, you can start judging when I've actually got out the content I want."

Sinha goes on to talk about the times when the right words do not come. "You can sometimes feel unable to do something. You're trying to achieve an effect, or write something very powerfully, but it won't become powerful. You can throw all the words you like at it, and they all mill around, and none of them adds up to this powerful effect. Now many people think when they hit a brick wall, that it's bad news. But I would say, no, it's not, it's actually good news, because if it's this hard to break through, the victory is going to be that special. It's like your own inner deep judgement, not a superficial thing that sits on your shoulder like a critic, but a deep judgement saying, not yet, not yet, not yet. You're restless, you're fidgeting, you're depressed, you find all kinds of interruptions and excuses not to write, and then you start to feel very guilty about it. Nine times out of ten, it's that subconscious aspect of yourself saying, not yet, not yet, it hasn't happened inside, because the actual creativity does seem to happen at some deep level of the mind without the conscious being involved, and when it's ready it will come out and then words *aren't* a problem."

"I think I must have been trepanned at an early age," declares French. "I don't think I've got a little censor. I never consciously go around any feelings that I shouldn't do something. The basic principle that I have about writing is that you've got to be interesting, and by its nature that usually means being a bit controversial. So I always start off by thinking, how am I going to make somebody go, good Lord, how did he get away with that? Then, I just write it."

WHAT SHOULD YOU KNOW ABOUT WRITING?

William Wordsworth described the task of writing as "emotion recollected in tranquillity".

Cutting edge copywriters write alone, in one uninterrupted burst of concentrated thought. Abbott writes it as it comes out. Delaney writes in a flurry of scratches and scrawls. French's light burns till midnight.

You should trust your subconscious, but still make conscious preparations.

Great writers know that adverbs are the enemies of verbs, adjectives are the enemies of nouns. Hemingway learned to distrust adjectives as he "would later learn to distrust certain people".

In *The Railway Man*, Eric Lomax conveys his grief in sober prose:

> The passion for trains and railways is, I have been told, incurable. I have also learned that there is no cure for torture. These two afflictions have been intimately linked in the course of my life, and yet through some chance combination of luck and grace I have survived them both.

Lomax, a boy who loved trains, became a prisoner of the Japanese on the Burma Death Railway. Despite his suffering, he can describe torture with sparsity:

It's even more sickening when you see it in the flesh.

It takes about twenty minutes to torture a bull to death.

The picador starts the proceedings by stabbing the bull in the neck with a steel-tipped lance.

This is done to weaken the bull's neck muscles.

Next on are the banderilleros. They continue the picador's work by embedding six barbed spikes (or banderillas) into the bull's neck.

The weight of the banderillas ensures that the spikes tear at the bull's flesh every time the animal moves.

Finally, the matador enters the ring. It's his job to plunge a long, curved sword into the bull's heart, to kill it.

Usually, the sword misses the heart and the matador has to sever the bull's spinal cord with a dagger. This results in paralysis, followed by death by asphyxiation.

Why do they do this? For the sad and simple reason that some people want to watch it.

These people don't need to see a bullfight. They need to see a doctor.

If you're going to Spain, don't go to the bullfight. (RSPCA)

The minimal use of adjectives and adverbs makes Richard Foster's copy stronger. Abbott Mead Vickers, London.

> Torture, after all, is inconspicuous; all it needs is water, a piece of wood and a loud voice.

After several attempts, Raymond Chandler found these words to describe footsteps:

> After a while they got faint, then they got silent.

Rudyard Kipling brought his sombre description of a First World War battlefield to a powerful climax; he told of the British soldiers who would

> wear their red way through every yard of it.

Like art direction, writing is a craft of reduction. Rely on alliteration and assonance; the labial explosives of big-bellied *B*s; an accumulation of soft, subtle *S*s. Revisit *Under Milk Wood* for imagery and musicality; you might just hear Richard Burton reading:

> To begin at the beginning:
> It is spring, moonless night in the small town, starless and bible-black, the cobblestreets silent and the hunched, courters'-and-rabbits' wood limping invisible down to the sloeblack, slow, black, crowblack, fishingboat-bobbing sea. The houses are blind as moles (though moles see fine tonight in the snouting, velvet dingles) or blind as Captain Cat there in the muffled middle by the pump and the town clock, the shops in mourning, the Welfare Hall in widows' weeds. And all the people of the lulled and dumbfound town are sleeping now.
> Hush, the babies are sleeping, the farmers, the fishers, the tradesmen and pensioners, cobbler, schoolteacher, postman and publican, the undertaker and the fancy woman, drunkard, dressmaker, preacher, policeman, the webfoot cocklewomen and the tidy wives. Young girls lie bedded soft or glide in their dreams, with rings and trousseaux, bridesmaided by glow-worms down the aisles of the organplaying wood. The boys are dreaming wicked or of the bucking ranches of the night and the jollyrodgered sea. And the anthracite statues of the horses sleep in the fields, and the cows in the byres, and the dogs in the wetnosed yards; and the cats nap in the slant corners or lope sly, streaking and needling, on the one cloud of the roofs.
> Listen. It is night in the chill, squat chapel, hymning in bonnet and brooch and bombazine black, butterfly choker and bootlace bow, coughing like nannygoats, sucking mintoes, fortywinking hallelujah; night in the four-ale, quiet as a domino; in Ocky Milkman's lofts like a mouse with gloves ...

"Bible-black", "muffled middle", "dumbfound town", "bedded soft", "wetnosed yards", "slant corners" and "lope sly" are profound craft examples from Dylan Thomas. If you want to write like that, Jack Kerouac suggests you should "be crazy dumbsaint of the mind" and "remove literary, grammatical and syntactical inhibition".

Great writers can teach us about writer's block, too. Hemingway said, "Always leave some water in the well". Deliberately stop writing at a point where you know what will come next, so tomorrow you'll have a place to start and write on from.

To stimulate better writing, one aspiring young copywriter retyped dozens of award-winning ads so he could experience great copy emerging onto a page beneath his own fingers.

How Should Headlines Be Written?

Are there any formulae for headline writing? Some headlines play one sentence off another, or one fact off another. And as a rule of thumb, the longer the copy, the shorter the headline.

"I don't think I have a set approach," muses Abbott. "I sit down, and I surprise myself by starting a sentence, but I'm not conscious of what the end will be. Somehow it works out. Sometimes it's quite neat and I think, I wonder where that came from."

Abbott is a quick, disciplined writer. "I try to find something that's going to be persuasive and insightful, and that pleases me in a craft sense because I've chosen the right words and it's concise. I find myself writing them very quickly, and then looking again at them the next day, and changing bits and pieces. I've always been quite quick," he regrets, "and I think there's a danger that it's easy to settle for kind of 'good enough', because you have a facility which gets you to 'good enough' quite quickly. You think, well, I've done that, let's get on to the next thing. I think I might have been a better writer if I hadn't found it so easy."

Delaney looks for intelligence in headlines. "There is a kind of familiarity about the construction of headlines which is dubious. Everybody gets a bit bored with it. I want the *thought* in the headline to be an interesting thought, which is relevant to the proposition." Delaney identifies the strengths of great headlines: "Intelligence in the thought, a degree of intelligence in the construction, and some

The Don McCullin exhibition. Featuring the work of Idi Amin, Pol Pot and Ho Chi Minh.

For over twenty years Don McCullin travelled to the battlefields of the world armed only with a camera.

In Cambodia his pictures bore witness to the work of the Khmer Rouge and their fanatical leader Pol Pot.

In Vietnam he was party to both the horrors of war and the dangers of war coverage. Forty-five journalists and photographers were killed and another eighteen are still missing.

In the Congo he found himself embroiled in a conflict made all the dirtier by the involvement of gun-toting mercenaries.

And he visited places whose names have become synonymous with suffering: Beirut, Biafra and Bangladesh.

But if war and oppression gave us his most powerful pictures then surely peacetime has given us his most appealing ones.

From his travels in the East are photographs of New Guinea tribes, a religious festival on the banks of the Ganges, and scenes from the Sumatra Islands.

From our shores there are dramatic landscapes.

And from his own home there is a series of still lifes.

For this major retrospective includes McCullin photographs that have never been shown before.

McCullin used Olympus cameras for many of these pictures, and Olympus in return are proud to be sponsoring this exhibition.

His work can be viewed at The Royal Photographic Society, Milsom Street, Bath from June 29th to September 1st.

Don McCullin has seen it all. Now so can you. **OLYMPUS**

A straight line sets off a bent line, by Malcolm Duffy.
Collett Dickenson Pearce, London.

kind of originality, which sounds a bit difficult to achieve, but a way of combining the thought with the construction to create an original way of doing it."

Sometimes, as was the case with his Timberland Red Indian ad, headlines come out of body copy. "You might say that's a pretty nice thought, and you just keep it back." Choosing headlines has become intuitive. "Not because I'm brilliant, but because I've had experience at it. Someone will come in with twenty ads, they might be for Harrods or Porsche, and I've got to pick two. I will know instantly."

Being both creator and critic is an intuitive skill which all great copywriters possess. As Indra Sinha admits: "I would normally write a headline first. Sometimes, it's very hard to find a headline which will do justice to the subject, particularly if you're working in the field which I was for many years, which was human rights. You're writing about some very brutal things that have happened to people. Sometimes there just aren't words to describe what has happened, so one tends to let them emerge somehow. You can't be glib or clever about them," cautions Sinha. "Well, you can be, but it would be very inappropriate." He cites one example. "There was an ad with a headline which said *Kids, you can never find them when you want them.* When you learned the subject was actually about children who had been seized and kidnapped and murdered, then you saw that attempt to be clever was a rather desperate one. It was very superficial."

Substance, not superficiality, should be the copywriter's priority. "David Abbott's *The board and I have decided we don't like the colour of your eyes* was a wonderful headline. Also one of Tony Brignull's, a very subtle one, *The life of a designer at Dunne & Co. is one of continual self-restraint*, was a very dry, very lovely line. They are lines with some substance to them."

Sometimes, Bevins writes headlines after he has finished the copy. "In a sense, there are two kinds of copy. There's the kind of copy that supports the headline, or expands on the line. Then there's the kind of copy that's more like a story, that in itself is supported by the headline, and the headline may not be written until after you've written the story. There are lots of people who write books without knowing what the title of the book is going to be. Once you've

Before they're roasted in garlic and rosemary they're soaked in urine and excrement.

The trucks that carry livestock across Europe hold up to 800 sheep at a time.

The journeys can last over twenty-four hours, but the animals' bladders cannot. They begin to urinate and excrete inside the lorry..

One sheep produces around a litre of urine and 700 grammes of faeces a day.

And so do the other 799.

Since they are trapped in such a confined space their fleeces quickly become coated in droppings.

For the rest of the trip they're wet, cold and some even suffer skin burns.

Eventually the urinating stops, but only because the animals are given no water in transit.

The size of Continental trucks means that unfamiliar flocks are often mixed together (an unsettling experience for any animal).

In the crush the weaker sheep lose their footing, fall to the floor and are trampled by the others.

Some die.

And all this happens so European meat traders can squeeze a little, more profit from their livestock.

The sheep could be slaughtered close to their farms, refrigerated and then transported (a method favoured by many farmers).

But offal and hides fetch a slightly higher price abroad and freshly killed meat is also at a premium, so the practice continues.

At least until the law is changed. EC agriculture ministers are about to meet to discuss livestock transportation regulations.

The RSPCA want to see an eight hour limit on the transportation of live animals for slaughter enforced immediately across the European Community.

Britain's representative at the negotiations is Gillian Shephard and there's still time to let her know your views on the crucial issue of maximum journey time.

Which is why we need your help.

Please phone the number below for a free RSPCA information pack and to find out what further action you can take.

Perhaps we can then persuade Mrs Shephard to look after our sheep.

STOP THE NEEDLESS TRANSPORTATION OF ANIMALS. PHONE 0500 34 35 36.

This whippet is a victim of recession.

It used to be a labrador.

When this picture was taken Sally weighed 26lbs.

The normal weight for a one year old labrador is about 60lbs.

The RSPCA inspector who rescued her found that every one of her ribs was visible and estimated that she had not been fed by her owner for over three weeks.

There is no excuse for this behaviour, but there is an explanation.

The owner in question had been made redundant and could not afford to feed the animal.

We were able to bring a successful prosecution banning him from owning a pet for five years.

But it was a long, expensive process, and only one of many we have to deal with every week.

Which is why we desperately need your help.

Our business is booming in this recession. Our uniformed inspectors are constantly being called upon to cope with its effects on animals.

Animals locked inside repossessed houses with no food or water.

Animals abandoned in remote lay-bys. Animals in pain whose owners cannot afford to pay vets' fees.

Our policy is never to refuse a call for help. But it's a policy that costs money.

We receive no aid from the Government and depend entirely on donations from the public.

Ironically, at a time when people have less money to spare, our need for it has massively increased.

Please send us whatever you can.

If you cannot help us, please don't hinder us by taking on a pet you cannot afford or giving an animal as a Christmas present.

And then, perhaps, the RSPCA will be starved of cases like this one.

Please tick the box if you are already a supporter.
Please use my donation to fight animal cruelty.

£100   £50   £25   £10   other £

I wish to give via
Visa/Access No:

Signature _____ Expiry _____

Name _____ Date _____

Address _____

To: RSPCA, Dept LTDT, Freepost,
Bristol BS3 3YY.

RSPCA
REG CHARITY 219099

Headlines by Peter Souter, using horrific juxtapositions.
Abbott Mead Vickers, London.

written the story, the challenge then is to find the best way to get people into it." Very often, Bevins finds his headlines are inspired by what people say. "I was at a Bankers Trust seminar and one of the speakers was describing the share market. He said, 'A rising tide lifts all boats, but a falling tide lets you see who's been swimming naked'."

"There's always the old style of copywriting," Ben Hunt reminds us. "You sit there and write twenty headlines. The best one becomes the headline, and the other nineteen appear in the body copy."

How Should the Copy Begin?

Classic book openings tell us everything we need to know.

> It was the best of times, it was the worst of times.

> I first remember being sexually abused by my father when I was about 3. It may have happened before, I don't know.

> Last night I dreamt I went to Manderley again. It seemed to me I stood by the iron gate leading to the drive, and for a while I could not enter, for the way was barred to me.

The first lines of a book are the most important. They communicate the flavour of what is to follow. Authors know they have only one chance to capture your imagination, or leave you cold, in which case you will not bother to read further and you will not buy the book.

In the first quote, Charles Dickens began *A Tale of Two Cities* with a cryptic observation of the times.

In the third, Daphne du Maurier's compelling narrative portends events in *Rebecca*.

The second quote is actually from an ad, a chilling account of child abuse written by Mike Boles at Saatchi & Saatchi, London, for the NSPCC. Boles, like other great copywriters, knew he had only one chance to hook his readers.

All well and good, some copywriters might argue, but shouldn't the selling proposition appear early in the copy? John the Evangelist thought so. The first sentence of "copy" in his Gospel puts the "product" into context immediately:

> Before the world was created, the Word already existed; he was with God, and he was the same as God.

324

What's it like to be raped as a 3 year old? A victim explains.

I FIRST remember being sexually abused by my father when I was about 3. It may have happened before, I don't know.

I can see it now, me lying in bed, with that big face coming towards me. He'd kiss me good-night, but he didn't stop at kissing.

He used to tell me it was our secret. And if I ever told anyone about it I'd be sent away.

But even as a child I knew something wasn't right. It was those words, "I'll protect you." How could he be protecting me? He was bloody hurting me.

It's strange really, he was my enemy, but at the same time my only friend in the world. He made me depend on him. He controlled me. My body was his toy for more than 9 years.

At school I found it hard to mix. I felt different. I'd never let anyone get close to me. In the changing rooms after P.E. I hated people seeing my naked body. I was so ashamed, thought they might be able to tell what had been happening to me and call me a poofter.

Even when I managed to find a girlfriend I still wasn't sure if I was heterosexual. I was terribly rough with her. I suppose I wanted to be in control of someone, like my father was with me.

Sex terrified me. Having an orgasm just made me think of what my father did inside of me. And that big smiling face.

I met someone else eventually. We got married. After 2 years she left me. She said I was cold and didn't understand her.

But that's how I was. I just wasn't aware of causing or feeling mental or physical pain. Some-thing inside me had been switched

off long ago. There were times when I could actually cut myself with a knife and not feel a thing.

After the divorce, I turned to drink. It was a way of escaping. But I still suffered deep depressions.

Last year, my father finally died. I think that's what made me contact the NSPCC. I was 53 years old, and it was the first time I'd ever told anyone about my childhood.

Once a week for 6 months a Child Protection Officer worked with me. He got me to tell him everything about my experience. Talking about it was very painful. For over 40 years I guess I'd been trying not to think about it.

Eventually though, it started to work. He made me realise that what happened wasn't my fault.

For the first time I can ever remember I actually began to feel good about myself. It was just like being let out of a dark and lonely cell.

I'll never forget what happened to me. But at least I can start to live my life.

For further information on the work of the NSPCC, or to make a donation, please write to: NSPCC, 67 Saffron Hill, London, EC1N 8RS or call 071 242 1626.

To report a suspected case of child abuse, call the NSPCC Child Protection Helpline on 0800 800 500.

NSPCC
Act Now For Children.

A compelling first-person narrative by Mike Boles. Saatchi & Saatchi, London.

Four sentences later, John advances his selling proposition:

> The light shines in the darkness, and the darkness has never put it out.

Text that stark and powerful, free of adjectives and adverbs, is worthy of emulation, but not easy to achieve.

"I've spent an extremely long time on openings," recalls Sinha, "usually two or three hours working on two or three sentences, just writing them over and over again with different word orders. What I've found is, when I've needed to do that, I've then thrown them away, because it's obvious that anything that needs to be written that many times is no good."

"Just write off the headline, or off the thought, and you'll find out whether it's good or not by the fact that it can sustain the argument or the creative platform," advises Delaney. "It was a kind of myth of copywriting that you write the ad, then take out the first paragraph, or the first five. I've never done that. I've always liked my first paragraphs." Not that it was always so easy, as Delaney readily admits. "When I was trying to become a copywriter years ago, and not very confident at it, I used to share a room with this old buffer. In the morning he used to come in and sit down, put a bit of paper in the typewriter, and just type all day and go home. And he used to do it all day, just type and smoke. He'd come and have a talk with me, and he saw I was stuck one day, and he said, what's the matter? And I said, I can't do it. And he said, just keep writing. What he taught me was absolutely true, which is what you do when you can't write, or even can't start, is *start anyway*. So I started. I used to literally sit down and say something which related to the headline and the story. I'd just write it down. Could be a question, rhetorical, ever wondered why this thing happens; or, there was a time when et cetera, et cetera. And I'd just write on. And I'd keep going, as though I didn't want anyone to interrupt me, I'd write it by hand, write, write, write, write, write."

Abbott wants to get into the argument that flows from the headline as quickly as possible. "I don't sit down and say, I've got to write the first great *War and Peace* opening line. I'm not conscious of that."

French advocates a "little bit of a slide in" from the headline. "It doesn't have to be the next expected line, but some relevance to the headline would be really nice. The whole point is, to get someone to read the copy, *you have to be interesting all the time.* So if your headline is interesting enough to get them in, don't blow your advantage in your first paragraph."

"I very much believe in that," says Sinha. "You have a duty *not* to bore the reader. Therefore you must start with something that will capture the imagination immediately, and often it may appear to have no connection with the headline. It doesn't matter, so long as the proposition that you've advanced in the headline is done justice to somewhere in the ad; preferably, don't leave it too long before you pick up the thread. Often if you find you've been working very hard on a piece of copy and you cut away the opening you've been working on until you come to the part where the real story starts, that's where your powerful opening is."

"I think the headline *is* your first paragraph." Redman draws an analogy with books. "When somebody reads a book, they don't have the advantage of reading a headline. So some of the great lines, like *Lolita*, they're the headlines that start off the book. So because the headline has dragged people kicking and screaming into the story, I think you need intriguing ways to keep them reading. Novelists do it as well; they mess with the chronology of the plot, so they will have one scene, which was ten years ago, jump to thirty years hence. It keeps the reader involved. And that's an interesting factor: you're playing with them, and if you do it right, they *enjoy* the fact that you're playing with them. It's the same with an ad. If you've said it in the headline, and you've got people interested with the headline, there's no reason then to have your first sentence repeat the same thought. I've seen that a lot in ads, and it's tedious. And what I've learned is once someone's written the copy, a lot of the time the first two or three paragraphs can be chopped."

It is far better for the writer to be ruthless with the copy, than the reader.

HOW SHOULD THE COPY CONTINUE?

"This is a kind of heresy," admits Delaney, "but I believe you write ads by sitting down to write them. You don't start knowing what an ad should be until you write it. *It's a voyage of discovery.* I think you embark with some information you have trust in, and you sit down, and then you start writing, and you simply do not know which way you're going. It's not to say you're going to wander off strategy, because that's part of what you sit down with; but it's only when you start writing, and thinking, and doodling, that you get to the point of what an ad should be. It isn't ever in the brief."

Delaney writes by hand. "That's the way I've always done it. I'm not a typing copywriter. My thoughts go faster than I can type. I want to scratch them out. I just want a ruled pad and a Pentel, and I can write really quickly then. I tear through it. Nothing interrupts me. I don't have to look at the screen. It's all just absolutely concentrated. It's a scrawl, I can hardly read it myself. It's all about hand extension of brain, not about how it looks, not about how many paragraphs, or anything like that."

Long copy is relatively easy to write if you enjoy doing it, Delaney believes. "But I think a lot of people can't do it, therefore they don't enjoy it. Steve Dunn always used to say to me, here's how much copy you need to write, and I'd go and write it. I can always write it to the length; if someone says, do me this much, I can write it almost without looking at it. What happens is, I go through it all, re-read it as I'm going, and then keep going. Then I go back and fix this bit, cut that bit, or whatever. It doesn't take me long."

Delaney's job, as he sees it, is to tell a story. "If it's about Porsche engines, it's about linking. You've got all the facts arrayed in front of you that you want to impart, and you just lay them out in front of the reader the best way you can. What I'm doing is assuming interest, which is presumptuous, but you *have* to do that because if you worry about interest, you'll think, my God, they'll never read it. So you have to tell the story in an entertaining way, use all the powers you've got as a writer to keep them entertained and feed them information they'll find relevant, and keep building, and then come to some kind of conclusion."

Samuel Goldwyn said a story should start with an earthquake and work its way up to a climax. Bevins takes the point. "If you've given them a great headline, you have to keep giving, and giving, and giving. It's a constant process of handing out small gifts, whether you're giving them something to make them laugh, or information they can *truly* use, not trite, shallow information. At the end of the

YOU WILL NEVER forget this masterpiece. It tells the story of Bathsheba and King David. It was painted by REMBRANDT in 1654. A fateful detail is the letter being read by Bathsheba. It is from King David. ▪ × × × × × × ▪ ▪ It asks that she meet him in secret. The consequences for Bathsheba – already wed – can only be tragic. But there is an even more fateful detail, discovered only recently. It gives new meaning to the brooding poignancy of "BATHSHEBA." ▪ Look closely at the model's left breast. Can you see the dimpling? This detail, recorded unknowingly by Rembrandt, is advanced breast cancer. ▪ × ▪ ▪ The consequences for the model? Well, she died several years later. ▪ × × × × × × × ▪ ▪ She was *Hendrickje Stoffels*. She was also Rembrandt's common-law wife and, within a year of the painting, mother of his daughter. (Was she pregnant as she posed?) ▪ In those days, neither model nor artist, nor anyone, had heard of breast cancer. Expert medical opinion now is that, almost certainly, she died of breast cancer. ▪ × × × × × × × ▪

family history of breast cancer. ▪ × × × × × × × × × × ▪ ▪ *Screening mammograms* are not covered by Medicare unless symptoms are present or unless there is that family history. ▪ If you are under 40, with no family history of breast cancer, your doctor is the best person to talk to about breast health and a detection regimen most appropriate for you. ▪ × ▪

TO AN ART LOVER,
THIS IS A CLASSIC REMBRANDT.
TO A DOCTOR,
IT'S CLASSIC BREAST CANCER.

A WOMAN'S BEST *PROTECTION* IS EARLY *DETECTION*.

Breast cancer is the most common cancer in women. ▪ ▪ ▪ These days, doctors can detect breast cancer long before it becomes even an unseen, unfelt lump. And long, long before it becomes the classic *"orange peel dimpling"* recorded by Rembrandt. For many women early detection can mean a complete cure. ▪ ▪ ▪ Early DETECTION is your best PROTECTION from the consequences of breast cancer. It can save your life, often without the need for a mastectomy.

THE ONLY EARLY DETECTION THAT WORKS IS REGULAR *SCREENING MAMMOGRAMS*.

Regular screening mammograms are recommended for women over 40 and for younger women where there is a

THE MBF SYDNEY SQUARE BREAST CLINIC.

MBF is determined to provide for its members what Medicare does not. For this reason, MBF recently acquired the respected Sydney Square Diagnostic Breast Clinic, now the MBF SYDNEY SQUARE BREAST CLINIC. Subsidised screening mammograms for MBF members, according to the medical guidelines above, are now available. ▪ × × × × × × × ▪ ▪ The fee is JUST $20. (Screening mammograms are available to non-members for the standard $60 fee.) ▪ × × × × ▪

ADVANCE BOOKING ESSENTIAL. CALL (02) 285 9999.

There is a limit to the number of screening mammograms that can be carried out. ▪ × × × × ▪ ▪ Not because of the equipment – MBF can always buy more equipment to meet the demand of its members. The limiting factor is the *highly-skilled personnel* essential to perform and interpret the X-rays. ▪ × × × × × × × × ▪ ▪ MBF acquired the Clinic for its members because it is run by some of Australia's most skilled and experienced breast health experts and *specialist radiologists*. ▪ × × × × × × × × × ▪ ▪ The Clinic views more than 10,000 X-rays each year. The MBF Sydney Square Breast Clinic can currently handle 100 screening mammograms a week, so naturally, advance booking is essential. For more information, call the Clinic on (02) 285 9999. ▪ × × × × × × × × ▪ ▪ If you are an MBF member, please have your membership number handy.

John Bevins invites us to detect cancer in a classic painting.
John Bevins Advertising, Sydney.

read, there mustn't be a sense of disappointment." Bevins says ads have the same potential as movies, books and even jokes to either enrich or impoverish their audience. Something in the ad should touch the reader's spirit. "I once did an ad for Microsoft Word, back in the early days, about 1984, and it was trying to get writers to use word processors and show them what a word processing programme could do. I'd found this list of words which Shakespeare had actually invented. I'd had no idea that words like suspicious, critical, distrustful, were originally created by him. So the headline was something like, *Suspicious, critical, distrustful of people who invent words?* And it went on to say that every word in the ad in italics was a word invented by Shakespeare. When they got to the coupon, the word *Hurry* was also in italics; yes, he invented that, too. At the end of it, people could say, I'm glad I read that, because I've really got something out of it beyond what it is I'm meant to get out of it, which is I should throw away my typewriter and use it as an anchor for my dinghy."

What distinguishes great long copy? More than anything else, its readability.

"For me, the transmission of the idea is the job," states John Salmon. "The form of it is less important than the content. I'm not given to puns or verbal constructs. I write in the tone of voice of the target audience in *easily transmitted language.*"

"The most important thing for me is to craft every paragraph and the point you're making in that paragraph," says Redman. "Some long copy ads might take a day to write, others a week, before they read well."

"The difference between good copy and bad copy for me," Hunt says, "is that good copy will have a flow in it. It will sound like it's not lecturing you; it will speak to you as a person."

"The copy has to flow," confirms Bildsten. "If you want people to read something continuously, it must flow as a continuous piece of writing. If it feels like you're just cobbling things together, then you're going to lose people."

"Avoid unnecessary diversions and indulgences designed to make the writer look good rather than the product," insists Fishlock. "Keep the reader interested at all times. One point leads to another, then to another. Think fishing: if the line goes slack, you lose them."

Graham Warsop is adamant that copy should reward the reader. "No matter how much factual information it contains, the reader should sense that it was written with care by somebody who wished to repay them for taking the trouble to read it. All too often, one reads body copy in advertising that looks as if the client had written it and the art director simply set it into the layout."

How does Sinha make his copy flow?

"I *don't* do it by one of the ways which is quite common, which is to link the end of one sentence to the beginning of another with a little bit of wordplay, or a little piece of irony. If it's done in a very accomplished way, I suppose you don't notice it so much, but when it's not done very well, which is mostly the case, it's clunky, and almost obscene and insulting. In fact, I don't think you would read on because it's patronising to have these heavy-handed links made for you. The way I'd keep a person reading on is I'd vary the *rhythms*, I'd look at the *musicality* of the words, I'd try and make the language *interesting*. More than anything else, I'd make sure there was an idea in every single bit of every paragraph, so the reader was propelled onwards by a flow of ideas, and if you don't have ideas, you're writing empty words and you won't keep anyone's attention."

Sinha's advice is to read your copy aloud. "If you have an ear for language, you hear rhythms of sentences, the way they flow onwards from one another. It's instinct. The very good trick actually is to read out aloud what you've written, and if it doesn't read well, if it sounds awkward or embarrassing, then you know you've got a problem. It's the best acid test of all. Read it aloud, and listen to it, and everything sorts itself out, because the words want to tumble out in a way that's attractive."

Abbott agrees. "I read my copy aloud, which is the old piece of advice. I've always done that. You spot the *false notes*, and you also check the flow, and you can hear when it doesn't flow, and that's the point of copy, to impart information in the most effortless way possible for the readers because they're not buying the magazine or newspaper for your contribution. It's very silly not to make it an easy diversion, an easy, rewarding one." Abbott still writes by hand. "I don't really think very much about how I write, I just do it. Usually I'm quick. Nine hundred to a thousand words, you work a bit harder

Twenty fascinating but utterly useless facts you really don't need to know about skin.

1. The smoke from burning giraffe skin is used to treat nosebleeds among some tribes in Africa. These tribes always travel with a spare giraffe and a box of matches, in case they bump into a tree.

(Not really: I made that last bit up.)

2. Surprisingly, elephant skin is extremely sensitive to sunburn. Now, why nature should have decided that this was a good plan for a large animal living exclusively in very sunny climates is a mystery. But there it is.

Take it or leave it.

3. Sharks have skin that is smooth when rubbed in one direction and abrasive when rubbed in the other. In fact, it was used as sandpaper, before they invented sandpaper. Not a lot of people know that.

So if you leave a trail of sawdust every time you scratch your back, you're probably a shark.

4. Lots of animals, (snakes and tarantulas, for instance), shed their skins every so often. They just clamber out of it, like overdue-for-laundry long woolen underwear, and walk away.

Well, not all of them. Frogs and salamanders *eat* their old skin. Words, frankly, fail us.

5. Polar bears are black. No kidding, they've got black skin but wear white fur coats, like Puff Daddy. Polar bears do not wear shades or indulge in rapping, to our knowledge.

6. How do mommy-hedgehogs have baby-hedgehogs? Going, "ouch!" quite a lot, one would think. But no: baby-hedgehogs are born in a little bag. So that they don't hurt mommy.

Isn't that just un*beardly* cute?

7. The Burmese Python has heat sensors in its lips. This apparently helps them locate prey. Which, presumably, they then kiss to death. Anyway, a popular python nickname is 'Hotlips'. Try it out next time you meet one.

8. The skin of the Crested Newt tastes horrid. This is said to be a defense against predators. On the other hand, since this wouldn't work until you were actually being eaten, it seems a somewhat questionable means of defense.

Revenge maybe.

9. The African Plated Lizard is usually sort of brownish. But in the breeding season, its head turns purply-pink. A similar phenomenon in humans can be observed in New York singles bars.

10. The New Guinea Pitohui has a toxic secretion on its skin and feathers, making it the world's only known poisonous bird. So if you see a 'Pitohui Vindaloo', on a menu, probably avoid it.

11. How do hedgehogs make love? "Carefully" is the accepted answer. So it's kinda strange that some African tribes use hedgehog skin as a fertility-charm. But then, these are people who inhale giraffe-smoke to cure nosebleeds, so what do *we* know?

12. Frogs don't drink. That's a fact. Alcoholics anonymous have very few members who are of the frog persuasion. They do, however, absorb moisture through their skin, and consequently have terrible trouble keeping their swimming pools full.

13. The Hagfish exudes slimy, gluey stuff, which apparently ensnares predators. How in the world it ever seemed like a good idea to *stick* yourself to the animal that intends eating you, is beyond us. It would seem to make you a sort of take-away lunch, but still...

14. Amazingly, the salamander does the same trick...only his secretion has the strength and bonding-speed of rubber cement. This explains why you see so many animals wandering about with their faces festooned in salamanders.

Not.

15. The Golden Poison Arrow Frog, from Colombia, has a skin-secretion so deadly that it cannot even be touched by bare hands. Guess what local hunters use this secretion for: Attaching little bells to party-hats?

Nope. Try again.

16. The Sumatran Rhinoceros is the only rhino with any noticeable hair on its body. Very butch, the Sumatran rhino, but this also explains why none of them have ever turned out to be Olympic swimmers.

17. The bullfrog breathes through its skin while underwater. As soon as it gets out of the water, it starts breathing through its nostrils. Nobody knows why it doesn't just go on breathing through its skin, but possibly it doesn't want to become a slave to habit.

18. Hognose snakes play dead when threatened. They not only lie very still but also exude a really disgusting, foul, rotting-flesh smell.

It probably works, but frankly, you wouldn't want your daughter to marry one.

19. Some toads have rather knobbly skin that exudes hallucinogenic slime.

Devotees avail themselves of this 'high' by scraping the slime from the back of the animal, or, in more urgent cases, licking the toad. Our question has always been what sort of a person would think it a great idea to lick a toad in the first place, *before* the dubious properties of its sweat were discovered.

20. The average female human has about four pounds of skin, which, if spread out, would cover about fifteen square feet. And if filled with feathers, would make an attractive duvet.

Mind you, if you used your skin as a bedspread, all your bits would fall out, and you'd have to carry them about in a large plastic bag. Which is easily obtainable from a local supermarket.

21. And one you do.

(Dove is all you need to know about skincare.)

Skin Fact Nº21

The smoke from burning giraffe skin is used to treat nosebleeds among some tribes in Africa. These tribes always travel with a spare giraffe and a box of matches, in case they bump into a tree.

(Not really: I made that last bit up.)

(Dove is all you need to know about skincare.)

Skin Fact Nº37

Some toads have rather knobbly skin that exudes hallucinogenic slime.

Devotees avail themselves of this 'high' by scraping the slime from the back of the animal, or, in more urgent cases, licking the toad. Our question has always been what sort of a person would think it a great idea to lick a toad in the first place, before the dubious properties of its sweat were discovered.

(Dove is all you need to know about skincare.)

Neil French using long copy ads to build Unilever's Dove skincare brand. French also art directed the campaign. O&M Malaysia.

on that. It's usually written as it comes out. I'm always a bit suspicious of copy that I have to rework."

French writes by hand, too, but directly onto the layout. He selects a pen which lets him replicate the font and type size of the finished setting. "I write to fit the ad, and I develop my argument as I go on, and when I see the final bit of the last column looming up, I wrap it up and get off," he laughs, "or switch to a finer nib and continue in 6-point."

French hardly ever rewrites an ad. "Although," he admits, "I have got to a point where I've done an ad and finished up a column short, and I can't waffle any more, so then I throw away the lot and do it again in bigger letters."

French writes and art directs his own work. His methodology is a fusion of both disciplines. Like Delaney and Abbott, he writes the entire piece in one sitting, but with the added advantage of being able to assess the reading experience during the writing experience.

"Generally speaking, I have a rough idea of what the thing should look like, and I know the type size it ought to be to make it look as though I've got something interesting to say. You can't do an ad in 24-point and hope that anybody will mistake it for an interesting ad. But if you do something in 12- or 18-point, people go, gosh, they've got a lot to say, and there's a complete difference. *Double the amount of words can sometimes look far more interesting.*"

The copy as visual, and the copy as copy, are French's dual pre-occupations. "I always start off thinking, well, it's going to be some-where between 12- and 18-point, and then, just on the basis of the look of the ad, I'll decide how many words it's going to be. Then, I'll start in the top left corner and carry on until I get to the bottom right corner, and work around the logo, if there is one." As he writes, French is acutely aware of his target audience and their sensibilities: blue rinses or football hooligans or bankers. Holding their interest may call for an occasional icon, or some visual respite from words, although French's work is usually without artifice. "If ever you see a large logo on any of my ads," he quips, "it's because I couldn't think of enough to write."

If flow is the greater priority in copy, content comes a close second. Communicating dozens of facts in a continuous piece of writing can

PEOPLE WHO ABUSE ANIMALS ARE CAUGHT SOONER OR LATER.
BUT NOT NECESSARILY FOR ABUSING ANIMALS.

What is the difference between a boy who kicks a dog and a man who beats his wife?

Apparently, just a matter of time.

Studies conducted over the last three decades show that people who abuse animals invariably go on to abuse humans.

When the FBI analysed the lives of violent criminals and serial killers on death row, they found that almost all of them had tortured cats and dogs when they were young.

Other research shows consistent patterns of animal cruelty among people who commit child abuse or spouse abuse.

A survey of fifty-seven families under treatment for child abuse revealed that in 88% of the families, at least one person had abused animals.

People who counsel battered women report that up to 70% of the women with pets have had their dogs and cats beaten, choked, mutilated, tortured, dismembered, hanged or shot by their husbands.

What does an abuser gain by attacking helpless animals?

He gets revenge. He gets a feeling of power and control. And when he discovers he can get away with it, he gains the confidence to start attacking people.

And the violence doesn't just progress from animals to humans.

It is also passed on from generation to generation.

An abused child, in turn, becomes an abusive child. He vents his anger and frustration on dogs, cats and smaller children at school.

When he grows up, he becomes an abusive husband and an abusive parent. In the process, he produces another generation of violent children.

How do you stop this vicious cycle?

Organisations like the Humane Society International stress the importance of correcting abusers early. Cruelty to animals, whether by a child or an adult, should never be ignored. It is a warning sign.

Not only is it a sign of a mentally disturbed individual, it is also a sign of a troubled family where child and spouse abuse may already be happening.

If you witness any act of animal cruelty, please call the SPCA or the police. Please remember that animals are never the only victims of animal abuse.

SOCIETY FOR THE PREVENTION OF CRUELTY TO ANIMALS.

Jagdish Ramakrishnan establishes a connection between animal abuse and human violence. Saatchi & Saatchi, Singapore.

be either a dull regurgitation or a vibrant reading experience. As Bildsten warned, the facts cannot be just cobbled together.

"I refuse to allow myself just to write the bald fact down," says Sinha. "I have to think, what does the fact signify? If you ask yourself what the fact signifies to you, the writer, that's one thing. But ask yourself, what does it signify to the reader? After all, you're telling the reader for a purpose. You have to turn facts, and numbers, into people's personal experiences."

When Frank Sinatra died, the media reported that millions of Americans were mourning his death. However, one correspondent reported that probably half the American population had been conceived while their parents were listening to a Frank Sinatra record.

"A perfect example of how to take what is otherwise a fairly sterile fact, and turn it into something which adds a whole dimension to what Sinatra was about," Sinha maintains. "A perfect example of how to present a fact."

But first, the facts have to be found. "I was doing research for our Save Water campaign, and I stumbled across the fact that some strange speakers had been invented which emulated the sound of flushing toilets." Redman turned it into a long copy ad, *Read on to find out what Japanese women do in the toilet*. "Which is something that has always interested me. If you read it, you don't think it's a water ad, which is the first rule. Then the copy goes on to describe their source of embarrassment." From this bizarre and seemingly trivial beginning, Redman had to steadily shift the reader into the serious consequences of wasting water. "If you just string facts together, it reads like a list; people will switch off. The best jokes don't tell you the punchline at the start. You have to link the facts in a way that's talking to a person, telling them things they never knew, twists of fate like water, the source of life, is bringing death. And you have to do it very reasonably, and ask for the reader's help, in this case, to treat water with respect." The ad took over a week for Redman to write.

Sinha can relate to that. "Unlike Neil French, I'll rarely get it right first time. I tend to rely on many drafts. I'll throw words at the computer screen and revise and revise. What's quite useful, having struggled with the material for a long time, is to put aside everything

READ ON TO FIND OUT WHAT JAPANESE WOMEN DO IN THE TOILET.

A polite Japanese lady will cover her mouth when she giggles.

She will bow her head to hide her eyes when embarrassed.

One could only imagine the crisis this creature faces inside the ladies' room.

She enters the cubicle, closes the door, pulls the latch and sits. Soon, the crowded washroom reverberates with the sound of her urine splashing into the water at the bottom of the toilet bowl.

An unavoidable nuisance of modern life you may say. A source of deep humiliation if you happen to be a Japanese woman.

Her solution for years has been to conceal the noise. Not by a well-timed cough.

But by flushing the toilet whilst relieving herself. The familiar commotion created by the gurgling cistern drowns out her business.

But by flushing the toilet whilst relieving herself. The familiar commotion created by the gurgling cistern drowns out her business.

Depending on the length of her stay, the toilet may be flushed up to three or four times.

And she may walk out quietly, without anyone knowing of the noise she has made.

Her face saved.

Unfortunately, the water is not. With each flush, 10 litres of water disappears into the sewerage. That's 30 litres a visit. And over 100 litres daily.

Now multiply that by the number of women in all of Japan.

A self-conscious avoidance of shame results in a shameful loss of pure drinking water.

And water is now one of the most precious commodities in the East.

Over 70% of India's water supplies are contaminated. In New Delhi, the Yzmuna River is deluged with 50 million gallons of untreated sewerage, 5 million gallons of industrial effluent and 125 thousand gallons of DDT. Not in a year. But each hopeless day.

The mighty Ganges swallows the raw human waste of no less than 114 crowded cities.

Shanghai spends millions piping clean water to its vast urban sprawl from over 900 miles away.

So too does Singapore and Bangkok. The Philippines and Indonesia inexplicably lose over one third of all water pumped to their thirsty cities.

Saudi Arabia's supply will be exhausted early next century. The next war in the Middle East won't be over crude black oil, but crystal clear water.

India and Pakistan are almost certain to find themselves in a similar position as they attempt to resolve the competition for the thick murk that flows through the Hindus River basin.

Hong Kong has the pleasure of possessing more Rolls Royce automobiles per capita than any other country. Yet you risk your life by drinking from the tap there.

Ironic then, that the source of life brings death. Bubbling with disease, fouled water robs the lives of 25 thousand Asians daily. 10 million a year.

The majority of them small children too frail to fight.

The World Bank estimates it will cost at least $128 billion in the next 10 years to simply meet the basic drinking and sanitation needs of Asia.

The World Bank estimates it will cost at least $128 billion in the next 10 years to simply meet the basic drinking and sanitation needs of Asia.

An amount almost beyond comprehension.

The crisis is real. It will not go away.

It calls for us all to re-evaluate how we use the clean water that is available.

And for the more ingenious ones amongst us to find solutions.

In Japan, electronic gadgets are now installed in the ladies' rooms. Attached to these gadgets are speakers. They emulate the sound of a flushing toilet.

Now there is no need for the timid women to flush any more than is necessary.

The Fuji Bank has installed this system and already reports a $70,000 saving on water bills each year.

How can you begin to change things? The battle begins in your home.

Everytime you turn on a tap, look at that stream. You wouldn't last three days without it.

More than food, or love, or wealth, you need water to survive.

(TREAT WATER WITH RESPECT)

Antony Redman discovers a bizarre connection between modesty and water conservation.
Batey Ads, Singapore.

I've been doing on it, and then just write a draft straight off, off the top of the head, and it usually flows because by then I'm *desperate* to say all the things I need to say and I'm not concerned with all the trying-to-be-clever's and curlicues and what-have-you's."

How Long Should the Copy Be?

"The great writers like Richard Foster seem always to write to the right length," Abbott reflects. "They seem to know when the job is done." Abbott instinctively knows when to end his own copy. "I suppose when it begins to bore me. Then I go back and cut another third out of it."

"What a lot of people refer to as long copy is, in fact, a paltry flea-bite of copy," argues Sinha. "What I call long copy is thousands of words. That's when you're really into it. I've begun lately, out of sheer bloody-mindedness, to say, look, you are just going to have to read three thousand words or whatever. And I'm not going to do that usual paragraphing trick any more! I'm going to write it like proper joined-up stuff. I'm afraid you are going to have to read ten-sentence paragraphs sometimes."

"I'm never afraid of long copy being used," confirms Mackay. "If someone is in a magazine or newspaper, they are there to read. And readers, generally speaking, love the word. They love print. They love the reading."

Mackay cites a successful long copy campaign in Australia for Bankers Trust created by John Bevins Advertising, Sydney. The ads are dense with copy.

"They're intentionally made to look difficult to read," explains Bevins, "so there's actually a sense of achievement in the readers when they've finished reading. I've never necessarily subscribed to the view that copy has to be broken up by subheads. I've never believed that every paragraph has to be one sentence. The reader should be seduced from the start." In fact, the reader has to contribute as well, Bevins says. "It's like telling a joke. It's not just given to somebody, they have to get it. The audience has to complete the circle."

Bevins advises writers to show people their work and gauge their response. "My team will always tell me when to stop."

Bildsten suggests an alternative to the traditional long copy

Only one annual award show takes place every eighteen months.
Oddly enough, it's not Irish.

Begorrah.

And alamak, lah, too.

Does anyone remember that rare moment of inspiration, when the last Creative Circle Committee decided, either in their wisdom, or from the depths of their ignorance, that the Gong Show should be postponed for six months?

The rationale for this whimsical flight of creative calendar-shuffling was apparently that agencies didn't have time to put enough work together to make the show worthwhile.

Meaning, of course, that they hadn't done enough stuff, now they came to look at it, that was likely to beat Ball.

So they gave themselves another six months.

The fact that this gave Ball another six months seemed, at the time, to have escaped them.

Look what happened. Wipe-out.

Murphy's Law, lah.

So now we've established that the best-laid plans end up in the shredder, shall we go back to being sensible?

Or have we inadvertently stumbled on the secret of eternal youth? A year is eighteen months. Neil French likes the idea a lot.

It makes him a thirty-year-old.

This year, instead of making the decision unilaterally we've decided to pass the buck. You decide.

There are several reasonable points of view on both sides of the argument, so here are some of them.

Read and make your choice.

The 18-month argument

At least it's original. Really not such a bad criterion for an event that is supposed to applaud creative ideas.

It gives plenty of time for each and every agency in town, regardless of size, to amass a body of work that it feels can truly represent its ability and talent. In other word, no excuses.

An annual show is very expensive to enter. A real drain on the bottom line. A system of two events every three years is easier to afford. And it allows for creative accounting.

It's too much to expect the sponsors to pay up once a year, every year.

It's a devil of a job for the elected chairman & his committee. There's a good six months work involved in setting-up every show, and then producing an annual. An extra gap of six-months would be a kindness to the poor souls.

There, it's all up to you, now. Fill in the little coupon, and tell us what to do.

To add to the confusion, we might as well air a few other thoughts which seem not to fit comfortably into either column:

Is it pointless having Singapore awards at all? Since our work is now internationally recognised, should we concentrate instead on regional and international competitions?

Or should we just ask Ball not to enter, and lower the standard, to give the rest of us a chance? It's a thought.

The 12-month argument

It's illogical. Annual is annual, and a year is twelve months, and that's the end of it.

If we can't do enough decent work in a year, let's admit it. Stretching it to eighteen months will just give some of us undeserved illusions of adequacy.

So enter less work. And better work. In any case, some ads judged on an eighteen-month basis would be two years old. That's archaeology. If not necrophilia. Not advertising, anyway. You're second-guessing. Ask them.

The Chairman & committee change every year. So the point's irrelevant. Agreed, if we grovel sufficiently to Jim Aitchison, he just might agree to do it again. In which case it's not fair to ask him to start tomorrow. Or is it? Yes, it is. Get on with it, Jim.

On a more positive note, can we parlay our success into something even bigger?

One idea, for instance, is to replace The Gong Show with World Press Awards. There's no such scheme at present, and with our reputation on a roll right now, can we capitalise on it?

Entries would have to be in English of course, or judging wouldn't be fair. But agencies in the U.S.A., the United Kingdom, Canada, Australia, and every other English-speaking country would feel far more comfortable sending their work to us than to each other. We're neutral territory.

As we do now, we could attract the very best in the world as judges, (who wouldn't like a trip to Singapore?) and the occasion could soon be an annual mecca for the advertising industry. Just as Cannes is for film, so Singapore could be for the print medium.

The concept fits in neatly with the new drive towards a creative reputation for the country, too. Think about it, eh?

You should tick *one* of the first three, *plus* number four, if you like the idea.

1. A twelve-month Gong Show ☐
2. An eighteen-month Gong Show ☐
3. Cancel the Gong Show ☐
4. Start the World Press Awards ☐

Name _____
Position _____
Company _____
Address _____

Signature _____

Mail to Florence Tay, M. Tay & Co, 1 Sophia Road, #05-03, Peace Centre, 0922. To arrive by May 31st, 1991.

Trade ads don't have to be boring, as Neil French's appeal to the Singapore advertising industry demonstrates. Note the icon in the text.

"When you see a man about to be murdered and he's looking at you and crying, you are naked."

Don McCullin has been photographing wars and human rights disasters since 1964, when he took his camera to Cyprus, and the Congo. He has often risked his life to bring back pictures to show the world what was happening, pictures which he hoped might help to end the horrors he witnessed. In these pages, Amnesty International invites Don to talk about his work and say what he thinks all of us can do to help.

PHOTOGRAPHS BY DON McCULLIN

Amnesty International working worldwide for the release of prisoners of conscience, fair trials for political prisoners and an end to torture, extra-judicial executions, "disappearances" and the death penalty.

Below.

The Congo, 1964.

A young man is tortured and humiliated by soldiers before being shot and by body, thrown into the river.

Minutes before this picture was taken, this man and others had been dragged behind trucks by rope tied to their groins.

The first time I saw a dead body was in Cyprus. Someone had shot this old man and his two sons. They were lying in a little house, warmed by the Mediterranean sun and when I opened the door, the sweet stench of fresh blood drenched my nostrils. In the next room there was a burning straw bed and the mixture of smoke and blood have stayed with me to this day. Often, if I get near a bonfire in the garden, I'm suddenly transported into a daylight dream of murder and death.

"The dead make their own statement."

I can see that scene now: the bodies on the floor, a woman standing there crying. It's her new husband she's looking at; they'd just got married. I'd let myself into that house quietly having knocked several times. I thought, my God, they're really going to punish me for intruding on this terrible scene but they didn't. They gave me a sign to stay and go ahead and record it, as if they wanted people to see. They wanted a record. The dead make their statement and my picture records it. The dead don't choose to give their statement like that, but it's the only way left for them.

I wanted my pictures to bring messages from the dead and the near-dead in prisons and death camps, to the rest of us as living, saying 'For god's sake do something.' It's the same job Amnesty does. The world's in a worse state today than when I started taking pictures and Amnesty is the only answering service out there, picking up on those feeble cries for help.

"What's your name, soldier?"

When I take a picture I may be the eyes of the newspaper's readers, but I can't be their conscience. It's hard living with my own.

The picture on this page, I took in the Congo. My baptism was the wicked experience of seeing what was done to those young men by

mercenaries in Stanleyville, now Kisingani.

I'd disguised myself and flown up on a secret aeroplane which was bringing mercenaries in from Leopoldville, now Kinshasa. I got to the airfield at dawn. A tropical thunderstorm was just finishing, the ground was wet, it was warm and everyone was sleepy. There was a platoon of men standing in the dawn, and this I foresaw stirring up, waiting to go. A man came down: the line with a clipboard and said, 'What's your name soldier?' I thought, I'm in trouble now. I said 'McCullin' and he said 'Not on the list! How do you spell it?' So I spelt it and he said, 'Right, climb on.' When we got to Stanleyville there was fighting going on. We drove from the airport past a lot of dead bodies to an old hotel by the river. There was terrific commotion, coming and going, distant explosions. After ten minutes a jeep screamed onto the compound and said, 'Any guys just in from Leopoldville, get down to the docks, we've got problems, the C.O. wants you over the river.'

"They were dragging them by the penis."

I was carrying a little twenty camera bag with two cameras, twenty rolls of film and a meter. A mercenary came up and said 'Have you got a weapon?' I said 'No' and he said 'Well get one.' I ignored him because it was abhorrent to me to carry a weapon. I jumped on this truck with all the soldiers and got down to the docks. I was young, easily impressed and I hadn't declared myself. I kept my camera in my little bag, but my eyes were wide wide open to all that was going on around me.

Out of the corner of my eye I saw a huddled bunch of human beings, all bleeding and shaking. It was a most distressing scene. A mercenary said, 'Haw, you should have been up here ten minutes ago, they were dragging them around behind trucks by their groins.' He told me 'That lot are for the chop. They'll shoot them and kick them in the river.' And I was in shock because it doesn't matter how tough you think you are, there's no kind of preparation that can get you ready for such sorrowful things.

"It's appalling to witness a murder."

To witness people about to be killed is appalling because you see them looking at you, pleading with their eyes. They sense your pity, their eyes get bigger, appealing to you to help, to get them out of this terrifying plight and of course there is absolutely nothing you can do.

You lose something of yourself when you witness people die. You walk away injured. There's a danger, since people have had so much realism from certain disgusting Hollywood directors that reportage pictures will be looked at as art. I've never considered my work art. I have watched too many people die. I've seen people murdered in front of me and I've seen public executions. You can never learn how to behave under those circumstances, because there's no way to behave, other than be outraged.

"The last air in his body was calling for God."

The old, famous cherry question is 'Do you ever help anybody?' The tragedy of my work, of thirty years photographing wars and human rights disasters is that I could never save the people I photographed.

I often wept secretly, when no-one could see. Once in Beirut I saw two men standing in a stair well with their hands up, while their families were being dragged down stairs. The families were looking at the men as they came

"I've never considered my work art, I have watched too many people die."

down. I went with the families and came back just in time to see these two men being shot in cold blood at point blank range. I can never forget that one of them had an Astrakhan hat on and a kind of light raincoat, and that the other was saying Allah as he was dropping. It was as if the last air in his body was calling for God. I went into the stairwell and gripped the wall and said to myself, take a hold of yourself, because this is only the beginning of... of what's going to happen here today.

"They were celebrating the death of a girl."

There was a day in Beirut when they killed several hundred Palestinians. I saw some of them die, but there was no way the camera was going up to my eye because a gunman came up and said 'If you take pictures you'll be killed yourself - I suggest you leave this area.' As I left, I heard the sound of a lyre being played. They were celebrating the death of a Palestinian girl about twenty years old lying in the winter mud and rain of the street. I thought my God, if I take this picture it could cost me my life, I looked over my shoulder very quickly

and furtively and thought I can't walk past this. So I whipped that camera to my eye and took one frame and hurried away and as I went I heard somebody pleading behind me, and got fire and I turned to see an old man falling; he was shot in the stomach at point blank range. I thought I must get out of here. You walk away from those situations and thank God you're alive, and feel guilty because somebody else paid the price for this mayhem. Next day I went back and there were mounds of corpses.

"When you think you're going to be killed..."

It's eerie, walking round a city where human life and human rights mean nothing. You walk round several corners and it looks normal, and then you walk round a corner and the most extraordinary things are going on - you see men being hustled to their deaths. I went up to one man, a gunman from East Beirut with whom I'd spent the previous day, and I said 'What's going on with these men?' He said 'They're going to get the chop' and I said 'No, please don't do this.' The press are here, everyone can see what you're doing, this is wrong, please don't do this.' He said 'Listen my friend, go away, it is none of your business and they took these men into the yard but I pushed my way in behind them. It had been raining and this old factory yard was all wet and damp under a wood sky. I saw one of the Palestinians looking at a gunman loading a fresh magazine into his rifle. I've often tried to transplant myself into that man's position. The shock of his: that goes through you when you think that you're going to be killed at just...unthinkable. It's unthinkable. I know that from Uganda when I thought I was going to get murdered in the Makindi prison. I know what that poor man felt like seconds before he was put to death.

"I thought my God, this is the end of my life."

In Uganda, I was arrested. They came to my room and made me pack my bags. I was dragged out and chucked into a jeep and driven to the Kampala police station, which was chock-a-block with people and two or three other journalists. About seven, when the day was beginning to fade, a man in a check jacket walked into the police station - he must have been a plain clothes security man. He asked the sergeant, 'Who are these people?' And the sergeant said 'They are journalists.' He said, 'Journalists! They are dirty people.' I was sort of staggering. But a few minutes later we were pushed and punched outside and squeezed into an army jeep. It sped out of the police compound up the hill and I thought 'They're going the wrong way, the airport's the other way.' They took us to the military prison at Makindi where a bunch of soldiers were drinking beer. They all grabbed sticks and rushed up shouting 'Get out of the car, get out of the car.' We were made to set on the floor cross legged, heads bowed and they started kicking us. Luckily they had rubber combat boots so we didn't get any broken ribs but they were whacking us with their sticks. Then they took us down into the courtyard, well inside the prison. They stood us against the wall and that's when I thought 'My God this is it, you know: the end of my bloody life.' My mouth was as if someone had emptied a tube of superglue in it because nothing dehydrates you quicker than fear. It completely locks your jaw.

"I lay on this mattress covered in blood."

But they took us down to some cells. We were there four days. There was a man lying on the bed. He looked in a bad way. Another man told us 'Take no notice of him, he's for the chop. He's a Tanzanian cop they caught at the border.' I heard the rattle of keys and marching feet and I ran and lay in the cell which had no lights. I heard them beating him. It went on and on and I heard the plaza and the screams and the thudding blows. Then they left. The

"You are just going to have to read it," says Indra Sinha.
Chaos Communication, UK for Amnesty International.

HOW MARGIN LENDING CAUSED THE SAD SEPARATION OF NORM AND MARGE.

№ 1* THIS IS A CAUTIONARY TALE of love, lust and having a lend. How two destinies were torn apart by a powerful yet greatly misunderstood force: margin lending. But first, let's get a good description of the culprit.

A Margin Lending mugshot.

Margin lending is simply borrowing money to invest in shares and managed funds. You increase your potential for wealth because you're investing with more than you would with just your own funds.

You get the capital growth and dividends or distributions from a *larger* investment (a), while paying the interest on the loan (b). As (a) gets bigger in relation to (b), you get wealthier, faster. Of course, if (a) *falls* in value, your losses are also compounded.

That said, the good news is that arriving at the first scenario may not be as fraught with danger as you may think.

Norm and Marge.

Rewind to January 1991. Tom and Nicole were newlyweds, Paul and Annita were in the Lodge, and Norm and Marge both had $50,000 to invest.

What to do?

They both decided to invest in shares, and for simplicity's sake, let's say that both their

investments mirrored the movements of the All Ords index.

Norm promptly invested his $50,000 in shares. Marge, on the other hand, took out a BT Margin Loan for *another* $50,000 to buy *more* shares.

This meant she now had $100,000 to invest, yet like Norm, she hadn't spent a cent over $50,000.

In margin lending parlance, she was *geared at 50%*, because she had a loan comprising 50% of the total (Marge could

have geared up to as much as 70% on many shares and 65% on managed funds).

So what happened?

The first year or so wasn't easy for Marge. Interest payments were often higher than the dividends she was receiving.

Nevertheless, her investments were ahead on paper through capital growth from a steadily growing market.

It was always her plan to reinvest any dividends in order to get the benefits of compounding returns, but that takes a little time to get up a head of steam.

Norm, too, reinvested his dividends (admittedly half those of Marge's) and enjoyed the capital growth from that same market. While Marge was ahead, there were times when it looked like their paths would cross again.

Like in late 1992, just before the new US President, Bill Clinton, took office.

Norm had even considered a margin loan but was scared away by all the talk of a 'falling market'.

Sound familiar?

So they both stuck to their own paths. And the rift widened. The bond market crash of '94 sent the market into a spin, but it still didn't re-acquaint Norm and Marge.

By now Marge's interest payments were well outpaced by the dividends she was receiving from her growing investments. Even in that lean year of 1994 her dividend income was greater than her interest payments by more than $3,000. She managed her risk carefully, never borrowing up to her limit, keeping a diversified portfolio of good quality assets and paying her interest regularly.

The rest, as you can see, is obvious. As the fireworks began exploding to welcome the new millennium, Marge's net return including interest payments and the $50,000 she

borrowed, was $271,873†, while Norm (still celebrating but with slightly cheaper champagne) had a net return of $213,214†.

Epilogue.

The moral of the story is to carefully consider margin lending as a very practical tool for creating wealth. Of course as with any investment, there are risks involved, but the risks are manageable, and BT can help. BT is Australia's most experienced margin lender with more than 21 years experience.

Advisers will recommend BT by choice, not by connection. They cite a team of more than 70 helpful BT client support people as just one of the reasons.

As for Marge and Norm, well, they never did get it together. In fact as far as we know, they never even met each other. And you know what? She *still* got the house and car. Go figure.

For more information, speak to your adviser, phone BT on 1800 622 910 or visit www.btmarginlending.com.au. Or clip this coupon and send to:

Reply Paid, BT Margin Lending, PO Box H157, Australia Square, NSW 1215. Or send by fax to (02) 9259 9709.

Mr/Mrs/Ms _____

Address _____

_____ P/code_____

Phone (BH)_____ (AH)_____

This information does not account for your investment objectives, particular needs or financial situation. These should be considered before investing and we recommend you consult a financial adviser. ‡ Chart based on monthly data for the ASX All Industrials Accumulation Index from 1/1/1991 to 31/12/2000. Lump sum of $50,000 invested for 10 years with no gearing, and 50% gearing (the loan amount remains fixed). Allowed for BT Margin Lending rates for the period. No tax or imputation credits.

▶ BT Margin Lending

A MEMBER OF THE PRINCIPAL FINANCIAL GROUP

'№ 1 IN A SERIES 'INSIGHTS FOR INVESTORS', BROUGHT TO YOU BY BT MARGIN LENDING.

Bankers Trust ads are deliberately crafted to look daunting by John Bevins Advertising, Sydney.

presentation. "Instead of writing it as a continuous piece, you can give *bursts of information*, bites of copy." He references Chiat/Day's Nissan Pathfinder campaign. "You visually tease people to read the copy bites."

SHOULD THE LAST LINE REPRISE THE HEADLINE?

Conventional wisdom says the copy should always end by reprising or reflecting back to the headline. One popular device is to express that reflection with a pun or a wordplay. If we accept the fact that copy should avoid insincerity, isn't this little trick too trite, too precious? Doesn't it smack too much of technique?

"I'm in two minds about it," debates French. "When I started to learn how to write copy, I was an account executive, the lowest form of life next to an amoeba, and I realised, luckily, that I didn't know anything, which was probably what set me aside from most account executives. So I went out and bought all the award books. If you read all the award books then, all the copy ended up with a reflection, in some way, of where it started. The copy made a nice, neat circle, and so I believed that was what you had to do. I copied it, slavishly. For more years than I care to admit, I ground out copy and reprised it at the last minute, so the damn stuff would have some relevance to the headline. It's only been in the last decade or so that I realised this was time wasted really, that Joe Consumer didn't give a toss, and the fact you'd led him in with one idea didn't mean you had to leave him with the same idea. In fact," French concludes, "leaving him with an entirely *different* idea suddenly struck me as a far more adventurous and rebellious use of copy. It was like leading them in with 'Come and see the naked lady', and turning them out wanting to buy the Encyclopaedia Britannica."

Abbott is more concerned with the way the argument is rounded off, rather than whether it reflects back to the headline. "There is a right way to conclude an argument," he advises. "It's not necessary to refer back to the headline. Once you had to end with the great pun or the great little twist. I still don't disbelieve in that, although I believe a lot less in puns."

"It depends whether you've formed an argument that's kept in contact with the headline," says Delaney. "There is a kind of formula

NO SURGEON IN THE WORLD CAN HELP THIS BLIND MAN SEE. BUT A DOG CAN.

Try going blind.

Walk to the corner of the street with your eyes closed.

Post a letter with your eyes closed.

Buy a loaf of bread with your eyes closed.

Discover how the simplest tasks become a nightmare with your eyes closed.

Now walk to the corner of the street and post a cheque with your eyes wide open.

THE GUIDE DOGS FOR THE BLIND ASSOCIATION
Department 3, 9 Park Street, Windsor, Berkshire SL4 1JR.

Persuasive copy, rounded off with an appropriate request.
Saatchi & Saatchi, London.

which is found in lots of advertising copy, and I've followed it myself, which is to wrap with a kind of reference back, because they always did it on Volkswagen. It's like the last chapter of a book; it's got to reflect something of the premise of the book. But if you've moved on from the premise of the headline, and found a different thing to talk about, then just finish naturally."

"The last line of the copy should act like the ribbon that wraps up the gift," considers Warsop. "It may not necessarily reprise the headline, although I have seen many ads in which that technique works to excellent effect."

"I think *every* paragraph should reflect the headline." If it does not, warns Mike Lescarbeau, the ending will stand out very awkwardly if it has to reach all the way back to the headline. The entire ad should be a continual amplification of the premise. "The end line should just be the end of a clever piece of copy."

Bevins believes it is instinctive to wrap with a reflection. "But I don't think it's a rule."

Redman is sceptical. "I think writers only do it to show how clever they are. It looks tricky. If you can do it brilliantly and make people go, wow, you're the best writer in the world, give it a shot. But if you're writing about a serious subject, your cleverness might just ruin the effect you've had on the reader. Sometimes it's best just to end soberly, and sincerely."

"It's conventional, and usually it rounds off the copy quite nicely." However, Sinha does not consider it mandatory. "There are times when it's quite appropriate *not* to do it. There's a very fine murder story by a Hindi writer and the last sentence of it has got nothing to do with the story at all. It's about riding in a car after the event, a description of the way the countryside was passing by the window. And yet, because it has no apparent connection, it gains a kind of surreal power. That apparently irrelevant ending casts the whole story into stark relief. If you study the work of great writers, if you can learn something from them about how to open and end things, you can apply those lessons, even though there is a world of difference between a literary short story and an ad."

While opinions differ, one rule is mandatory. Whether or not it reflects the headline, the last line should ask the reader to *do* something: either to buy the product, or boycott the bullfight, or save water, or send money.

"What makes you get your cheque book out isn't how loud they speak, but how well they speak." Abbott discusses the discipline of public service advertising and why young copywriters should adopt what he calls *rationality with passion*. "I think when you're young, there's more blood coursing through your veins at a faster rate, and you get angry. You get angry in print and you use exclamation marks. But it's like when you meet an angry person. Usually, they don't actually persuade you, whereas somebody who may be passionate about something, but speaks in a quieter voice, and bungs in some reasons, some rationality with passion, is usually more persuasive, and you get your cheque book out. They've said something which either makes you feel guilty, or sad, or happy, or nostalgic, or whimsical, or giving, and you want to bloody *do* this thing. Part of the process of making people respond to cause advertising is not just to tell them there's a problem, but suggest to them that if *they* do something, there's a good chance that the thing could be solved, and that they will have played a part, and that their money isn't going to go into some central administration fund. It isn't just giving for giving's sake, because there's a great deal of cynicism about charities."

SHOULD COPYWRITERS BE INVOLVED IN THE ART DIRECTION?

How their words appear on the page is a fundamental issue for copywriters, stresses Delaney. "I'm usually given a word count to write to, then from a word count I move to a letter count. I usually spend time down on the Mac with the guy putting it together, and we'll move letters and words and everything around to make it all fit. The fitting part of copy is a fundamental part of what you do for a living. Every sentence has to fit. That's what crafting is."

Salmon was once a typographer. "I made it my business to find out what was legible and what wasn't. There is so much rubbish talked." Salmon believes there is an inherent conflict of interest between copywriters and art directors. "Some are more concerned with the copy's appearance as texture or design, rather than with its transmission as language. Helmut Krone, who was probably the greatest art director of all time, would make sure that the copy was broken up into short paragraphs, with lots of widows, lots of broken lines. It would look like it'd be *nothing* to read it. Whereas George Lois, another great art director, would be inclined to have wide measures and treat the type as a patch of texture."

Writers, and their art directors, should learn basic editorial techniques, not only to keep readers reading, but so their ads slip into the editorial texture. Subheads work like signposts, promising more rewards in the text ahead. Indented paragraphs make the reading experience more familiar; so do justified copy settings. Judicious widows let air into the text. Quotations set in italics signal fresh surprises. Icons help pace the read, segmenting the argument; French once used a chilli and a shamrock, Andrew Clarke used a burning match. In his Metropolitan Police campaign, Neil Godfrey even ran editorial-style introductions in a larger type size across three columns. It is not mandatory to use these techniques, but it makes sense to know what they are.

"Because people aren't predisposed to read advertisements, because they've got no particular reason to want to do so, you've got to catch them." Sinha discusses the benefits of one-sentence paragraphs. "They break up what otherwise might be quite dense text and make it look typographically attractive on the page. They also give a sense that there's a lot to say. By writing like that, you can take a relatively short number of words, two or three hundred, which in editorial terms is nothing, but when you lay them out like that in a nice, large type size with lots of easy, relaxed leading, you can fill a page and it looks like long copy."

Redman has reservations. "I've spent many a day sitting in front of a computer, trying to rewrite lines so they fit into the column, so there are no widows, no big holes left in it. But then you look at some of the best copy that's written, and it's got widows, and it's got holes, and it's not justified, so I think it can be a little bit fussy when you start worrying about that too much because it also can destroy the flow of the ad. I've seen type set ragged, I've seen it set across the entire width of the page rather than broken into two or three columns, and it still works. The *major* priority is to select a typeface and a type size that makes it readable."

Has Copywriting Ceased to Evolve?

One who makes traditions absolute runs the risk of making them obsolete.

And so it is with copywriting. The craft is riddled with convention. Construction is predictable. Tonality rarely changes. Puns, twists, techniques are staples. Experimentation is discouraged.

"We have fallen into a mould," charges Sinha. "What idiot says that because it's a paid for space, it has to be written in a paid for way, with a potato in the mouth, talking down to '*you*'? You can put absolutely *anything* you like in that space. You can write journalism. Neil Godfrey and I did a campaign for the Metropolitan Police. One of those was a skinhead spitting at a policeman. It won a lot of awards, but it wouldn't have, had it been left to one of the people on the jury who is a very famous English art director, well known for being a dumb blonde, who said, this isn't advertising, this is journalism. To which I say, thank you very much, that's the best compliment that you could have paid me, it's far better than that Pencil you gave me."

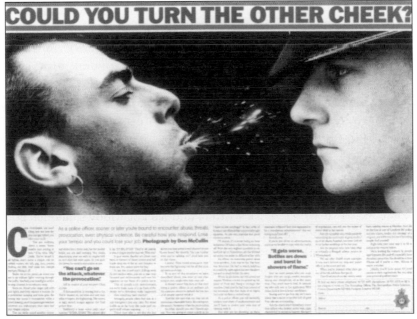

Indra Sinha wrote journalistically and Neil Godfrey used editorial-style art direction for the Metropolitan Police. Collett Dickenson Pearce, London.

Unlike art direction, where visuals are being pushed to extreme limits, copywriting has failed to evolve. It is all too easy to blame the audience; to argue that they are a visual not verbal generation. Yet more books are being sold than ever before. More people are reading than ever before. Audiences are better educated, more sophisticated, more inclined to enjoy great copy. The truth is more painful. The genre has largely self-destructed. Over the years, writers have failed to reward the readers.

"One of the reasons the craft has wallowed over the years, why it's dying out, is because copywriters just picked up styles from other copywriters," argues Bevins. "I think they should be inventing their own styles. It's one of the really interesting opportunities in copywriting. There are things we haven't tried, we don't experiment enough, and that's one of the offences of long copy."

Hunt agrees. "Copywriter is probably a good word because you copy other writers when you start. When I came to Asia, I was working with Neil French. He was an influence on me. And it's not just advertising writers. If you're reading Hemingway, you suddenly find your sentences are getting shorter." Hunt believes the hardest thing is *not* to copy. "Anybody can sit down, and with a bit of practice, write like somebody else. It's like singers. A lot of singers can sound like Ella Fitzgerald, but there's still only one Ella Fitzgerald. Hopefully, as the years go by, you grow out of it. You develop your own voice. Your writing starts to sound different, but it's not immediately obvious."

French can view the issue from both a writing and art perspective. "If you look at something that Indra writes, it's classic, and it could have been written by Hemingway or Scott Fitzgerald. If you look at the kind of drivel that I churn out, it's some guy talking, which is why it's full of my own 1950's-learned throwaways. We never grow out of what we learn when we discover language. I'm still Old Bean'ing people like an old fighter pilot, and that in itself has a credibility because they think, well, this guy's for real, nobody would write like that on purpose. The music and nuances of language change with the times, but they don't necessarily outdate themselves. The visual part of life changes from year to year; we don't wear drainpipes, but we still talk very much the same as we did in the 1960s."

If art directors dare to be different, why don't copywriters? As Delaney observes: "Advertising is very conservative, incredibly conservative, given that its role is to represent commerce, and commerce is moving, being pushed by consumers. Nike have done pioneering work with all kinds of communication. They've hired intelligent writers. They've done things which once I didn't like very much, but which I've come to admire them for, after writing for sports products myself. You're talking to a young audience where it's not a matter of writing and sounding cool, because that's really corny, but where you look for new ways to express yourself which aren't the conventional advertising structures or prose structures. It's a matter of adopting certain styles, a certain conviction, looking to other writers from other areas." But if it feels self-conscious, Delaney warns, it will fail.

Perhaps writers, by nature, are even more conservative than the industry they serve. Could it be that the desire to produce something which is new, different and good is outweighed by the fear it will be new, different and bad?

"This may sound indulgent," cautions Hunt, "but new, different and good, and new, different and bad, it doesn't matter; as long as it's new and different. I try to do a spectrum of work, the classic work, and some esoteric work, just to try to push back the boundaries. I've just written some stuff that I thought was over the top. When I was writing it I thought, I can't present this, it's off the wall, but the client just bought it. An eight hundred-word stream of consciousness ad, for an ice cream."

"I think that genuinely new work wins through in the end," affirms Sinha, "but it seems to be the case that it may not catch on for the first couple of years of its life." The Benson & Hedges surrealistic work, he says, which was very innovative when it first came out, was not taken seriously for awards until it became acceptable to do so.

"If you had a moratorium on awards for ten years," suggests Sinha, "if you said there will be no awards for the next ten years, and said that after those ten years there will be awards for the most new and original things that had emerged, then you might find that within those years all the new ways of expressing ourselves will just come out, because there would no longer be any compulsion to impress juries who are steeped in the old, conventional ways."

9

THE GLOBAL VIEW

The final challenge for cutting edge creativity is the global campaign. Advertising on a global level, we are told, cannot hope to speak with a cutting edge voice.

Usually, the argument is that one culture's creativity cannot be imposed on another. Cutting edge work is far too "clever"; it would never be understood outside more sophisticated Western markets.

Oddly enough, comprehension is not the issue. True cutting edge advertising is all about clarity, simplicity and imagination. Brands which have adopted it have become the new international icons.

As always, resistance to cutting edge work resides in a mix of fear and vested interests.

CAN THE SAME IDEA WORK UNIVERSALLY?

"It strikes me as odd," observes John Hegarty, "that if Hollywood manages to do it, music manages to do it, and Picasso managed to do it, yet advertising can't. And yet advertising is the one industry which is supposed to be able to bring people together. Physical borders are put up by people. The skill of great advertising is to come up with an idea that does cross borders. If you accept all the problems that that has, then you would never produce something great. You should look for the things that *unite* us, not divide us. Then you can create advertising that crosses borders."

Simon Sherwood continues: "If you start out by looking for the differences between people, be they political, ethnic, or religious, you'll find them. They're there. There are differences between the French and the Germans, between the Vietnamese and the Thais, but there are also some similarities. Our view has always been that when it comes to consumer behaviour, when it comes to consumer response to brand messages and what they want out of brands, those similarities are *stronger* than people up until now have believed."

Sherwood asserts that global agency networks have been structured around the differences rather than the similarities. "The way agencies have built their networks reflects the belief that different markets are different from each other. They all argue, oh, but that wouldn't work here. So the conventional agency network is there to recognise the differences, and what we've tried to do is look at it from the other end of the telescope."

At Leo Burnett, Singapore, chairman Linda Locke believes universal ideas will work if the product itself is universal. "If you're selling Levi's jeans, you're selling that same American lifestyle. Ads written for the British market have also worked in our market. But when people design ads with the global village in mind, that's when it seems to come unstuck. It's better when you stay *true* to what the brand is all about."

Ian Batey discusses one such brand: Singapore Airlines. "We've been heavily involved in the brand for over thirty years. It is a brand that is the same wherever it goes around the world. It flies with the same equipment, it flies with the same people, and it provides the same consistent service, so we can run the same ads everywhere. Now one could argue that your appeal varies in different markets and societies; that you are different things to different people. And it's a fair enough argument. But my view is, you are what you are what you are. If what you offer is not something that appeals in certain markets, rather than change your offer, rather than try to change who you are, you just stop going into those markets."

What concerns Batey is the need to remain consistent in a shrinking world. "We all know the world is shrinking by the hour in terms of our communication abilities, it's shrinking by the hour in the views we have on life, the world is shrinking in so many areas that I think you *can* spread the gospel according to what you feel is right globally, and it will work. The people who have found this extremely hard to bite on are the Japanese. Outside of Japan, they didn't really know what to do with their global brands. Therefore, they decided in America to do it the American way, in Europe to do it the European way. As we all know, that has been partly successful; but in the medium to long term, I think you need a *consistent* voice, so that wherever you are, whoever you talk to, there is a consistent personality and a consistent voice. You've just got to make sure that you get it right to begin with."

WHAT SORT OF IDEAS WORK UNIVERSALLY?

Food, shelter and income are basic universal needs. But every year, in newly developing nations, millions of consumers are progressing beyond them. They are acquiring new wealth and new, higher expectations. But when wealth ceases to coexist with sophistication, how should brand values be communicated?

According to conventional wisdom, newly rich consumers in newly developing markets can hardly be expected to understand advertising concepts beyond their personal fields of reference.

In Batey's view, it is horses for courses. "If you go into Bangladesh with a population of forty to fifty million, and you're advertising high ticket brands like expensive cars or air travel, you always automatically know that all you're talking to is five hundred thousand people. And you don't change your tune to them because they're highly educated, very international, very urbane people. Even with mass consumption brands, you're selling a dream. You can reach out and connect with people, no matter how low on the scale of education or income they might be." Batey distrusts conventional consumer focus groups. "Marketers have to learn to say, let's blow people's minds out. The new Asian is grabbing onto all the things he can get from the West with an extraordinary amount of appetite. He sees them as symbols of success, and he wants to exhibit his success. He's jumping in like Flynn. Whatever we think is successful in the West, I'll bet you by and large will be successful in the East."

Sherwood is convinced that advertising has to lead people. "When advertising just recognises that people aren't very sophisticated, it becomes crude and simplistic. Really effective communication is about giving people a point of view. It's not about holding up the mirror, it's about getting in front of people, and leading them. Great advertising should present *a vision that people want to share*."

Yet conventional global advertising has steered towards the lowest common denominator. The myth has always been that cutting edge work would *not* work.

The lowest common denominator has always been the problem in advertising, Hegarty observes. "How do you create something that has integrity to it, and has drama to it, yet talks to as many people as possible? That's what makes the job so challenging and so difficult." Hegarty believes people are able to accept much more than agencies and advertisers give them credit for. "There are always going to be cultural differences, and Heaven forbid, there should always be. But people are able to operate on a global basis as well as on a local basis. It's not a case of giving up one for the sake of the other."

How the Cutting Edge Cuts Through

By seeking similarities in their global target audiences, marketers can liberate themselves from the lowest common denominator in advertising.

Sherwood tells how. "If you go all around the world, which we've done, and talk to 15- to 19-year-olds, Levi's core target market, you'll find that while they're hugely different in some ways, they're remarkably the same in others. And I'm not talking about lowest common denominator similarities. For example, they share the same anxieties about growing up. They're concerned about the same issues. Their relationships with their parents. How they relate with schools, with authority. If you can find messages that touch those areas, you can talk to a much broader group, globally, in ways that you might not have thought possible."

Visual narratives, like the agency's work for Levi's, Sherwood suggests, offer the most potent opportunities for cutting edge global print and television.

"When mankind passes down its history from one generation to the next," he explains, "very often words have not been the medium to do it." From simple cave paintings to ornate works of art, the human condition has been preserved visually. "One of the things that we've developed is the visual narrative, coming up with ideas that have a powerful visual presence, that tell a story visually."

"If you want to aim for superior global advertising," says Locke, "it's got to be something on a *human* level, with human insights." Locke describes a telecommunications commercial shot by Leo Burnett, Thailand. "It was about a father on the phone in an airport lounge, enacting a bedtime story for his daughter. When the camera tracked around, you saw he was actually using a videophone. That emotional connection could be shown anywhere on the planet, and every father and mother in the world would get exactly the same thing out of it. Something which *touches the emotions*, something with the use of *humour*, will start to separate you from the competition, and the more rational work will probably become a thing of the past."

Much global advertising is still rational. But, as brand building itself changes, so will communications. Rather than trying to transmit fixed, dogmatic brand characteristics around the world, brands will offer relationships.

The way those relationships are offered by global advertisers will also change. Flexible control will replace rigid, centralised control. Mercedes-Benz has long practised this policy; tonality and certain layout specifics are carefully engendered globally, while individual markets generate and share ideas. The brand can speak with consistency and flexibility wherever it appears.

Locke cites the experience of British Airways. "In order for people to understand the new vision at British Airways, they had to have centralised control. When better work came out of the local offices, it was allowed to run." Locke believes that advertisers with organised global marketing structures and a commonly understood vision can gain more by allowing local markets to "explore a bit". However, she adds, "If they're very unstructured, with different advertising saying different things all over the world for a brand which is universally recognised, they'd probably need to go the other

Ihr guter Stern auf allen

Unser meistgebrauchtes Ersatzteil.

One of the world's most recognised brands maintains tonality, encourages flexibility.
Springer & Jacoby, Hamburg.

way, and put in some tight controls until everyone understood what the brand was all about."

New York adman Robert Gibralter has worked in Europe and Asia, and formerly headed global advertising at Avon Products, Inc. He has no qualms about cutting edge creativity being able to communicate with consumers in different markets across the world. His enthusiasm is underscored by what he sees as a "fascinating time in the history of consumers, global brands and commercial creativity". At Avon, Gibralter tapped local markets to help create a corporate image that was unified yet diverse enough to appeal to consumers all over the world.

Does he favour any particular strategic planning model? "I like the Brand Balance concept, to help understand the rational and emotional sides of a brand, and to lay the architecture for creative minds from around the world." But Gibralter is pragmatic. "Everyone seems to have a proprietary model. However, in the scheme of things, the model is merely a diving board for great creatives to soar, a brush in the hands of painters. Ultimately, each of the great creative masters has the edge within themselves and actually smash their own models to deliver outstanding work."

The Universal Truths

Disrupting conventions and achieving creative breakthroughs are possible in every market and in every language. There are no exceptions. Conventions exist everywhere. Creativity exists everywhere. The Greatest Lies are still The Greatest Lies, wherever they are told. The step-by-step path to cutting edge creativity applies universally.

In terms of execution, global cutting edge print should be more visual than verbal.

As Neil French advises: "If you base something on a line, especially an *idiom*, then you are definitely going to lose its power in other parts of the world. It is very difficult for an idiom, which makes so much sense to one country, to be translated or bent in some way to the thoughts of another country. Suddenly, it loses all its power. But if you base your campaign on a thought, or an attitude, then it doesn't necessarily lose its power and its life. Attitude travels, words don't necessarily travel."

Sometimes, simple English words like *Always* or *Just do it* can be used in non-English speaking markets, but, as French warns, there is no guarantee that they will be fully comprehended. Even the simplest English phrases such as *Just do it* cannot be translated literally into languages like Chinese. The abstract use of *it* in English has no word-for-word Chinese equivalent.

Humour probably is the most exportable commodity. When America's One Show staged an exhibition in Taipei, Little Caesar's TV commercials had the predominantly non-English speaking audience in stitches. When the Japanese entered their famous Nissin Cup Noodle *Hungry?* campaign at Cannes, it won the Best of Show. Every year, humorous print and television work from all over the world wins major prizes at the London International Advertising Awards and the New York Festivals. In their home markets, humorous print ads usually represent the cutting edge.

Simplicity should be another tenet of cutting edge global print, Guido Heffels stresses. "Focus on the major content. You can't throw five different balls at a consumer in every ad." Heffels votes for visual communications. "Why take the long way round?"

Bob Isherwood believes the power of a single-minded idea will communicate with people everywhere. "With more local markets accepting global ads, agencies have to acknowledge that it's not good enough to compete with the guy down the street. They actually have to compete with the guys across the ocean. Which means there's only one standard, a world class standard."

If Isherwood is right, what does it take to become a world class communicator?

"If you want to talk to millions of people," says Hegarty, "you must know how to talk to *one* person. And when you can talk to one person, then you can talk to millions of people."

GLOBAL PRINT PERSPECTIVES

China. "What was outside people's radar in China a few years ago, no longer is," asserts creative director Andrew Bell who has worked in Hong Kong, Singapore, Thailand and Malaysia. Major cities like Beijing and Shanghai are increasingly more sophisticated. "Chinese consumers are hungry for information, they're driven to discover

Cutting edge creativity from China, targeting blue-collar workers and farmers.
Breaking the category rules by not showing the product, it positions Jinling
"Clean God" as the washing machine that can clean their dirtiest clothes.
Campaign theme: "There are no dirty clothes that can't be washed."
Creative directors: Seah Chee Kiat and Chen Shao Tuan. Agency:
Guangzhou Jiamei Advertising.

new information, especially in the provinces. They read the ads as part of the paper." Bell cites a long copy print campaign produced for Carlsberg by Leo Burnett, Hong Kong. "The ads were about the brewery, how the beer is made. Consumers read every word. *China is a nation of new consumers.* They even read every word on the packaging. If something is new to them, they want to know what it will do for them."

Chinese-language guru Lim Sau Hoong has created many cutting edge campaigns for China from her Singapore agency, 10AM Communications. She maintains there are no differences between creating great Chinese- and English-language print campaigns. "A great ad is a great ad. It has to be effective, with a creative, fresh idea, well executed." She says the print ads that work best in the Chinese market are those that touch "both the brain and the heart".

Write down the ten most important things in your life.

1
2
3
4
5
6
7
8
9
10

We've got friendly neighbours. We've got strong allies. We've got good defence. And, frankly when we look around, there are no visible threats to our country.

But if we're honest, we'd have to ask: What has luck got to do with it?

In truth, nothing.

Because, since 1967, our freedom has been guaranteed by our citizens' armed forces.

And today, it's by no means a matter of luck that the Singapore Armed Forces safeguards our economy, our jobs, and our way of life.

The fact that we've survived and prospered all these years is the result of people sharing the responsibility for their own independence.

And making an occasional sacrifice.

People who recognise that the effort is worth it. Because if they don't make it, no one else will.

Imagine if the people of Kuwait had been asked that question, twenty-four hours before the Iraqi invasion.

Probably, their answers would have been much the same as yours.

But, twenty-four hours later, how many of the things they valued would still have been in existence?

It's a fact of life in today's world, a fact that's been repeated continually in history, that people never really know what they've got until it's gone.

Perhaps, in Singapore, we're luckier.

Singapore. We can't take it for granted.

写下你生命中
最重要的十件事

1
2
3
4
5
6
7
8
9
10

或许我们是幸运的。我们的邻国友善。 盟友强大。国防军事。环顾四方。似乎没 有什么内外患。

但让我们扪心自问：难道这一切都是 偶然的吗？

绝对不是。

因为自1967年开始。我们的人民武装部队就一直担起了保家卫国的重任。

今天。新加坡武装部队坚持确保我们 经济繁荣。工作稳定。生活安定。也绝不是偶然的。

而我们之所以能生存到今天。�32至今 享和人成果。靠的不是到的。正是人们坚 守国家独立。人民自由的信念与责任。

因为只有你们。才让每个新加坡人深 信：这一切都是值得的。只有你们继续努 力。我们才有今天。更有明天。

新加坡。我们岂能视以轻心？

试想想，倘若科威特人民在伊拉克攻 战他们的前二十四小时内有机会回答同样的问题。他们的答案会是什么？

也许和你的一样。

但是，二十四小时之后，他们所珍视 的一切，又仅存多少？

事实上，在不断重演的历史中，人们往往对所拥有的一切不加珍惜，直到有一天失去了，才能全图追回，一切却已经太迟。

When concepts are based on human truths, not wordplays, the same ad — with the same layout — can work in different languages. The argument in the copy was universally applicable, and presented with the same tonality in each language.
Euro RSCG Partnership (The Ball Partnership), Singapore.

Scandinavia. "Visually-led ads work best, simply because the pace of society is so much faster than just a few years ago," advises Erik Heisholt, executive creative director of Leo Burnett Oslo. Print is a very popular medium, and still engages local consumers. Scandinavia has won international fame for cutting edge television; its print work is now gaining similar recognition thanks to world-class print agencies such as Leo Burnett Oslo in Norway, and Lowe Brindfors Stockholm and Forsman & Bodenfors Gothenburg in Sweden. Heisholt believes intelligent humour works in his market and subscribes to the view that not every ad in a print campaign has to look the same. "There are no rules," he adds.

Eastern Europe. "The work that stands out is invariably produced locally," asserts Basil Mina, Leo Burnett's executive creative director for Central and Eastern Europe based in Prague, Czechoslovakia. "Most of the multinational work I see here is just bland, lowest common denominator work, internationally-sanctioned, and visually-based." Originally from South Africa, Mina has worked in Toronto, Hong Kong, and Chicago. He has won Cannes Lions with work done out of three continents – Asia, Africa and Europe. "I passionately believe that one does not have to live in London, New York or Madrid to produce great work. The trick is to find a fundamental human truth and dramatise it in a way that brings a smile to your target audience's mind. I am most excited by great work I see out of places like Egypt, Peru and Romania."

Mina believes print campaigns can cross borders and work across different socio-cultural markets. "If you dramatise a basic human truth in a powerful way there is no reason why it should not cross borders. The Mercedes-Benz SLK ad done from Leo Burnett London would still connect in the most remote market – people in Kiev would get that one! The same can be said about much of the Nike work." He also has faith in long copy ads working "as long as you have something relevant to say and you can say it very, very well. The great Amnesty International work done out of London all those years ago still resonates and it always will. Same can be said for the great Timberland work."

Because he is shaping a generation of creatives in markets where advertising is still a relatively new phenomenon, Mina is concerned

The way we were ... Celebrating the Czech Republic's freedom, Leo Burnett Prague's campaign for the Museum of Communism replicated graphics used during decades of Communist propaganda.

about the homogenisation of creativity. "I strongly believe that if you can speak in the local lexicon or work within a local idiom – whether verbal or visual – you are far more likely to connect. I worry that international award shows are homogenising the work. Last year's finalists at Cannes all looked disturbingly similar. We seem to be stuck in this post-modern phase where all the ads are visually driven, with minimalist copy and stripped down type. It's a good thing in that it establishes an international standard of excellence, but a bad thing in that most of the good creative people model their work on the international standard at the expense of finding their own unique voice." Mina offers an analogy: "You've never seen anything quite as awful as a South African rap band, or quite as beautiful as a traditional Zulu choir."

The Philippines. "Our market has been very exposed to a lot of cutting edge Western stuff," says Philippine creative guru David Guerrero, co-founder of premier creative agency BBDO/Guerrero Ortega. "People here are much more sophisticated than marketers give them credit for."

Guerrero reports that newspaper readership appears high. "The top three broadsheets each sell around 200,000 copies. Each province has its own local daily. Tabloids and freesheets are on the rise, too. But compared to the total population of 80 million, newspapers can be seen as something of an elite medium." Newspapers, it seems, are very diverse, densely packed with text, and liberally pull down cabinet ministers and celebrities with glee. "Telecoms, banks, cars and insurance will regularly use newspapers. Soft drinks, washing powders, shampoos and fast food restaurants less so. This is a country where the 30-second commercial on network TV still rules. On the other hand, Filipinos are the world's most avid text message senders according to Nokia, and the billboard medium is growing exponentially."

While Philippine print creativity is improving, logo size is often equated with "branding", laments Guerrero. "Celebrity endorsements are rife, and an awful lot tends to be crammed into a small space. However, there is a great tradition of public service and pro-bono work and its influence is often felt in mainstream product work."

Guerrero maintains everything needs to be visually-led, even a headline ad. Long copy has become a visual style of its own, he says. "The realities of production and reproduction in this country make it hard to achieve international standards. It puts an *extra responsibility on the idea* rather than being able to rely on stunning execution."

When it comes to ideas, apparently Philippine creatives have a lot to leverage. "Filipinos hate planning and love to improvise. They don't take life too seriously, even on occasions when they should. They worry terribly what others think of them. 'Face' and keeping up

Adidas and Baygon from BBDO/Guerrero Ortega,
the premier creative agency in The Philippines.

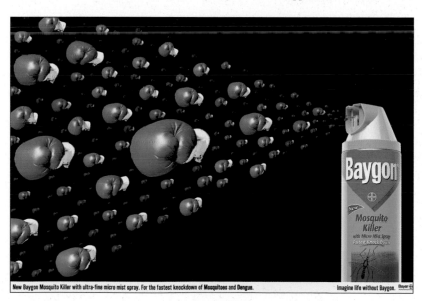

with the neighbours are important. Patriotism is fine as long as it's not too serious. Everybody loves the underdog. Then there's a huge Catholic transcendent belief in love, the church and the family, in the name of whom all things are forgivable."

Singapore. According to conventional wisdom, Chinese advertising should not be funny. Concepts should be based on superstition, good luck and prosperity. By applying some lateral thinking and humour, a dental hygiene campaign broke that convention.

Chinese readers opened their newspapers to find a rather incongruous message. At first glance, it did not appear to have any connection with dental health, or anything else for that matter. Translated line by line, the large Chinese characters read "14 is 14, 40 is 40, 14 is not 40, 40 is not 14", which is quite meaningless. However, as any student of Mandarin knows, it is a Chinese tongue twister when read aloud:

"Shí sì shì shí sì,

"Sì shí shì sì shí,

"Shí sì bù shi sì shí,

"Sì shí bù shi shí sì."

The tagline in small print reads: *Try saying that without your real teeth.* Chinese readers loved it; it was the only ad in the paper that gave them a chuckle. In the local advertising awards, it won Best of Show for Chinese-language print.

十四是十四

四十是四十

十四不是四十

四十不是十四

（如果没牙齿，看你怎么念。）

牙齿不珍惜，后悔来不及。
要重视你的牙齿。

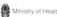 Ministry of Health

Breaking conventions with Chinese humour. Ketchum Advertising, Singapore.

No Jam

Double A paper, with evenly distributed fibres that make it the smoothest paper ever, is guaranteed to come out of your photocopier each time.

Double Quality Paper

No Jam

Double A paper, with evenly distributed fibres that make it the smoothest paper ever, is guaranteed to come out of your photocopier each time.

Double Quality Paper

No Jam

Double A paper, with evenly distributed fibres that make it the smoothest paper ever, is guaranteed to come out of your photocopier each time.

Double Quality Paper

A singular proposition, simply expressed, and relevant to the target audience. The universal truths of advertising were harnessed to launch Double A, a new brand of jam-free paper. Creative director: Norman Tan. Agency: J. Walter Thompson, Singapore.

Asian public service campaigns. BBDO/Guerrero Ortega fought air pollution for the Bantay Usok (Pollution Watch) Group, resulting in 34,233 SMS reports of offending vehicles. Meanwhile at TBWA Shanghai, creative director Eddie Wong focused attention on species endangered by Chinese medical practices for the World Wildlife Fund.

HAS CREATIVITY BECOME TOO HOMOGENISED?

Globalisation is seductive, but brings with it the risk we will all sound and look the same. And the issues are as compelling for advertising creatives as they are for authors and filmmakers:

How can I plug into the universal mainstream, but retain my own voice and culture?

If I want to achieve an international standard, do I really have to imitate the West?

Can my own culture evolve and find its own space within the wider marketplace?

Too often, bad advertising is excused, even justified, simply because it is "local", which is an insult to the culture in question. What we have to remember is that British advertising is "local" at its point of origin, and so too is American work. British advertising is so often brilliant because it is unashamedly British. Likewise, American advertising speaks with an American voice and attitude.

It's a question of applying the universal truths – singularity of proposition, simplicity of expression, and relevance of message – within your own cultural context. You don't have to slavishly copy Western ideas, or make your ads look like they were created in London or New York. The Brazilians have embraced the universal truths and found their own voice. So have the Japanese, the Thais, the Australians and New Zealanders. The Indians, Chinese and many others are beginning to.

It is not as difficult as it seems. Scottish author and Booker Prize nominee Ali Smith explains: "You go as local as you can, the thing becomes huge, it becomes the world. That's the key. Small things are big in our small lives. Little details are gold dust. We think things happen in a big way in our lives. Actually, things happen all the time in small, random and disparate ways."

If a New Zealand movie telling a New Zealand story can win the Academy Award, and if an Indian writer writing about India and an Australian author writing about Australia can win the Booker Prize, then the message is clear. Cutting edge creatives should be true to themselves and their own cultural context, while taking on board the universal truths of great advertising as their *guiding principles*. Rather than imitate, they will then innovate. The world is waiting.

10

THE CUTTING EDGE AGENDA

What does it take to be a cutting edge print communicator? Certainly not comfort. Comfort equals oblivion.

Being in the right agency will help. As Dean Hanson recalls: "I started in a very bad agency, which was a very good thing. You can gain an appreciation. It's healthy to be frustrated a little bit, as long as it doesn't crush you. I know so many people in this business who are really good, but they've never been given a shot."

Having great clients helps. "Love your clients to death" was chairman Michael Ball's edict at The Ball Partnership. When you find clients who appreciate and approve your work, treasure them. Neil French used to send the clients and suits to pick up the awards. Without their trust and support, the work would never have happened.

Having talent helps. New York headhunter Judy Wald says: "Execution can be learned; concepts are what you have to have, cutting edge concepts."

Above all, resilience. John Bevins wrote his first ads in school for surfboards. He is still writing. Antony Redman could not get in to show creative directors his book; but when he posed as a court official with a fake summons, all doors opened.

Not everyone succeeds. The great English actor Sir Alec Guinness left advertising after working "in a very minor capacity" for thirty shillings a week.

Those who have succeeded tell us how.

CHAPTER 10

HEROES AND HERESIES

Roy Grace. Roy Grace joined as an art director and left twenty-three years later as executive creative director of DDB Worldwide and chairman of the American company. In that time, he contributed twenty-five spots to "The Hundred Best Commercials of All Time" and four of the seventeen commercials enshrined in the Museum of Modern Art's permanent collection. His Volkswagen *Funeral*, Alka-Seltzer *Spicy Meatball* and American Tourister *Gorilla* are American legends. He is chairman of Grace & Rothschild, New York.

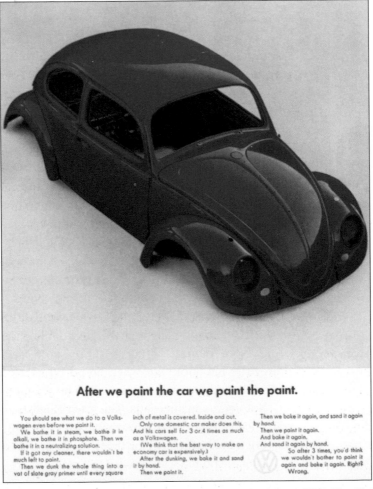

After we paint the car we paint the paint.

You should see what we do to a Volkswagen even before we paint it.
We bathe it in steam, we bathe it in alkali, we bathe it in phosphate. Then we bathe it in a neutralizing solution.
If it got any cleaner, there wouldn't be much left to paint.
Then we dunk the whole thing into a vat of slate gray primer until every square

inch of metal is covered. Inside and out.
Only one domestic car maker does this. And his cars sell for 3 or 4 times as much as a Volkswagen.
(We think that the best way to make an economy car is expensively.)
After the dunking, we bake it and sand it by hand.
Then we paint it.

Then we bake it again, and sand it again by hand.
Then we paint it again.
And bake it again.
And sand it again by hand.
So after 3 times, you'd think we wouldn't bother to paint it again and bake it again. Right? Wrong.

Roy Grace joined the Hall of the Gods, and became one of them. DDB, New York.

"I have been doing this since I was seventeen-years-old. I'm having trouble with the math because I don't want to believe it. Forty-four years, too goddamn long. My first agency job was at Benton & Bowles for a year, then Grey Advertising for a year, and then twenty-three years at Doyle Dane Bernbach. Before I went to DDB, I'd had twenty-five different jobs in advertising, promotion, graphics, publishing, always as an art director. I'd never felt I was able to do the kind of work that really satisfied me until I went to DDB. It was like coming home. I was free to do my best because the agency was so disorganised at the time. You were pretty much an individual who would succeed or fail on your own merits. Very little politics. It was chaotic. I had a supervisor, but I never showed him any work. He was too busy doing his own work, he didn't care. You'd do your work, sometimes you'd show it to Bernbach, sometimes not. It was just a wonderful place to work at the time."

Bill Bernbach's quotes still echo along creative corridors in every country of the world. "I don't know if he ever said anything profound in my presence other than 'I like it' or 'I don't like it'. Before he got into advertising, he wrote speeches for one of the New York governors, that's where his eloquence came from. He was an excellent speaker. He was a man who was dedicated to doing the best, provocative, graphically exciting advertising. He did it not as a necessity, but because of love and enthusiasm. And it was just a delight to work for him. What Bill was, was a great judge of advertising, and a great leader in advertising. He never was a great creator of advertising. The couple of times I worked on ads with Bill, he would come up with the most God awful ideas. He was very, very strong in his opinions and beliefs. He was a tough man. He would say, 'Fire that guy', and make sure he was out on the day it happened. He was not a pussycat."

Bernbach was already a legend when Grace joined. He had already changed the face of American advertising, but did he have any sense of his own importance? "Oh, he sure did. Later on, significantly so. It was a fascinating place to work, not only because of Bernbach. It was the level of talent in all the people around you. It was extraordinary. The level of competition was very strong, good, clean, open and honest. We needed Bernbach as a legend, as an icon. We not only perpetuated Bernbach's genius, we enlarged it. He was our battering ram against clients, against the threshold of creativity, and we used him in ways I don't think he could have fulfilled because he was only a human being, trying to run a business. We were always disappointed that when a client didn't buy an ad, Bernbach wouldn't resign the account on the spot, because that was *our* legend."

Art director Helmut Krone was another towering figure at DDB. "A very complicated man. I loved Helmut. But after working with Helmut for about fifteen years, I finally understood how Helmut's mind worked. Helmut could always be expected to say and do the opposite of what you'd expect. This was true in his work and in his life. Once you understood that about Helmut, you could deal with him. I don't think there's ever been anyone like him for print art direction. I don't think there'll ever be anyone like him again. A fierce dedication, absolute passion for excellence."

According to legend, Krone invented layouts, including the famous Volkswagen layout. "He didn't invent them, he rediscovered them at the appropriate time. Helmut would say things like, 'Everything I do I stole from somebody'. He was a great researcher. I believe that everything that exists existed at one time or another before in another form. Helmut would unearth forgotten devices at the appropriate time, and I learned that from him. It was okay not to steal, but to be *influenced*. He just had a unique mind and a unique way of working. It was hell for writers to work for him. You could sit in a room with Helmut for days and he'd never say a word. No matter what you said to him, he wouldn't answer you. Why? I think two things. Helmut was a difficult person, and I think Helmut was *trying* to be difficult. He was trying to feed his own legend and reputation, and he did a very good job of doing it. It took a long time for me to get to know Helmut well, to be able to go out to lunch with him and have a normal conversation with him. He was a very shy, introverted, very bright person."

There were other giants, too. "I remember David Abbott. He was in the early, filthy dirty, stinking offices at DDB. You could see then he was talented. He was very young, and he was in a foreign country, and he was in the Hall of the Gods, but he was good and it was a shame he didn't stay. David Abbott in one office, Mary Wells in another. Great, great people."

Looking at the industry, Grace is critical of conventional agency structures. "There is too much bureaucratic nonsense. The more a bureaucracy attains size, the more negative its impact becomes. A lot of these large agencies aren't advertising agencies in my sense of the word; they produce commodities. The people doing the work are overly supervised. They get terrible guidance. But I'm a fond believer in the genius of Man, in water always seeking the path of least resistance. Whenever you have something that reaches a level of mediocrity, another way pops up that's better."

Grace talks about sustaining a career in advertising. "There's an internal editorial process that you must have. You must be brutally honest, brutally objective, to maintain a certain level of quality, because it's always easy to say, *this* ad is not important. I wanted so desperately to be good at advertising. I think it was not so much fear of failure, but fear of not succeeding. I wanted to be bulletproof in what I did, so I became the worst critic I could imagine. It's the need to be absolutely certain that you're right and to ask the questions before the client asks them, to ask the questions before the marketplace asks them, about your premises and your execution. I have always believed you work for somebody. The great thing about working for DDB, I had finally found that somebody – Bill Bernbach. Long after Bernbach died, I was still working for him. I would say, what would Bill think? Would Bill like it? Now I'm still working for somebody, and it's taken a long time, and it's me."

David Abbott. "When you see young people coming into advertising now, they all seem to me much better prepared than we were. Most of us arrived via other jobs. I came via university, via running my father's shops when he died. I had no idea about ads or advertising, I'd never really written an ad, whereas now the kids seem absolutely passionate and bright. I had to be in advertising to discover that there was a different sort of advertising over in America. I lapped it up. I knew the body copy by heart. Somehow the rhythms of Volkswagen ads were in my head like a tune, so when I got the chance to write on it, I knew it. I knew how many lines there were in a column, I knew what the cadences were, I knew what the tone of voice was, because I literally read those ads every day. Now the people joining us from art colleges and copywriting courses do the same."

Before joining DDB, David Abbott worked at Mather & Crowther. "The writers and art directors were on different floors. I sat in an office full of copywriters and we fed out our paper which went into the art directors in the studio. I wrote my first commercial, which won an award, but I had nothing to do with it once the script left the copy office."

Neil Godfrey was the first person to be sent to DDB's New York office. Abbott followed. "We were real guinea pigs. Doyle Dane was the first agency where I worked in the art director-writer partnership. I was working with an art director on Volkswagen. I'd done some reasonable jobs, and my first ever Volkswagen TV commercial was for the square-backed sedan, about an eloping couple in the middle of the night, and I thought we were doing pretty well. One Monday morning I came in and my partner said, 'I've been in to see Roy Grace and told him I can't work with you any more, we're not cracking it'. Then Roy called me in and said I'd be going back to London soon, and he moved me on to something else. I thought I'd failed."

Abbott admits that he was permanently terrified. "I had arrived on a Friday and started work on the Monday. My wife was seven and a half months pregnant. It was July, it was stinking hot. We were living in a hotel for seven weeks. At the end of the day I used to get the *New York Times* and try to find a sublet. Whatever impression I gave of being assured, I was trembling inside. I used to cheat. I used to go home at night and stay up until four o'clock writing lines, then I'd go in and pretend they were impromptu. I'd say things like, 'I don't know what you think of this, maybe it just needs a bit more work', and I'd been polishing it for about four hours. Until I got one ad through, it was nerve-racking. But I was absolutely thrilled to be there, totally overawed. There were thirteen hundred people, seventy creative teams, at the office party in Christmas, 1966. All the corridors were full of heroes. They asked me to stay on. I was tempted, but I wanted to get back to England. I had by that time three little children."

Despite an outwardly gentle manner, Abbott recognises a restless, competitive streak. "If we're doing a pitch, I still tense up. I still don't want to get beaten. I think we are now quite a hard agency to beat. I think we've got used to winning our fair share of things. There's a kind of history of standards which you don't want to betray, which we do betray of course, I betray them all the time, but by and large you don't want to stop trying. This is a very dissatisfied agency, and I think that stems from a part of me. I'm much more conscious of all the things that *aren't* right than the things that are right. It's the things we *don't* do well that preoccupy me more than the things that we do do well."

If Abbott's first experience working with an art director had left him unnerved, a few years later he would commence the longest creative partnership in British advertising. "When we started this company, I had never worked with Ron Brown. He was at Young & Rubicam and I rang him up. He'd worked at Doyle Dane, but after I'd left. We had a chat, and I didn't know whether we'd get on or not, but anyway he agreed to come. And he's been prepared over the years to work my way of working, which is quite difficult for an art director because I've been doing lots of other things as well as writing ads. We don't sit down all day across the table with each other. It's grabbing moments, or it's me coming in, I'm afraid, with bits of paper and saying, 'Do you think this will work, Ron?' And if he'd been a different personality, he might have said, this is not a true partnership. In fact, it *has* been a true partnership because he's made an enormous contribution, and he's written lines, and he's just grown up about what I've had to do, and he's been prepared to put up with it. I wouldn't have been able to do what I've done without an art director like Ron. I suspect I probably would have stopped doing ads. My aim has always been to go on doing ads, so it was luck that we could work together and there was no jealousy or resentment. He's a very even-tempered man. He's also a great craftsman, which I've always admired, and I don't think I could work with an art director who wasn't meticulous, and didn't care a lot about the details, and be quietly passionate about the craft."

Neil Godfrey. "I came straight out of the Royal College of Art as a painter, so I really was very naïve in the ways of how advertising worked. I saw the page as the equivalent of a painting, as a space to put shapes and textures in. I'd been working for a few months at Doyle Dane in London, then they sent me to New York. The people who I thought would be the stroppiest and strongest were exactly the opposite."

Godfrey's immediate supervisor was Krone. "Everyone was in awe of Helmut because of his great Volkswagen and Avis campaigns. I was just amazed whenever he asked my opinions on things. I was surprised that Helmut could be a bit unsure. He'd been working on one particular job for a year. He'd tied a piece of washing up soap to a scented toilet soap with string, and by strapping them together he was saying the new product had the right combination of both of them. The agency had just hired a new, young account guy. He knocked on the door and went into Helmut's office which was very Bauhaus, severe white with tubular furniture. He said, 'Look, Mr. Krone, you've been working on this for long enough now, the client has been asking for this job, so can I give him a date?' Apparently Helmut stood up, put on his jacket, and went home. A week later he called up and said, 'Is that man out of my office yet? If he is, I'll come back'."

Godfrey describes how DDB created an inspiring atmosphere. "Instead of people pitting themselves against each other, and being rather petty and jealous, everybody was interested in what the other person was doing, just to see the great ideas that were coming out, and to want to do better through admiration rather than through jealousy. I remember walking past Roy Grace's office one day and he showed me this Volkswagen ad he'd done. It was a pencil line drawing of the top of a Volkswagen and the caption was *How much longer can we hand you this line?* And he said to me, 'I'm not sure about it, is it too simple?' I said I thought it was terrific, and he said, 'Okay, well maybe I'll think about doing it'. And it turned out to be one of the classic Volkswagen ads."

Client relationships were different, too. "What was particularly great about DDB and Collett's, in the 1960s and 1970s, was that clients couldn't wait to meet the creative people. I went out to dinner many times with clients and their wives. We used to do it because they thought we were geniuses. There's a slightly different attitude now. The clients all have Camcorders and think that they're movie producers. That film that used to be a bit of magic, you can't give them that any more. But there's still an opportunity in print to work the magic for them."

Tim Delaney. "I'm fifty-two and I started in the mailroom of an agency just off Park Lane when I was fifteen. I've been writing ads for thirty-four of those years and it's weird in the sense that I still really enjoy it. It's really strange."

Tim Delaney travels light. "I don't keep any of my ads at all. I don't regard them once I've done them. I don't give them any value. I don't have a reel, I've never had one. I don't see it as something which is about the best or worst, I kind of see it as a job, but it's a job I really enjoy. I like the work other people do as well. I don't see the work as some kind of testimony to me, or some kind of legacy to other people. I don't see it in any other terms than what's in *front* of me, and maybe that's why I enjoy it."

Delaney still signs off every brief in the agency. He questions them if they aren't right. He expects his people to be demanding of themselves. "Creative people often don't work hard enough. They go to lunch, whinge, and go home. They should be more prolific. Our agency did forty-five television commercials last year. If people want to write, they have to write and write and write. Creative people should take greater interest in not just the business of advertising, but the business of *business*. Go to clients, to boardrooms, learn the culture of clients, earn the respect of clients, not just in the advertising sense, but the business sense. It won't turn you into a suit, or make you less creative; it will make you a more perceptive, better connected creative."

How can creative people sustain a career in advertising? "It's not a lot different from sustaining a career in other areas. Fundamentally, you've got to *like* what you do, and if you're lucky in life, you can like what you do. I suspect that only about five percent of the people employed like what they do. So if you like advertising, that will sustain you. If you're in an area of advertising that you like, and one of the things about copywriting or creating ads is that it's very stimulating, you are constantly finding means of expression, that will sustain you. If you're good at it, then you'll get people to buy your ads, because they'll like them and they'll run them, and that will sustain you. If you're bad at it, they won't, and that'll make you very unhappy and then you should leave. If you've got a talent, you should find a place where that talent is appreciated by the agency, and *used* by the agency, and appreciated and used by their clients. That will make you happy because it means you're not doing something which is completely futile, so that should sustain you. Finally, you can be sustained by the fact that that is a relatively rare thing, and therefore you'll get paid handsomely, and therefore that will give you a lifestyle which you may not get if you become a milkman."

Neil French. "I never had any training to do anything except be a rent collector and a bullfighter. I never had any training to be a bouncer. I never had any training to be an advertising man. I left school when I was fifteen, I had no 'A' level English. I didn't go to art school, didn't go to art college, don't know nothing about nothing. But I understand people. I understand people *very well*."

As a student of human nature, Neil French qualified with honours. "In a long and varied career, I've mixed with so many different types of people of different educational levels, and of different financial levels, that I'm able to actually put myself in the position of talking to one of those people every time I do an ad. I can almost picture the person I'm talking to. And I find that an ad is a bit like a conversation, or telling a joke, if you like, or telling a story. You *vary* the way you tell it according to the audience, and it's those little variations that make the thing work for that particular audience. I learned those things especially when I was a singer; you'd look out at the audience, and you'd see the blue rinses, and you'd do a completely different delivery than you would if the place was full of football supporters. Although the material would be the same, the way you delivered it would vary. And so that's the same with an advertising campaign. I try and look at who I'm talking to, like the poor bald men; of course, in their case, I not only know how they think, I am one."

One group of people, French admits, have escaped his radar. "I think less and less these days I'm capable of talking to young people, because I don't have any kids, and I don't know anybody much under twenty-five, so I probably wouldn't be any good these days selling young stuff. I'm not sure I ever was. I think I probably missed out being young at some point. I think I went straight from being a schoolboy to being an adult."

French reflects on young creative people entering advertising. "Knowledge of the consumer is the most important thing, and it's one of the sad things that you see these days. Kids come out of art college with a lot of knowledge about computers, and *no* knowledge at all about the people to whom they're going to be speaking."

Gary Goldsmith. "I started off in the business as a writer. I couldn't think visually at first. It seemed like every ad in my first student book was a big line and a little product shot. I worked in a not-very-good agency, and all the art directors were ruining my ads, not that they were that good to begin with, so I decided to become an art director. For me, it was really a process of having to *force* myself to think visually. Even to this day I have to force myself to think outside of words. I think a lot of us tend to think in terms of words. Actually, it's much harder to think visually, at least for me it is."

Over the years, Gary Goldsmith has developed a theory that people should do work outside what their tendency is. "I tend not to use people in my advertising. And I thought about why I never did, and it's because of the ads I've seen that I have this predisposition that they're all corny and hokey and contrived, and the people are all very artificial looking and not like anybody we ever knew. I always resented the idea of an ad trying to tell me what I looked like, or what I should be dressed like, or how I should behave. A client once asked me, 'How come there are no people in this ad? We need people in there, so people can relate to them', and I told him, well, there *is* somebody in the ad, and the somebody in the ad is the reader, *that's* the person that's in the ad, because we're creating a situation where they're putting themselves in it, as opposed to having them see a mirror image of something that's not them. But I have forced myself a few times to use people. I've said, how can I use people in a campaign that's not like the conventional way? Sometimes you have to do an exercise with yourself where you say, okay, these are my tendencies, these are the things I typically do, and I'm not allowed to do any of those things on this assignment, I'm going to have to go against those things. If you generally use small, tasteful type, then use big, ugly type, and somehow make that work. And that's what I did with myself about using people. I'm going to do some campaigns with people if it's the last thing I do, and do it in a way that's my *own* way. And it was good because it forced me to do something I wouldn't have done, and it forced me to deal with a different side of solving the problem."

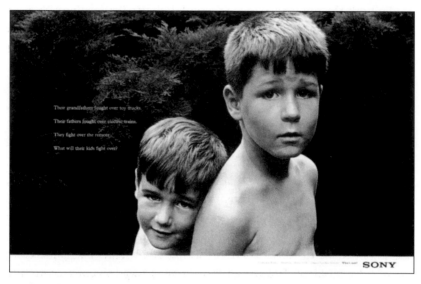

Gary Goldsmith, working outside his tendency. Lowe & Partners, New York.

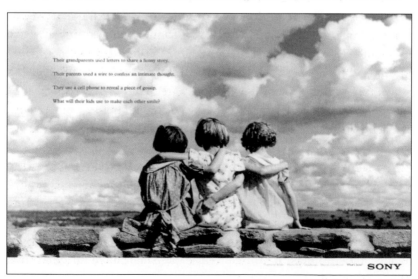

Goldsmith believes young people joining the business often lack resilience. "The schools are preparing them in such a way that they're actually *more* prepared than we were when we got out of school. They're doing ads that look like finished ads when they're in school. Their expectations are very high. They think they're going to get out, get a job, and everything is going to proceed very smoothly. A very talented kid came to see me with a nice portfolio, came out of art school, showed me his work, and his main concern was that he might go to an agency that would try to change his style. I asked him how many campaigns he'd produced, real campaigns, real ads, and he said, 'None'. And I said, well, you don't have a style then. After you've been in the business ten years, and you have twenty campaigns, then you'll have a style. You have to go into it open minded, try to learn from everyone you can, do work without thinking about your style, just think about solving each problem and let your style become what it will become. But if you're twenty-two, and your style is set after only working on your book, you've got the wrong attitude. My advice would be, *be patient and impatient at the same time.* Always be fighting to try to do more work, good work, but cut yourself a break. Don't expect that you're going to get out and be the world's best writer or art director in the first year. Give yourself a chance. Be resilient. People get discouraged way too early now. Just go in every day and try to do something good."

Bob Isherwood. "I left school at thirteen and a half, and I was an apprentice motor mechanic for two years. I was the worst motor mechanic that Ford had ever seen. I didn't have many skills, except I used to like to draw. I knew someone who had just finished art school and become an animator. He said I should go to art school, too, and I was so desperate to get out of being a motor mechanic, I thought, yeah, that's what I should do, and I got into art school, and that changed my life completely. After four years in art school I worked for a year, then I left Australia. I went straight to London, and I just looked up anything that had advertising in its name in the phone book. The first place didn't give me a job, but the next one did, Advertising Design Associates. I worked there doing pharmaceutical advertising design. But my first real job in advertising was at Young & Rubicam. I think I had work in the second volume of D&AD, but that was as a graphic designer."

Bob Isherwood, Saatchi & Saatchi's worldwide creative director, was originally based in the Sydney office. "We feel very much that a company doesn't have boundaries, and that includes geographical ones. I have always worked on the basis of getting people who are better than you are, regardless of where they happen to be. Don't just get someone because they happen to be down the street and easy."

David Droga. Recruited by Isherwood, David Droga was twenty-seven when he was appointed Saatchi & Saatchi's regional creative director for Asia. Within a matter of months, his Singapore office was named International Agency of the Year by *Advertising Age*. He became executive creative director of the London agency, and is now global creative director of Publicis Worldwide.

"I don't think talent itself is the key to success. It's a competitive nature, having a real drive, wanting to compete on a global basis, not just with the agency down the road. I inherited a competitive spirit, I'm the youngest of five boys. My four older brothers all got scholarships to Cambridge. The way I'd describe myself is that I have an immense ego, but also immense insecurities, and that's the combination that drives you along. When I sit down to do an ad, I'm always thinking, how can I do something great? And in the back of my mind, I'm thinking, but what if you *don't*? That's what pushes you to work the midnight hours, trying to surprise yourself. I've always been a selfish writer, I've always wanted to do the ideas myself."

As a loner, Droga is wary of the traditional creative pairing. "It is a dangerous scenario. Nothing can outdo a great team, but sometimes similar personalities clash, sometimes somebody won't want to voice an opinion because it might sound foolish. If you're stuck with the wrong partner, it can be an awkward situation, especially if the teaming has been thrust on you. At OMON, the writers did the ideas, the art directors art directed them. When I came to Singapore, I experimented with the teams, I shuffled them. We did what Fallons do, different people worked with each other, so they experienced new people, new things."

Droga keeps fresh by setting his goals higher and higher. "I had a lot of goals when I first got into the business at OMON. I wanted to be the best at the agency, then I wanted to be the best in Sydney, then the best in Australia. Then I looked for a bigger canvas, which was Asia. There are some agencies that have done good stuff in Asia, but it's still a new market, relatively unexplored. And I also keep surrounding myself with new, young people, to keep the pressure on myself, having people push you as much as you push them. You've got to be cynical about advertising, but you've also got to respect it. It's also not taking yourself too seriously. Some people just want to get to the top because they're very competitive."

Can young creatives expect resistance from older, more entrenched creatives? "To a degree. But I was sheltered at OMON because we were all young, all arrogant, going against the grain. There are certain older people who believe you have to pay your dues and have the battle scars to warrant certain positions. My argument is, well, bringing freshness and naïvety to the table is where you get new perspectives. I don't think you should ever carry too much luggage with you."

Nick Cohen. "I think that it's really important to understand that everyone is only as good as the *next* bit of work they're going to do. Our business is one where people do some good work, and then they feed and live off that for the rest of their careers. If you look inside yourself, you realise it's a young person's business. What you did a few years ago is irrelevant to what's going on now. If you really are good and you want to prove yourself, you have to do something that's vital now. Maybe if people shelved their egos and had a bit more humility …"

Tom Lichtenheld. "You've got to find what you love and let it kill you. It's tough, getting tougher, and schools are turning out students who are ready to start doing ads. I couldn't get into this business now with the book I had when I started."

Lichtenheld values humility. "Judging an award show is very humbling. It makes you feel most of your own work is mediocre. It makes you think, I could have done a better idea, I could have executed it better, I could have stuck to my guns better, I wasn't tenacious enough to talk to the print production person about that gutter space, there were too many gaps between those words."

Norman Alcuri. "You should break *thinking* rules, not art direction rules. Art direction is about communicating, because we're still salesmen, and also about appetite appeal. There's a German saying, the eye eats along. I think you should absorb everything around you: movies, CD covers, editorial designs. I still look through award books, even though those guys have always had more time and money than me, and they're better."

Alcuri shares one of his golden rules. "It took me a long time to learn this, and somebody should have told me, years ago, but if ever you have any doubt about what typeface to use, or what styling to use, just look at the pack or the logo. Make a link between the ad and the pack. Use a background colour, or a border colour, that matches the colour of the pack or the logo. Somebody has spent thousands on designing that pack, and the logo, which has a typeface attached to it."

Bruce Bildsten. Bruce Bildsten has spent most of his career at Fallon since graduating from college in 1981. An award-winning copywriter, he is now a creative director. "You have to make sure you're not judging work on what clients think is good, especially when you have as much contact with clients as I do. You have to look at things from their perspective, but be careful not to do that too much. I'm around them so much, the biggest trap I can get into is to start to think like them, or become a filter for them internally."

Bildsten seeks his inspiration from design. "I like to look at design annuals instead of ad annuals, to be quite honest, because I like to think more visually. I find them more inspiring and less of a trap than looking in ad annuals. It's also more helpful to look at foreign work than American work."

What sacrifices will lie ahead for cutting edge communicators? "*Sacrifices* is a good word. A lot of young people go to schools where they think they've learned everything. They think it will be easy, that opportunities will be handed to them on a platter. The number of opportunities available to people here at Fallon now, versus when I started, is just astronomical. Everyone has got opportunities with huge TV budgets within a few months of landing here, and they can be right out of school. The most successful people here stay humble and they really work hard. You can get so sucked up into the world of production, for example, and be so conscious of the hotel you're staying at, the places you're going, and the directors you're working with, in the end you can just end up with nothing.

Generally, and maybe this is just the old curmudgeon in me, I don't think people are as willing to work as hard as we were, not willing to go through as much as we were. They don't generate as many ideas to begin with. There's the belief that it's easier than it really is. There are art directors now who cannot draw a thing, period. It worries me because when they come to me as a creative director, I can't even begin to judge their ideas unless they take them another step further. Sometimes the ideas might be so utterly brilliant that I can overlook that, but generally there's so much that's missing, and sometimes they may get it right in the end, but sometimes they may not."

Indra Sinha. "I think that it's tempting if you do one sort of thing very well, to always do it. I'm accused a lot of writing extremely long copy ads when maybe it's not necessary. I believe in the power of the word, and therefore I actually want to write. It's not a conscious decision that I have done successful ads for one campaign, therefore I'll do it the same way again. Probably, I'm best known in the industry for doing things like the Metropolitan Police ads, and Amnesty ads, but actually they're not the things that are closest to my heart. The closest ads to my heart were some silly little ads I wrote for an Indian bookshop, which were written in the first person in an Indian dialect, full of things like, 'He speaks English like a native'. They were character sketches of my friend who ran the bookshop. We used to do six or eight a year. They were very scurrilous, they made fun of people. One year, I put three of them into D&AD, and they all got in."

Bill Oberlander. "My advice to art directors is to go back to school and study design. There are too many poseurs, too many fake art directors in this business, too many copywriters with a set of markers or some Mac skills who don't understand how graphic tension on a page can really change the way people feel. I'm training designers to be art directors, and I'm having art directors think more like designers."

His advice to creative directors and agency heads? "Recruit younger people who keep you young. Recruit the right kind of clients who keep you believing that it's possible. If you recruit the wrong clients time and time again, you're going to get more cynical, more bitter, more jaded, and more dispirited, and then you just give up."

389

Gerard Stamp. "Study all the award books. In magazines and newspapers, rip out ads you like. Rip out ads you don't like, too, and work out what they are trying to say and do it better. Don't worry about building a portfolio full of highly finished mock-ups. Just use a big black Pentel pen and get the idea across on a layout pad. Please, try to avoid the easy fix on a computer. If you think you can't draw, just use stick men. A child can draw stick men, and sometimes a child-like layout is the best. Keep it simple. If in doubt, take it out. Learn to love type as much as photographs and illustrations. Type is very often the key that unlocks a layout."

Basil Mina. "I forget who it was that said 'only write about what you know', but they really nailed it. Open your eyes and see what is going on outside your own door, to the human drama playing out in Bucharest or Bratislava. Open your eyes on the trams, in restaurants, at the sandwich bar, wherever. That's where you will find your most original ideas, and more simple, original human truths than any advertising annual you can get your hands on. Consume the art directors' annuals and award show books for the *technique*, but open your eyes to what's in front of you. Don't steal ideas. Be inspired by the *principles* behind the great work, but find your own voice."

Mark Tutssel. "Consumers haven't lost their ability to read, the industry has lost its ability to write." Tutssel argues that colleges must begin producing copywriters again. His advice to young creatives:

"Become a student of print advertising. Study the award show annuals. Go back in time and study the work of the great copywriters, from a time when there was no shortage of craftsmen. Copywriters who could do full justice to the medium. Read and read again the copy written by the greats – David Abbott, Ed McCabe, Tim Delaney and Bob Levenson, to name a few. *Don't imitate. Study and learn.*"

Tutssel balances that advice with another imperative. "Go out and experience life and bring it to your work. Stay so tuned into popular culture and new thinking that you amass a reservoir of ideas to call on."

Simplicity, he reminds us, is the key to a great print ad. "Great ads never let anything get in the way of a powerful, believable message.

There are a lot of rules for making a great print ad, but when you see a great one, it throws out all the rules."

Graham Warsop. "I recently had the good fortune to judge the Singapore Creative Circle Awards with some of the world's top creatives, including John Hegarty. During a conversation, he remarked how important it is for creatives not to become fixated with advertising, where their staple reading diet is advertising annuals. He's absolutely right. One will find far more inspiration from going to a ballet, climbing a tree, walking through a busy market or any one of a hundred other activities that let one observe people, life, nature and culture."

Warsop believes the time has arrived when creatives should approach the crafts of communication more broadly and with greater discipline. "However naturally talented they may be, there is always enormous scope for improvement and learning. Fortunately today there are more books written on the various different disciplines in communication than ever before, one example being *Is Anybody Out There?* I would recommend to young creatives that they should endeavour to read at least one book, not an awards annual, on aspects of communication every two months, and one book that is completely unrelated to advertising every two months."

How Others See Us

Anthony Vagnoni, former editor-at-large of *Advertising Age*, wrote about nothing else but people who make ads. "The best people do not, repeat, do not take themselves too seriously. They have healthy, grounded egos. They live in the real world. They don't live and breathe advertising."

Vagnoni believes too many young creatives are so obsessed by advertising that they have become desensitised to life. "The best work doesn't breed off itself. It's fresh. You've got to find insights in the real world and apply them to products. You've got to have a healthy sense of yourself; you're not finding a cure for cancer, you're not Francis Ford Coppola." He suggests two role models. "Jeff Goodby, because he's not from the self-referential school of advertising. And Cliff Freeman, because he has had consistent success throughout his career, not just one great campaign."

In London, Gee Thomson, founder of *Shots*, thinks advertising must move forward rapidly. "People see the machinery of advertising too easily. It's been very clumsy in the past. Images like sex and fast cars have worn thin. They are too blatant and not acceptable to the new, young people of today. Advertising needs to come from new, unexpected angles."

Thomson believes the people who stand out in advertising are usually very individual. "Advertising has absorbed difficult people, off-the-wall people. Above all else, they are truly original thinkers. They have themes in their heads which they pursue."

Michael Lynch, publisher of Australia's *Campaign Brief*, identifies the qualities of great advertising people: "If you take a local example, Lionel Hunt and the Campaign Palace, it's about not compromising, not taking every client there is. Put everything into your ads and let the money come later. Talent helps, which is found early in life; a hack usually never becomes anything more."

Lynch says doing ads self-sustains. "The great names still do ads. It's like doing it for the first time, every time. If I was young and wanted a career in advertising, I'd beg, I'd starve, until I got into the right agency. Don't do the middle stuff, the drivel." Lynch cites Droga as a role model. "He's only been in advertising ten years. He was only at OMON for the ads, not the money. Then he was let loose at Saatchi's." Lynch advocates going to Cannes. "Not for a job, but to see the tricks, pick the trends." Great suits, Lynch believes, learn what great ads are by reading creative books, watching *Shots* reels, developing instincts for breakthrough ideas.

Former publisher of Asia's *Media & Marketing*, Ken McKenzie, argues that the most successful creative people have inquiring minds, a down-to-earth manner that unlocks doors everywhere, and the quiet confidence to stand by the right idea. "They realise that every task, no matter how mundane or distasteful, is a building block in their career. They don't go round saying how passionate they are, they don't have begrudging scowls, and they don't trash hotel rooms."

McKenzie calls for the return of the creative superstar. "The new messiahs are sorely needed, because there is an industry waiting to follow. They'll not only need strong personal intuition and creative mystique, but leadership abilities and the techniques of trial lawyers to bring clients into line."

Over to You

Hundreds of great writers, art directors, account service people, planners and clients have defined the cutting edge for you. Now the industry needs your contribution.

If success comes easily, in a "baptism of caresses" as Will Self called it, be wary. Be especially wary of imitating your own success.

Lee Strasberg's advice for actors holds true for creative people everywhere: "Neither life nor talent stands still. Standing still leads inevitably to retrogression. The actor does things that he has done before, perhaps more easily, but without the electrifying spark that usually arises in young people when they do their first productions. We then see the terrifying struggle that almost always begins with success, when the actor begins to repeat and to imitate, if not someone else, what is even worse, to imitate himself and thus pay a terrible price in his most important commodity, the very thing that singled him out at the beginning, his talent."

If creativity is a destructive process, if it means tearing down what has gone before and rebuilding afresh, what better place to start than with ourselves?

BIBLIOGRAPHY

Bond, Jonathan, and Richard Kirshenbaum. *Under the Radar: Talking to Today's Cynical Consumer*. John Wiley & Sons, 1998.

Dru, Jean-Marie. *Disruption: Overturning Conventions and Shaking Up the Marketplace*. John Wiley & Sons, 1996.

Ehrenberg, A. S. C. Repetitive Advertising and the Consumer. *Journal of Advertising Research*, April 1979.

Festinger, Leon. *A Theory of Cognitive Dissonance*. Row, Peterson, 1957.

Hall, Oakley. *The Art & Craft of Novel Writing*. Story Press, 1989.

Krugman, Herbert E. The Impact of Television Advertising: Learning without Involvement. *Public Opinion Quarterly*, Vol. XXIX, No. 3, Fall 1965.

Mackay, Hugh. *The Good Listener*. Pan Macmillan Australia, 1998.

INDEX